UNIVERSAL WISDOM

---

*A Journey through
the Sacred Wisdom
of the World*

Selected and Introduced by

BEDE GRIFFITHS

Fount
An Imprint of HarperCollins*Publishers*

Fount is an Imprint of
HarperCollins *Religious*
Part of HarperCollins*Publishers*
77–85 Fulham Palace Road, London W6 8JB

First published in 1994 by Fount in Great Britain
and by HarperSanFrancisco in the USA

1 3 5 7 9 10 8 6 4 2

Copyright in the compilation, introduction
and commentary © 1994 Bede Griffiths

For copyright information on the various extracts,
please see 'Acknowledgements'

A catalogue record for this book is
available from the British Library.

UK ISBN 0 00 627679 2
USA ISBN 0 00 627815 9

Photoset in Linotron Ehrhardt
by Rowland Phototypesetting Ltd
Bury St Edmunds, Suffolk

Printed and bound in Great Britain by
HarperCollinsManufacturing Glasgow

CONTENTS

INTRODUCTION

The religions of the world are meeting today in a way they have never done before. Each religion grew up in a particular cultural setting, Hinduism and Buddhism in India, Taoism and Confucianism in China, Judaism and Christianity in Palestine, Islam in Arabia. But in the course of time each religion grew and extended its influence. Hinduism remained largely confined to India, but the meeting of Aryan people from the north with the Dravidian and other indigenous people from other parts led to a continuous growth and enrichment of their religion, which gave it a universal character. Likewise the two opposite traditions of Taoism and Confucianism in China led to the growth of a profound, universal wisdom which united the whole of China. Buddhism, beginning in India, spread to Sri Lanka, Burma, Thailand and Vietnam, and then with the growth of Mahayana doctrine to Tibet, Korea, China and Japan. Judaism and Christianity both began in Palestine, but Judaism spread in the "diaspora" over the Middle East and Europe and north Africa and eventually the whole world. Christianity spread first of all westwards over the Roman Empire and eastwards over Syria, Mesopotamia and Persia and as far as India and China, while in the west it became the dominant religion of Europe and America. Islam, beginning in Arabia, spread westwards to north Africa as far as Spain and eastwards over Syria, Turkey and Iraq to Iran, India and Indonesia. With this geographical extension there took place an extraordinary development of doctrine. The primitive Vedic mythology developed in Yoga, Vedanta and Tantra into an elaborate system of mystical philosophy, moral discipline and an immense ritualistic religion. The earlier Buddhist doctrine, with its limited view of individual salvation in Nirvana, evolved into the Mahayana doctrine of universal salvation, with the Bodhisattva making a vow not to enter Nirvana until every living being has been saved. Judaism developed in the Talmud an elaborate system of law and later in the Kabbala a subtle mystical doctrine. Christianity, under the influence of Greek philosophy and Roman law, developed a vast system of ritual and doctrine which shaped the history of Europe and America and extended to the European colonies in Asia and Africa. Most remarkable of all in some ways the primitive religion of the Quran, from its contact with the civilization of Syria, Egypt, Iraq and Iran, developed a sophisticated culture, and by absorbing the philosophy of Plato and Aristotle produced its own unique philosophy and theology.

But in spite of this extraordinary expansion of each religion, it is only today that these different religious traditions are beginning to mix freely all over the world and are seeking to relate to one another, not in terms of rivalry and conflict but in terms of dialogue and mutual respect. One of the greatest needs of humanity today is to transcend the cultural limitations of the great religions and to find a wisdom, a philosophy, which can reconcile their differences and reveal the unity which underlies all their diversities. This has been called the "perennial philosophy", the eternal wisdom, which has been revealed in a different way in each religion.

The perennial philosophy stems from a crucial period in human history in the middle of the first millennium before Christ. It was then that a breakthrough was made beyond the cultural limitations of ancient religion to the experience of ultimate reality. This reality which has no proper name, since it transcends the mind and cannot be expressed in words, was called Brahman and Atman (the Spirit) in Hinduism, Nirvana and Sunyata (the Void) in Buddhism, Tao (the Way) in China, Being (*toōn*) in Greece and Yahweh ("I am") in Israel, but all these are but words which point to an inexpressible mystery, in which the ultimate meaning of the universe is to be found, but which no human word or thought can express. It is this which is the goal of all human striving, the truth which all science and philosophy seeks to fathom, the bliss in which all human love is fulfilled.

It was in Hinduism, or rather in the complex religion which later became known as Hinduism, that the first great breakthrough occurred. In the Upanishads in about 600 BC the ancient religion based on the fire-sacrifice (*yajna*) was transformed by the *rishis* (seers), who retired to the forest to meditate, and who were concerned in this way not with the ritualistic fire outside but with the inner fire of the spirit (*Atman*). The ancient Brahman, the hidden power in the sacrifice, was discovered to be the hidden power in the universe, and the spirit of man, the Atman, the inner self, was seen to be one with Brahman, the spirit of the universe. A little later Gautama Buddha, discarding alike the mythology and the ritual of the Vedas, pierced through with his mind beyond all phenomena, which he described as transient (*anitta*), sorrowful (*dukka*) in the sense of giving no lasting satisfaction, and insubstantial (*anatta*), having no basis in reality, to the infinite, eternal, unchanging reality which he called Nirvana. In China the author of the Tao Te Ching (*The Book of the Power of the Way*), whatever its origin may be, was able to go beyond the conventional moral philosophy of Confucius and discover the nameless mystery which he called the Tao, as the subtle source of all wisdom and morality. In Greece Socrates and Plato, going beyond all previous philosophers, who had tried to find the origin of the world in a material form, whether water, air or fire or the four elements together, awoke to the reality of the mind as the source alike of the material universe and of the human person. Finally the Hebrew prophets, rejecting the gods of the ancient world, revealed the presence of a transcendent Being, whose only name was "I am" as the supreme person, the Lord of the universe. Thus in India, China, Greece and Palestine at almost the same time the discovery of the ultimate reality, beyond all the changes of the temporal world, dawned on the human race.

In the course of time these unique insights were developed by philosophers and theologians over a period of more than a thousand years into great doctrinal systems. In India Sankara in the eighth century AD unified the system of Vedanta and set it on the course of further development in the different systems of philosophy which have gone on growing to the present day. In Buddhism, Nagarjuna, the Brahmin philosopher from South India, devised a logical system which was to provide a basis for the Mahayana doctrine of China and Tibet. In China, Taoism and Confucianism, interacting over the centuries, developed the Neo-Confucian system which dominated China until the coming of Marxism. In Greece the new vision of Socrates and Plato led to the growth of the Neoplatonism of Plotinus and became of decisive importance in the growth both of Christianity and of Islam. The Greek fathers, Clement, Origen and Gregory of Nyssa, building on the mystical insights of St Paul and St John, developed a profound mystical theology under the influence of Neoplatonism, which was to flower in the great mystical tradition of the Middle Ages. Finally in Israel and in Islam the religion of the patriarchs and the prophets underwent a vital transformation, as it encountered the cultural tradition of Greece and the oriental world.

In each religion therefore we can trace the development of a comparatively simple and unsophisticated religion into a subtle and complex system of philosophy, which shows a remarkable unity underlying all the differences. This philosophy, which prevailed in almost all parts of the world until the fifteenth century, was rejected in Europe in the sixteenth century and a new system of philosophy based on the findings of western science has taken its place. But the philosophy of western science itself has now begun to disintegrate, as a result of the new scientific developments in relativity and quantum physics. As a result the world today is left with no basic philosophy which can give meaning to life, and we are in danger of losing all sense of meaning and purpose in human existence. When to this is added the devastating effect of western technology on the ecology of the planet, which threatens to destroy the world, on which we depend for our very existence, it can be seen that the need of a philosophy, a universal wisdom, which can unify humanity and enable us to face the problems created by western science and technology, has become the greatest need of humanity today. The religions of the world cannot by themselves answer this need. They are themselves today part of the problem of a divided world. The different world religions – Hinduism, Buddhism, Judaism, Christianity and Islam – have themselves to recover the ancient wisdom, which they have inherited, and this has now to be interpreted in the light of the knowledge of the world, which western science has given us.

It is hoped that the texts which have been gathered together in this volume, illustrating the basic insights of the perennial philosophy, may provide a source book for the new vision of reality, which the world is seeking today. It does not pretend to be a work of scholarship for academic study. It is rather a collection of texts in convenient translations which illustrate the fundamental wisdom underlying the religious traditions of the world. People today have to grow accustomed to reflecting on the scriptures of the world religions. No religion can stand alone. Each has undergone a long evolution in the course of history and today we realize that religions are interdependent. Each religion has its own unique insight into ultimate truth and reality. As we meditate on these texts, our vision is enlarged. We see our own religion in a new light and we begin to discern how humanity today could grow in mutual understanding, towards that unity which is our common goal. This demands a certain detachment from our own culture and religion, a recognition of the changing elements in each religious tradition and an opening of heart and mind to the transcendent truth, which is revealed in every genuine religious tradition. At the same time we have to take account of the changes which western science, whether physics, biology, psychology, sociology or metaphysics, has brought to our lives. It is only the patient meditation on the texts of the perennial philosophy which can give us the insight which we need and enable us to discern the changes which must take place in our lives. Only then can we hope to realize the deep unity which underlies all our human differences and recover our sense of solidarity with this vast universe, which has been given us as our home and for which we are responsible.

The Origin of Religion

The study of comparative religion, especially of pre-historic and tribal religion, such as Mircea Eliade has undertaken,[1] can enable us to go behind all the later developments of religion and discover the basic experience from which all religion springs. Rudolf Otto in his *The Idea of the Holy*,[2] has come near to uncovering this hidden source of religion. Human beings, faced with the vastness of this mysterious universe, awaken to what he calls *mysterium tremendum et fascinans*. It is first of all a "mystery". Human beings, faced with the presence of the unknown, could not but be filled with awe, not simply with fear of the unknown, but with a sense of the vastness, the unfathomable immensity of the world around them. The world was fearful – *tremendum* – but also fascinating – *fascinans*. It forced one to try to explore it, to fathom its immensity. It awoke desire, longing, yearning for something inexplicable. Later more sophisticated people have felt the same sense of awe in the presence of nature. Especially in the romantic movement in England and Germany in the nineteenth century this sense of the primordial mystery was awakened in both poets and philosophers. Even before this, Pascal with his mathematical genius was led to cry out: *Le silence éternel de ces espaces infinis m'effraye* – "the eternal silence of these infinite spaces makes me afraid" – and Kant could rise above all the abstractions of his philosophy to acknowledge his awe in the presence of "the starry firmament above and the moral law within".

This acknowledgement of the dual character of the mystery is extremely important. We have inherited from Descartes and the scientists of the seventeenth century a belief in a world divided into a physical world outside us and an inner world of subjective experience – what Descartes called *res extensa* – "extended substance" – and *res cogitans* – "thinking substance". But we are discovering today that this division is illusory. Actually the division goes back beyond Descartes and western science to the Greek philosophers of the sixth and fifth centuries BC. It was then that the rational, analytical mind first began to awaken and the idea of the division between mind and matter arose. Before that time humanity as a whole enjoyed a unitive vision of reality. However far we go back in comparative religion, we find a common sense of the universe as an integrated whole. Humanity was conceived as one with nature and with the universal Spirit pervading the human and the physical world, plants and animals, earth and sky and sea. This is the primordial vision of the universe reflected in all ancient religion.

Mircea Eliade has shown how among tribal people today there is a common understanding of a cosmic power which manifests itself alike in nature and in man.[3] It is called *mana* among the Melanesian islanders. It manifests itself in the whole creation but especially in any extraordinary phenomena such as thunder or lightning or a tempest, and in human beings who have exceptional powers, such as a shaman or a chief of a clan, and again in the spirits of the ancestors or the souls of the dead. This power is present in the whole universe, but breaks out, as it were, in certain people and in particular events. This gives rise to a belief in a divine world, a world of spirits, which govern the course of nature and are responsible for the fertility of the earth and the changes of the seasons. These beings are said to be endowed with infinite prescience and wisdom. The moral law, and often the tribal ritual, are said to have been inaugurated by them. All this, as Mircea Eliade insists, is not the result of rational, logical deduction but comes from the experience of the "sacred". It is given immediately to consciousness as humanity discovers itself and takes cognizance of its position in the universe. They are not products of the conscious mind but experiences of the whole person, mediated through the rituals and customs of the tribe and revealed at the time of initiation.

We come here upon the fundamental difference between the mind of western man and that of the people of the ancient world. I say "western man", because this development is typical of a male patriarchal culture. Ever since the time of ancient Greece, the human being in the west has been described as a "rational animal", that is, an animal being with body and soul, of which the faculty of reason is considered to be the highest power. For modern western people the rational, analytical, logical, mathematical mind is considered to be the typical faculty of human understanding and no knowledge is considered to be scientific which does not depend on this. Yet this mode of knowledge is largely a product of the last three centuries in the west and was unknown to humanity in the thousands of years of its early history. As Jacques Maritain has pointed out,[4] the intelligence of primitive man, that is, of human beings before the age of reason, was under the primacy of the imagination. The imagination, the image-making faculty, is the mode in which most people even today come to know the universe. We all form images of people and of things around us, and it is through these images that we come to know the universe. Jung has shown how it is through the images or archetypes of the unconscious that all human beings from the earliest times have come to know the universe, and the typical mode of expression of the imagination is the myth. It is in the myth that the source of all knowledge and religion is to be found. The mind of people in India today is still shaped by the great myths of the Ramayana and the Mahabharata, shown on television, as they were once recited and dramatized in all the villages of India; and Christian people all over the world still live by the great myths of the Bible – the Creation and the Fall, the Exodus and the Promised Land, the Messiah and his Kingdom. In these great myths a profound wisdom is contained, a wisdom which guides and shapes human existence, but it is a wisdom in which reason is implicit not explicit. Reason proceeds by abstraction, by "drawing out" the rational concept from its embodiment in the imagination. The wisdom of a great poet, a Homer, a Vergil, a Dante, a Shakespeare is an imaginative wisdom, a wisdom which grasps reality not in abstract concepts but in concrete images. It is so also with the great scriptures of religion, the Vedas, the

Quran, the Bible. In all of them Reality is made known, is revealed, not in the concepts of abstract reason but in the living language of the imagination, which touches not merely the analytical mind but the senses, the feelings and the imagination. The basis of all myth is to be found in symbols. A symbol is defined as a sign by which reality is made present to human consciousness. The most obvious example of this is the word. What distinguishes a human being from an animal is the capacity for speech. Every human child has this capacity and if left to itself will create its own language. This accounts for the amazing variety of languages among primitive people. Every little tribe will have its own language and it is only very slowly, even today, that a common language can be established. Now words in their original sense always represent concrete reality. It is only at a very late stage – we have seen in the first millennium before Christ – that abstract thought arises and words come to represent abstract ideas. In the early stages of human existence words represent – that is, make present to consciousness – concrete reality. Consciousness itself is simply the capacity to represent – to make present to oneself – the world which we experience through our senses. This is why the Hebrew, especially in the Psalms, always uses concrete terms and will say for instance: "My tongue shall praise you with joyful lips." But in fact, all ancient language is concrete in this way. Words make present to consciousness the concrete world which surrounds us. This is why myth is the typical language of archaic thought. The myth makes present in concrete terms the reality of the world, which the human person encounters. The "archetypes of the unconscious", of which Jung speaks, are simply concrete images of the world encountered in human consciousness. It is from these archetypal symbols, arising in the unconscious and brought into consciousness by the myth, that all human knowledge arises, and abstract ideas are only the refinement by the human reason of these primeval images. But in coming into consciousness, these images are illumined by the intelligence. They give meaning to life and enable human beings to understand – to "stand under" and so give focus to – the world in which they live.

In every advanced language a distinction is made between reason and the intellect, between *ratio* and *intellectus* between *dianoia* and *nous*, and in India between the *manas* and the *buddhi*. The *manas* is the measuring mind, from the root *ma*, found in the "moon" which measures time, and "matter" which measures space. But beyond the manas is the Buddhi, the source of light (the Buddha is the enlightened one), the intelligence which has in-sight, which "sees into" reality. The seers of the Vedas were called *rishis* because they had this insight. The intellect is the faculty which "knows", which does not merely "conjecture" or form a hypothesis, but which grasps the real by direct reflection on itself. The human mind, beyond the power of reason, has the power to reflect on itself, to know itself in its acts. We all reflect on our actions and on our experience day by day and this reflection gives us direct knowledge of our selves and our environment. Reason can then develop this knowledge by logic and analysis and mathematical theory and so evolve a scientific method, but the whole structure of science depends on the initial knowledge, the original knowledge of the self in its reflection on its acts. Descartes was right in a sense in saying: "I think, therefore I am", but he was wrong in limiting thought to reason. To think is to reflect on oneself, to grasp oneself in the totality of one's being in the world.

It is here that the function of the imagination is found. The imagination reflects the world not by means of abstract concepts but by images which make reality present to us in its concrete existence. It was this that led Coleridge in his *Biographia Literaria* to speak of the imagination as "the living power and prime agent of all human perception, a repetition in the finite mind of the eternal act of creation in the infinite 'I am'". The whole creation is an act of imagination in the divine mind, an image of the eternal reality, which becomes present to us in this form. In the same way Wordsworth could speak of "imagination which in truth/ is but another name for absolute power/ and clearest insight, amplitude of mind/ and reason is her most exalted mood". In the western mind as a whole the imagination has been seen as an inferior power, always subordinate to higher power of reason. But Wordsworth, like Coleridge, and Goethe saw the imagination, that is, the creative imagination in art and poetry, as above the normal exercise of reason.[5] In the great poet, as in the prophets and seers of religion, the logical reason is transcended and becomes the instrument of a higher faculty of the mind. Today we are recognizing the difference between the right and the left brain, and realizing that the left brain with its linear thinking is only a part of the greater brain which gives insight into the total reality.

This has given us a new insight into the meaning of the ancient myths and the values of primitive religion. The people of ancient times did not think with a small part of their brain, as we have learned to do. They experienced the world in its totality with the totality of their being. A myth is not a fanciful story about the beginning of the world or some supposed divine event. It is the concrete presentation of the reality of the world as manifested in the imagination and engaging all the faculties of the human being. To understand the myth one had to be initiated into a total way of life and through it discover the meaning of human existence. Today we are searching for a myth which will give meaning to our lives, now that the myth of western science has betrayed us. Western science created the myth of a universe of solid bodies moving in space and time, obeying mathematical laws, but this myth has collapsed. As science itself has discovered, we know now that matter is energy, and time and space are concepts by which we try to organize our perceptions of the material world. The universe appears as a vast ocean of energy organized by an intelligence, of which our human intelligence is a reflection. We are coming back therefore to the ancient understanding of matter as energy – *dynamis* in Aristotle's terms – organized by intelligence (*nous*) in the shape of "forms" or "morphogenetic fields" as Rupert Sheldrake has called them,[6] which structure the universe. This is very near to the understanding of the perennial philosophy found in Greek and Arabian philosophers and the Christian theologians of the Middle Ages. The intelligences forming the universe came to be known in Christianity as angels; and in Greece, as India today, as gods.

The concepts of gods and angels are strange to us now, but this is only because western science has tried to persuade us that the universe is composed of dead matter subject to mechanical laws. In reality, as we are discovering again, the universe is a living organism, undergoing continuous evolution, and informed by intelligence at every level. We are thus recovering the sense of the universe composed of powers and presences, which touch every aspect of our lives, both physical and psychological. This takes us back to the understanding of ancient, tribal people, as Christopher Dawson has noted, "Primitive man does not look upon the external world in the modern way as a passive, mechanical system, a background for human energies, mere matter for the human mind to mould. He sees it as a living world of mysterious forces greater than his own . . . which manifest themselves both in external nature and his inner consciousness".[7] This is the real world which we all inhabit and which the perennial philosophy has made known to us.

It is generally understood today that this universe began in an explosion of energy at an intense heat which, as it cooled down, developed into particles of matter such as photons, protons, electrons, and these gradually coalesced so as to form atoms and molecules, which structured the material universe. But these atoms and molecules have been found to be structured with mathematical precision and the material universe can be seen to obey mathematical laws. This means that there is an intelligence at work in matter. Mathematical laws are known by intelligence, and if the human intelligence finds mathematical laws at work in the universe, it must mean that something akin to human intelligence is present in matter from the beginning – unless all science is based on illusion. This has always been the view of the perennial philosophy. Aristotle and the Arabian philosophers spoke of the stars as "intelligences", that is, they recognized in the stars the presence of intelligent powers which govern the universe. In the Christian tradition these intelligences or "cosmic powers" came to be known as "angels" or "messengers". That is, they were seen as the agents of a cosmic intelligence, a universal power, which was responsible for the organization of the universe.

This again takes us back to the beginning of history and of all religion. Though most people have recognized many "gods", that is powers or spirits, operating in the universe, there is a universal tendency to reduce all these powers and spirits to one supreme power and spiritual presence. This is found in almost all African religions, where a supreme creator God is recognized above all the spirits of ancestors and other beings which dominate the world, though in practice little attention may be paid to him. But as Mircea Eliade again has shown, the presence of a "sky-god", a "divine, celestial being, creator of the universe, who guarantees the fertility of the earth by the rains which it sends", is found in all parts of the world. This being was known in the Vedas as Dyauspita, the "sky-father", the letter "d" being found in all Aryan languages as in Zeus (gen *dios*) in Greece, and Jupiter (*diupiter*) in Latin, the letter "d" becoming "sk" in Norse. So everywhere we find the presence of a sky-father, and when Jesus taught his disciples to pray, he could find nothing better than to say: "Our Father in heaven" (Greek *ouranos*, the sky).

This raises an important point. When people in the ancient world spoke of "heaven", they meant both the sky – the firmament on high – and the power and the presence of the sky. We have grown accustomed to separating the material aspect from the spiritual. We think of the sky as a material phenomenon, a vault, a space, however we may describe it, which has been emptied of all spiritual reality, of power and intelligence. But for the ancient world there was no separation between mind and matter, between the phenomenon and the numenon, the material world and the power and intelligence which governed it. This division is due partly to the influence of Greek philosophy, especially Plato, but also to that of the Hebrew mind in the Bible. The people of Israel originally believed like other peoples in many gods, as can be seen in the Hebrew word for God, *Elohim*, which is plural. But gradually they were taught to believe in one supreme God, *Yahweh*, and worship of no other god was tolerated. But this led to a separation of God from the created world; a dualism was introduced, perhaps under Persian influence, which separated God from nature and left the natural world without any divine presence in it. It is this that has led to the western view of nature as an inanimate being separate from God, which has brought such disaster to the world today.

The Vedic Mythology

Religion in India took a quite different direction. The Vedas are generally supposed to have been brought to India in the second millennium by Aryan people, akin to the Greeks and Romans, from the west. The Vedic seers themselves look back to patriarchs of ancient times from whom they received this wisdom and no one can say from where it came. But this is not of great importance. The word *Veda* means knowledge (from the root *vid*, to "see" or "know") and the Vedas are held to be eternal (*nitya*). Like all ancient people they believed that the source of their religion did not come from the temporal world, the world of passing phenomena, but from the eternal. The Vedas were also said to be *sruti* (from the root *sr*, to hear). They were not invented by man but "heard" or "seen"; that is, they came by direct inspiration (though through a human instrument). They were also said to be *apauruseya* – without human authorship. This reminds us that all authentic knowledge comes not from the senses but from the mind, the intelligence, which reflects the divine intelligence, the source of creation. Though knowledge normally comes through the senses and through the whole apparatus of the brain, its source is in the mind itself, the intelligence with its capacity for self reflection, which gives knowledge not only of itself but also of its source in the universal, cosmic intelligence. It is this which we find in the Vedas – the rishis, the "seers", were accustomed to reflect on themselves, and in meditation to discover the source of their knowledge, the prime intelligence or cosmic consciousness, from which human consciousness is derived. It is in the Vedas that we can best trace the passage from the ancient world of mythology, when the human mind was under the dominion of the imagination, to the philosophical understanding of ultimate truth and reality, which emerged in the Upanishads in the sixth century before Christ. The seers of the Vedas began like all ancient people with the belief in many gods, or powers and presences, both in the world of nature and in the human being. But from the earliest times they tended to see beyond all these gods to the one Reality, which lay behind them. A famous verse in the Rig Veda says: *ekam sat vipra bahuda vadanti* – "the one being the wise call by many names". It was this "one being" which haunted the mind of the Vedic seers, so that all "gods" were seen as but "names and forms" of this one Reality.

This one Reality came to be known in course of time as Brahman. The word *brahman* comes from the root *brh*, to grow or swell, and it seems first of all to have been applied to the mantra, the sacred word, which rose in the mind of the priest who offered the sacrifice. The centre of the Vedic religion was the fire-sacrifice, the *yajna*, in which a ritual altar was built and offerings made in the fire. Agni the god of fire was believed to consume the offerings. But Agni was not only the physical fire but the fire in the mind of the priest who offered the sacrifice. He had a physical body with his "flaming hair", but he was also the "god who knows", the priest who carried the sacrifice to the gods. In other words, Agni was the name of the primal energy in the universe, of which fire is the most obvious form, but he was also the energy of the mind, the intelligence, which orders the universe. Finally he becomes a symbol, like all the gods, of the primordial power and wisdom which shapes the universe. It was in this way that the *brahman*, the sacred utterance through which the sacrifice was enacted, became a symbol of the divine power, present in the sacrifice and in the whole universe and in the mind of man.

The Vedic myth develops this concept of Agni as the divine fire (or energy) in the universe into the story of the conflict between Agni and Vrata. Vrata represents the contrary force, the power which holds humanity captive and imprisons the mind in the hard rock of matter. Later Agni was replaced by Indra, originally, like Yahweh in Israel, a god of thunder – the power of the sky-god – but later recognized as the Lord of the gods, the power of the mind. In the story of the myth Indra with his thunderbolt (*vajra*) breaks through the hard rock at the base of the mountain and sets free the waters and the cattle imprisoned there. Indra here represents the divine mind, the supreme intelligence, which breaks through the hard rock, the dark matter, of the unconscious and sets free the waters, symbol of the life of the mind, and the cows, symbol of the fertility of consciousness. Cows in the Vedas are always symbols not only of fertility but of light. The dawn is said to release the cows from their pen with the rising of the sun.

Jeanine Miller in her book on the Vedas[8] has shown how the Vedic seers in their meditation were able to transcend the limits of conventional religion and discover the hidden source of religion in the divine mind. The human mind has been subject from the beginning to the senses and the imagination. But always there is a hidden power in human nature which can transcend the senses and the imagination and open the human being to the intelligence which transcends the conscious mind. This breakthrough beyond sense and imagination occurred in the first millennium before Christ and the human mind awoke to full consciousness, to the experience of ultimate reality. Each of the great religions of the world, building on this foundation, established a way of life by which humanity could be set free from the forces of the unconscious and attain to truth and reality. But in the sixteenth century in the west this movement was reversed. The human mind began again to subject itself to the material world. The object of science became not to know the supreme reality and to understand the material world in its light, but to explore the material world in the light of a limited human reason – limited to the observation of phenomena. The result has been that scientists today are cut off from the sources of knowledge and confined to the knowledge of phenomena interpreted by the rational mind.

Karl Popper, one of the leading philosophers of science, in his book with John Eccles on *The Self and its Brain*,[9] has tried to go beyond the materialism of western science. He recognizes three "worlds" or spheres of reality – the physical world observed by the senses and scientific instruments, the mental world of human reason, which analyses the physical world, and the world of "mental objects", that is scientific theories which must have reality, because they are seen to act upon and transform the material world. But he still remains imprisoned in the world of reason and can conceive of no knowledge, which is ultimately not due to "conjecture" and "hypothesis". But this undermines the whole basis of science and can only lead to universal scepticism. He acknowledges that human beings have the power of reflection, so as to form a self, a self-reflective being. But he does not see that this power of self-reflection is the basis of all certainty, and therefore of all science. I do not "conjecture" to my own existence or to that of a physical world. I know myself and the world in a direct act of self-reflection. I am present to myself and the world around me by direct experience, that is, by a reflection on myself in the act of my existence, I not only know that I exist; I know that I know. To know oneself is to experience oneself and one's world immediately. This is the basis of all human knowledge and of all properly human existence.

It is true that I do not know my "essence", that is, what I am. It is here that reason comes in and scientific conjecture and hypothesis, and such knowledge is always growing. But the knowledge of my existence and that of the world which I experience is given by direct intuition ("seeing into"). The reason why the western mind cannot grasp this is because it has been accustomed for centuries to observe external phenomena and to imagine that all knowledge comes from the senses. It has lost the art of meditation. But many scientists today are beginning to recover this lost art, of which David Bohm is the most eminent example. Apart from being an expert physicist, he is also a disciple of Krishnamurti and learned the practice of meditation. Meditation consists precisely in learning to go beyond the senses and the reason, which works through the senses, and to observe the action of the mind itself. It is then that one discovers the source of the mind, the ground of consciousness. David Bohm has described this in terms of the implicate and the explicate order.[10] What we normally observe is the explicate order of the world, the world "unfolded" to human consciousness. But when we enter into meditation we go beyond the manifold world of sense and reason (that is of all "scientific" knowledge) and discover the world not explicated through the senses but in its original state of "implication". The world is found in the self and the self in the world.

The Wisdom of the Upanishads

It was this experience of the self in its ground or source, in its original being, which was the discovery of the Upanishads. They called this self *atman* from the root *an* (as in *animus* and *anima*) to "breathe". In meditation it is through the breath that one learns to go beyond the senses and the mind. By concentrating on the breathing all images and thoughts and feelings are brought to rest, and then in the silence, in the emptiness of all thought, the knowledge of the spirit dawns, the pure consciousness from which all conscious knowledge comes, the source of the activity of the mind. The Isa Upanishad speaks of seeing the "self" or "spirit" in all beings and all beings in the "self". It then goes on to show the danger of dwelling either on transcendence, that is consciousness of a transcendent reality above this world, or on immanence, that is experience of the world as immanent in human consciousness. It is only when we learn to see the immanent (the material world) in the transcendent (the divine) and the transcendent in the immanent, that we find the truth. Both materialism and idealism can lead us astray. It is the consciousness which transcends the opposites and all dualities that reaches the truth.

The Kena Upanishad gives a beautiful example of how the problem of polytheism was solved in the Vedic tradition. The three gods, Agni, Vayu and Indra, the powers of fire and of the air and of thunder, win a victory which they attribute to themselves. But Brahman, the supreme reality, appears to them and shows that they owe all their powers to him, or to "that", which has no form or name. The discovery was made that the "gods" are nothing but names and forms of the one Reality beyond name and form. This is a lesson for all religions. Each religion tends to exalt one particular name and form, Yahweh or Allah or Christ, above every other name and to forget that the supreme Reality has properly no name or form. It transcends all human understanding. This was discovered in the course of time in each religion, and we shall see how in each of them a process took place which led to the transcendence of all limitations and the recognition of one supreme truth or reality, which has no name. In India this was the achievement of the Upanishads. We can see it most clearly in the Katha Upanishad, where Nachiketas, the young man in search of truth, goes down to the world of the dead, thus dying to the world, as every seeker of the truth must do. Death, the guide to life, teaches him to leave everything behind and instructs him in the truth of the Atman, the spirit who is "difficult to be seen, who has entered into the dark, who is hidden in the cave, who dwells in the abyss, as God" and thus awakens him to the eternal truth, the mystery hidden at the heart of the world. It is this journey into the darkness, to death, which we all have to undergo, if we are to experience re-birth to life eternal.

The Mundaka Upanishad speaks of this mystery in terms of light, but it is in the Mandukya Upanishad that the most penetrating insight is given into human consciousness. There a distinction is made between the waking state of normal consciousness, the dream state and the state of deep sleep. But beyond these states of consciousness is the "fourth state", the state of transcendent consciousness. It is this which is the goal of human existence. We have all to learn to transcend our present mode of consciousness, with its dependence on the senses and the imagination, and to experience the state of transcendent wisdom. This is a state which cannot be described. We have to experience it to know what it is. Yet it is present all the time in all human consciousness and every religion seeks to open the way to it. But as long as we remain in our present mode of consciousness, we cannot know the truth. Religion can point to it and show the way but only direct experience can convince us of the truth and lead to final liberation.

It is in a later Upanishad, the Svetasvatara, that we find the most comprehensive answer to the whole question. It begins by asking: "What is the source of the universe? What is Brahman? From where do we come? By what power do we live? Where do we find rest? Who rules over our joys and sorrows?" It then lists the various answers which have been given to these questions. "Shall we think of time, or of the nature of things, or of a law of necessity, or of chance or of the elements?" Having rejected all these answers, which modern science has given to the problem of life, it goes on to say: "By the yoga of meditation and contemplation the wise saw the power of God" – the *devatmasakti*, literally "the power of the spirit of God" – hidden in his own creation. "It is he who rules over all the sources of this universe, from time to the soul of man." This illustrates precisely the approach of the Upanishads to the basic problems of life. It is by the "yoga of meditation and contemplation" that we come to the deepest understanding of life. Science and philosophy can only take us so far, dependent as they are on the senses and the rational mind. But in meditation we go beyond the senses and the rational mind and encounter the source of reality, the divine power hidden in creation and in the mind. This is the insight which gives knowledge of the truth and sets us free.

The Svetasvatara Upanishad then goes on to describe the three worlds – the world of matter, the world of mind or the soul, and God, the ruler of all. But it goes on to say that God, the world and the soul are all contained in the mystery of Brahman. For many people today the personal God, whether Jewish, Christian or Muslim, is a problem, since he so obviously reflects the limitations of the human mind. But in India from the earliest times it has been recognized that the personal God, whatever form he may take, is a reflection in the human mind of the one, transcendent reality, the Brahman. In the Svetasvatara Upanishad there is a magnificent revelation of a personal God, who here comes to be identified with Siva. He is said to be pure consciousness, the creator of time, all powerful, all knowing, the lord of the soul and of nature, but he is also the loving protector of all, the God of love. But at the same time he is recognized to be a form of Brahman, of the supreme mystery which transcends human understanding. We shall see how in each religion, in spite of the dominance of the personal God, this insight is always to be found.

The Revelation of the Personal God

It is in the Bhagavad Gita, the Song of the Lord, that the great revelation of the personal God in India is to be found. The Bhagavad Gita appears in the great epic poem, the Mahabharata, which was composed between 400 BC and AD 400. It belongs not to *sruti*, the revelation of the Vedas, but to the later development of religion in India known as *smriti* (from the root *smr*, to remember). In it Krishna is revealed as the form of the personal God. The source of the Krishna legend is not known. There is more than one Krishna mentioned in earlier times. But by this time he has come to be seen and worshipped as the one supreme God, the creator of the universe, the source of all wisdom and the power of salvation. In the Gita a clear distinction is made between the divine nature of Krishna, his invisible spirit, and his visible nature, manifested in all creation. The language used may often seem pantheistic – "I am the taste of living waters, and the light of the sun and the moon." But one must always remember in reading Hindu texts that, though the language may be pantheistic, seeming to identify God with nature, the actual doctrine is "pan-en-theistic", that is a belief that God is *in* everything. As Manikkar Vasakar, the great Tamil mystic, put it: "You are all that is and You are nothing that is." A great deal of misunderstanding has been caused by labelling Hindu doctrine "pantheistic". But in reality it is a constant witness to the profound fact that God is *in* every being, as the ground of its existence, and the great insight of the Upanishads, as we have seen, was the recognition of this one supreme reality as the ground and source of all creation and of human existence. In the Bhagavad Gita Krishna is exalted as the personal God, the "friend of all", dwelling in the heart of every creature and offering salvation – that is final liberation – to all who call on him. Yet at the same time this personal God who reveals himself as love, is one with the infinite Brahman, the eternal spirit who sustains the universe. This revelation of the personal God in the Bhagavad Gita, like that of Siva in the Svetasvatara Upanishad, has to be compared with that of Yahweh in the Jewish tradition and that of Allah in Islam, and finally we have to see how they all relate to the mystery of the Trinity in Christian tradition.

The Challenge of Buddhism

Buddhism presents the greatest challenge to all religions, especially to those which believe in a personal, creator God. Gautama Buddha coming at the end of the Vedic period (563–483 BC) rejected all the traditional beliefs and practices of religion. The Vedic gods, the ritual sacrifices, the Brahmin priesthood and the whole caste system, which has provided the religious basis of Hindu society ever since, were all rejected in favour of a negative philosophy, which might be considered a sort of nihilism. The great insight of Buddha was into the transitoriness of the world. "All is passing (*anitta*), all is sorrow (*dukka*), all is unreal (*anatta*)." This was the basis of Buddha's teaching. The end of all things is nirvana, the "blowing out", the extinction of all being, the eradication of all desire. It might be said that this was the most radical philosophy ever propounded. It strikes at the root of existence as we know it. Yet behind this negative philosophy there is a profound insight. Nirvana is the end of all becoming, of all desire, of all that makes life worth living for most people. Yet when all change and becoming has ceased, when all desires, all "clinging" to life, has come to an end, there is an experience of absolute bliss. This was the experience of Buddha, as he sat beneath the Bo tree. He entered into deep meditation. He allowed all movement of the senses to cease, put an end to all desire, and then in the silence and solitude of the mind he experienced the bliss of pure consciousness. He entered into the depth of the soul, the ground of consciousness, and there found the peace, the joy, the fulfilment for which he had been seeking. This is the message of Buddhism today. As long as we remain engrossed in the world of the senses, ever seeking the fulfilment of our desires, we can never find peace. All over the world today, as in all Asia in the past, this message of "enlightenment", of inner peace, is being heard. The teaching of Buddha was handed on by his disciples by word of mouth and only came to be put into writing after several centuries, but the essential teaching has come down to us particularly in the Dhammapada, the Path of the Law.

The teaching of the Dhammapada is clear. It is not the body or the senses but the mind which is the cause of all human problems and it is the mind which is also their cure. As long as the mind attaches itself to thoughts and feelings and desires, it is carried away into a world of illusion and becomes subject to passion and desire. But when the mind withdraws from the impressions of the senses and realizes its own inherent nature, it experiences inner joy and peace and fulfilment. The note of joy sounds all through the Dhammapada, the joy of those who have renounced passion and desire and all attachment to the material world, and have found inner peace and freedom, and who know the truth. The western mind has concentrated its attention on the material world, to understand its working by science, to control it by technology and to make life in this world as attractive as possible. It has succeeded beyond all its dreams in analysing matter down to its minutest particles, in exploring the furthest limits of time and space, in unifying the human world and creating a standard of life which has never been known before. But all this has been done at the cost of polluting the earth, the water and the air, of destroying innumerable species of plants and animals, and of using up the resources on which human life depends. All this is the result of following a philosophy which made the knowledge and control of the material world its goal. The western world has now to undergo a *metanoia*, a change of mind, which will enable it to recover the ancient wisdom, the perennial philosophy, on which human nature actually depends.

Buddhism, first in the Hinayana tradition and then in the Mahayana, is one of the sources of this eternal wisdom. Buddha broke through the bondage of the human mind to the senses and the material world and set it free on the path of truth and peace. Buddhism may seem to be a religion without God or creation or a soul, but Buddha set the human mind free from its attachment to the body and the material world and opened it to truth and life. There is no God in Buddhism and no Creator, but there is in the peace of Nirvana infinite wisdom and infinite compassion, and what else do we mean by "God"? This is the challenge which Buddhism presents both to the religion and to the science of the west. Buddha saw that all the images and concepts of "God" and all the rituals and practices of religion have no value, unless they are sustained by the mind, which goes beyond all images and concepts, and realizes its true nature, not as dependent on the body and senses but as the source of the life of the body and the intelligence of the brain. Western science has grown up under the illusion that there is a material world "outside" the mind. It is now slowly learning, what the perennial philosophy has known all along, that the world, which appears to be outside us, is inconceivable apart from the mind which observes it. It was the experience of physicists in the present century working with quantum physics, which finally made it clear that the world which the scientist observes is not reality in itself but reality exposed to human consciousness, to the mind and the brain of the scientist.

It was this discovery of the independence of the mind from the senses for which Buddha was responsible. In the early Hinayana tradition the emphasis was on the practical aspect of this discovery. Buddha saw humanity imprisoned in the world of the senses like people trapped in a burning house, and his aim was to set them free, to teach them by the "eightfold noble path" how to be free from the pain, the sorrow of this world. His was a message of salvation for suffering humanity. Everything depends on the Knowledge of the "four noble truths", of suffering, the cause of suffering, the end of suffering and the way to the end of suffering. This way depended essentially on knowing the nature of the mind, and it was the exploration of the nature of the mind which led to the great development of Mahayana doctrine. This development took place many years after the passing of Buddha, but one may hold that it was implicit from the beginning. There is a vast literature of Mahayana doctrine, not only in Sanskrit but also in Tibetan and Chinese, but beneath all its complications there is an essential truth proclaimed in it and it is this that we need to understand. We have chosen the treatise on the Awakening of Faith by Ashvaghosa as an example of it, but perhaps this quotation from the Lankavatara Sutra can indicate its essential message.

> When all appearances and names are set aside and all discrimination ceases, then that which remains is the true and essential nature of things, and as nothing can be predicated of the nature of essence, it is called Suchness (*tathata*) of Reality. This Universal, undifferentiated, inscrutable Suchness is the only Reality, but it is variously called Reality (*dharma*), Body of Reality (*dharmakaya*), Noble Knowledge (*arya jnana*), Noble wisdom (*arya prajna*). This Dharma of the image-lessness of the Body of Reality is the Dharma which has been proclaimed by all the Buddhas, and when all things are understood in full agreement with it, one is in possession of perfect knowledge (*prajna*) and is on the way to the attainment of the noble knowledge (*arya jnana*) of the Tathagatas

(that is, the Buddhas, who have "attained to that" or reached the goal of Reality). This is the essential teaching of the Mahayana, which, as we shall see, is found alike in Hindu, Chinese and Greek philosophy, that when we pass beyond the "discriminating" or analytical knowledge of science and philosophy, we come to the knowledge of reality itself in pure consciousness.

The Chinese Way

The Tao Te Ching, the Book of the Way and its Power, as Arthur Waley translates it, is perhaps the most mysterious book ever written. Its author is unknown, its date is unknown, and its meaning is uncertain, and yet it presents what has been called "perhaps the most profound conception which has ever entered the human mind". The earliest tradition is that it was written by Lao Tzu, a contemporary of Confucius. He is said to have been born in 602 BC and to have died at the age 160 in 442 BC, but many scholars today question his very existence and claim that the book was written in the third or fourth century BC and was the work of more than one author. This is all to the good, as the exact date and authorship of the book are not important. It belongs essentially to that great breakthrough in human consciousness which occurred in the first millennium before Christ, and is a supreme example of that great mystical tradition which underlies all religion. The Tao Te Ching begins by affirming, as the Upanishads and Buddha had done, that the ultimate reality has no name – "Tao, the Way, is the 'by-name' which we give it". Yet this in itself is significant. Both Hinduism and Buddhism speak of ultimate reality as Brahman or Nirvana in metaphysical terms, but the Chinese, with their more practical character, prefer to speak of it as the Way. Tao is the "rhythm" of the universe, the "flow" of reality, more like the "ever living fire" of Heraclitus or the field of energies of modern physics. Its character is the union of opposites, the Yin and the Yang, the passive and the active, the female and the male. This leads in Chinese philosophy to a profound sense of the complementarity of all existence. The western world, based on the Hebrew and the Greek, thinks in terms of opposites, of good and evil, truth and error, black and white. Its way of thinking is logical, based on the principle of contradiction. But the Chinese mind, and with it the eastern mind as a whole, thinks more in terms of complementarity. It is aware of the Unity which transcends and yet includes all dualities, of the whole which transcends and yet unites all its parts. But we need to remind ourselves that the west also attained to this insight in the great Christian philosopher, Nicholas of Cusa, a cardinal of the Roman church, who spoke of the *coincidentia oppositorum* – the "coincidence of opposites".

The Tao Te Ching is always aware of this unity behind the multiplicity of the world, but it is a dynamic unity. "There was something", it says, "formlessly fashioned, which existed before heaven and earth. Without sound, without substance, dependent on nothing, unchanging, all pervading, unfailing. One may think of it as the Mother of all things under heaven. Its true name we do not know. Tao is the by-name which we give it." It is significant that it is called the Mother. We have grown up in a patriarchal civilization and our images of God, the supreme reality, are all masculine. The Hebrew people, from whom the western world received its religion, belonged to a patriarchal culture and saw their God in masculine terms, consciously reacting against the cult of feminine deities, among the surrounding peoples. But the Tao is essentially feminine. It is the Root, the Ground, the Receptive. The most typical concept in the Tao Te Ching is that of *wu wei*, that is "actionless activity". It is a state of passivity, of "non-action", but a passivity that is totally active, in the sense of receptive. This is the essence of the feminine. The woman is made to be passive in relation to the man, to receive the seed which makes her fertile. But this passivity is an active passivity, a receptivity which is dynamic and creative, from which all life and fruitfulness, all love and communion grow. The world today needs to recover this sense of feminine power, which is complementary to the masculine and without which man becomes dominating, sterile and destructive. But this means that western religion must come to recognize the feminine aspect of God.

The Tao is compared to water, which "is excellent in benefitting all things" (the source of all fertility) "and always takes the lowest place". "There is nothing weaker than water, but for overcoming things that are hard and strong, there is nothing that can equal it, nothing that can take its place." This is the virtue of humility, the poverty of spirit of the Sermon on the Mount, to which the kingdom of heaven belongs. This leads to the paradox of the value of emptiness. "We make pots of clay," it is said, "but it is the empty space in them which makes them useful. We make a wheel with many spokes joined in a hub, but it is the empty space in the hub which makes the wheel go round. We make houses of brick and wood, but it is the empty spaces in the doors and windows that make them habitable." This again is the value of "non-action", what Gandhi called *ahimsa*. According to the Tao Te Ching a country should not be ruled by violence or by any action on the part of the ruler. The more the state is organized, the more resistance it encounters. "A large kingdom must be like the low ground towards which all streams flow. It must be a point towards which all things under heaven and earth converge. Its part must be that of female in its dealings with all things under heaven. The female by quiescence conquers the male; by quiescence gets underneath." This is a strange paradoxical view of human society, but may it not be that of which the world today stands in need?

A favourite symbol for the Tao is the Uncarved Block, that is the Original Nature. That is the Root, the Ground of being, the Centre on which all things converge. It is identified with the Void and the Quietness, all alike being terms which point to the hidden mystery of the universe. So it is said: "Push far enough towards the void, hold fast enough to the Quietness." This in turn is called the mystic female. "The Spirit of the Valley", it is said, "never dies. The gateway of the Mystic Female is called the root of heaven and earth." And again it is said: "Can you in opening and shutting the heavenly gates [that is, the gates of consciousness] always play the female part?" This may sound very paradoxical and unreal, but for centuries now the western world has been following the path of Yang – of the masculine, active, aggressive, rational, scientific mind – and has brought the world near to destruction. It is time now to recover the path of Yin, of the feminine, passive, patient, intuitive and poetic mind. This is the path which the Tao Te Ching sets before us.

The Monotheism of India

The breakthrough in human consciousness which took place in India and China in the first millennium, also appeared in Greece at the same time. The Greek philosophers from Thales onward in the sixth century before Christ were the first people in the west to develop a strictly rational mode of thought. In the fifth century this movement came to a head in Socrates and Plato, who established the rational mind as the criterion of truth and morality. Unfortunately, the Greeks were always inclined to stop short with rational thought expressed in concepts and judgements. But there was always a deeper movement of thought which went beyond the rational mind. Plato himself acknowledged that we must see in Egypt the source of the more mature wisdom of the west. In Egypt the god Thoth, known in Greece as Hermes Trismegistos, the Thrice-Great Hermes, was conceived as the source of a profound spiritual wisdom, which was preserved in Greece in what is known as the Hermetic tradition. This was a genuine mystical tradition, which was able to transcend the rational mind and discover the source of all wisdom and knowledge in the Nous, the intuitive mind, which itself was seen to derive from a primordial principle beyond human understanding. This insight was developed in Neoplatonism, especially by Plotinus in the third century AD. This philosophy, which reflects the same insight as the Hindu and Buddhist masters, was to have a profound influence on the religion of the west, affecting especially Islam and Christianity, both of which developed a mystical tradition akin to that of Hinduism and Buddhism in the east, and forming an essential part of the *philosophia perennis*, the universal wisdom at the base of all religion.

But before we consider this mystical tradition in western religion, we need to reflect on the development of a pure monotheistic religion in India. The Bhagavad Gita, as we have seen, had laid the foundation of faith and devotion to a personal, creator God. In the course of time this religion of *bhakti*, of fervent love and devotion, spread all over India and in the Middle Ages developed in the Sant movement into a form of pure monotheism. For the Hindu, the personal God was normally conceived in a human form as an *avatara*, a "descent" of God, in the form of Rama or Krishna or some other being. But in the Sant movement the personal God was conceived as totally without form, infinite, eternal, unchanging, transcending the universe yet immanent in it and revealing himself to his devotees as an immanent presence in the heart. The great exponent of this religion was Guru Nanak, the founder of the Sikh religion, which though largely confined to India yet contains within itself the principles of a universal monotheism. What is remarkable about this religion is that though it stems from Hinduism, it was able to transcend the limitations of traditional Hinduism and embrace elements of Islam, especially of Sufi doctrine, and include both Hindus and Muslims among its followers. What is still more important, it could transcend caste and include out-castes among its saints. In this way it became a truly universal religion. It was able also to transcend the dualism implicit in most monotheistic religion.

In order to uphold the transcendence of God, the supreme Being, monotheists feel impelled to see the world as separate from God. Thus religions tend to fall either into dualism or into monism. In order to avoid saying that God and the world are Two, the monist will deny the reality of the world and hold that all multiplicity is an illusion. But the mono-theism of Guru Nanak and all authentic religion holds that God, the absolute Reality, is both transcendent and immanent. The world has no reality in itself – as such it is *maya*, an illusion – but its reality is from God and in God. God – or Brahman or Tao or whatever name we give to the absolute reality – exists in himself, and the universe and humanity exist only in relation to the one Reality. This is the doctrine of Guru Nanak. God, the eternal Truth, is manifested in the creation and in the human mind, but yet remains transcendent beyond word and thought. Knowledge of God comes through meditation on the universe and the human heart, but only the grace of God, the divine illumination, can reveal the hidden mystery. We give extracts from the morning, noon and evening prayer of Guru Nanak from the Adi Grant as an example of his spiritual legacy, together with some hymns of other later Gurus, and of Kabir who combined the Hindu and the Muslim traditions, and the cobbler Ravidas. There are six words which express the true nature of Guru Nanak's religion. The first is *Sabad* (Skt *Sabda*), the Word. God the transcendent Mystery is ineffable but he expresses himself in his Word, which is revealed in all creation and makes itself known in the human heart – the *man* or manas of Hindu tradition. This Word is said to be *anahat* that is "unheard" in the sense that it is an interior word. The Word in turn is expressed in the Name (*Nam*). This is the content of all God's revelation, reflected in all the creation and made known in the human heart. Both the Word and the Name are revealed by the Guru. The Guru is a key concept of Sikh religion as of Hinduism, but it must be understood primarily of the inner guide. The external Guru, whoever he may be, exists only to awaken the disciple (the *Sikh*) to the Guru within, the inner light and truth. The Guru reveals the will of God, the *hukam*, which is the divine order in nature. To discern this divine order beneath all the changing phenomena of the world is to know the Truth

(*Sach*, Skt.*Sat*), and this in turn is a gift of divine Grace (*nadar*). Here we have a complete philosophy for the world today. We look out on the world around us, the world both of nature and of humanity, and beneath all the violence and conflict we discern a divine order, which is the truth, the reality behind all appearances. This discernment of the divine will comes to us through the guidance of the Guru, whoever he may be, who awakens us to the inner light, the word of truth within, and enables us to know his "name", the character, the person, of the indwelling spirit, and all this comes to us by the "grace" of God. This contact with the supreme mystery guides and directs our life, if we empty ourselves, surrender our ego (the *haumai*) and allow the divine truth (the *Sach Khand*) to take possession of our being.

It only remains to add that the God of Guru Nanak, though personal, has no human form. He is formless – *nirankar*. In other words he is like the nirguna Brahman of Hindu tradition, that is "without attributes" or beyond all human expression. Yet he expresses himself in his Word, his self-manifestation in creation, by which he becomes *saguna* with attributes, revealing himself in human nature and making known his "name". His Name again, like his Word, is not a particular name; it is the universal Name, the content of the divine revelation. This is an austere religion. There are none of the satisfactions of a man-like God, with whom human beings can relate. He is approached by *bhakti*, that is, loving devotion, but it is the devotion of total self-giving, and the union between the human and the divine – the *sahaj* – is a mystical union which cannot be expressed in words. It is here that the Nath tradition, the theory of yoga, which was part of the Sant religion, enters in. For the yogi, union with Brahman was not a theory or a doctrine which could be expressed in words. It was an experience of the person in the depth or ground of its being. Thus religion ends as it began, in mystery. It is the meeting of the transcendent mystery at the heart of the universe with the mystery hidden in the heart of humanity. It is the passage beyond the space-time universe, beyond human reason and understanding, beyond the created world into the uncreated, timeless, spaceless reality which is life and truth and love.

Semitic Monotheism

When we turn to the monotheism of Judaism and Islam, we encounter different approaches to the same reality. Both religions stem from a very primitive society, polytheistic and polygamous, consisting of petty tribes for whom war was the normal way of settling disputes and in which women were subjected to men. It was the great achievement of each religion that it was able to rise to the conception of one God, all powerful and all knowing, the creator of heaven and earth, that is, of the spiritual and material universe. This God was a "righteous" God, upholding the moral law, and a "holy" God, demanding total submission (Islam) on the part of his followers. In both religions their God was held to be "merciful and compassionate"; these are, in fact, the primary attributes of God repeated daily in the opening prayer of the Quran. But the mercy and compassion of God were held to be strictly reserved to those who believed in him; the rest were condemned to everlasting punishment. It is this moral dualism in the Semitic religions which has caused so much trouble in the world, and this in turn is based on a metaphysical dualism. God is wholly transcendent, separate from the world, and though his mercy and compassion may draw his faithful followers to him, the division between God and humanity can never be overcome.

There can be no doubt that this dualism springs from the very primitive conditions in which each religion originated. Yahweh was the "Lord of hosts", that is, of the armies of Israel, who led them in war against their enemies. In the same way Muhammad had to fight for his followers against the clans who defied them. Thus violence and conflict were built into each religion from the beginning, and their God inevitably reflected the mind of his followers. Both in Israel and in Islam this policy of war and conquest was able to build up a people, uniting many tribes and clans, and eventually many nations and peoples, in a religious community which has been able to resist all the forces of disruption through loyalty to their faith in the one God, to whom they have entrusted their lives. Still more remarkable has been the way in which they have been able to construct a doctrine and a discipline, which has brought them into contact with the great tradition of wisdom in India and in Greece, which we have been studying.

Islam and the Sufi Doctrine

In Islam this was the work of the Sufi mystics. Within a hundred years of the death of Muhammad an ascetic movement arose in Islam, influenced, no doubt, by the Christian monks encountered in Arabia, Egypt and Ethiopia, which became known as Sufism from the woollen garment (*suf*) which they wore. As Islam spread westward across north Africa to Spain and eastward to Palestine, Syria, Turkey, Iraq and Iran, it encountered both the philosophical tradition of Greece, especially of Neoplatonism, and the refined poetic and artistic culture of the Middle East. It was then that a spiritual movement awoke in Islam which was to develop one of the most profound forms of the perennial philosophy which has ever been known. The Sufi mystics drew out the symbolic meaning of the Quran much as the Christian mystics developed the symbolism of the Bible. We give the text from the Quran on the Light, which inspired many of the mystics, especially Al Ghazali (1058–1111), who wrote a profound commentary on it. Al Ghazali exercised the greatest influence on the development of Sufism, since being one of the leading doctors of Islam he converted to Sufism and made it acceptable to the orthodox Muslim. He left us the story of his conversion, of which we print the most important part. But the person in whom the mystical doctrine of Islam found its most perfect expression was the "great sheik", Ibn al Arabi. Born in Spain in AD 1165, he travelled through north Africa to Mecca and the Middle East and finally settled in Damascus, where he died in 1240. He was not only a profoundly learned man but was the subject of mystical experiences and divine revelations. His great work *The Meccan Revelations* contains 2500 pages and has not yet been translated. His smaller work, *The Bezels of Wisdom*, has recently been translated into English and reveals a mind of extraordinary intellectual power. In other words, he is an example of a mystic who is also a philosopher, and can give a coherent and intelligible form to his mystical insight.

The basic principle of his philosophy is his conception of the Oneness of Being (*Wuhdat al wujud*). According to this principle all difference, distinction and conflict are but apparent facets of a unique reality. In other words he reached the same understanding of ultimate truth and reality which had been reached by the great Hindu and Buddhist philosophers. The dualism inherent in orthodox Islam was overcome and Islam learned to speak the language of the universal wisdom. This "Oneness of being", in which all opposites are reconciled, is the supreme insight of the perennial philosophy. It cannot be known by reason, but where the heart is opened in faith to the supreme Reality, it is known with intellectual clarity. Ibn al Arabi calls this principle *al haqq*, the Reality, while the personal God, Allah, is the form of the Reality when conceived in relation to the created world. Ibn al Arabi speaks of the "God created in belief" to distinguish this form of God from the Reality which embraces God and the world in one. The problem for all monotheism has been how to reconcile the one absolute, supreme Reality, the personal God, with the created world of time and space, of change and becoming. For orthodox Islam the human being is a Slave (*abd*) of God, created separate from God and for ever incapable of sharing the divine nature. But for Ibn al Arabi a link was found between the human and the divine in what he calls the "isthmus" (*barsakh*). This was what is called the Perfect Man (*al Insan al Kamil*). The Universal or Perfect Man is the archetypal man. In sufi theory every created being has its archetype, its "idea", in the all-creating mind, and the archetypal man is the being in whom the form or nature of man is revealed. In a beautiful image he is said to be the eye by which the divine subject sees himself and the perfect mirror which reflects the divine light. We have to recognize that beyond the individual human mind, which reflects through the body and its senses, there is always the universal mind, the source of truth, of logic and mathematics, of metaphysical and moral insight. This is the source of all certainty in human experience. This is the *buddhi* of Hindu tradition, the *prajna* of Buddhist tradition, the *nous* of Greek tradition. It is interesting to notice that Ibn al Arabi uses the word *khayal*, which has been translated "creative imagination". This recalls the power of Imagination which we observed in Wordsworth, Coleridge and Goethe, the power to "mirror" the creation. It is by this power of Imagination that the divine mind mirrors the creation and the creation reflects the divine mind. The Perfect Man therefore is the image in which the divine being reflects the creation and created being reflects the mind of God. Following Islamic tradition, Ibn al Arabi sees in Muhammad the image of the Perfect Man, but he also has the interesting idea of the "saint", as one who sees beyond the God "created in belief" to the ultimate truth and the reality, from which the prophet and apostle derive their mission.

Jewish Mysticism – The Kabbala

Israel like Islam began as an extremely primitive religion. Its God, Yahweh, was a tribal god, who was responsible for the massacre of the first-born of a whole people and who led the armies of Israel in the invasion of Palestine, where they were commanded to destroy the cities and kill both men, women and children. Yet from this barbarous religion there emerged under the leadership of Moses a profound doctrine of God, as the creator and Lord of the universe, who was "holy", and "righteous", the author of the moral law. The problem, however, remained, that as their God was exalted in holiness, the opposing power in the universe came to be projected as a power opposed to God in the form of Satan. Originally Satan, as in the Book of Job, was one of the "sons of God", but in the course of time, perhaps under the influence of Persian dualism, he came to be seen as an independent power of evil, the devil (the *diabolos* or destroyer who "throws apart" or divides the world as opposed to the symbol, the *symbolon*, which "throws together" or unites the world). This created a fundamental moral dualism in Judaism, which led to belief in an eternal reward for the "righteous" and eternal punishment for the "wicked". Yet in Judaism as in Islam a remarkable doctrine emerged in the Middle Ages, particularly in Spain, in the form of the Kabbala, in which, like the Sufis in Islam, the Jewish mystics were able to transcend this dualism and enter into the main stream of the universal wisdom which had come down from India and Greece.

The supreme Reality came to be known in the Kabbala as *En Sof*, the "Infinite". In this infinite, eternal Reality, a division arises, which is nothing less than the emergence of self-consciousness. It is from this self-consciousness of the Eternal that creation arises. In the infinity of Being there is an infinite variety of possible beings, finite forms or manifestations of the one infinite Being. These original forms of being were conceived in the Kabbala as emerging from the ten *Sefirof*, the ten spheres of divine manifestation, a kind of spiritual universe, which preceded the manifestation of the created universe. This constituted the archetypal world from which the created world, as we know it, is derived. In a view which reminds us of the "void" (*sunyata*) of Mahayana Buddhism, the source of this manifestation of the infinite was conceived as "nothingness". This nothingness is the abyss of being, the divine darkness of a later tradition, from which all forms of manifestation emerge. It is interesting to find that the origin of manifestation is to be found in a "point", in which the whole creation was originally folded up. This reminds us of David Bohm's conception of the universe being the explication, the unfolding, of the implicate order, in which the whole creation was originally "folded up".

In the Jewish tradition this source of the manifestation of the infinite was identified with the Wisdom (*hokhmah*) of God. In this eternal wisdom the essences or ideas, the archetypes, of all created being, are held to exist. Once more we come upon the fundamental idea that before the material space-time world comes into existence, it is conceived in the mind of the infinite and eternal Being. In the divine Wisdom all the forms or ideas of created Being exist in an undifferentiated state. The principle of differentiation by which the separate forms of being – both material and human – come into existence is known among the Sephiroth as *Bina*, the Intelligence. Once again the Intelligence or Intellect, the Nous, is seen as the source of division, of analysis, which separates the individual being from its matrix, the divine mother, who conceives the creation in her womb. But this "point" from which all creation comes, is a dynamic point, which is compared to a fountain. It is the mystical Eden, the Paradise, from which the waters of the divine life flow over the creation. All these streams of divine life are held to fall into the "great sea", the *Shekhinah*, the symbol of the divine presence in creation. It is of great interest that the Shekhinah was conceived as feminine, so that the Kabbala was able to overcome not only the dualism of God and creation, but also the dualism of male and female, and to recognize a feminine aspect in God. As one of the Kabbalists declared: "If one contemplates things in mystical meditation, everything is revealed as one."

It must be emphasized that this is in no sense a form of pantheism. For pantheism the world in its diversity and multiplicity is conceived as

God. This is clearly opposed to any forms of monotheism. For the Kab-
balist, on the other hand, as for the tradition of the perennial philosophy
as a whole, the world is conceived as one with God only when it is known
in its original unity in the divine mind before any form of multiplicity or
diversity appears. We have to recognize that the world of phenomena, of
things as they appear to the senses and the rational mind, as western
science is beginning to discover, is an illusion, while the Reality is that
which gives existence and meaning to phenomena, and that Reality is
what monotheists call God. It is interesting that the Kabbala also develops
the doctrine of Man as the Image of God and conceives Adam Kadmon,
the Original Man, like the Perfect Man of the Sufi Tradition and the
Purusha of Hindu tradition as the image of God. We can therefore see
how in each religion an identical doctrine emerges, which can rightly be
called the Universal Wisdom, or what in India is called the *Sanatana
Dharma*, the eternal religion.

The Holy Trinity and the Body of Christ

Christianity emerged as a separate religion from Judaism only by slow
stages. Jesus of Nazareth was born of a Jewish family, said to have been
descended from the line of David. He grew up as a Jew, speaking Aramaic
and studying the Jewish scriptures, no doubt in Hebrew. His mind and
character were formed according to Jewish tradition and he thought and
spoke in terms of the traditional religion of Israel. He accepted the Law
of Moses as a sacred inheritance and interpreted his own life and destiny
in the light of the prophetic revelation. He made his own the Jewish
expectation of a Messiah, who would redeem the world and reveal God's
final plan of salvation. In particular he saw in the "suffering servant" of
Isaiah the figure of his own person and destiny, and in the Son of Man
of the book of Daniel, who was to come in the clouds of heaven and
usher in the kingdom of God, the sign of his own calling to establish the
kingdom of God. As the fortunes of Israel declined and their country
was conquered first by the Babylonians, then by the Persians and Greeks,
and finally by the Romans, the hopes of Israel turned towards a divine
intervention, which would put an end to the present world and inaugurate
a new age. Such was the expectation of Israel at the coming of Christ.

But rooted, as he was, in the tradition of the Law and the Prophets,
Jesus yet felt himself called to break with the traditions of Israel in many
ways. There was first of all the custom of the observance of the Sabbath.
This had become very restrictive and often defeated the very purpose for
which it had been instituted. Again and again Jesus is seen rejecting the
strict observances of the sabbath and declaring that "the sabbath was
made for man, not man for the sabbath". This applied to the whole

observance of the Law. The Law of religion was relativized and made subordinate to the one, universal law of love of God and of one's neighbour. But this inevitably changed Jesus's attitude to people under the law. He deliberately associated with "sinners", people who were prevented by their status or occupation from observing the law. This led him to show compassion to prostitutes and to a woman caught in the act adultery. This led him in turn to break down the barrier between the Jew and the Samaritan, an ancient religious division which had divided Israel in two. Finally he came to the point of accepting women – even a Samaritan woman – on terms of equality with men. It is difficult for us to imagine the effect of this revolutionary attitude on the people of his time, but one can understand how it brought him enemies on every side, particularly among those who upheld the Law. Thus the whole problem of religion and morality today was focused in Jesus's life as a Jew, in his time.

But a problem remains in trying to interpret the life and teaching of Jesus today. Jesus himself spoke Aramaic (a Semitic dialect akin to Hebrew) and his message was given to a small group of disciples in Palestine. As the Christian community spread outside Palestine to the cities of the Roman Empire, the disciples, who were no longer Jews, spoke Greek, and the life and teaching of Jesus was recorded in what is called the New Testament – as distinguished from the Old Testament of Jewish religion – not in Aramaic but in Greek. As a result we know only of the life and teaching of Jesus through the gospels, which were composed during the second half of the first century in Christian communities, which inevitably interpreted them in the context of their own situation. It cannot be denied that an authentic portrait of Jesus as a man and of his basic teaching comes down to us in the four gospels – four distinct accounts written under different circumstances, yet all basically consistent with one another. Yet the differences remain and how much each account was influenced by the situation and circumstances of the writer, it is impossible to say.

This is especially evident when we come to consider the relation of Jesus to orthodox Judaism. In Matthew's gospel, which was always considered to be the first gospel and clearly has an Aramaic background, the Jewish impact on Jesus's teaching is very clear, especially in the harsh judgement on "sinners", where we are continually reminded of their being cast into the "outer darkness" with "weeping and gnashing of teeth". It is possible that Jesus used such language, but it is much more probable that this is a Jewish interpretation of his teaching with the pronounced dualism of traditional Judaism. At any rate in Mark's gospel, which most critics now regard as the earliest, and which was probably written in Rome, the centre of the "gentile" world, this element scarcely occurs, and Luke, who also writes from a Hellenistic perspective, presents above all the compassionate character of Jesus, as seen, for instance in the parable of the Good Samaritan and the Prodigal Son. This becomes extremely important for our understanding of Jesus today. There is nothing more alienating than the concept of a vengeful God condemning people to eternal punishment. This concept seems to be an inheritance from a Semitic monotheism, which was unable to overcome the dualism inherent in this system of thought.

When we turn to the fourth gospel, probably composed in Ephesus at the end of the first century, we are in another world. Ephesus, in what is now Turkey, was a centre of what is known as gnosticism and the fourth gospel bears every sign of being composed in this milieu. Gnosticism took many forms, Hellenistic, Jewish and Christian, but essentially it was a form of *gnosis* an awakening to the ancient wisdom, the divine knowledge or *jnana* in Hindu terms, which came down through Persia and Egypt to the west. Much of it became very debased in the process, but a spark of wisdom or transcendent knowledge remained. It is this which we find in the fourth gospel. In the prologue the writer speaks of Jesus as the Word or Logos of God, thus linking him with the Logos of Heraclitus and the Stoic philosophers, but also with the Wisdom of the later Writings of Judaism. After the Law and prophets the Jewish scriptures included the Writings, in which they drew on the ancient wisdom of Egypt and Babylonia and thus extended the horizon of their thought. In the wisdom literature of the Old Testament we encounter an authentic witness to the ancient tradition of Wisdom, and the fourth gospel places the life and teaching of Jesus in this context. It is above all a symbolic story. The writer has no hesitation in altering times and places, putting the cleansing of the temple at the beginning of Jesus's ministry, for instance, instead of at the end. In this he is simply recovering the ancient tradition of symbolism, in which the symbol is seen as a sign under which reality becomes present, and reveals its deeper meaning.

In the fourth gospel all the words and actions of Jesus are given this symbolic character. Jesus himself is a symbol of God, a sign by which the divine mystery makes itself present and becomes known. The western mind is accustomed to abstract thought, by which truth is communicated through universal concepts but, as we have seen, in the ancient world reality was made known through concrete symbols – a symbol being precisely a sign by which reality is made present to human consciousness. In the fourth gospel therefore Jesus's words and actions are all seen as "signs", by which the divine Reality, the absolute Truth, makes itself present to those who are capable of receiving it. It is not addressed to the rational, analytical, scientific mind, which will always miss its meaning. It is revealed to the deeper intuitive mind, the *nous* or *intellectus* or rather beyond the mind to the centre of the human person, the spirit, the *pneuma* of St Paul, the *atman* of the Hindu tradition, which is the true Self, the inner reality of the human being.

It is of particular importance that in the fourth gospel the Logos, the Word, is said to have "become flesh". There is always the danger that Reality should be reduced to an abstraction. It can become a universal idea, which, however profound it may be, does not touch the "flesh", the concrete reality of the human person. This is the peculiar revelation of the fourth gospel, that the Reality, the Truth, the Word, is revealed in the flesh and blood of a human being, who sheds his blood on the cross and rises to eternal life in the flesh. This does away for ever with the view that this world of flesh and blood, of suffering and death, is unreal in the light of the perennial philosophy. The world of science is an unreal world: it is a world of sense phenomena and mental abstractions. But in the real world, while the reality of sense experience and rational know-ledge is not lost, it is taken up into the world of personal being, of the whole, from which sense and reason derive their reality. This is the world of the fourth gospel, as of all the forms of ancient wisdom. It is the world which we know, when we cease to be dominated by the rational mind and allow the light of the eternal truth to shine in the heart. Jesus in the fourth gospel is seen always open to this divine light: "You shall see the heavens opened and the angels of God ascending and descending on the Son of Man." The angels are, of course, the manifestations of the divine presence (like the Sephiroth in the Kabbala) and the Son of Man is the eternal Man, the primordial Person, who is present in Jesus of Nazareth.

Jesus in the fourth gospel refers himself at every stage to his source in the Father. The Father is the Source, the Origin, the One. Jesus receives his being from the Father. He is God (*theos*) from God (*ek tou theou*). Gradually through the gospel this relationship of Jesus to the Father is unfolded. He is the Way that leads to the Father, the Truth that reveals the Father, the Life that flows from the Father. He tells the Samaritan woman that "the Father seeks those who will worship him in spirit and truth" and speaks of a "fountain of water springing up to eternal life". He feeds the hungry with bread and speaks of a "bread that comes down from heaven". Always the reference is to the transcendent reality, the one Light, the one Life, the Source of all. He speaks of giving his "flesh for the life of the world", of "eating his flesh and drinking his blood". All this is spoken of the flesh and blood of eternal life, for "my flesh is meat indeed, my blood is drink indeed", that is, in truth, in reality, not under temporal appearances. This language is almost impossible for people to understand today. We have come to mistake the appearances of the spatio-temporal world for reality, and it is hard for us to see behind the appearances to the Reality which is always there.

It is important to emphasize this dependence of Jesus on the Father. A custom has grown up of speaking of Jesus as God, but this is quite contrary to the usage of the New Testament. In the New Testament, almost without exception, the word "God" is reserved to the Father – the Source and Origin of all. Jesus never speaks of himself as God, but emphasizes all the time his total dependence on God. "The Son can do nothing of himself but only what he sees the Father doing." "I can do nothing on my own authority." When he was accused of making himself God, his reply was not that he was God, but that it was said in the Old Testament "you are Gods and all of you sons of the most High", thus emphasizing that the divine life is offered to all, while he is the one "whom the Father has consecrated and sent into the world". Yet with this total dependence on the Father, Jesus receives everything from the Father, the Father has "given all things into his hands". This is the deep meaning behind this language of Father and Son. The Son is the image, the self-expression, the self-consciousness of God. As the earlier gospels of Matthew and Luke had recorded: "No one knows the Son but the Father and no one knows the Father but the Son", and they add "he to whom the Son chooses to reveal him".

This brings out a further dimension in the mystery of the Son. Jesus is not Son in an exclusive sense. Every human being is created in the "image and likeness" of God. Every human being is a capacity for God. Jesus comes to reveal the destiny of all humanity. Jesus speaks of himself in terms of utmost intimacy with the Father. "I am in the Father and the Father in me", "He who sees me, sees the Father", "I and the Father are one." Here we have expressed in the clearest terms the "non-duality" of Jesus and God. He is one with the Father and yet he is not the Father. This is neither monism, a simple identity, nor dualism, a real separation. It is "non-dualism", the mystery revealed in the Hindu and Buddhist and Taoist scriptures and discovered in Judaism and Islam. Here we are at the heart of the cosmic revelation. Jesus makes this clear when he prays for his disciples "that they may be one, as thou, Father, art in me and I in thee, that they also may be in us". This is the destiny of all humanity, to realize its essential unity in the Godhead, by whatever name it is known, to be one with the absolute Reality, the absolute Truth, the infinite, the eternal Life and Light.

But this unity cannot be known without the pain of self-sacrifice; it demands "nothing less than all". Jesus had warned his disciples: "He who would save his life will lose it; he who will lose his life for my sake will find it", and he himself took the path of self-sacrifice to the point of death. This was accompanied by a tremendous struggle, when he "sweated blood", as his human nature rebelled against the pain, humiliation and death, which he had to endure; and he prayed "let this cup pass away", but immediately added, "not my will but thy will be done". This is the cost of surrendering the self, the separated, individual self, which has to die, if the true self is to be found. But there was still one last trial for Jesus to undergo. He had been rejected by his own people, condemned by the Roman government, forsaken by his disciples, but he had still to make a final sacrifice. He had still to lose his image of God. As he lay dying on the cross, he cried out, "My God, my God, why have you forsaken me?" This is the last trial of every spiritual person, to surrender his image and concept of God and to face the Reality which lies beyond all images and concepts. Only then could he say: "It is finished".

When he parted from his disciples Jesus had promised to send them the Spirit (Greek *pneuma* from the root *pnu*, to breathe or blow, like the Sanskrit *Atman*, the Buddhist *nirvana*, the "blowing out", the Latin *animus* and *anima*, the Hebrew *ruah*). The Spirit is like the wind or the breath – "no one can see whence it comes or whither it goes" – it is invisible. Jesus had to depart in the flesh to become present in the spirit. In every religion there are rituals and doctrines by which the Spirit makes itself known, but we have always to go beyond all rituals and doctrines to the Reality which they represent. We cannot do without the rituals and doctrines, but if we remain at that level we become idolaters, not discerning the truth. So the Spirit in all religion is the Reality, which gives meaning to all observances. But there is one expression of the Spirit which is more meaningful than all others and that is love. Love is invisible, but it is the most powerful force in human nature. Jesus spoke of the Spirit which he would send as Truth but also as Love. "If anyone loves me, my Father will love him and we will come to him and make our abode with him." This is the love, the *prema* and *bhakti*, which was proclaimed in the Bhagavad Gita, the compassion (*karuna*) of Buddha, the rapturous love of the Sufi saints. Ultimately a religion is tested by its capacity to awaken love in its followers, and, what is perhaps more difficult, to extend that love to all humanity. In the past religions have tended to confine their love to their own followers, but always there has been a movement to break through these barriers and attain to a universal love. The Universal Wisdom is necessarily a message of universal Love.

Eventually it can be said that the mystery of the Godhead, of ultimate Truth and Reality, is to be found not in a personal God nor in an impersonal Absolute but in inter-personal relationship, or a communion of love. The universe has been called a "complicated web of inter-dependent relationships" (Capra), and humanity as a whole can be described as a web of inter-personal relationships. Every being seeks spontaneously to express and communicate itself, and the whole universe can be conceived as the mode of expression and communication in space and time of the one infinite, eternal reality. In a human being this expression and communication comes through consciousness which manifests itself in knowledge and love. The supreme Being or absolute Reality therefore comes to be conceived as expressing itself in an eternal Word or Wisdom, which is manifested in the structure of the universe and in the human heart, and communicating itself in a Holy Spirit or divine energy, which is manifested in all the energies of the universe and in human beings above all in the energy of love. It is in this way that the Godhead comes to be conceived as a Trinity. The Father, the Ground and Source of being, expresses himself eternally in the Son, the Word or Wisdom, which reveals the Godhead, and the Holy Spirit is the Energy of love, the feminine aspect of God, by which the Godhead eternally communicates itself in Love. All human wisdom and love is a manifestation in space and time of this eternal Wisdom and Love. In Christian tradition the Word of God is conceived to have received its full and final revelation in Jesus Christ, and the Spirit of God to have been revealed in the fullness of love manifested in his sacrifice on the Cross and present in the Church as the Spirit of love, communicated to every Christian.

It is here that the feminine aspect in God is revealed, though it has rarely been recognized in Christian tradition. If the Son is "begotten" of the Father, there must clearly be a Mother in whom he is conceived. In the Incarnation the Son was conceived in the womb of the Virgin overshadowed by the Holy Spirit.

In Eternity the Son is begotten of the Father and conceived in the womb of the Mother, the Holy Spirit, just as in creation the Father sows the seed of the Word in matter, and the Holy Spirit, the Mother, nourishes the seed and brings forth all the forms of creation. In the Hindu tradition the world comes forth from the union of Purusha and Prakriti, the Male and Female principles, and in Sufi doctrine the world is brought into being by the "Breath of the Merciful". In Semitic religions the fear of sex as a disruptive force in human life has often led to the suppression of women and a failure to recognize the presence of the feminine in God. But the inclusion of the Song of Songs in the sacred Writings of Israel opened the way to the recognition of the essential holiness of sexual love, as shown in the Christian commentaries on the Song of Songs from the time of Origen in the third century to Sister Bernard in the twelth. In Hindu and Buddhist tradition sexual love has always been seen as a symbol of divine love. Ibn al Arabi's expression "Breath of the Merciful" (*nafas al rahman*) is especially significant, since the word *rahman* comes from the root *rahima*, which means the "womb". The "merciful" is thus conceived as the womb from which all the potentialities in the divine mind are released in creation.

We can thus discern a basic pattern in all the great religious traditions.

There is first of all the supreme Principle, the ultimate Truth, beyond name and form, the Nirguna Brahman of Hinduism, the Nirvana and Sunyata of Buddhism, the Tao without a name of Chinese tradition, the Truth of Sikhism, the Reality – al Haqq – of Sufism, the Infinite En Sof of the Kabbala, the Godhead (as distinguished from God) in Christianity. There is then the manifestation of the hidden Reality, the Saguna Brahman of Hinduism, the Buddha or Tathagata of Buddhism, the Chinese Sage, the Sikh Guru, the personal God, Yahweh or Allah, of Judaism and Islam, and the Christ of Christianity. Finally there is the Spirit, the *atman* of Hinduism, the "Compassion" of the Buddha, the Grace (*Nadar*) of Sikhism, the "Breath of the Merciful" in Islam, the *Ruah*, the Spirit, in Judaism and the *Pneuma* in Christianity. But in each religion this universal truth is embodied in a community, in which it receives a particular structure of ritual and doctrine, which separates the religions from one another. In Christianity the divine revelation in Christ was embodied in the Church. This Church took various forms, as it spread through the Roman Empire and then through Europe and beyond. But at an early stage there arose a conception of the Church as a universal community. This appeared particularly in the Letter to the Ephesians, which stemmed from the same gnostic environment as the fourth gospel. The Letter to the Ephesians takes up from the Letter to the Colossians, which stems from the same milieu, the conception of the *pleroma*, the "fullness", corresponding with the Sanskrit *purnam*. This signifies the absolute fullness of reality, but it is now said that this fullness dwells in Christ – "in him dwells the fullness of the Godhead bodily". This is a remarkable text revealing a conception of the "godhead", as in Meister Eckhart, beyond the personal God, and this fullness is said to dwell "bodily" in Christ, that is, the divine fullness or ultimate reality is present in its fullness in a human being. The Letter to the Ephesians goes on to say that this fullness is found in the Church, "which is his Body, the fullness of Him who fills all in all". We have here the conception of a human community, which embraces all creation, for according to the Letter to the Colossians, in Christ "all things were created, in heaven and on earth ... all were created through him and for him." This is a truly cosmic vision embracing the whole created world, which we now know to be an integrated whole, and this forms a Body, a living organism, which is capable of embracing all humanity. We have therefore the conception of a universal community capable of embodying the Universal Wisdom and uniting all humanity in one Body, one living whole, in which the "fullness", the whole, of the Godhead dwells.

In practice, of course, the Church has become divided into innumerable little churches, each with its own limited horizon and cut off from the wider religious traditions of the world. But today we are able to see how the Christian churches, while recognizing the values of each Christian tradition, could transcend these divisions, and at the same time open themselves to the values and insights of other religions. Each religion has to undergo a death and resurrection – a death to its historical and cultural limitations and a resurrection to a new life in the Spirit, which would embody the traditions of the Universal Wisdom in a way which responds to the need of humanity today. No doubt we are all very far from realizing this unity, but as the different religions of the world meet today, we are discovering our common heritage and becoming aware of the unity which binds together the whole human race and makes it aware of its responsibility for the whole created universe. The concept of one world, one human race, and one religion based on the Universal Wisdom, has acquired a new significance, as a way to escape from the disastrous conflicts which are dividing the world today.

I

HINDUISM

Upanishads
Bhagavadgita

The classical Upanishads composed between 600 BC and 300 BC mark the first great breakthrough in human consciousness to the infinite, transcendent mystery of Being, the ultimate Reality beyond word and thought. The *rishis* (seers) called this supreme Being *Brahman*, a word which originally signified the utterance of prayer, the mantra, by which the divine mystery was invoked in the sacrifice (*yajna*), but which came to signify the divine mystery itself as the source of being and consciousness. The rishis looked round on the world of the senses, the phenomenal world, and saw beyond it to the source of all phenomena, the ground of being, which they called Brahman, and beyond the body and the senses to the source of consciousness, which they called Atman, the Spirit, the Self. Finally the great discovery was made that "this Atman is Brahman", the source of being and consciousness is one and the same. In the course of time this supreme reality was described as Sacchidananda, being (*sat*) realized in full consciousness (*cit*) and experienced as absolute bliss (*ananda*). Yet beyond all words and concepts it was realized that this supreme mystery of being could only be described in negative terms as *neti, neti,* "not this, not this". However far we penetrate towards the truth, we have to acknowledge in the end, that it is an absolute mystery, beyond human comprehension. Yet though it could be described in impersonal terms, it was seen from the first that it had a personal character and was called Pursusha, the cosmic Person, who sustains the universe by his indwelling presence. This personal aspect of the mystery of being was named in a later Upanishad (the Svetasvatara) as Siva the "auspicious" or "kindly one" and gave birth to the school of Saivism, while in the Bhagavad Gita, the Song of the Lord, it was conceived as Vishnu, who manifested himself in the form of Krishna, and this became the source of the school of Vaishnavism. Still today Hindus are divided between Saivites and Vaishnavites, but beyond all these differences of name and form, the Hindu still recognizes the Brahman and the Atman as the ultimate ground of being and consciousness.

UPANISHADS

Isha
Kena
Katha
Mundaka
Mandukya
Svetasvatara

ISHA

Translated from the Sanskrit by
W. B. Yeats and Shree Purohit Swami

That is perfect. This is perfect. Perfect comes from perfect. Take perfect from perfect, the remainder is perfect.

May peace and peace and peace be everywhere.

Whatever lives is full of the Lord. Claim nothing; enjoy, do not covet His property.

Then hope for a hundred years of life doing your duty. No other way can prevent deeds from clinging, proud as you are of your human life.

They that deny the Self, return after death to a godless birth, blind, enveloped in darkness.

The Self is one. Unmoving, it moves faster than the mind. The senses lag, but Self runs ahead. Unmoving, it outruns pursuit. Out of Self comes the breath that is the life of all things.

Unmoving, it moves; is far away, yet near; within all, outside all.

Of a certainty the man who can see all creatures in himself, himself in all creatures, knows no sorrow.

How can a wise man, knowing the unity of life, seeing all creatures in himself, be deluded or sorrowful?

The Self is everywhere, without a body, without a shape, whole, pure, wise, all knowing, far shining, self-depending, all transcending; in the eternal procession assigning to every period its proper duty.

Pin your faith to natural knowledge, stumble through the darkness of the blind; pin your faith to supernatural knowledge, stumble through a darkness deeper still.

Natural knowledge brings one result, supernatural knowledge another. We have heard it from the wise who have clearly explained it.

They that know and can distinguish between natural knowledge and supernatural knowledge shall, by the first, cross the perishable in safety; shall, passing beyond the second, attain immortal life.

Pin your faith to the seed of nature, stumble through the darkness of the blind; pin your faith to the shapes of nature, stumble through a darkness deeper still.

The seed of nature brings one result; the shapes of nature another. We have heard it from the wise, who have clearly explained it.

They that know and can distinguish between the shapes of nature and the seed of nature shall, by the first, cross the perishable in safety; shall, passing beyond the second, attain immortal life.

They have put a golden stopper into the neck of the bottle. Pull it, Lord! Let out reality. I am full of longing.

Protector, Seer, controller of all, fountain of life, upholder, do not waste light; gather light; let me see that blessed body – Lord of all. I myself am He.

Life merge into the all prevalent, the eternal; body turn to ashes. Mind! meditate on the eternal Spirit; remember past deeds. Mind! remember past deeds; remember, Mind! remember.

Holy light! illuminate the way that we may gather the good we planted. Are not our deeds known to you? Do not let us grow crooked, we that kneel and pray again and again.

KENA

Translated from the Sanskrit by
W. B. Yeats and Shree Purohit Swami

1

Speech, eyes, ears, limbs, life, energy, come to my help. These books
have Spirit for theme. I shall never deny Spirit, nor Spirit deny me. Let
me be in union, communion with Spirit. When I am one with Spirit, may
the laws these books proclaim live in me, may the laws live.

The enquirer asked: "What has called my mind to the hunt? What has
made my life begin? What wags in my tongue? What God has opened
eye and ear?"

The teacher answered: "It lives in all that lives, hearing through the
ear, thinking through the mind, speaking through the tongue, seeing
through the eye. The wise man clings neither to this nor that, rises out
of sense, attains immortal life.

"Eye, tongue, cannot approach it nor mind know; not knowing, we
cannot satisfy enquiry. It lies beyond the known, beyond the unknown.
We know through those who have preached it, have learned it from
tradition.

"That which makes the tongue speak, but needs no tongue to explain,
that alone is Spirit; not what sets the world by the ears.

"That which makes the mind think, but needs no mind to think, that
alone is Spirit; not what sets the world by the ears.

"That which makes the eye see, but needs no eye to see, that alone is
Spirit; not what sets the world by the ears.

"That which makes the ear hear, but needs no ear to hear, that alone
is Spirit; not what sets the world by the ears.

"That which makes life live, but needs no life to live, that alone is
Spirit; not what sets the world by the ears."

2

"If you think that you know much, you know little. If you think that you
know It from study of your own mind or of nature, study again."

The enquirer said: "I do not think that I know much, I neither say
that I know, nor say that I do not."

The teacher answered: "The man who claimed that he knows, knows
nothing; but he who claims nothing, knows.

"Who says that Spirit is not known, knows; who claims that he knows, knows nothing. The ignorant think that Spirit lies within knowledge, the wise man knows It beyond knowledge.

"Spirit is known through revelation. It leads to freedom. It leads to power. Revelation is the conquest of death.

"The living man who finds Spirit, finds Truth. But if he fail, he sinks among fouler shapes. The man who can see the same Spirit in every creature, clings neither to this nor that, attains immortal life."

3

Once upon a time, Spirit planned that the gods might win a great victory. The gods grew boastful; though Spirit had planned their victory, they thought they had done it all.

Spirit saw their vanity and appeared. They could not understand; they said: "Who is that mysterious Person?"

They said to Fire: "Fire! Find out who is that mysterious Person."

Fire ran to Spirit. Spirit asked what it was. Fire said: "I am Fire; known to all."

Spirit asked: "What can you do?" Fire said: "I can burn anything and everything in this world."

"Burn it," said Spirit, putting a straw on the ground. Fire threw itself upon the straw, but could not burn it. Then Fire ran to the gods in a hurry and confessed it could not find out who was that mysterious Person.

Then the gods asked Wind to find out who was that mysterious Person.

Wind ran to Spirit and Spirit asked what it was. Wind said: "I am Wind; I am the King of the Air."

Spirit asked: "What can you do?" and Wind said: "I can blow away anything and everything in this world."

"Blow it away," said Spirit, putting a straw on the ground. Wind threw itself upon the straw, but could not move it. Then Wind ran to the gods in a hurry and confessed it could not find out who was that mysterious Person.

Then the gods went to Light and asked it to find out who was that mysterious Person. Light ran towards Spirit, but Spirit disappeared upon the instant.

There appeared in the sky that pretty girl, the Goddess of Wisdom, snowy Himālaya's daughter. Light went to her and asked who was that mysterious Person.

4

The Goddess said: "Spirit, through Spirit you attained your greatness. Praise the greatness of Spirit." Then Light knew that the mysterious Person was none but Spirit.

That is how these gods – Fire, Wind and Light – attained supremacy; they came nearest to Spirit and were the first to call that Person Spirit.

Light stands above Fire and Wind; because closer than they, it was the first to call that Person Spirit.

This is the moral of the tale. In the lightning, in the light of an eye, the light belongs to Spirit.

The power of the mind when it remembers and desires, when it thinks again and again, belongs to Spirit. Therefore let Mind meditate on Spirit.

Spirit is the Good in all. It should be worshipped as the Good. He that knows it as the Good is esteemed by all.

You asked me about spiritual knowledge, I have explained it.

Austerity, self-control, meditation are the foundation of this knowledge; the Vedas are its house, truth its shrine.

He who knows this shall prevail against all evil, enjoy the Kingdom of Heaven, yes, for ever enjoy the blessed Kingdom of Heaven.

KATHA

Translated from the Sanskrit by
W. B. Yeats and Shree Purohit Swami

Part One

1

May He protect us both. May He take pleasure in us both. May we show courage together. May spiritual knowledge shine before us. May we never hate one another. May peace and peace and peace be everywhere.

Wājashrawas, wanting heaven, gave away all his property.

He had a son by name Nachiketas. While the gifts were passing, Nachiketas, though but a boy, thought to himself:

"He has not earned much of a heaven; his cows can neither eat, drink, calve nor give milk."

He went to his father and said: "Father, have you given me to somebody?" He repeated the question a second and a third time; at last his father said: "I give you to Death."

Nachiketas thought: "Whether I die now or later matters little; but what I would like to know is what happens if Death gets me now."

Wājashrawas would have taken back his words but Nachiketas said: "Think of those who went before, those that will come after: their word their bond. Man dies and is born again like a blade of grass."

Nachiketas went into the forest and sat in meditation within the house of Death. When Death appeared his servant said: "Lord! When a holy man enters a house as guest it is as if Fire entered. The wise man cools him down. So please give him water.

"If a holy man comes into a fool's house and is given nothing, the fool's family, public and private life, ambitions, reputation, property, hopes, alliances, all suffer."

Thereupon Death said to Nachiketas: "A guest should be respected; you have lived three days in my house without eating and drinking. I bow to you, holy man! Take from me three gifts and I shall be the better for it."

Nachiketas said: "I will take as my first gift that I may be reconciled to my father; that he may be happy; that he may keep no grudge against me but make me welcome."

Death said: "I shall so arrange things, that when your father gets you back he shall sleep well at night, his grudge forgotten and love you as before."

Nachiketas said: "There is no fear in the Kingdom of Heaven; because you are not there, nobody there is afraid of old age; man is beyond hunger, thirst and sorrow.

"Death! you know what Fire leads to heaven, show it, I am full of faith. I ask that Fire as my second gift."

Death said: "I will explain it, listen. Find the rock and conquer unmeasured worlds. Listen, for this came out of the cavern."

Death told him that out of Fire comes this world, what bricks and how many go to the altar, how best to build it. Nachiketas repeated all. Death encouraged ran on:

"I give you another gift. This Fire shall be called by your name.

"Count the links of the chain: worship the triple Fire: knowledge, meditation, practice; the triple process: evidence, inference, experience; the triple duty: study, concentration, renunciation; understand that everything comes from Spirit, that Spirit alone is sought and found; attain everlasting peace; mount beyond birth and death.

"When man understands himself, understands universal Self, the union of the two, kindles the triple Fire, offers the sacrifice; then shall he, though still on earth, break the bonds of death, beyond sorrow, mount into heaven.

"This Fire that leads to heaven is your second gift, Nachiketas! It shall be named after you. Now choose again, choose the third gift."

Nachiketas said: "Some say that when man dies he continues to exist, others that he does not. Explain, and that shall be my third gift."

Death said: "This question has been discussed by the god, it is deep and difficult. Choose another gift, Nachiketas! Do not be hard. Do not compel me to explain."

Nachiketas said: "Death! you say that the gods have discussed it, that it is deep and difficult; what explanation can be as good as yours? What gift compares with that?"

Death said: "Take sons and grandsons, all long-lived, cattle and horses, elephants and gold, take a great kingdom.

"Anything but this; wealth, long life, Nachiketas! empire, anything whatever; satisfy the heart's desire.

"Pleasures beyond human reach, fine women with carriages, their musical instruments; mount beyond dreams; enjoy. But do not ask what lies beyond death."

Nachiketas said: "Destroyer of man! these things pass. Joy ends enjoyment, the longest life is short. Keep those horses, keep singing and dancing, keep it all for yourself.

"Wealth cannot satisfy a man. If he but please you, Master of All, he can live as long as he likes, get all that he likes; but I will not change my gift.

"What man, subject to death and decay, getting the chance of undecaying life, would still enjoy mere long life, thinking of copulation and beauty.

"Say where man goes after death: end all that discussion. This, which you have made so mysterious, is the only gift I will take."

2

Death said: "The good is one, the pleasant another; both command the soul. Who follows the good, attains sanctity; who follows the pleasant, drops out of the race.

"Every man faces both. The mind of the wise man draws him to the good, the flesh of the fool drives him to the pleasant.

"Nachiketas! Having examined the pleasures you have rejected them; turned from the vortex of life and death.

"Diverging roads: one called ignorance, the other wisdom. Rejecting images of pleasure, Nachiketas! you turn towards wisdom.

"Fools brag of their knowledge; proud, ignorant, dissolving, blind led by the blind, staggering to and fro.

"What can the money-maddened simpleton know of the future? 'This is the only world,' cries he; because he thinks there is no other I kill him again and again.

"Some have never heard of the Self, some have heard but cannot find Him. Who finds Him is a world's wonder, who expounds Him is a world's wonder, who inherits Him from his Master is a world's wonder.

"No man of common mind can teach Him; such men dispute one against another. But when the uncommon man speaks, dispute is over. Because the Self is a fine substance, He slips from the mind and deludes imagination.

"Beloved! Logic brings no man to the Self. Yet when a wise man shows Him, He is found. Your longing eyes are turned towards reality. Would that I had always such a pupil.

"Because man cannot find the Eternal through passing pleasure, I have sought the Fire in these pleasures and, worshipping that alone, found the Eternal.

"Nachiketas! The fulfilment of all desire, the conquest of the world, freedom from fear, unlimited pleasure, magical power, all were yours, but you renounced them all, brave and wise man.

"The wise, meditating on God, concentrating their thought, discovering in the mouth of the cavern, deeper in the cavern, that Self, that ancient Self, difficult to imagine, more difficult to understand, pass beyond joy and sorrow.

"The man that, hearing from the Teacher and comprehending, distinguishes nature from the Self, goes to the source; that man attains joy, lives for ever in that joy. I think, Nachiketas! your gates of joy stand open."

Nachiketas asked: "What lies beyond right and wrong, beyond cause and effect, beyond past and future?"

Death said: "The word the Vedas extol, austerities proclaim, sanctities approach – that word is Ôm.

"That word is eternal Spirit, eternal distance; who knows it attains to his desire.

"That word is the ultimate foundation. Who finds it is adored among the saints.

"The Self knows all, is not born, does not die, is not the effect of any cause; is eternal, self-existent, imperishable, ancient. How can the killing of the body kill Him?

"He who thinks that He kills, he who thinks that He is killed, is ignorant. He does not kill nor is He killed.

"The Self is lesser than the least, greater than the greatest. He lives in all hearts. When senses are at rest, free from desire, man finds Him and mounts beyond sorrow.

"Though sitting, He travels; though sleeping, is everywhere. Who but I, Death, can understand that God is beyond joy and sorrow.

"Who knows the Self, bodiless among the embodied, unchanging among the changing, prevalent everywhere, goes beyond sorrow.

"The Self is not known through discourse, splitting of hairs, learning however great; He comes to the man He loves; takes that man's body for His own.

"The wicked man is restless, without concentration, without peace; how can he find Him, whatever his learning?

"He has made mere preachers and soldiers His food, death its condiment; how can a common man find Him?"

3

"The individual self and the universal Self, living in the heart, like shade and light, though beyond enjoyment, enjoy the result of action. All say this, all who know Spirit, whether householder or ascetic.

"Man can kindle that Fire, that Spirit, a bridge for all who sacrifice, a guide for all who pass beyond fear.

"Self rides in the chariot of the body, intellect the firm-footed charioteer, discursive mind the reins.

"Senses are the horses, objects of desire the roads. When Self is joined to body, mind, sense, none but He enjoys.

"When a man lacks steadiness, unable to control his mind, his senses are unmanageable horses.

"But if he control his mind, a steady man, they are manageable horses.

"The impure, self-willed, unsteady man misses the goal and is born again and again.

"The self-controlled, steady, pure man goes to that goal from which he never returns.

"He who calls intellect to manage the reins of his mind reaches the end of his journey, finds there all-pervading Spirit.

"Above the senses are the objects of desire, above the objects of desire mind, above the mind intellect, above the intellect manifest nature.

"Above manifest nature the unmanifest seed, above the unmanifest seed, God. God is the goal; beyond Him nothing.

"God does not proclaim Himself, He is everybody's secret, but the intellect of the sage has found Him.

"The wise man would lose his speech in mind, mind in the intellect, intellect in nature, nature in God and so find peace.

"Get up! Stir yourself! Learn wisdom at the Master's feet. A hard path the sages say, the sharp edge of a razor.

"He who knows the soundless, odourless, tasteless, intangible, formless, deathless, supernatural, undecaying, beginningless, endless, unchangeable Reality, springs out of the mouth of Death."

Those who hear and repeat correctly this ancient dialogue between Death and Nachiketas are approved by holy men.

He who sings this great mystery at the anniversary of his fathers to a rightly chosen company, finds good luck, good luck beyond measure.

Part Two

1

Death said: "God made sense turn outward, man therefore looks outward, not into himself. Now and again a daring soul, desiring immortality, has looked back and found himself.

"The ignorant man runs after pleasure, sinks into the entanglements of death; but the wise man, seeking the undying, does not run among things that die.

"He through whom we see, taste, smell, feel, hear, enjoy, knows everything. He is that Self.

"The wise man by meditating upon the self-dependent, all-pervading Self, understands waking and sleeping and goes beyond sorrow.

"Knowing that the individual self, eater of the fruit of action, is the universal Self, maker of past and future, he knows he has nothing to fear.

"He knows that He himself born in the beginning out of meditation, before water was created, enters every heart and lives there among the elements.

"That boundless Power, source of every power, manifesting itself as life, entering every heart, living there among the elements, that is Self.

"The Fire, hidden in the fire-stick like a child in the womb, worshipped with offerings, that Fire is Self.

"He who makes the sun rise and set, to Whom all powers do homage, He that has no master, that is Self.

"That which is here, is hereafter; hereafter is here. He who thinks otherwise wanders from death to death.

"Tell the mind that there is but One; he who divides the One, wanders from death to death.

"When that Person in the heart, no bigger than a thumb, is known as maker of past and future, what more is there to fear? That is Self.

"That Person, no bigger than a thumb, burning like flame without smoke, maker of past and future, the same today and tomorrow, that is Self.

"As rain upon a mountain ridge runs down the slope, the man that has seen the shapes of Self runs after them everywhere.

"The Self of the wise man remains pure; pure water, Nachiketas, poured into pure water."

2

"Who meditates on self-existent, pure intelligence, ruler of the body, the city of eleven gates, grieves no more, is free, for ever free.

"He is sun in the sky, fire upon the altar, guest in the house, air that runs everywhere, Lord of lords, living in reality. He abounds everywhere, is renewed in the sacrifice, born in water, springs out of the soil, breaks out of the mountain; power: reality.

"Living at the centre, adorable, adored by the senses, He breathes out, breathes in.

"When He, the bodiless, leaves the body, exhausts the body, what leaves? That is Self.

"Man lives by more than breath; he lives by the help of another who makes it come and go.

"Nachiketas! I will tell you the secret of undying Spirit and what happens after death.

"Some enter the womb, waiting for a moving body, some pass into unmoving things: according to deed and knowledge.

"Who is awake, who creates lovely dreams, when man is lost in sleep? That Person through whom all things live, beyond whom none can go; pure, powerful, immortal Spirit.

"As fire, though one, takes the shape of whatsoever it consumes, so the Self, though one, animating all things, takes the shape of whatsoever it animates; yet stands outside.

"As air, though one, takes the shape of whatsoever it enters, so the Self, though one, animating all things, takes the shape of whatsoever it animates; yet stands outside.

"As the sun, the eye of the world, is not touched by the impurity it looks upon, so the Self, though one, animating all things, is not moved by human misery but stands outside.

"He is One, Governor, Self of all, Creator of many out of one. He that dare discover Him within, rejoices; what other dare rejoice?

"He is imperishable among things that perish. Life of all life, He, though one, satisfies every man's desire. He that dare discover Him within, knows peace; what other dare know peace?"

Nachiketas asked: "Where shall I find that joy beyond all words? Does He reflect another's light or shine of Himself?"

Death replied: "Neither sun, moon, stars, fire nor lightning lights Him. When He shines, everything begins to shine. Everything in the world reflects His light."

3

"Eternal creation is a tree, with roots above, branches on the ground; pure eternal Spirit, living in all things and beyond whom none can go; that is Self.

"Everything owes life and movement to Spirit. Spirit strikes terror, hangs like a thunderbolt overhead; find it, find immortality.

"Through terror of God fire burns, sun shines, rain pours, wind blows, death speeds.

"Man, if he fail to find Him before the body falls, must take another body.

"Man, looking into the mirror of himself may know Spirit there as he knows light from shade; but in the world of spirits It is known distorted as in a dream, in the choir of angels as though reflected on troubled water.

"He who knows that the senses belong not to Spirit but to the elements, that they are born and die, grieves no more.

"Mind is above sense, intellect above mind, nature above intellect, the unmanifest above nature.

"Above the unmanifest is God, unconditioned, filling all things. He who finds Him enters immortal life, becomes free.

"No eye can see Him, nor has He a face that can be seen, yet through meditation and through discipline He can be found in the heart. He that finds Him enters immortal life.

"When mind and sense are at rest, when the discrimination of intellect is finished, man comes to his final condition.

"Yoga brings the constant control of sense. When that condition is reached the Yogi can do no wrong. Before it is reached Yoga seems union and again disunion.

"He cannot be known through discourse, nor found by the mind or the eye. He that believes in His existence finds Him. How can a man who does not so believe find Him?

"Go backward from effect to cause until you are compelled to believe in Him. Once you are so compelled, truth dawns.

"When the desires of the heart are finished, man though still in the body is united to Spirit; mortal becomes immortal.

"When the knot of the heart is cut, mortal becomes immortal. This is the law.

"The heart has a hundred and one arteries; one of these – *Sushumnā* – goes up into the head. He who climbs through it attains immortality; others drive him into the vortex.

"God, the inmost Self, no bigger than a thumb, lives in the heart. Man should strip him of the body, as the arrow-maker strips the reed, that he may know Him as perpetual and pure; what can He be but perpetual and pure?"

Then Nachiketas having learned from Death this knowledge, learned the method of meditation, rose above desire and death, found God: who does the like, finds Him.

MUNDAKA

Translated from the Sanskrit by
W. B. Yeats and Shree Purohit Swami

Part One

1

Lords, inspiration of sacrifice! May our ears hear the good. May our eyes see the good. May we serve Him with the whole strength of our body. May we, all our life, carry out His will. May peace and peace and peace be everywhere.

The Creator came first; He created Himself as Creator; then called Himself the Protector of the world. He gave the knowledge of Spirit, foundation of all knowledge, to his eldest son Atharwa.

Atharwa gave it to Angee; Angee to Satyawaha Bhāradwāja; Satyawaha Bhāradwāja to Angiras.

That famous man the householder Shounaka said to Angiras: "What is it that when known, makes us know everything in the world?"

Angiras said: "Those who know Spirit say that there are two kinds of knowledge, a lower and a higher.

"The lower is the knowledge of the four Vedas and such things as pronunciation, ceremonial, grammar, etymology, poetry, astronomy, The higher knowledge is the knowledge of the Everlasting.

"Of that which has neither tangibility, nor antecedent, colour, eyes, ears, hands, feet; of that which is prevalent everywhere, immeasurably minute, self-evident, indestructible, always alive; of that which the wise name the Source.

"As the web springs from the spider and is again withdrawn, as the plant springs from the soil, hairs from the body of man, so springs the world from the Everlasting.

"Brooding Spirit creates food, food life, life mind, mind the elements, the elements the world, the world Karma, Karma the Everlasting.

"He looks at all things; knows all things. All things, their nourishment, their names, their forms, are from His will. All that He has willed is right."

2

"The Sages studied the rituals described in the Vedas, went beyond them to the truth. You may find it better to stay with them; if you seek the reward of your actions, stay with them.

"When the sacrificial fire has been kindled, set it ablaze with butter, pour an oblation, then let the butter set it ablaze again.

"If the worshipper does not offer his sacrifice, according to the rules, during the new moon, or full moon, or at the rainy season, or at harvest time, if he offer it without regularity or at other seasons, or not at all, if he entertain no guests at the sacrifice, his people for seven generations shall be unlucky.

"There are seven tongues of fire, the ruinous, the terrible, the swift, the smoky, the red, the bright, the flickering.

"If the sacrifice has been made at the right time, the tongues, emblem of the solar rays, carry the devotee into paradise.

"'Welcome! Welcome!' cry his pleasant flattering good deeds, as the tongues, emblem of the solar rays, carry him. 'Look upon what we have made for you, look upon this beautiful paradise.'

"Those sacrifices with their crew of eighteen men, are unseaworthy ships, belong to a trivial karma. The fool fixes his hopes upon them; goes to wreck.

"Fools brag of their knowledge, proud, ignorant, dissolving; staggering to and fro, blind and led by the blind.

"Dunces think, in their pride, that they have solved every problem; the passionate never learn. All these, the merit of their sacrifice exhausted, are thrust from paradise into the misery of life.

"These dunces think ritual and alms are enough, they know nothing of the good itself; when ritual and alms have done their work, they fall into their old human life or it may be lower still.

"The wise and the clean, content with what they get, or living in solitude, practising austerities, go to the Deathless, through the gates of the sun.

"He that understands the results of action, wants to renounce them all. Activity cannot attain the Inactive; therefore, with hands folded, let him go to some teacher who lives in Spirit and in whom revelation lives.

"To such a pupil, humble, master of mind and sense, the teacher can teach all he knows, bringing him to the Deathless."

Part Two

1

"This is the truth: the sparks, though of one nature with the fire, leap from it; uncounted beings leap from the Everlasting, but these, my son, merge into It again.

"The Everlasting is shapeless, birthless, breathless, mindless, above everything, outside everything, inside everything.

"From Him are born life, mind, sense, air, wind, water, earth that supports all.

"He is the inmost Self of all. Fire, His head; sun and moon, His eyes; the four quarters, His ears; revelation, His voice; wind, His breath; world, His heart; earth, His feet.

"Fire is from Him, its fuel sun, moon from sun, rain from moon, food from rain, man from food, seed from man; thus all descends from God.

"From Him are hymns, holy chants, ritual, initiation, sacrifice, ceremonial, oblation, time, deeds, everything under sun and moon;

"From Him, gods, angels, men, cattle, birds, living fires, rice, barley, austerity, faith, truth, continence, law;

"From Him seven senses like ritual fires, seven desires like flames, seven objects like oblations, seven pleasures like sacrifices, seven nerves like habitations, seven centres in the heart like hollows in the cavern.

"From Him, seas, rivers, mountains, herbs and their properties: in the middle of the elements the inmost Self.

"My son! There is nothing in this world, that is not God. He is action, purity; everlasting Spirit. Find Him in the cavern; knaw the knot of ignorance."

2

"Shining, yet hidden, Spirit lives in the cavern. Everything that sways, breathes, opens, closes, lives in Spirit; beyond learning, beyond everything, better than anything; living, unliving.

"It is the undying blazing Spirit, that seed of all seeds, wherein lay hidden the world and all its creatures. It is life, speech, mind, reality, immortality. It is there to be struck. Strike it, my son!

"Take the bow of our sacred knowledge, lay against it the arrow of devotion, pull the string of concentration, strike the target.

"Ôm is the bow, the personal self the arrow, impersonal Self the target. Aim accurately, sink therein.

"Into His cloak are woven earth, mind, life, the canopy, the Kingdom of Heaven. He is alone and sole; man's bridge to immortality.

"Come out of all the schools. Meditate upon Ôm as the Self. Remember He takes many shapes, lives in the hub where the arteries meet; and may His blessing bring you out of the darkness.

"He knows all, knows every particular. His glory prevails on earth, in heaven, in His own seat, the holy city of the heart.

"He becomes mind and guides body and life. He lives in man's heart and eats man's food. He that knows Him, in finding joy, finds immortality.

"He that knows Him as the shaped and the shapeless, cuts through the knot of his heart, solves every doubt, exhausts every action.

"In a beautiful golden scabbard hides the stainless, indivisible, luminous Spirit.

"Neither sun, moon, star, neither fire nor lightning, lights Him. When He shines, everything begins to shine. Everything in the world reflects His light.

"Spirit is everywhere, upon the right, upon the left, above, below, behind, in front. What is the world but Spirit?"

Part Three

1

"Two birds, bound one to another in friendship, have made their homes on the same tree. One stares about him, one pecks at the sweet fruit.

"The personal self, weary of pecking here and there, sinks into dejection; but when he understands through meditation that the other – the impersonal Self – is indeed Spirit, dejection disappears.

"When the sage meets Spirit, phallus and what it enters, good and evil disappear, they are one.

"The sage who knows Him as life and the giver of life, does not assert himself; playing with Self, enjoying Self, doing his duty, he takes his rank.

"The Self is found by veracity, purity, intelligence, continence. The ascetic, so purged, discovers His burning light in the heart.

"Falsehood turns from the way; truth goes all the way; the end of the way is truth; the way is paved with truth. The sage travels there without desire.

"Truth lies beyond imagination, beyond paradise; great, smaller than the smallest; near, further than the furthest; hiding from the traveller in the cavern.

"Nor can penance discover Him, nor ritual reveal, nor eye see, nor tongue speak; only in meditation can mind, grown pure and still, discover formless truth.

"The Self shines out of the pure heart, when life enters with its five fires and fills the mind.

"A pure man gets all he wants. A man with mind fixed upon some man who knows the Self, gets all he wants."

2

"The daring man adores the knower of that Spirit, wherein the world lives and is bright; knows him escaped from the seminal fluid.

"He who desires one thing after another, brooding over them, is born where his desires can be satisfied; but the Self attained, one desire satisfied, all are satisfied.

"The Self is not known through discourse, splitting of hairs, learning however great. He comes to the man He loves; takes that man's body as His own.

"Blunderers, charlatans, weaklings, cannot attain the Self. He is found by the pure, daring, cautious man.

"He who has found Him, seeks no more; the riddle is solved; desire gone, he is at peace. Having approached from everywhere that which is everywhere, whole, he passes into the Whole.

"When the ascetic has mastered theory and practice, he forgets body, remembers Spirit, attains immortality.

"His phases return to their source, his senses to their gods, his personal self and all his actions to the impersonal imperishable Self.

"As rivers lose name and shape in the sea, wise men lose name and shape in God, glittering beyond all distance.

"He who has found Spirit, is Spirit. Nobody ignorant of Spirit is born into his family. He goes beyond sorrow, sin, death; the knots of his heart unloosed.

"The Rig-Veda says 'Tell this to those that know the Vedas, do their duty, obey the law, make themselves an oblation to the sole Fire.'

"This is that ancient Truth," sage Angiras declared. "Obey the law and understand."

> We bow down to you, Great Sage!
> Bow down to you, Great Sages!

MANDUKYA

Translated from the Sanskrit by
W. B. Yeats and Shree Purohit Swami

Lords! inspiration of sacrifice! May our ears hear the good. May our eyes see the good. May we serve Him with the whole strength of our body. May we, all our life, carry out His will.

Peace, peace, and peace be everywhere.

Welcome to the Lord!

The word Ôm is the Imperishable; all this its manifestation. Past, present, future – everything is Ôm. Whatever transcends the three divisions of time, that too is Ôm.

There is nothing that is not Spirit. The personal self is the impersonal Spirit. It has four conditions.

First comes the material condition – common to all – perception turned outward, seven agents, nineteen agencies, wherein the Self enjoys coarse matter. This is known as the waking condition.

The second is the mental condition, perception turned inward, seven agents, nineteen agencies, where in the Self enjoys subtle matter. This is known as the dreaming condition.

In deep sleep man feels no desire, creates no dream. This undreaming sleep is the third condition, the intellectual condition. Because of his union with the Self and his unbroken knowledge of it, he is filled with joy, he knows his joy; his mind is illuminated.

The Self is the lord of all; inhabitant of the hearts of all. He is the source of all; creator and dissolver of beings. There is nothing He does not know.

He is not knowable by perception, turned inward or outward, nor by both combined. He is neither that which is known, nor that which is not known, nor is He the sum of all that might be known. He cannot be seen, grasped, bargained with. He is undefinable, unthinkable, indescribable.

The only proof of His existence is union with Him. The world disappears in Him. He is the peaceful, the good, the one without a second. This is the fourth condition of the Self – the most worthy of all.

This Self, though beyond words, is that supreme word Ôm; though indivisible, it can be divided in three letters corresponding to the three conditions of the Self, the letter A, the letter U, and the letter M.

The waking condition, called the material condition, corresponds to the letter A, which leads the alphabet and breathes in all the other letters. He who understands, gets all he wants; becomes a leader among men.

The dreaming condition, called the mental condition, corresponds to the second letter U. It upholds; stands between waking and sleeping. He who understands, upholds the tradition of spiritual knowledge; looks upon everything with an impartial eye. No one ignorant of Spirit is born into his family.

Undreaming sleep, called the intellectual condition, corresponds to the third letter, M. It weighs and unites. He who understands, weighs the world; rejects; unites himself with the cause.

The fourth condition of the Self corresponds to Ôm as One, indivisible Word. He is whole; beyond bargain. The world disappears in Him. He is the good; the one without a second. Thus Ôm is nothing but Self. He who understands, with the help of his personal self, merges himself into the impersonal Self; He who understands.

SVETASVATARA

Translated by Juan Mascaro

Part One

The lovers of Brahman ask:

What is the source of this universe? What is Brahman? From where do
we come? By what power do we live? Where do we find rest? Who rules
over our joys and sorrows, O seers of Brahman?

Shall we think of time, or of the own nature of things, or of a law of
necessity, or of chance, or of the elements, or of the power of creation
of woman or man? Not a union of these, for above them is a soul who
thinks. But our soul is under the power of pleasure and pain!

By the Yoga of meditation and contemplation the wise saw the power of
God, hidden in His own creation. It is He who rules over all the sources
of this universe, from time to the soul of man.

And they saw the Wheel of His power made of one circle, three layers,
sixteen parts, fifty spokes, twenty counter-spokes, six groups of eight,
three paths, one rope of innumerable strands, and the great illusion.

They also saw the river of life impetuously rushing with the five streams
of sense-feelings which come from five sources, the five elements. Its
waves are moved by five breathing winds, and its origin is a fivefold
fountain of consciousness. This river has five whirlpools, and the violent
waves of five sorrows. It has five stages of pain and five dangerous wind-
ings and turnings.

In this vast Wheel of creation wherein all things live and die, wanders
round the human soul like a swan in restless flying, and she thinks that
God is afar. But when the love of God comes down upon her, then she
finds her own immortal life.

Exalted in songs has been Brahman. In him are God and the world
and the soul, and he is the imperishable supporter of all. When the seers
of Brahman see him in all creation, they find peace in Brahman and are
free from all sorrows.

God upholds the oneness of this universe: the seen and the unseen,
the transient and the eternal. The soul of man is bound by pleasure and
pain; but when she sees God she is free from all fetters.

There is the soul of man with wisdom and unwisdom, power and powerlessness; there is nature, Prakriti, which is creation for the sake of the soul; and there is God, infinite, omnipresent, who watches the work of creation. When a man knows the three he knows Brahman.

Matter in time passes away, but God is for ever in Eternity, and he rules both matter and soul. By meditation on him, by contemplation of him, and by communion with him, there comes in the end the destruction of earthly delusion.

When a man knows God, he is free: his sorrows have an end, and birth and death are no more. When in inner union he is beyond the world of the body, then the third world, the world of the Spirit, is found, where the power of the All is, and man has all: for he is one with the ONE.

Know that Brahman is for ever in thee, and nothing higher is there to be known. When one sees God and the world and the soul, one sees the Three: one sees Brahman.

Even as fire is not seen in wood and yet by power it comes to light as fire, so Brahman in the universe and in the soul is revealed by the power of Ôm.

The soul is the wood below that can burn and be fire, and Ôm is the whirling friction-rod above. Prayer is the power that makes Ôm turn round and then the mystery of God comes to light.

God is found in the soul when sought with truth and self-sacrifice, as fire is found in wood, water in hidden springs, cream in milk, and oil in the oil-fruit.

There is a Spirit who is hidden in all things, as cream is hidden in milk, and who is the source of self-knowledge and self-sacrifice. This is Brahman, the Spirit Supreme. This is Brahman, the Spirit Supreme.

Part Two

Savitri, the god of inspiration, sent the mind and its powers to find truth. He saw the light of the god of fire and spread it over the earth.

By the grace of god Savitri, our mind is one with him and we strive with all our power for light.

Savitri gives life to our souls and then they shine in great light. He makes our mind and its powers one and leads our thoughts to heaven.

The seers of the god who sees all keep their mind and their thoughts in oneness. They sing the glory of god Savitri who has given every man his work.

I sing the songs of olden times with adoration: may my own songs follow the path of the sun. Let all the children of immortality hear me, even those who are in the highest heaven.

Where the fire of the Spirit burns, where the wind of the Spirit blows, where the Soma-wine of the Spirit overflows, there a new soul is born.

Inspired then by Savitri let us find joy in the prayers of olden times: for if we make them our rock we shall be made pure of past sins.

With upright body, head, and neck lead the mind and its powers into thy heart; and the Ôm of Brahman will then be thy boat with which to cross the rivers of fear.

And when the body is in silent steadiness, breathe rhythmically through the nostrils with a peaceful ebbing and flowing of breath. The chariot of the mind is drawn by wild horses, and those wild horses have to be tamed.

Find a quiet retreat for the practice of Yoga, sheltered from the wind, level and clean, free from rubbish, smouldering fires, and ugliness, and where the sound of waters and the beauty of the place help thought and contemplation.

These are the imaginary forms that appear before the final vision of Brahman: a mist, a smoke, and a sun; a wind, fire-flies, and a fire; lightnings, a clear crystal, and a moon.

When the Yogi has full power over his body composed of the elements of earth, water, fire, air and ether, then he obtains a new body of spiritual fire which is beyond illness, old age and death.

The first fruits of the practice of Yoga are: health, little waste matter, and a clear complexion; lightness of the body, a pleasant scent, and a sweet voice; and an absence of greedy desires.

Even as a mirror of gold, covered by dust, when cleaned well shines again in full splendour, when a man has seen the Truth of the Spirit he is one with him, the aim of his life is fulfilled and he is ever beyond sorrow.

Then the soul of man becomes a lamp by which he finds the Truth of Brahman. Then he sees God, pure, never-born, everlasting; and when he sees God he is free from all bondage.

This is the God whose light illumines all creation, the Creator of all from the beginning. He was, he is and forever he shall be. He is in all and he sees all.

Glory be to that God who is in the fire, who is in the waters, who is in plants and in trees, who is in all things in this vast creation. Unto that Spirit be glory and glory.

Part Three

There is ONE in whose hands is the net of Maya, who rules with his power, who rules all the worlds with his power. He is the same at the time of creation and at the time of dissolution. Those who know him attain immortality.

He is Rudra, he alone is the ONE who governs the worlds with his power. He watches over all beings and rules over their creation and their destruction.

His eyes and mouths are everywhere, his arms and feet are everywhere. He is God who made heaven and earth, who gave man his arms and who gave to the birds their wings.

May Rudra, the seer of Eternity, who gave to the gods their birth and their glory, who keeps all things under his protection, and who in the beginning created the Golden Seed, grant us the grace of pure vision.

Come down to us, Rudra, who art in the high mountains. Come and let the light of thy face, free from fear and evil, shine upon us. Come to us with thy love.

Let not the arrow in thy hand hurt man or any living being: let it be an arrow of love.

Greater than all is Brahman, the Supreme, the Infinite. He dwells in the mystery of all beings according to their forms in nature. Those who know him who knows all, and in whose glory all things are, attain immortality.

I know the Spirit supreme, radiant like the sun beyond darkness. He who knows him goes beyond death, for he is the only path to life immortal.

His infinity is beyond what is great or small, and greater than him there is nothing. Like a tree everlasting he stands in the centre of heaven, and his radiance illumines all creation.

Those who know him who is greater than all, beyond form and beyond pain, attain immortality: those who know not go to the worlds of sorrow.

All this universe is in the glory of God, of Siva the god of love. The heads and faces of men are his own and he is in the hearts of all.

He is indeed the Lord Supreme whose grace moves the hearts of men. He leads us unto his own joy and to the glory of his light.

He is the inmost soul of all, which like a little flame the size of a thumb is hidden in the hearts of men. He is the master of wisdom ever reached by thought and love. He is the immortality of those who know him.

He has innumerable heads and eyes and feet, and his vastness enfolds the universe, and even a measure of ten beyond.

God is in truth the whole universe: what was, what is, and what beyond shall ever be. He is the god of life immortal, and of all life that lives by food.

His hands and feet are everywhere, he has heads and mouths everywhere: he sees all, he hears all. He is in all and he is.

The Light of consciousness comes to him through infinite powers of perception, and yet he is above these powers. He is God, the ruler of all, the infinite refuge of all.

The wandering swan of the soul dwells in the castle of nine gates of the body and flies away to enjoy the outer world. He is the master of the universe: of all that moves and of all that moves not.

Without hands he holds all things, without feet he runs everywhere. Without eyes he sees all things, without ears all things he hears. He knows all, but no one knows him, the Spirit before the beginning, the Spirit Supreme everlasting.

Concealed in the heart of all beings lies the Atman, the Spirit, the Self; smaller than the smallest atom, greater than the greatest spaces. When by the grace of God man sees the glory of God, he sees him beyond the world of desire and then sorrows are left behind.

I know that Spirit whose infinity is in all, who is ever one beyond time. I know the Spirit whom the lovers of Brahman call eternal, beyond the birth and rebirth of life.

Part Four

May God, who in the mystery of His vision and power transforms his white radiance into His many-coloured creation, from whom all things come and into whom they all return, grant us the grace of pure vision.

He is the sun, the moon, and the stars. He is the fire, the waters, and the wind. He is Brahma the creator of all, and Prajapati, the Lord of creation.

Thou this boy, and thou this maiden; thou this man, and thou this woman; thou art this old man who support himself on a staff; thou the God who appears in forms infinite.

Thou the blue bird and thou the green bird; thou the cloud that conceals the lightning and thou the seasons and the oceans. Beyond beginning, thou art in thine infinity, and all the worlds had their beginning in thee.

There is nature, never-born, who with her three elements – light, fire and darkness – creates all things in nature. There is the never-born soul of man bound by the pleasures of nature; and there is the Spirit of man, never-born, who has left pleasures behind in the joy of the Beyond.

There are two birds, two sweet friends, who dwell on the self-same tree. The one eats the fruits thereof, and the other looks on in silence.

The first is the human soul who, resting on that tree, though active, feels sad in his unwisdom. But on beholding the power and the glory of the higher Spirit, he becomes free from sorrow.

Of what use is the *Rig Veda* to one who does not know the Spirit from whom the *Rig Veda* comes, and in whom all things abide? For only those who have found him have found peace.

For all the sacred books, all holy sacrifice and ritual and prayers, all the words of the Vedas, and the whole past and present and future, come from the Spirit. With Maya, his power of wonder, he made all things, and by Maya the human soul is bound.

Know therefore that nature is Maya, but that God is the ruler of Maya; and that all beings in our universe are parts of his infinite splendour.

He rules over the sources of creation. From him comes the universe and unto him it returns. He is the Lord, the giver of blessings, the one God of our adoration, in whom there is perfect peace.

May Rudra, the seer of Eternity, who gave to the gods their birth and their glory, who keeps all things under his protection, and who in the beginning saw the Golden Seed, grant us the grace of pure vision.

Who is the God to whom we shall offer adoration? The God of gods, in whose glory the worlds are, and who rules this world of man and all living beings.

He is the God of forms infinite in whose glory all things are, smaller than the smallest atom, and yet the Creator of all, everliving in the mystery of His creation. In the vision of this God of love there is everlasting peace.

He is the Lord of all who, hidden in the heart of things, watches over the world of time. The gods and the seers of Brahman are one with Him; and when a man knows Him he cuts the bonds of death.

When one knows God who is hidden in the heart of all things, even as cream is hidden in milk, and in whose glory all things are, he is free from all bondage.

This is the God whose work is all the worlds, the supreme Soul who dwells forever in the hearts of men. Those who know Him through their hearts and their minds become immortal.

There is a region beyond darkness where there is neither day nor night, nor what is, nor what is not. Only Siva, the god of love, is there. It is the region of the glorious splendour of God from whom came the light of the sun, and from whom the ancient wisdom came in the beginning.

The mind cannot grasp Him above, or below, or in the space in between. With whom shall we compare Him whose glory is the whole universe?

Far beyond the range of vision, He cannot be seen by mortal eyes; but He can be known by the heart and the mind, and those who know Him attain immortality.

A man comes to Thee in fearful wonder and says: "Thou art God who never was born. Let Thy face, Rudra, shine upon me, and let Thy love be my eternal protection.

"Hurt not my child, nor the child of my child; hurt not my life, my horses, or my cows. Kill not in anger our brave men, for we ever come to Thee with adorations."

Part Five

Two things are hidden in the mystery of infinity of Brahman: knowledge and ignorance. Ignorance passes away and knowledge is immortal; but Brahman is in Eternity above ignorance and knowledge.

He is the ONE in whose power are the many sources of creation, and the root and the flower of all things. The Golden Seed, the Creator, was in his mind in the beginning; and he saw him born when time began.

He is God who spreads the net of transmigration and then withdraws it in the field of life. He is the Lord who created the lords of creation, the supreme Soul who rules over all.

Even as the radiance of the sun shines everywhere in space, so does the glory of God rule over all his creation.

In the unfolding of his own nature he makes all things blossom into flower and fruit. He gives to them all their fragrance and colour. He, the ONE, the only God who rules the universe.

There is a Spirit hidden in the mystery of the Upanishads and the Vedas; and Brahma, the god of creation, owns him as his own Creator. It is the Spirit of God, seen by gods and seers of olden times who, when one with him, became immortal.

When a man is bound by the three powers of nature, he works for a selfish reward and in time he has his reward. His soul then becomes the many forms of the three powers, strays along the three paths, and wanders on through life and death.

The soul is like the sun in splendour. When it becomes one with the self-conscious "I am" and its desires, it is a flame the size of a thumb; but when one with pure reason and the inner Spirit, it becomes in concentration as the point of a needle.

The soul can be thought as the part of a point of a hair which divided by a hundred were divided by a hundred again; and yet in this living soul there is the seed of Infinity.

The soul is not a man, nor a woman, nor what is neither a woman nor a man. When the soul takes the form of a body, by that same body the soul is bound.

The soul is born and unfolds in a body, with dreams and desires and the food of life. And then it is reborn in new bodies, in accordance with its former works.

The quality of the soul determines its future body: earthly or airy, heavy or light. Its thoughts and its actions can lead it to freedom, or lead it to bondage, in life after life.

But there is the God of forms infinite, and when a man knows God he is free from all bondage. He is the Creator of all, everliving in the mystery of his creation. He is beyond beginning and end, and in his glory all things are.

He is an incorporeal Spirit, but he can be seen by a heart which is pure. Being and non-being come from him and he is the Creator of all. He is God, the God of love, and when a man knows him then he leaves behind his bodies of transmigration.

Part Six

Some sages speak of the nature of things as the cause of the world, and others, in their delusion, speak of time. But it is by the glory of God that the Wheel of Brahman revolves in the universe.

The whole universe is ever in his power. He is pure consciousness, the creator of time: all-powerful, all-knowing. It is under his rule that the work of creation revolves in its evolution, and we have earth, and water, and ether, and fire and air.

God ended his work and he rested, and he made a bond of love between his soul and the soul of all things. And the ONE became one with the one, and the two, and the three and the eight, and with time and with the subtle mystery of the human soul.

His first works are bound by the three qualities, and he gives to each thing its place in nature. When the three are gone, the work is done, and then a greater work can begin.

His Being is the source of all being, the seed of all things that in this life have their life. He is beyond time and space, and yet he is the God of forms infinite who dwells in our inmost thoughts, and who is seen by those who love him.

He is beyond the tree of life and time, and things seen by mortal eyes; but the whole universe comes from him. He gives us truth and takes away evil, for he is the Lord of all good. Know that he is in the inmost of thy soul and that he is the home of thine immortality.

May we know the Lord of lords, the King of kings, the God of gods: God, the God of love, the Lord of all.

We cannot see how he works, or what are the tools of his work. Nothing can be compared with him, and how can anything be greater than he is? His power is shown in infinite ways, and how great is his work and wisdom!

No one was before he was, and no one has rule over him; because he is the source of all, and he is also the ruler of all.

May God who is hidden in nature, even as the silkworm is hidden in the web of silk he made, lead us to union with his own spirit, with Brahman.

He is God, hidden in all beings, their inmost soul who is in all. He watches the works of creation, lives in all things, watches all things. He is pure consciousness, beyond the three conditions of nature, the ONE who rules the work of silence of many, the ONE who transforms one seed into many. Only those who see God in their soul attain the joy eternal.

He is the Eternal among things that pass away, pure Consciousness of conscious beings, the ONE who fulfils the prayers of many. By the vision of Sankhya and the harmony of Yoga a man knows God, and when a man knows God he is free from all fetters.

There the sun shines not, nor the moon, nor the stars; lightnings shine not there and much less earthly fire. From his light all these give light; and his radiance illumines all creation.

He is the wandering swan everlasting, the soul of all in the universe, the Spirit of fire in the ocean of life. To know him is to overcome death, and he is the only Path to life eternal.

He is the never-created Creator of all: he knows all. He is pure consciousness, the creator of time: all-powerful, all-knowing. He is the Lord of the soul and of nature and of the three conditions of nature. From him comes the transmigration of life and liberation: bondage in time and freedom in Eternity.

He is the God of light, immortal in his glory, pure consciousness, omnipresent, the loving protector of all. He is the everlasting ruler of the world: could there be any ruler but he?

Longing therefore for liberation, I go for refuge to God who by his grace reveals his own light; and who in the beginning created the god of creation and gave to him the sacred Vedas.

I go for refuge to God who is ONE in the silence of Eternity, pure radiance of beauty and perfection, in whom we find our peace. He is the bridge supreme which leads to immortality, and the Spirit of fire which burns the dross of lower life.

If ever for man it were possible to fold the tent of the sky, in that day he might be able to end his sorrow without the help of God.

By the power of inner harmony and by the grace of God Svetasvatara had the vision of Brahman. He then spoke to his nearest hermit-students about the supreme purification, about Brahman whom the seers adore.

This supreme mystery of the Vedanta which was revealed in olden times must only be given to one whose heart is pure and who is a pupil or a son.

If one has supreme love for God and also loves his master as God, then the light of this teaching shines in a great soul: it shines indeed in a great soul.

BHAGAVADGITA

BHAGAVADGITA

Translated by Kees W. Bolle

Part One

DHTARĀṢṬRA:
1. In the land of the right tradition, the land of the Kurus,
   my men and the men of Pāṇḍu met,
   Ready to fight.
   What did they do, Saṃjaya?

SAṂJAYA:
2. The king, Duryodhana, surveyed
   the Pāṇḍava army drawn up for battle.
   Then he went to his mentor
   and said:

3. "Master, see that mighty army
   of Pāṇḍu's men.
   Your skilful pupil, the son of Drupada,
   arrayed them.

4. "They have heroes, mighty bowmen,
   matching Bhīma and Arjuna in battle:
   Yuyudhāna and Virāṭa,
   and Drupada, the great chariot fighter;

5. "Dhṛṣṭaketu; Cekitāna;
   the valiant king of Kāśī;
   Purujit; Kuntibhoja;
   the Śibi king, foremost among men;

6. "And the courageous Yudhāmanyu,
   and the heroic Uttamaujas,
   The son of Subhadrā; Draupadī's sons –
   all great chariot fighters.

7. "But, most venerable nobleman,
    observe all those men of distinction
Who are on our side, the captains of my army;
    let me identify them for you.

8. "There are yourself, Bhīṣma, Karṇa,
    and the victorious Kṛpa;
Aśvatthāman, Vikarṇa,
    and the son of Somadatta;

9. "And many other heroes,
    willing to lay down their lives for me,
Armed with various missiles and spears,
    all skilled in battle.

10. "The other army is not equal to us
    in spite of its protection by Bhīma, the Terrible.
This army of ours, commanded by Bhīṣma,
    the Awe-Inspiring, outnumbers them.

11. "Let all of you, above all,
    guard Bhīṣma,
In whatever division you are stationed,
    in all movements of the battle front."

12. Duryodhana listened with delight when Bhīṣma,
    the Kuru elder, the majestic grandsire,
Blew his conch-shell,
    roaring loudly like a lion.

13. Then all at once, conch-shells,
    drums, cymbals, trumpets,
Sounded forth,
    and the noise grew wild.

14. Kṛṣṇa and Arjuna,
    standing on their mighty chariot
Yoked with white steeds,
    blew their divine conch-shells.

15. Kṛṣṇa blew his "Horn of Pañcajana",
    Arjuna blew his "Gift of God".

And Wolf-Belly, the Worker of Terror
  blew his great shell "Wild One".

16. King Yudhiṣṭhira, Kuntī's son,
    blew "Everlasting Victory",
  And Nakula and Sahadeva blew
    "Sweet Tone" and "Gem-Flower".

17. The king of Kāśī – superb bowman –
    Sikhaṇḍin – the great chariot fighter –
  Dhṛṣṭadyumna, Virāta,
    and the unvanquished Sātyaki,

18. Drupada, and Draupadī's sons,
    and the warrior son of Subhadrā
  One by one sounded their conches
    in every direction at once.

19. The wild roar
    that made heaven and earth ring
  Rent the hearts
    of Dhṛtarāṣṭra's men.

20–21. Arjuna, known by the monkey in his banner,
    looked upon Dhṛtarāṣṭra's men in battle order
  – Arrows had already begun to fly –
    lifted his bow
  And then spoke to Kṛṣṇa:
    "Unshakeable One,
  Halt my chariot
    between the two armies,

22. "While I survey
    those pugnacious troops arrayed for battle
  With whom I am to wage
    this great war.

23. "Let me look at those who are assembled here
    and who will fight,
  Who are eager to please in battle
    Dhṛtarāṣṭra's perverse son."

24. Kṛṣṇa heeded
    Arjuna's request.

He halted the superb chariot
between the two armies,

25. In front of Bhīṣma, Droṇa,
and all the princes of the earth,
And said: "See, Son of Pṛthā,
the assembled Kurus."

26. In that place Arjuna saw
fathers, grandfathers,
Mentors, uncles, brothers,
sons, grandsons, playmates,

27–28. Fathers-in-law, and close friends
in both armies.
Seeing all these kinsmen
in array, the son of Kuntī
Was overwhelmed by emotion
and in despair he said:
"O Kṛṣṇa, when I see my relatives here
who have come together and want to fight,

29. "I feel paralysed,
my mouth becomes dry,
I tremble within,
my hair stands on end;

30. "The bow Gāṇḍīva slips from my hand,
my skin feels hot,
I cannot keep steady,
my mind whirls.

31. "O Keśava, I see
but evil signs,
I see nothing good resulting
from slaying my own people in combat.

32. "I have no desire for victory, Kṛṣṇa,
nor for kingship and its joys.
What is kingship worth to us, Govinda,
and pleasures, or life?

33. "These men here drawn up in battle
      giving their lives and possessions
    Are the ones for whose sake we desired
      kingship, pleasures, happiness.

34. "Teachers, fathers, sons,
      grandfathers,
    Uncles, fathers-in-law, grandsons,
      brothers-in-law, and other kinsmen –

35. "If they killed me,
      I still would not wish to kill them,
    Not for kingship over heaven, air and earth!
      How much less for the sake of the earth
      alone!

36. "What joy could we have, Stirrer of Men,
      if we should slay Dhṛtarāṣṭra's party?
    The atrocity would pursue us if we killed
      those men who are aiming their bows at us.

37. "We do not have the right to slay
      Dhṛtarāṣṭra's men, our own kin.
    For how could we be happy
      after slaying our relatives?

38. "Even though they see no wickedness
      in annihilating their kin,
    In betraying friends,
      since greed has clouded their wits,

39. "Should we not be wise enough
      to turn back from this evil,
    O Stirrer of Men, as we see before us
      the wickedness of annihilating the entire family?

40. "With the disruption of the family,
      the eternal family tradition perishes.
    With the collapse of the tradition
      chaos overtakes the whole race.

41. "Such predominance of chaos leads to
      the corruption of women in the family.

When the women are corrupted
the whole society erodes.

42. "This erosion leads to hell
for the family and those who destroyed it
Their ancestors end up in hell too,
because the ancestral rites are discontinued.

43. "The crimes of those who destroy their kinsfolk
cause promiscuity;
They overturn the rules governing caste
and the eternal family traditions.

44. "Surely, Janārdana, men
who overturn the family traditions
Will end up in hell.
This is what we have been taught.

45. "Alas! We are determined
to commit a great crime,
Now that we have come out to kill our own people
out of greed for kingship and pleasure.

46. "I would be happier
if Dhṛtarāṣṭra's men killed me in the battle,
While I was unarmed
and offered no resistance."

47. With these words Arjuna sank down on his seat
in the midst of the battle.
He had let go of his bow and arrows.
Sorrow had overwhelmed him.

Part Two

SAMJAYA:
1. When sentiment had thus overcome him,
while he despaired – his sight blurred,
His eyes filled with tears –
Kṛṣṇa, the Slayer of Madhu, answered:

THE LORD:

2. How is it possible that at a time of crisis
     you, Arjuna, should become so weak!
   Noblemen detest such weakness.
     It does not lead to heaven. It is degrading.

3. Be a man, Son of Pṛthā!
     This impotence does not suit you.
   Cast off this abject faintheartedness.
     Stand up, you Conqueror!

ARJUNA:

4. O Slayer of Madhu, Slayer of Enemies,
     how can I fight Bhīṣma and Droṇa?
   How shall I send my arrows at those two,
     worthy of my worship?

5. It would be better
   To live on alms
   Without having slain
   Our spiritual guides,
   Men of authority –
   But after killing my elders,
   Even if they were greedy,
   My food here in this world
   Would taste of blood.

6. Still we do not know
   Which is best,
   Whether we should win
   Or they.
   There they are,
   Dhṛtarāṣṭra's men,
   Drawn up before us.
   If we slay them,
   We'll no longer wish to live.

7. I am not myself:
   I am afflicted
   With feelings of pity.
   I am confused.
   What should be done?
   I ask you:

Which is best?
Tell me that
With certainty.
I am your pupil.
Teach me.
I have thrown myself at your feet.

8. For I cannot see
Anything at all
That could dispel this sorrow
Which lames me.
I cannot imagine
Anything to dispel it
Even if I attained
Prosperous kingship
Without a rival on earth,
Or even lordship
Of the gods.

SAṂJAYA:

9. Thus the thick-haired warrior
    spoke to Kṛṣṇa,
And he concluded: "I shall not fight!"
    Then he was silent.

10. Hṛṣīkeśa seemed to smile
    when he answered
The desperate man
    between the two armies:

THE LORD:

11. You have spent your sorrow on beings who do not
    need it
    and pay lip-service to wisdom.
Educated men do not sorrow
    for the dead nor the living.

12. There was no time at which I was not
    nor you nor these princes.
Nor shall any of us
    ever cease to be.

13. Just as a person changes from
        childhood to youth to old age in the body,
    He changes bodies.
        This does not upset the composed man.

14. The world our senses touch, Son of Kunti,
        is hot or cold, pleasant or unpleasant.
    Sensations come and go. They do not last.
        Learn to endure them, Son of Bharata!

15. They do not shake the composed man
        to whom unpleasantness
    And pleasure are alike.
        He is fit for immortality.

16. What is not cannot come into being,
        and what is has no end.
    Men who see things as they are
        perceive the limit of both.

17. But you must know that which is imperishable
        and which stretched forth the whole world.
    No one is able to destroy that
        which is everlasting.

18. Before you are the temporal bodies
        of the eternal, embodied one
    Who does not perish and cannot be measured.
        Therefore you must fight.

19. Who thinks this one a slayer,
        or who thinks of him as slain,
    Both lack understanding.
        He neither slays nor is slain.

20. He is never born.
    He never dies.
    You cannot say of him
    He came to be
    And will be no more.
    Primeval, he is
    Unborn,
    Changeless,

Everlasting.
The body will be slain,
But he will not.

21. How can the man who knows him as imperishable,
      eternal, unborn, and changeless,
    Kill anyone?
      Whom does he cause to be killed, Son of Pṛthā?

22. Just as a man discards
    Worn-out clothes
    And puts on others,
    That are new,
    The embodied leaves behind
    Worn-out bodies
    And enters others,
    New ones.

23. Swords cannot wound him,
      the fire cannot burn him,
    Water cannot dampen him
      nor the wind parch him.

24. He cannot be cut or burned,
      not moistened or dried.
    Subsisting always, everywhere, immobile,
      fixed is the eternal one.

25. He is unmanifest, unthinkable,
      and not subject to change.
    Therefore, once you have understood him in this way,
      you should not sorrow.

26. Or, even if you think he is born and dies
      continually,
    Even then, O Warrior,
      You ought not to lament him.

27. Whoever is born will certainly die,
      and whoever dies will certainly be born.
    Since this cannot be changed,
      your grief is inappropriate.

28. No one sees the beginning of things,
       but only the middle.
    Their end also is unseen.
       There is no reason to lament.

29. As by a miracle
    One may see him.
    Likewise by miracle
    One may
    Name and discuss him,
    And by miracle
    One may hear
    What is revealed of him.
    But even having heard,
    No one knows him.

30. That person existing in everyone's body
       is for ever inviolable.
    Therefore you should not sorrow
       for any creatures.

31. Considering also the duty of your own class
       you should not waver.
    To a warrior nothing is better than
       a just battle.

32. Happy the warriors, Son of Pṛthā,
       who find such a battle
    Offered unsought –
       a gate to heaven wide open.

33. But if you will not engage
       in this just war,
    You give up your duty and your fame
       and will incur demerit.

34. Also, the world will talk
       of your everlasting dishonour,
    And dishonour is worse than death
       to a man of fame.

35. The great warriors will think
       you deserted out of fear.

Those who held you in high esteem
   will snap their fingers at you.

36. Your detractors will say
   a number of unspeakable things,
Reviling all you stand for.
   What could be worse than that?

37. Slain, you will gain heaven;
   victorious, you will enjoy the earth.
Stand up, therefore, determined to fight,
   Son of Kuntī!

38. Realizing that joy and grief, gain and loss,
   winning and losing are the same,
Gird yourself for the battle.
   Thus you will not incur demerit.

39. I have given you this understanding through the teachings of
   Reason.
Now hear it in the tradition of Discipline.
Armed with its meditative knowledge you will be free
   from imprisonment by actions.

40. In Discipline no observance is lost,
   nor can any harm result from Discipline.
Even the least practice on this path
   can protect you from grave danger.

41. The knowledge meditation attains on this path consists
   in commitment and is whole.
Irresolute men have a fragmented
   and incomplete knowledge.

42–44. Undiscerning men, theologians
   preoccupied with Scriptural lore,
Who claim there is nothing else,
   utter words with ephemeral results;

Their words promise better births through cultic acts,
   dwell at length on various rites,
And aim at pleasure and power.
   These men are full of desire, zealous for heaven.

They cling to pleasures and power
  and are fooled by their own discourses.
They have no knowledge consisting in commitment,
  fixed in concentration.

45. The Scriptures speak to the world's weave of integrity,
    passion, and sloth. Transcend it, Arjuna,
  Free from opposites, forever in integrity,
    detached from things, in command of yourself.

46. All the Scriptures mean as much – no more, no less –
    to the discerning spiritual man
  As a water tank
    in a universal flood.

47. You are entitled to perform rituals,
    but not at all to their results.
  The results of rituals should not be your motive.
    Nor should you abstain from ritual.

48. Follow Discipline, and perform your rites
    with detachment, Pursuer of Wealth,
  Equal-minded to success or failure.
    Discipline means equanimity,

49. For ritual [performed for its effect] is far inferior
    to the Discipline of Meditation.
  Seek refuge in meditative knowledge.
    Wretched are men when results are their incentive.

50. A man with meditative knowledge
    leaves behind him both good and evil deeds.
  Therefore, practise Discipline.
    Discipline is skill in works and rites.

51. Intelligent men with meditative knowledge
    disregard the reward of cultic work,
  And enter a blissful state,
    freed from the imprisonment of births.

52. When your meditation gets across
    the thicket of delusion,
  You will no longer worry about

what the Scriptures have taught you or will teach
   you.

53. When your meditating mind, now bewildered
       by conflicting views of Revelationl
    Shall stand firm, unmoved in concentration,
       then will you attain Discipline.

ARJUNA:
54. Please describe the man of firm judgement
       who is established in concentration.
    How would a man of firm mind speak,
       or sit, or move about?

THE LORD:
55. A man is of firm judgement
       when he has abandoned all inner desires
    And the self is content,
       at peace with itself.

56. When unpleasant things do not perturb him
       nor pleasures beguile him,
    When longing, fear, and anger have left,
       he is a sage of firm mind.

57. That man has a firm judgement
       who feels no desire towards anything.
    Whatever good or bad he incurs,
       he never delights in it nor hates it.

58. When on all sides he withdraws his senses
       from the sensual world,
    As a tortoise draws in its legs,
       his judgement has become stable.

59. The realm of the senses recedes
       for the person who fasts.
    Only an inclination, a flavour, lingers.
       That leaves him only when he has seen the highest.

60. Even the wise man who exerts himself
       to attain perfection
    Has senses that harass him
       and carry away his mind.

61. One should sit down, restraining all senses,
    intent on me.
   Whoever controls his senses
    has a firm judgement.

62. A man gets attached to what the senses tell him
    if he does not turn his mind away.
   Attachment gives rise to desire,
    desire to anger.

63. Anger leads to a state of delusion;
    delusion distorts one's memory.
   Distortion of memory distorts consciousness,
    and then a man perishes.

64. But when a man wholly governing himself
    is roaming the sensual world
   With his senses under control, freed
    from likes and dislikes, he attains clarity.

65. In clarity, he is liberated
    from all unpleasantness,
   For the judgement of clear-minded men
    is unerringly steadfast.

66. The undisciplined does not meditate;
    he has no means of mental realization.
   And there is no peace for one without such means.
    Without peace, how can there be happiness for
    him?

67. For when a man allows his mind to obey
    the whims of the senses,
   It destroys his judgement
    like a storm destroys a ship.

68. Therefore, O Warrior,
    having your senses entirely withdrawn
   From the world of the senses
    means attaining a steadfast judgement.

69. The man of self-control is awake
    in what is night for all creatures;

And when they are awake,
  it is night for the seer.

70. The sea gathers the waters;
  It fills and fills itself . . .
  Its equilibrium
  Is undisturbed.
  So also
  The man into whom
  All desires enter –
  Not he who goes after desires –
  Finds peace.

71. The man who has given up all desire
    and moves about without wanting anything,
  Who says neither *mine* nor *I*,
    wins peace.

72. This, Son of Pṛthā, is divine stability.
    Whoso reaches it is not again confused.
  Whoso abides in it even at death
    gains the freedom that is God's.

Part Three

ARJUNA:
  1. If meditative knowledge
      or right judgement is superior to action,
    Why do you urge me
      to do this work of violence, Keśava?

  2. You confuse me
      with a tangle of words.
    Teach me the one thing
      by which I can attain what is highest.

THE LORD:
  3. O Blameless One, long ago have I revealed
      the twofold rule basic to this world:
    For men of reason, the way of Knowledge;
      for men of discipline, the way of Cultic Work.

4. Man does not overcome activity
    by refraining from ritual.
He does not become successful
    by renunciation alone.

5. For no one remains inactive
    even for a moment.
The states of all existence make everyone act
    in spite of himself.

6. A man who restrains his body's powers and functions,
    but who sits, turning over in his mind
The objects of sense, deludes himself.
    His conduct is pointless.

7. He is superior who with his mind
    restrains the senses, Arjuna, and engages
In the discipline of work
    with all his powers, not anxious for results.

8. Perform the required ritual work.
    Action is better than inaction.
Without action, the body
    would stop functioning.

9. It is true, this world is enslaved by activity,
    but the exception is work for the sake of sacrifice.
Therefore, Son of Kuntī, free from attachment,
    act for that purpose.

10. Long ago, the Lord of men brought forth
    men together with sacrifice and said:
"By this you shall multiply;
    let this be the source of your abundance.

11. "Please the gods by sacrifice
    and they must make you prosper.
While you and the gods sustain each other,
    you will reach the highest good.

12. "Sustained by sacrifice
    the gods will fulfil your desires.

Only a thief consumes their gifts
 without giving to them."

13. Good men eat the remnants of sacrifice
 and are cleansed of all impurities.
 The wicked, who cook merely for themselves,
 partake of evil.

14. From food, creatures arise.
 Rain produces food.
 Sacrice brings rain.
 Cultic work is the root of sacrifice.

15. Cultic work comes from the Divine,
 the Divine from the one supreme, subtle sound.
 Hence the Divine, although omnipresent,
 is ever established in the sacrifice.

16. Whoever does not turn with the wheel
 thus set in motion –
 That man lives in vain, Son of Pṛthā.
 He is of evil intent, engrossed in the senses.

17. But the man who takes pleasure in the self
 and is satisfied in its reality
 And is wholly content in it,
 has no real need for action.

18. For him there is no sense whatever in action
 nor in inaction.
 He does not rely on anything in this world
 for any end.

19. Therefore, do the work that is required, always
 free from attachments.
 Acting in that freedom
 man reaches the highest.

20. By cultic work Janaka and others
 attained complete success.
 Concerned alone with the upholding of the world,
 you should act.

21. Whatever the best man does,
    others do that also.
The world follows
    the standard he sets for himself.

22. There is nothing at all I need to do
    in the worlds, heaven, air, and earth.
There is nothing I need that I do not have.
    And yet I am engaged in work.

23. For if I did not engage in action,
    tirelessly,
People everywhere
    would follow my example.

24. If I did no work,
    these worlds would go down,
And I would surely wreak havoc;
    I would destroy these people.

25. Fools are wedded to cultic work.
    A wise man should act as they do,
But unattached,
    envisaging the totality of the world.

26. Unwise men are attached to ritual,
    and he should not unsettle their minds.
Being himself disciplined in his acts,
    the wise should encourage them in all their
      rites.

27. Always and everywhere, acts are done
    by the states arising in primal matter.
A man totally confused in his self-consciousness
    imagines: *I act.*

28. But he who knows how the forces of nature
    and cultic work are really divided, O Warrior,
Is free from them, for he is aware
    that nature's forces always move one another.

29. A man of full knowledge should not interfere
    with dullards, who know only part.

They are obsessed by the forces of nature
and entranced by their motions.

30. Cast all works on me, directing
your thought to the reality of your self.
Become free from desires, from selfishness,
and fight without anxiety.

31. Men who hold to this my teaching
with full confidence,
Without cavilling,
are no longer imprisoned by their acts.

32. But those who are irritated by my teaching
and do not follow it
Are fools; they are lost;
they are estranged from insight.

33. Even a wise man moves
according to his nature.
All creatures follow their nature.
Coercion will accomplish nothing.

34. Likes and dislikes are arrayed
in whatever our senses grasp.
A man should not come under the sway
of likes and dislikes. They are his opponents.

35. One's own duty in its imperfection
is better than someone else's duty well-performed.
It is better to die in one's own duty. . . .
Another's duty is perilous.

ARJUNA:
36. Then what or who makes man do wrong
even without wanting to,
As if he were driven by force,
Son of Vṛṣṇi?

THE LORD:
37. It is desire, and it is anger, and arises
from the state of being known as passion.
It devours much and is a great evil.
That is the enemy.

38. This enemy covers the world
    as smoke conceals the fire,
As dirt clouds a mirror,
    or a membrane envelops an embryo.

39. This constant enemy of the wise
    keeps wisdom hidden.
It appears as desire.
    It is an insatiable fire.

40. The senses, the mind, our concentration,
    uphold this enemy.
By means of them the enemy conceals
    wisdom and deludes a man.

41. Hence you must slay that destroyer
    of wisdom and discrimination.
You must slay it after first
    conquering your senses, Strongest of Bharatas.

42. They say the senses are high,
    yet the mind higher than the senses.
The power of concentration transcends the mind.
    Still, there is he who is beyond that power.

43. Thus understanding him who is beyond concentration,
    you yourself, gaining strength by yourself,
You, Warrior, must slay
    the formidable enemy in the form of desire.

Part Four

THE LORD:

1. Long long ago I taught Vivasvant [the man of
    mythic times] this ceaseless discipline.
Vivasvant gave it to Manu [the first perfectly righteous man]
    and Manu gave it to Ikṣvāku [who founded one of the two
    royal dynasties].

2. The discipline thus sacredly handed down
    was understood by the royal seers.

Then, after a long presence in this world,
    it was lost.

3. This same discipline of ancient days
    today I give to you,
Because you are my devotee and friend.
    And indeed, this highest of all matters is secret.

ARJUNA:

4. Your birth is something recent;
    Vivasvant's happened long ago.
How can I make sense of what you say,
    that you taught this long, long ago, in the beginning?

THE LORD:

5. You and I have had
    many births, Arjuna.
I know them all.
    You do not.

6. Unborn, imperishable in my own being,
    and Lord over finite lives,
Still I take as my basis material existence
    and appear through my own power.

7. For whenever
    right languishes
And unright ascends,
    I manifest myself.

8. Age after age I appear
    to establish the right and true,
So that the good are saved
    and the evildoers perish.

9. When a man knows my divine birth and work
    thus, as they really are,
After this life he is not reborn,
    but comes to me.

10. Many people, freed of passion, fear, and anger,
    full of me and relying on me,
Have been purified by the fire of wisdom
    and have come to my mansion.

11. Men seek refuge with me in various ways.
     I grant them grace.
    All round you,
       men are following my path.

12. Wanting their cultic acts to succeed,
       they offer sacrifices to the gods,
    For here in the world of men successful results
       come quickly and easily through ritual.

13. I brought forth the four great divisions of men
       according to their qualities and rituals.
    Although I made all this,
       know that I never act at all.

14. Actions do not pollute me;
       desire for results is unknown to me.
    He who understands me thus
       is not ensnared by his ritual acts.

15. With this in mind, men in ancient days did cultic acts
       while aspiring for release.
    And therefore you must imitate
       the men of ancient times.

16. Even sages have been confused
       by the meaning of "active" and "inactive".
    Therefore I shall explain what action is.
       Knowing this will free you from evil.

17. One must understand what right action is
       and what wrong action is.
    One must know also about nonaction. It is difficult
       to understand the nature of action.

18. Whoever sees quiescence in the prescribed cultic acts
       and effective acts in inaction,
    He is understanding among men.
       Doing all right acts, he is disciplined.

19. The man whose undertakings have lost
       desire and calculation

Is called educated by those with understanding.
His actions are consumed in the fire of wisdom.

20. Not caring for the results of his work,
    always content, not in need of support,
Even when he becomes engaged in action,
    he does not really do anything.

21. Without wishes, with mind and body under control,
    with no claim upon anything,
Involved in no activity other than that
    of the body alone, he cannot incur demerit.

22. Pleased by whatever comes his way, outside the realm
    of opposites, free from selfishness,
Even-minded in success and failure,
    even when he has acted, his act does not imprison him.

23. The actions of this man all vanish.
    He has no attachment any more. He is free.
His mind is held steady in wisdom. He does
    what should be done for the sacrifices.

24. The dedication of the sacrifice is God.
    The oblation itself is God. God pours it into God's fire.
God is bound to be attained by one
    who concentrates on God's cultic work.

25. The discipline of some is to revere
    the sacrifice itself.
Some follow the rules of sacrifice
    but offer it upon God's spiritual fire.

26. Some offer up their sense of hearing
    and the other senses upon the fires of self-
    restraint.
And some offer up sound and the other objects
    of their senses to the fire of the senses.

27. Some offer up all sensual acts
    and all activities of life
Upon the fire that is lit by wisdom,
    the fire of the discipline of self-control.

28. Next to those who sacrifice things,
       those who sacrifice with asceticism,
    And those who sacrifice
       through discipline,
    There are still others,
       devotees faithful to their vows
    Whose sacrifice goes on
       through study or the pursuit of wisdom.

29. There there are those who give themselves
       to breath control,
    Checking the course of their breath
       up and down.
    They offer the life-breath they inhale
       in the exhalation,
    And, likewise, their exhalation
       in their breathing-in.

30. Others abstain from eating, and thus
       offer nothing but their breathing.
    All these truly know sacrifice.
       Their impurities are taken away by sacrifice.

31. Enjoying the food of immortality left over
       from sacrifice, they go to the eternal godhead.
    A man who does not sacrifice
       has no part in this world. How could he enter the other?

32. Thus many kinds of sacrifice are made
       and give direct access to God.
    Know them as born from action,
       and knowing this you will be freed.

33. Better than sacrifice of matter alone
       is sacrifice carried out through understanding.
    All action, Conqueror, without exception,
       is contained and completed in understanding.

34. You must learn this by humbly submitting yourself,
       by asking questions and rendering service.
    Then those who have understanding,
       who see things as they are, will teach you.

35. When you have learned it,
       you will not be confused like this again.
    This understanding will show you that all exists,
       in yourself and also in me.

36. Even if you are the worst
       of all evildoers,
    You will cross over evil and deceit
       with the boat of understanding.

37. Once the fire is kindled,
       it reduces the firewood to ashes.
    Just so, understanding
       consumes all action.

38. There is no purifier like understanding.
       Accomplished in discipline,
    A man has all he needs to find it
       in himself in the course of time.

39. He who trusts in his spiritual guide
       gains understanding. He holds it highest,
       constantly,
    Controlling his senses. Having gained understanding,
       he soon reaches supreme peace.

40. But a man full of doubts, lacking
       understanding and trust, perishes.
    The man full of doubts has neither this world
       nor the next, nor happiness.

41. Actions do not imprison him who
       through discipline has renounced action.
    Understanding has dissolved his doubts.
       He has control of himself.

42. Therefore, with the sword of understanding
       put an end to the product of your ignorance –
    That wavering in your heart. And then,
       begin your discipline. Arise!

Part Five

ARJUNA:

1. You praise the renunciation of acts, and then,
    you speak in praise of discipline!
   Tell me plainly, without ambiguity,
    which of the two is better?

THE LORD:

2. Both, renunciation and discipline of action
    lead to supreme bliss.
   Yet discipline of action
    surpasses the renunciation of it.

3. Clearly, constant renunciation is part of a man
    when he knows neither disgust nor desire.
   Free from the sway of opposites,
    he is easily freed from his prison.

4. Not the educated, but foolish men speak of
    reason and discipline as separate.
   Whoever has made a serious beginning with only one,
    gains the fruit of both.

5. The place men of reason arrive at
    is reached also by men of discipline.
   Reason and discipline are one.
    Who sees this is wide awake.

6. However, renunciation is difficult
    to achieve without discipline.
   Trained in some discipline,
    a wise man soon reaches God.

7. If a man is trained in a discipline,
    becomes wholly purified,
   Learns to control himself
    and his senses,
   His own individual existence
    now being the existence of all –
   Even when he acts,
    he is not stained.

8. Disciplined, knowing the nature of things,
    he will think: "I don't do anything!"
  When all the while he sees, hears, touches, smells,
    eats, goes about, sleeps, breathes,

9. Talks, voids, grasps something,
    opens and shuts his eyes;
  He knows full well
    that the senses merely play on the objects of sense.

10. Resting his acts in God,
    he has lost his attachment. He acts,
  But evil clings to him no more
    than water to a lotus leaf.

11. Disciplined men do act with their body, thought,
    meditation, or even their senses alone,
  But they do so to purify themselves,
    and without attachment.

12. The disciplined man gives up the results of his acts
    and attains perfect peace.
  The undisciplined man acts out of desire; he is
    attached to the results; his acts imprison him.

13. Mentally freed from all acts,
    the person dwells happily in the body –
  Lord in the city of nine gates –
    not acting at all, nor causing action.

14. Neither acting nor acts nor
    the link of people with the result of their acts
  Comes from the lord.
    They are the dominion of material nature.

15. The lord does not take on
    the fault or merit of anyone.
  Ignorance veils wisdom,
    and misleads people,

16. But when knowledge of the self destroys
    that ignorance in men,

Their knowledge like the sun
lights up that which is highest.

17. They direct their meditation, their whole being,
toward it.
They make it their whole aim.
They are wholly intent on it. Cleansed by
wisdom,
they enter the estate of no return.

18. The educated see no difference between
men of purest birth, of knowledge and good
conduct,
And cows, elephants,
foul dogs, and foul eaters of dogs.

19. Men who can hold their thought in such
balance
have overcome the world of birth right here.
God is flawless and in balance,
so they live in God.

20. Such a man will not exult when he is lucky
nor be afflicted when unlucky.
Steady of mind, wide awake,
the knower of God abides in God.

21. When wholly free from outer contacts
a man finds happiness in himself,
He is fully trained in God's discipline
and reaches unending bliss.

22. The experiences we owe to our sense of touch
are only sources of unpleasantness.
They have a beginning and an end.
A wise man takes no pleasure in them.

23. That man is disciplined and happy
who can prevail over the turmoil
That springs from desire and anger,
here on earth, before he leaves his body.

24. That disciplined man
with joy and light within,

Becomes one with God
and reaches the freedom that is God's.

25. Seers whose stains are washed away
win the freedom that is God's.
Their doubts are ended. They have dominion
over themselves. They delight in the well-being of all beings.

26. God's freedom surrounds men of sustained efforts,
who release themselves from desire and anger,
Who control their thought
and know themselves.

27, 28 The wise man who dispels outer contacts,
who concentrates his sight between his brows,
Who evens out his breathing
in and out,
Who masters his senses, thought, and meditation,
and is intent on freedom,
And is already freed from desire, fear and anger,
who is like this always; he is set free.

29. Knowing me, the enjoyer of sacrifice
and spiritual exertion, the great lord
Of the universe and friend of all beings,
he enters peace.

Part Six

THE LORD:
1. That man knows renunciation and is disciplined
who does the required cultic acts not counting on their
results,
Not he whose sacrificial fire is extinct
and who avoids all liturgy.

2. What people call renunciation
is really liturgical discipline,
For a man acquires no discipline whatever
without detaching himself from the purpose of the ritual.

3. Cult is the way for the sage
   who aspires to discipline.
   When he has advanced to discipline,
   his way is stillness.

4. He has advanced to discipline
   and has renounced all purpose,
   When he is no longer obsessed
   with sense objects and ritual works.

5. Man should discover his own reality
   and not thwart himself.
   For he has the self as his only friend,
   or as his only enemy.

6. A person has the self as friend
   when he has conquered himself,
   But if he rejects his own reality,
   the self will war against him.

7. A man who has conquered himself
   has a self that is fully present,
   In heat and cold, comfort and discomfort,
   in honour, and disgrace also.

8. The man of discipline, abundantly endowed
   with wisdom and sense, solitary
   And unshakeable, controlled, has true harmony.
   Lumps of earth, rocks, gold, are alike to him.

9. Honour to him who is disposed equally
   toward personal friends, allies, and opponents,
   Those standing aside or caught between,
   foes, kinsmen, the good, and the wicked even.

10. The man of discipline will train himself,
    continually, in a secret place,
    Alone, restraining himself and his thoughts completely,
    without having or wishing for anything.

11. In a clean place he prepares a firm seat for himself,
    neither too high nor too low,

Covered with cloth, a skin, and sacred grass
[such as one sits on at sacrifices].

12. On this seat, restraining the function
of his thought and senses,
he fixed his mind on one point. He will practise
discipline to purify himself.

13–14. He is immobile, holding body, head, and neck straight,
motionless.
He rests his gaze between his eyebrows
without attention to the world around him;
In total peace, without any fear,
faithful to the vow of his sacred study,
He will sit disciplined, intent on me,
controlling his mind, his thought set on me.

15. The man of discipline who in this manner
incessantly disciplines himself,
Controlling his mind, attains the summit of freedom,
the peace that is in me.

16. A man who overeats has no discipline,
nor does a man who does not eat at all.
Likewise a man addicted to sleep,
and one who wants to be for ever awake.

17. Only he acquires the discipline that ends sorrow
who is disciplined in eating, relaxation,
Disciplined in acts, disciplined
in sleep and wakefulness.

18. When thought is checked and focuses
on one's own reality alone,
Then a person is called disciplined.
He is freed from all desires.

19. A lamp in a windless place has a still flame.
This is the traditional image
For the disciplined man of controlled mind
who practises the discipline of the self.

20. His thought comes to rest
checked by the practice of discipline,

And he is happy in himself
perceiving his self's reality;

21. He knows that boundless bliss
beyond the senses which meditation can grasp;
He holds on and does not swerve
from its truth;

22. And having seized upon it,
he prizes nothing more.
Abiding in it, he is not moved
by sorrow, however heavy;

23. He will know that this loosening
of sorrowful ties is discipline.
He must practise it resolutely,
without losing heart.

24. He gives up all desires, regardless,
that are the outgrowth of conscious, stated purposes.
His will restrains the horde
of the senses completely.

25. Gradually he will come to rest through
his firm meditative power.
He fixes his mind on the self,
and he will think of nothing.

26. Whenever the fickle, unstable mind
goes astray,
He subdues it and brings it
under control in himself.

27. For utmost joy comes to that disciplined man
whose thought is at peace.
Passion has quieted. He has
become one with God, pure.

28. Thus the man of discipline, cleansed,
constantly trained himself.
He easily reaches God
and tastes limitless joy.

29. Wholly immersed in discipline
    seeing the same in all things,
    He sees himself in all beings,
    and all beings in himself.

30. I do not let him go;
    I never desert him
    Who sees me in all there is
    and sees all in me.

31. Who has attained oneness and loves me
    who am in all beings –
    Whatever his circumstances,
    that man of discipline lives in me.

32. Who sees the same in all there is,
    whether pleasant or unpleasant,
    And in the image of his own reality,
    that man of discipline is supreme, I say.

ARJUNA:

33. Man is fickle. Hence I fail to see
    how this discipline
    That you describe as sameness
    could be firmly established.

34. Man's will is fickle,
    stirring about, impetuous, set in its ways.
    It is quite difficult to restrain it, I think.
    It is like curbing the wind.

THE LORD:

35. Surely, the mind or will
    is hard to control and fickle.
    But by training and ascetic practice
    it is possible to control it.

36. In my opinion discipline
    is difficult for a man without self-control;
    But a man with self-control who makes an effort
    can attain it by some means.

ARJUNA:

    37. If a man is full of trust, yet makes no effort,
         and his mind strays from discipline,
      And he achieves no enduring success –
         where does he end up, Kṛṣṇa?

    38. Could it not be that he is lost both ways
         and fades like a torn cloud [emptied of its rain]?
      He has no sure foothold
         and he is lost on God's path.

    39. Please, Kṛṣṇa, resolve my uncertainty
         once and for all,
      For there is no one but you
         to sweep away this uncertainty.

THE LORD:

    40. That man will not be ruined, Pārtha,
         whether in this world or beyond it,
      For no one who has done anything salutary
         ends up badly, dear friend.

    41. He reaches the regions of the meritorious
         and he lives there for endless years.
      Then he who strayed from discipline is reborn
         in the home of pure, auspicous folk.

    42. Or else, he grows up in the house
         of wise people, men of discipline.
      For such a birth is still more difficult
         to attain on earth.

    43. There he takes up that inclination
         that was within him before.
      He strives still more toward complete success,
         Joy of the Kurus,

    44. For his former training carries him on
         even without his will.
      The mere desire to know discipline
         takes him beyond the externals of religion.

45. However, the man of discipline makes
       a serious effort. He becomes pure.
    After a number of births, perfected,
       he reaches the highest goal.

46. The man of discipline is more than the ascetics,
       more also than men of wisdom.
    He excels the men of ritual work.
       Therefore, become a man of discipline!

47. Of all men of discipline,
       the one who trusts me and loves me
    With his inmost self,
       him I hold most disciplined.

Part Seven

THE LORD:
  1. There is no doubt that you will know me
       in my total being when you persist
     In discipline, and rely on me,
       and when your thought clings to me. Listen.

  2. Without holding back anything, I shall teach you
       wisdom, and explain how it can be attained,
     Knowing which,
       there is nothing left to be known.

  3. One out of thousands
       may strive for success.
     And even of these only a few
       may know me as I really am.

  4. My earthly world is eightfold,
       divided into earth, water,
     Fire, air, ether, mind, the faculty
       of meditation, and self-awareness.

  5. This is lower nature. My higher
       nature is different.
     It is the very life
       that sustains the world.

6. Do not forget that this is the source
      of all existence.
   I am the genesis and the end
      of the entire world.

7. There is nothing higher than I am,
      O Conqueror of Wealth!
   The world is strung on me
      like pearls on a string.

8. I am the flavour in water,
      the radiance in the sun and moon,
   The basic, sacred word in sacred texts,
      the sound in the highest element,
   And, Arjuna, I am
      what makes men *men*.

9. I am the scent of promise in the earth
      and the burning strength in the fire,
   The life in all creatures
      and the ascetic fire in holy men.

10. Son of Pṛthā, know me as the
       perennial seed in all that lives.
    I am the understanding of those who understand,
       the majesty of the majestic.

11. I am the strength of the strong,
       free from lust and passion,
    And I am, Strongest of Bharatas,
       the right desire in living beings.

12. States of mind arise from
       integrity, passion, and sloth.
    They come from me, for certain, yet
       I am not in them; they are in me.

13. These three states, made up of integrity,
       passion, and sloth, mislead the world.
    It does not recognize me, because
       I am different and unchanging.

14. My veil, woven of these three strands,
    is divine and difficult to pierce.
    Yet those who seek my grace do get
    beyond its wizardry.

15. Workers of evil, people with obsessions,
    and vile men do not seek my grace.
    Because of this wizardry they have no wisdom.
    They are in an infernal state.

16, 17. People act properly and worship me
    when they have fallen into misfortune,
    Or when they are eager for wisdom,
    or eager for wealth, or when they are wise.

    Always disciplined, among these four types, the wise man
    stands supreme, devoted to me alone.
    The wise man loves me ardently,
    and I love him.

18. All four are worthy. Still I think
    of the wise man as my self,
    For he has trained himself,
    has come to me and entered upon the highest way.

19. The wise man submits to my grace
    at the end of many births.
    He realizes: God is all.
    This exalted person is exceptional.

20. When varied desires damage their wisdom,
    people seek grace in other gods than me.
    They resort to various regimens
    to satisfy their nature's need.

21. Any devotee may draw near
    any divine form in full trust.
    In each case, I endow him with
    unfailing confidence.

22. Filled with this trust he attends to
    the worship of his god,

And he obtains his desires from him,
   for in fact I grant these desires.

23. Lacking in wisdom, men do attain
   their goals, but their goals have a limit.
Making offerings to other gods, they go to other gods.
   My devotees ultimately come to me.

24. Men without understanding think I was
   unmanifest first and then came to exist.
They do not know my supreme
   changeless, most perfect being.

25. I am not given for everyone to see.
   I am concealed by the wizardry I apply.
This perplexed world does not recognize
   me, the unborn and unchanging.

26. I know previous existences
   and present and future ones,
But not a single person
   knows me.

27. All creatures enter delusion at birth –
   Conqueror of Enemies! –
For they are obsessed by the opposites,
   haunted by likes and dislikes.

28. But when men cultivate merit
   and the impure is exhausted,
They are set free from the delusion of opposites.
   They commune with me, steady in their vow.

29. Those who rely on me and strive for
   liberation from old age and death
Know the divine secret fully, and the entire
   ordained work, bearing on the self.

30. Who concentrate their minds and know me
   in my relationship to the principles of existence,
To the gods and sacrifice,
   truly know me, even at the time of their death.

Part Eight

ARJUNA:

1. What is that "divine secret"? What affects
   the self? What work is ordained?
   What can be said of the principles of existence?
   What relates to the gods?

2. How is one related to
   the sacrifice, here, in this body?
   And how shall men of self-control
   know you at their death?

THE LORD:

3. The divine secret is the imperishable [– the supreme,
   subtle sound behind the sacred texts].
   Highest nature affects the self.
   The world in its birth and existence
   Brings forth creatures and orders of being
   and is the ordained cultic work.

4. Historical circumstances make for
   the principles of existence.
   Man's spirit relates to the gods.
   Indeed, I myself,
   Here in body, relate to sacrifice,
   O you, supreme mortal!

5. And when a man leaves the body,
   thinking of me at the time of his death,
   There is no doubt that he
   will come to my estate.

6. Whatever estate he has in mind
   when in the end of leaves the body,
   That is the estate he enters, for that
   is the estate he has always dwelt on in his mind.

7. Therefore you must meditate on me
   always, and you must fight.
   No doubt you will come to me when your mind
   and meditation are fixed on me.

8. Meditating, with a practised mind,
    if seduced
  By nothing else, man reaches
    the Divine Being.

9. Who only meditates on the primordial Lord,
   The Ruler,
   Smaller than the smallest,
   Who ordained everything,
   Whom thought cannot fathom,
   Whose lustre is like the sun's,
   In whom there is no darkness –

10. He who meditates on the Lord
    at the time of death,
    With unwavering mind,
    Trained in devotion
    And in the strength of discipline,
    Concentrating well
    His breath,
    His life,
    Between
    His brows –
    That man reaches
    The supreme, Divine Being.

11. Men who know Scripture
    Call it
    The imperishable, the subtle sound.
    Ascetics who have
    Vanquished passion
    Enter it.
    Those who seek it lead
    A life of chastity.
    I shall tell you concisely
    About that state.

12. One should control all the openings of the body,
      check the thoughts of his heart,
    Concentrate his life's breath in his head,
      in short, concentrate on discipline.

13. He goes to the highest goal
     who leaves the body,
   Meditating on me, saying the divine secret,
     one syllable, Ôm.

14. I am easy to reach for him
     who is ever disciplined,
   Who thinks of nothing, ever, but of me,
     who meditates on me constantly.

15. Great men reach me and do not take a new birth
     fleeting and miserable.
   They have attained their
     perfect fulfilment.

16. On this side of God's abode
     worlds are cycles,
   Arjuna, but for those who reach me
     there is no repetition.

17. Who knows the Eternal's day
     and the Eternal's night,
   Each lasting a thousand ages, truly
     knows day and night.

18. At daybreak all things are disclosed.
     They arise from the unmanifest.
   At dusk they dissolve into
     the very same unmanifest.

19. Again and again, the whole multitude
     of creatures is born, and when night falls,
   Is dissolved, without their will,
     and at daybreak, is born again.

20. Beyond that unmanifest is
     another, everlasting unmanifest
   Which has no end, although
     every creature perish.

21. This is called the imperishable
     unmanifest and the highest goal.

Who reaches it does not return.
It is my supreme abode.

22. It is he,
accessible through unswerving devotion.
All creatures have their being in him.
Through him the world was made.

23. I shall tell you at what time,
upon dying,
Disciplined men will not return,
and when they will return.

24. People who know God reach God when they die
at the time of fire, light, day,
The bright half of the month, and the six months
when the sun rises from the North.

25. When a man of discipline passes on
to the light of the moon at the time of smoke and night,
The dark half of the month, the half year
of the sun's southern course, he returns.

26. For the world takes these two eternal
courses, the light and the dark.
By one a man leaves, not to return.
By the other does he return.

27. Knowing about these two courses,
no disciplined man becomes lost.
Therefore, see to it that you are
disciplined at all times.

28. Whatever merit is laid down
For study of Scripture,
For sacrifices, ascetic life,
And alms giving –
The disciplined man who understands
The lesson goes beyond all of it
And reaches the highest, the very first place.

Part Nine

THE LORD:

1. You are a man of good will, and I shall tell you
     the most secret wisdom,
   And explain how it can be attained.
     Then nothing will stand in your way.

2. It is the supreme purifier,
     the master science, the sovereign mystery.
   It is right and perfectly obvious,
     easy to do, and everlasting.

3. Men who do not trust
     in this which is right, O Conqueror,
   Do not reach me, and return
     to the endless round of deaths.

4. My shape is unmanifest, but I
     pervade the world.
   All beings have their being in me,
     But I do not rest in them.

5. See my sovereign technique:
     creatures both in me and not in me.
   Supporting beings, my person brings
     beings to life, without living in them.

6. I am omnipresent as the stormwind
     which resides in space.
   All beings exist in me.
     Remember that.

7. All creatures enter into my nature
     at the end of an aeon.
   In another beginning
     I send them forth again.

8. Establishing my own nature,
     time after time I send them forth,
   This host of beings, without
     their will, by dint of that nature.

9. This activity does not
      imprison me, O Fighter for Wealth!
   I appear as an onlooker, detached
      in the midst of this work.

10. Nature gives birth to all moving
       and unmoving things. I supervise.
    That is how the world keeps turning,
       Son of Kuntī!

11. Fools misjudge me when I take
       a human form,
    Because they do not know my supreme
       state as Lord of Beings.

12. Unconscious, they fall prey to beguiling nature
       such as belongs to ogres and demons,
    For their hopes are vain, and so
       are their rituals and their search for wisdom.

13. But great men resort to me,
       to divine nature.
    Thinking of no one else, they worship me,
       for they know me as the changeless source of existence.

14. Making my name great always,
       firm, not straying from their vow,
    Revering me in their devotion, constant
       in discipline, in reverence they know me.

15. Others know me in reverence,
       when thirsting for wisdom they bring their
       sacrifices,
    Knowing my unique form, my many and
       successive
       forms, my face turned toward everyone.

16. I am the rite, I am the sacrifice,
       the libation for the ancestors and the juice for the gods,
    The priest's verse and the sacrificial butter.
       I take the offering, I am the offering.

17. I am father and mother of the world.
        In ancient days I established it.
    I am what need be known, what purifies,
        the sacred syllable Ôm,
    The verse of the sacred books.

18. Your way and goal, upholder, ruler,
        witness, dwelling, refuge, friend,
    The world's origin, continuance
        and dissolution, abiding
    Essence, changeless seed.

19. I scorch. I stop and send the rain.
        I am deathlessness and death.
    O Arjuna, I am
        the entire world.

20. Cleansed of evil,
    Knowers of the holy Scriptures,
    Drinkers of sacred libations,
    Make sacrifice to me
    And seek to attain heaven.
    They reach the blessed world
    Of the Lord of the gods
    And in the divine world
    Taste the gods' divine enjoyments.

21. But after they have enjoyed
    The wide expanse of heaven,
    Their merit exhausted,
    They return to mortal life.
    Thus they follow the practice
    Of the Scriptures,
    They lust and desire
    And get what comes and goes.

22. Those who think on me with reverence,
        and think of nothing else,
    When their zeal is constant – I grant them
        a sure prize.

23. And when devotees have other gods
        and full of trust bring sacrifices

Outside the established liturgy,
   they sacrifice to none but me.

24. For I receive and I command
      all sacrifices.
    But not all sacrificers recognize me
      as I am. Hence they fail.

25. The gods' devotees go to the gods.
      Who vow to ancestral spirits go to those.
    Sacrificers to demons go to the demons.
      Who sacrifice to me come to me.

26. When you offer with love a leaf,
      a flower, or water to me,
    I accept that offer of love
      from the giver who gives himself.

27. Whatever you do, or eat,
      or sacrifice, or offer,
    Whatever you do in self-restraint,
      do as an offering to me.

28. Thus you will be freed from the prison
      of deeds and their results, good and evil.
    Wholly trained in renunciation,
      released, you will come to me.

29. I am equal-minded toward all beings.
      They neither enrapture me nor enrage me.
    But if they worship me lovingly,
      they are in me and I in them.

30. Even if a very wicked man worships,
      loving none but me –
    That man should be considered wise
      and good. He knows what he is about.

31. He soon becomes completely righteous.
      He is bound for everlasting peace.
    I am speaking to *you*. *Understand*:
      No devotee of mine gets lost.

32. For all who rely on me,
    no matter how vile their birth –
Women, artisans, labourers –
    go to the highest goal.

33. How much more my devotees
    who have merit by birth or are rulers with vision!
You have entered this fleeting, joyless world.
    Worship and love me!

34. Think of me, be devoted to me.
    Revere me while sacrificing to me.
Thus disciplining yourself, wholly
    intent on me, you will come to me.

Part Ten

THE LORD:

1. Listen again, warrior, to my supreme word,
    because you delight in it,
And I shall present it to you,
    for I desire what is best for you.

2. The multitudes of gods do not know where I come from,
    neither do the great seers,
For I am the universal beginning
    of the gods and the great seers.

3. When a man knows me as the unborn
    beginningless Lord of worlds and peoples,
He is free among mortals from all obsessions,
    released at once from all evil.

4. Understanding, wisdom, clarity,
    forbearance and truthfulness, inner control and peace,
Joy, grief, the arising and passing away of things,
    anxiety and courage.

5. Gentleness, equanimity, happiness,
    austerity, generosity, glory and shame –
Whatever exists is disposed to such states of mind,
    and all these varieties come from me.

6. The seven timeless sages
   and the four ancestors of mankind.
   Are born of my will and have their disposition in me
   and all creatures on earth are theirs.

7. Who knows this dominion of mine
   and its use as they really are,
   Is sure to be truly disciplined
   by applying himself without wavering.

8. I am the origin of all.
   Because of me everything lives.
   Intelligent men in the right state of mind
   know this and sing my praise.

9. They are happy and joyful, thinking of me,
   their whole life going out toward me,
   Instructing one another,
   constantly narrating my acts.

10. They never cease to be disciplined,
    delight in worshipping,
    And I bestow on them the right mind
    which leads them to me.

11. Tenderly – remaining in my true state -
    I put an end to their sloth,
    Which comes from ignorance.
    I do so with the bright light of wisdom.

ARJUNA:

12–13. You are God, the highest abode,
    the supreme sanctifier.
    All seers, and also the divine seer Nārada,
    and Asita Devala, and Vyāsa
    Call you the everlasting Divine Being
    who existed before the gods,
    The Lord without birth –
    and you yourself tell me so.

14. I believe
    all this you teach me is true.

Neither gods nor demons, O Lord,
    are able to envision your form.

15. You, Highest Being, who
    to yourself alone are known,
O source of living begins, Lord of life,
    God of gods, Lord of the world!

16. The abundant forms of yourself are divine.
    Please tell me then, and hold back nothing,
By what forms you continue
    to pervade this multiple world.

17. Meditating on you always,
    how may I know you – you in your mystic power?
And in what states of being
    should I envisage you?

18. Tell me more, and in detail,
    of your mystic power and mighty forms,
For I cannot listen enough, O Stirrer of Men,
    to your immortal word.

THE LORD:
19. My mighty forms are indeed divine, and
    of course I shall tell you
What they are in essence.
    My total extent has no end.

20. I am the reality that abides
    in the soul of all creatures,
And of all creatures I am
    the beginning, middle, and end.

21. Of the God of Heaven, I am Viṣṇu,
    of lights the brilliant sun.
I am the leading storm god.
    I am the moon among the stars.

22. Of Sacred Scriptures, I am the Book of Songs.
    I am king of the celestial race.
I am the mind presiding over the senses.
    Of all that evolved, I am awareness.

23. I am Śiva among the Terrifying Gods,
       Lord of Wealth among elves and goblins.
    Of the Radiant Gods I am Fire,
       of mountain peaks, Meru.

24. Know me as the chief of house-priests –
       the chaplain of the gods.
    Among generals I am the God of War,
       among great waters the ocean.

25. Of the great seers I am the greatest, Bhṛgu,
       of speech the one supreme, subtle sound,
    Of sacrifices the offering of whispered chants,
       of mountain-ranges Himālaya,

26. Of all trees the sacred fig-tree,
       of divine seers Nārada,
    Of the heavenly musicians Citraratha,
       of perfect wise men the sage Kapila.

27. Know me among horses as charger of Indra
       sprung from Immortality,
    Among elephants as the elephant of Indra,
       and among men as king.

28. Of weapons I am Indra's thunderbolt,
       of cattle Kāmaduh [the Cow of Plenty].
    Regarding procreation, I am the God of Love.
       Of serpents I am Vāsuki [their prince].

29. I am the primeval watersnake.
       Of the mighty beings of the waters I am Varuṇa.
    I am Aryaman heading the ancestral spirits.
       In restraint I am Yama [lord of death].

30. I am the devout prince of the gods' foes.
       Among men marking the seasons I am Time.
    Among wild beasts I am the lion.
       Of all that has wings I am [Viṣṇu's bird] Garuḍa.

31. I am the purifier in ritual purification,
       Rāma among warriors,

Of the sea's prodigies the Makara,
    among rivers the Ganges.

32. Of every world brought forth I am
    beginning, middle, and end.
I am that knowledge that affects the self,
    the true subject of learned debaters.

33. I am the A of the alphabet,
    in grammar the compound of perfect balance.
I am alone am imperishable time
    and I turn everywhere sustaining the world.

34. I am death that snatches all
    and the birth of all yet to be born.
Of feminine names Glory, Fortune, Divine Speech,
    Memory, Prudence, Constancy, Patience.

35. In ritual I am the perfect chant
    and the perfectly scanned verse
I am the first of months,
    among seasons the spring.

36. I am the dice-roll of the cunning,
    the majesty of the majestic,
The victory and the determined struggle,
    the integrity of courageous men.

37. I am Kṛṣṇa of the Vṛṣṇis,
    Arjuna of the Pāṇḍavas!
Of saintly hermits I am Vyāsa,
    of seers Uśanas

38. I am the justice stern masters mete,
    the statecraft of leaders who desire victory;
I am the silence of mysteries,
    the wisdom of the wise.

39. I am all that is
    the nucleus of any being.
Nothing moving or unmoving
    could exist without me.

40. There is no end to my divine,
       abundant, mighty forms,
    But I have given you a view
       of my dominion.

41. Learn this: Whatever radiates power
       or shows fortune or valour
    Surely reflects a small portion
       of my glory.

42. But there is no need to know everything!
       I have spread out this entire world
    And continue to support it
       with one fraction of myself.

Part Eleven

ARJUNA:
1. You have favoured me by disclosing
       the highest secret, concerning the self.
    Your words have cleared away
       the darkness of my mind.

2. For you have taught me at length
       the origin and end of creatures,
    And also about your glory,
       which is endless.

3. O highest Lord, I wish I could see you,
       your form as Lord,
    Just as you yourself say you are,
       Supreme Divine Being.

4. O Lord, if you think it is possible
       that I might see you —
    Then, Lord of mystic power,
       show to me your changeless self.

THE LORD:
5. Open your eyes and see
       my hundreds, my thousands of forms,

In all their variety, heavenly splendour,
   in all their colours and semblances.

6. Look upon the Gods of Heaven, the Radiant Gods,
   The Terrifying Gods, the Kind Celestial Twins.
  See, Arjuna, countless marvels,
   never seen before.

7. Here in my body, in one place, now
   the whole world –
  All that moves and does not move –
   and whatever else you want to see.

8. Of course, with the ordinary eye
   you cannot see me.
  I give you divine vision.
   Behold my absolute power!

SAMJAYA:
9. With these words, Viṣṇu,
   the great Lord of mystic power,
  Gave Arjuna the vision
   of his highest, absolute form –

10. His form with many mouths and eyes,
   appearing in many miraculous ways,
  With many divine ornaments
   and divine, unsheathed weapons.

11. He wore garlands and robes
   and ointments of divine fragrance.
  He was a wholly wonderful god,
   infinite, facing in every direction.

12. If the light of a thousand suns
   should effulge all at once,
  It would resemble the radiance
   of that god of overpowering reality.

13. Then and there, Arjuna saw
   the entire world unified,
  Yet divided manifold,
   embodied in the God of gods.

14. Bewildered and enraptured,
    Arjuna, the Pursuer of Wealth,
    Bowed his head to the god,
    joined his palms, and said:

ARJUNA:

15. Master! Within you
    I see the gods, and
    All classes of beings, the Creator
    On his lotus seat,
    And all seers and divine serpents.

16. Far and near, I see you
    without limit,
    Reaching, containing everything, and
    With innumerable mouths and eyes.
    I see no end to you, no middle,
    And no beginning –
    O universal Lord and form of all!

17. You, Wearer
    Of Crown, Mace, and Discus,
    You are a deluge of brilliant light
    All around.
    I see you,
    Who can hardly be seen,
    With the splendour of radiant fires and suns,
    Immeasurable.

18. You are the one imperishable
    Paramount necessary core of knowledge,
    The world's ultimate foundation;
    You never cease to guard the eternal tradition.
    You are the everlasting
    Divine Being.

19. There is no telling what is
    Beginning, middle, or end in you.
    Your power is infinite.
    Your arms reach infinitely far.
    Sun and moon are your eyes.
    This is how I see you.

Your mouth is a flaming sacrificial fire.
You burn up the world with your radiance.

20. For you alone fill the quarters of heaven
    And the space between heaven and earth.
    The world above,
    Man's world,
    And the world in between
    Are frightened at the awesome sight of you,
    O mighty being!

21. There I see throngs of gods entering you.
    Some are afraid,
    They join their palms
    And call upon your name.
    Throngs of great seers and perfect sages hail you
    With magnificent hymns.

22. The Terrifying Gods,
    The Gods of Heaven, the Radiant Gods,
    Also the Celestial Spirits,
    The All-Gods, the Celestial Twins,
    The Storm Gods and the Ancestors;
    Multitudes of heavenly musicians,
    Good sprites, demons and perfect sages
    All look upon you in wonder.

23. When the worlds see your form
    Of many mouths and eyes,
    Of many arms, legs, feet,
    Many torsos, many terrible tusks,
    They tremble,
    As do I.

24. For seeing you
    Ablaze with all the colours of the rainbow,
    Touching the sky,
    With gaping mouths and wide, flaming eyes,
    My heart in me is shaken.
    O God,
    I have lost all certainty, all peace.

25. Your mouths and their terrible tusks
    Evoke

The world in conflagration.
Looking at them
I can no longer
Orient myself.
There is no refuge.
O Lord of gods,
Dwelling place of the world,
Give me your grace.

26. And there the sons of Dhṛtarāṣṭra
Enter you,
All of them,
Together with a host of kings,
Bhīṣma,
Droṇa,
And also the charioteer's son, Karṇa –
And our own commanders,
Even they are with them!

27. They rush into your awful mouths
With those terrible tusks.
Some can be seen
Stuck
Between your teeth,
Their heads crushed.

28. As the many river torrents
Rush toward one sea,
Those worldly heroes
Enter
Your flaming mouths.

29. As moths hasten frantically
Into the fire
To meet their end,
So men enter
Your jaws.

30. Devouring all
With the flames of your mouths
Lapping and licking all around,
You fill the world
With effulgence,

And your awesome splendour is scorching,
O God!

31. I bow before you, supreme God.
    Be gracious.
    You, who are so awesome to see,
    Tell me, who are you?
    I want to know you, the very first Lord,
    For I do not understand what it is you are doing.

THE LORD:

32. I am Time who destroys man's world.
    I am the time that is now ripe
    To gather in the people here;
    That is what I am doing.
    Even without you,
    All these warriors
    Drawn up for battle
    In opposing ranks
    Will cease to exist.

33. Therefore
    Rise up!
    Win glory!
    When you conquer your enemies,
    Your kingship will be fulfilled.
    Enjoy it.
    Be just an instrument,
    You, you can draw the bow
    With the left as well as the right hand!
    I myself have slain
    Your enemies
    Long ago.

34. Do not waver.
    Conquer the enemies
    Whom I have already slain –
    Droṇa and Bhīṣma and Jayadratha,
    And Karṇa also, and the other heroes at arms.
    Fight!
    You are about to defeat
    Your rivals in war.

SAṂJAYA:

35. After these words of Kṛṣṇa,
    The wearer of the crown was overwhelmed.
    Joining his palms he honoured Kṛṣṇa.
    He bowed down, then spoke again,
    Stammering, overcome by fear:

ARJUNA:

36. It is right, Kṛṣṇa, that the world
    Revels in your glory,
    That demons are frightened
    And flee in all directions,
    And all the host of perfect sages
    Honour you.

37. Why should they not bow to you,
    O mighty one!
    For you are most worthy of honour;
    You impelled even the creator.
    O infinite Lord of the gods
    And abode of the world,
    You are the imperishable beginning,
    You are what exists and what does not
        exist,
    And you are beyond both.

38. You are the very first god,
    The primal Divine Being,
    The absolute foundation of all things,
    Knower and known,
    And the highest estate.
    You of infinite form
    Stretched out the world.

39. You who are Wind, Death, Fire,
    The God of Streams, the Moon,
    The Lord of living beings,
    Of creation,
    You should receive honour
    A thousandfold – Time and again,
    Honour, honour to you!

40. Let honour be given to you
    Before you and behind
    And on all sides.
    You who are all,
    Your might is boundless,
    Your strength unmeasured.
    You are all,
    For you fulfil all.

41. Whatever I blurted out,
    Carelessly or out of affection –
    Kṛṣṇa! Son of Yadhu! My friend! –
    Thinking of you as my companion,
    And unaware of this,
    Of your greatness.

42. And whatever I did improperly to you,
    Jokingly,
    In playing, resting, sitting, or eating,
    Either by myself or in public –
    O imperishable Lord,
    I ask your pardon for it.
    You are immeasurable.

43. You are the father of the world
    WIth all its moving and unmoving things.
    You are its spiritual guide,
    Most venerable and worthy of worship.
    There is none like you.
    How could there be anyone higher
    In the world above, in man's world,
    And in the realm between the two,
    O paramount Lord!

44. Therefore, I bow,
    I prostrate myself,
    I beg your grace,
    For you are the Lord to be worshipped.
    Please, God, be patient with me
    As a father with his son, a friend with his friend
    A lover with his beloved.

45. I have seen
    What no one saw before,
    And I rejoice.
    But my heart is stricken with fear.
    Show me
    That one usual form of yours,
    O God,
    Be gracious, Lord of gods,
    Refuge of the world.

46. I would like to see you
    Just like that
    With your crown and club
    And the discus in your hand.
    O you with thousand arms
    And of all forms,
    Appear again
    In that four-armed shape of yours.

THE LORD:

47. I am pleased with you, Arjuna,
    And by my own will
    I have shown you my supreme form.
    This is the form of my majesty.
    It is my universal form,
    Primordial and endless.
    No one but you has ever seen it.

48. No one but you, foremost of the Kurus,
    In the world of men
    Can see me in this form,
    Whether by knowledge of Sacred Texts,
    Or by sacrifices,
    Study, or acts of generosity,
    Or rituals, or grim austerities.

49. Have no fear, no anxieties,
    When you see this shape of mine,
    However terrifying it is.
    See, here is my usual form again.
    Your fear is dispelled,
    Your heart at ease.

SAMJAYA:

    50. Thus Kṛṣṇa spoke to Arjuna
        And showed his own form again.
        The mighty being
        Took on his agreeable form,
        And he comforted that frightened man.

ARJUNA:

    51. Now that I see this pleasant,
          human shape of yours, Kṛṣṇa,
        I regain my senses
          and become normal again.

THE LORD:

    52. Even the gods long
          to see this form of mine
        That is very difficult to see
          and that you have seen.

    53. The way you have seen me
          I cannot be seen
        By knowing sacred texts, by austerity,
          generosity, or sacrifice,

    54. But I can be known and seen in this way,
          as I really am;
        I am accessible through devotion
          directed to me alone.

    55. Who does his rites for me and is intent on me,
          who loves me without other desires,
        And has no ill will toward any creatures at all,
          he comes to me.

Part Twelve

ARJUNA:

    1. I understand how some devotees of steady
         discipline see and revere you,
       And others the very nucleus, the invisible nucleus
         of all things. But who knows discipline best?

THE LORD:

   2. Those are most disciplined
      who are endowed with greatest trust.
    They concentrate on me,
      and see and revere me, in constant discipline.

3, 4. Still, those who see and revere the unmanifest,
      which is imperishable, incomparable,
    Omnipresent, passing beyond understanding,
      the highest, changeless, lasting,
    They also reach me. They take pleasure
      in the well-being of all creatures.
    They have attained equanimity toward all
      and restrained their senses.

   5. These men, who focus their attention
      on the unmanifest, go through greater affliction,
    For souls in their human form have difficulty
      reaching an invisible goal.

   6. But those who are intent on me
      and dedicate all their rituals and doings to me,
    Who meditate on me, who revere and see me,
      disciplined towards none but me –

   7. Them I lift up from the ocean
      of the round of deaths
    As soon as they direct
      their thought to me.

   8. Keep your mind centred on me. Make
      your meditation enter me.
    From now on you will dwell in me
      for certain.

   9. Or, if you are not able to concentrate
      on me fixedly,
    You, Winner of Wealth, must try
      to win me by training.

10. And if you are not disciplined enough for training,
      give yourself wholly to rites for me.

> You will be successful
>> just doing cultic acts for my sake.

11. If you are not able to do even that,
     rely on the mystery of my devotion.
   Keep yourself in check, and cease anticipating
     the effects of all your rituals.

12. Although wisdom is better than training,
     and meditation excels the search for knowledge,
   Abandoning the outcome of rituals is worth more
     than meditating. It brings peace at once.

13, 14. I love my devotee –
     the man of discipline always happy,
   Controlling himself, firm of will,
     accepting all creatures
   With solidarity and compassion,
     not selfish, not self-centred,
   With equanimity toward pleasant and unpleasant things,
     thought and meditation directed toward me.

15. And I love the man who is free from the turmoil
     of joy, impatience, and fear,
   Who does not frighten the world
     and is not afraid of the world.

16. I love my devotee – the unperturbed
     onlooker, carefree, pure, intelligent,
   Able to give up
     all he undertakes.

17. I love that man of devotion who shows
     neither exhilaration nor disgust,
   Neither regret nor desire, and who can
     give up good as well as evil things.

18, 19. I love the man of devotion. He is
     equal-minded to friend and foe,
   To honour and shame, heat and cold,
     to pleasant and unpleasant things.
   He is a silent sage, equally unaffected
     by praise and blame. He is content

With whatever comes his way.
He has no home. His mind is steadfast.

20. I love those devotees who see and revere
what I have set forth
As true immortality.
They trust me beyond all the world.

Part Thirteen

THE LORD:

1. The human body is a field,
and someone knows this field.
Those who know him
call him the knower of the field.

2. I am knower of the field in all fields.
Knowledge of the field
And of him who knows the field –
that I call wisdom.

3. Learn from me in brief about this field,
what it is, its nature, how it changes,
How it came about, and learn
of the knower and his powers.

4. Often and in many ways seers
have sung of the field in sacred verses,
And in didactic verses about God,
well founded and certain.

5, 6. This sums up the field with its changes:
the gross elements; self-awareness;
The Great Principle and the unmanifest;
the ten senses of action and perception;

With these, thought; the five ranges of the senses;
desire, hate, pleasantness, unpleasantness;
The aggregates of sense and matter;
consciousness; mental steadiness.

7–11. To be wise, you should be modest,
sincere, gentle, forbearing, just.

You should venerate your spiritual guide
    and be pure, steadfast, self-controlled;

Turn away from what the senses tell you;
    stop seeing yourself in the centre;
Watch the evils of birth, death, old age,
    disease, and all unpleasantness;

Do not be attached, do not be fond
    of your son, wife, house, and the like,
Practice equanimity always,
    whether luck grants your wishes or not.

And, to be wise, practise unswerving love
    as a discipline toward me alone.
Visit solitary places and stay a while.
    Do not delight in crowds.

Cultivate knowledge pertaining to the self
    and a view to the meaning of reality.
All this together constitutes wisdom.
    What deviates from this is ignorance.

12. I shall teach you the goal of wisdom.
    When you know it you reach the immortal.
It is called "neither existent nor inexistent",
    It is the beginningless, the supreme, God.

13. It reaches and moves in all directions.
    It sees, rules, faces everywhere.
It hears universally.
    It never ceases to envelop all.

14. Without senses, it appears
    sentient in all its modes.
Transcendent and immanent at the same time,
    unattached, it supports all.

15. External, yet inside creatures,
    immobile and yet moving,
It is too subtle to be explained.
    It is distant and yet near.

16. Creatures have it undivided,
       and yet it seems divided among them.
    The goal of wisdom, it is their support.
       It consumes them. It creates them.

17. It is the very light of lights.
       It is beyond darkness.
    Knowledge, the goal of knowledge, of wisdom
       is seated in everyone's heart.

18. I have presented to you in short
       the field, wisdom, and its goal.
    My devotee understands
       and is fit for my estate.

19. Primal matter and spirit
       are both without beginning.
    The underlying states and changes in all things
       have a material origin.

20. A person acts and effects things
       on the basis of primal matter.
    He has his experiences because of the spirit
       in all unpleasantness and pleasure.

21. For when the spirit exists in primal matter
       it enjoys the states matter brings about.
    Its attachment to those states
       effects good and evil births.

22. With respect to the human body
       the supreme spirit is
    The great Lord who observes, approves,
       supports and enjoys.

23. Who thus knows the spirit
       and primal matter with its states
    Is not born again,
       no matter what he does in life.

24. Some perceive the reality of the self
       by themselves and in themselves

Through meditation, some through reason,
    some through ritual.

25. But others have a different understanding.
    They hear the word from others and accept it with reverence.
Their ultimate guide is revelation.
    These men also cross the ocean of death.

26. Know that any and every being
    moving or motionless that is born
Is born from the joining of the field
    and the master who knows the field.

27. He has the right vision who sees
    in all creatures alike the supreme Lord
Who remains and does not die
    when they die.

28. For when he sees the Lord dwelling
    in all and everything alike,
He cannot be at war with himself.
    Thus he is on his way to the highest goal.

29. Primal matter alone is at work
    in all that is done.
Who sees this and sees that he himself
    is not engaged in acts has true insight.

30. When he sees that creatures different in state
    and habitat are really in one place
And that they spread forth from there,
    he reaches the Eternal.

31. The changeless, supreme self, though dwelling in the body,
    does not act and is not affected by action,
For it has no beginning and is not subject
    to the states of matter.

32. Just as the ether, present everywhere,
    is too subtle to be polluted by anything,
The self, though pervading the whole body,
    is not polluted.

33. One sun illumines
    the entire world.
Likewise, the Lord of the field
    illumines the entire field.

34. Those who have the insight to know about this distinction
    between field and master of the field,
And about freedom from existence and matter,
    are on their way to the highest goal.

Part Fourteen

THE LORD:

1. Again, I shall set forth supreme knowledge,
    the very highest wisdom.
All sages who reached it, on departing from this world
    have reached supreme perfection.

2. They are not born when the world is born;
    they are not shaken when the world is destroyed;
They resort to this wisdom
    and have become just like myself.

3. The Great Principle, the Divine, is my womb;
    I cast the seed into it;
There is the origin
    of all creatures.

4. Whatever forms originate
    in any wombs,
The real womb is the Divine, the Great Principle.
    I am the father that gives the seed.

5. Integrity, passion, sloth; these are
    the states arising in primal matter.
They tie the changeless soul
    down to the body, O warrior.

6. Integrity gives light and health
    because it is pure.
It binds through the love for happiness
    and for knowledge, Blameless One.

7. Passion consists in desire
     arising from cravings and attachments.
   It binds the soul, son of Kuntī,
     by the love for action.

8. Sloth is born from ignorance.
     It deludes all souls.
   It binds, man of Bharata,
     by carelessness, idleness, sleep.

9. Integrity fastens the world to happiness,
     and passion to action, Bhārata,
   But sloth clouds wisdom
     and ties the world to carelessness.

10. Integrity arises
      growing beyond passion and sloth.
    Passion and sloth in turn arise
      by growing beyond the other two.

11. When the flood of light appears
      at all the gates of the body,
    Then you can tell
      the growth of integrity.

12. Greed, activities,
      initiative in actions, uneasiness, desire –
    These come about
      when passion is on the increase.

13. When sloth takes over,
      these things come about:
    Darkness and inertia,
      negligence and mere delusion.

14. Now if a person dies
      when integrity holds sway,
    He attains to the pure worlds
      of those who know the highest.

15. Dying under the sway of passion,
      he is born among people loving action,

And dying under the rule of sloth,
he is bound for an inert, misguided existence.

16. They say that rightly done works or cultic acts
have a result of purity and integrity.
The consequence of passion is pain.
Sloth leads to ignorance.

17. Wisdom is born from integrity,
and greed from passion.
Carelessness and delusions, obsessions,
and ignorance itself come from sloth.

18. Men of integrity ascend;
men of passion remain in the middle;
Men of sloth, who move in the lowest state,
end up below.

19. When a man opens his eyes and observes
that the states alone are the root of all activity,
When he knows that which is higher than the states,
he enters my realm.

20. A person gains release from the pains
of birth, old age, and death
When he goes beyond the three states
that come through bodily existence.

ARJUNA:
21. What marks the existence of man
when he has gone beyond these three states, Lord?
How does he behave, and how
does he transcend the three states?

THE LORD:
22. He does not become agitated about
the light of wisdom,
Activities, and delusions when they occur,
nor does he long for them when they are gone.

23. Involved, he seems an onlooker
The various states of being do not disturb him.
He knows they are just those states.
He is firm, unshaken.

24. Self-reliant, steady,
       dispassionate in pleasure and trouble;
    Clods of earth, rocks, pieces of gold are one to him;
       There is no difference between
    Desirable and undesirable;
       Praise for himself and invective are alike;

25. Poised in the face of honour and disgrace,
       allied and opposing parties,
    Able to abandon all undertakings –
       Such a man has transcended the states.

26. Who serves me with
       unfailing, loving devotion
    Goes beyond these states
       and is fit for the divine abode.

27. I am the ground of the divine,
       which is deathless, unchanging,
    And the eternal tradition,
       and unfailing bliss.

Part Fifteen

THE LORD:
  1. They say there is an eternal pipal-tree
       with roots on high and branches downward.
    The verses of Scripture are its leaves.
    Who understands this tree understands the Scriptures.

  2. It stretches its branches
    Upward and downward.
    The states of all things
    Nurture the young shoots.
    The young shoots are
    The nourishment of our senses.
    And below,
    The roots go far
    Into the world of men;
    They are the sequences of actions.

3. This understanding
   Of the tree's shape –
   Its end and its beginning,
   And its ground –
   Is not open to
   The ordinary world.
   The roots of that pipal
   Have spread far.
   With the strong ax
   Of detachment
   A man should cut
   That tree.

4. Then he should search
   For that place whence
   Men who have found it
   Do not return.
   He should search for it
   And reflect:
   "I take refuge
   In the very first
   Divine Being.
   The whole world came,
   The whole world stretched forth
   From Him."

5. Men without delusions
   Go to that
   Everlasting place.
   They are humble,
   Sincere people.
   They have overcome
   The damage
   Done by attachments.
   They are intent
   Uninterruptedly
   On that which is Real.
   Desires have dwindled away.
   From opposites as we know them –
   Joy, grief –
   They are set free.

6. Neither sun, moon, nor fire
   lights up the place they reach,

From which no one returns.
    That is my supreme abode.

7. Part of me has become the life of the world.
    Everlasting, yet in the world of the living,
This part absorbs the senses and mind,
    whose home is in matter.

8. Whatever body the Lord takes on, or, upon death, leaves,
    He grasps and holds those senses and mind
As the wind carries
    fragrances from place to place.

9. The Lord takes his stand upon
    hearing, sight, touch, taste, smell,
And upon the mind.
    He enjoys what mind and senses enjoy.

10. Deluded men cannot trace his course.
    Only the eye of wisdom sees him
Clothed in the states of existence, going forth,
    being in the body, or taking in experience.

11. Disciplined men can also make an effort
    and see his presence in themselves.
Senseless men, far from perfection,
    never see him, in spite of their efforts.

12. The splendour in sun, moon, and fire
    illumines the entire world.
That splendour
    is mine.

13. I enter the earth, and I uphold
    all creatures by my might.
I become Soma, the very sap of life,
    and I nourish all plants.

14. I become the fire of life
    and dwell in the bodies of the living.
Ignited by the breaths
    I digest all the four sorts of food.

15. And in everyone's heart
    I am present.
    For me come
    Knowledge of tradition,
    Wisdom
    And reasoning.
    I am the object
    Of all the Scriptures.
    I am the knower of the Scriptures.
    I have established their purpose.

16. There are two spirits in the world,
       one perishable, one imperishable.
    All creatures together form the perishable,
       the imperishable is that which is on high.

17. Other than these two is the highest being,
       known as the supreme reality.
    He, the eternal Lord, enters the threefold world –
       of gods, men, and the realm between – and
       carries it.

18. I go beyond the perishable,
       and I transcend also the imperishable.
    Therefore, the world and Scripture
       celebrate me as the Highest Being.

19. Whatever man free from all obsessions
       thus knows me as the Highest Being,
    Knows all. He loves and worships me
       in all ways of worship and love.

20. I have imparted to you, man without blame,
       the most secret teachings.
    If a man sees their light, he will be enlightened,
       and what he should do is done, son of Bharata.

Part Sixteen

THE LORD:
1–3. A man born to divine fortune is brave.
     He is inwardly purified.

With determination he cultivates spiritual knowledge.
   He is generous and shows self-restraint.
He performs the required sacrifices,
   studies the Scriptures,
Practises austerity
   and honesty.
He is gentle, truthful, not given to anger,
   able to give up possessions.
He has peace
   and does not slander anyone.
He has compassion toward all cratures,
   and no greed.
He knows mildness and humility,
   and is not fickle in his behaviour.
There is majesty in him.
   He is forbearing, firm, and pure,
Free from all treachery
   and conceit.

4. A man born to the demonic lot is
      deceitful, arrogrant, conceited,
   Wrathful, harsh in speech,
      and ignorant.

5. Divine fortune leads one to release;
      the demonic lot to bondage.
   Do not worry, son of Paṇḍu:
      You are born to divine fortune.

6. There are two orders of creation:
      one divine, the other demonic.
   I have spoken at length of the divine.
      Now hear what the demonic is like.

7. Demonic people do not comprehend
      religious acts or search for release.
   Purity as well as liturgy
      are foreign to them, and so is truth.

8. The world is without reality, they say,
      without foundation, without God;
   There is no causality;
      what ground does the world have but desire?

9. Stubbornly adhering to this view,
    these foolish people arise to harm the world.
Foes of the world, having lost the reality of their lives,
    they wreak havoc.

10. Wholly given to insatiable desire,
    deceitful, haughty, presumptuous,
They cling to false ideas because of their obsessions
    and go about their lives hugging impurity.

11. They devote themselves to endless fantasies and anxieties,
    though they may die today or tomorrow.
The enjoyment of desires is uppermost in their minds,
    for they think that that is all there is.

12. Hundreds of expectations ensnare them.
    They are trapped by desires and resentments.
They have criminal aspirations to amass money
    for the indulgence of their desires.

13–15. Their ignorance beguiles them. They think:
    "Today I got this wish fulfilled, tomorrow I'll get that;
This belongs to me, that also;
    I shall be rich.

    "I have slain that enemy,
        and I shall slay others too;
    I am in control; I enjoy the world;
        I am a success; I am strong and happy;

    "I am wealthy and highborn;
        who is my equal?
    I shall sacrifice, give proper gifts,
        and rejoice at the results."

16. Their many mental waves drive them to distraction.
    The net of delusion envelops them.
They are caught in the enjoyment of their lusts.
    They fall into a foul hell.

17. Suffering from megalomania, puffed up
    with the arrogance and presumption of wealth,

They make a show of sacrificing,
    vainly, not in the established liturgy.

18. These men, so full of scorn, rely on their ego, on force,
    on pride, on lust and wrath,
And they hate me
    in their own body and that of others.

19. Nothing ever prevents me from hurling the wicked
    into demonic births in the cycle of existence,
For they are vile, ruthless men,
    full of hostilities.

20. In their delusion they come to a demonic womb
    birth after birth
Without every reaching me, son of Kuntī;
    they then go to the lowest destination.

21. The gates of hell destroying the soul
    are threefold:
Desire, anger, and greed.
    Therefore man should avoid these three.

22. Released from these three gates of darkness,
    son of Kuntī, man
Practises what is good for his soul;
    then he attains the highest destiny.

23. If a man neglects the scriptural ordinances
    and lives according to his desires,
He cannot be successful
    or attain happiness or the highest goal.

24. Therefore, let the Scriptures be your criterion
    for distinguishing duties and violations.
You should perform actions and rites
    which you know are enjoined in the Scriptures.

Part Seventeen

ARJUNA:
1. Some people perform their sacrifices full of trust,
    but they neglect the liturgy given in Scripture.

What determines their place?
Is it integrity, passion, or sloth?

THE LORD:

2. All living souls have some kind of trust.
It is part of their nature
And is determined either by integrity, passion, or sloth.
Listen to what this trust is:

3. Everyone has a trust
conforming to his character.
Man consists in trust:
What he trusts in, that is what he is.

4. Men of integrity sacrifice to the gods,
men of passion to sprites and monsters,
And the others, the men of sloth,
to the spirits of the dead and hosts of dark creatures.

5. Deceitfulness and ego impel some men.
Desires and passions fortify them.
They practise dire austerities
not enjoined by the Scriptures.

6. These fools starve the elements
that stay together in the body,
And they starve me who am in the body.
People like this are of demonic resolve.

7. But the food all men like
is also of three kinds,
And so are their sacrifices, austerities, and gifts.
Hear what the differences are.

8. Men of integrity like food that strengthens life,
courage, stamina, health, bliss, and pleasure,
And that is tasty, substantial,
sustaining, and satisfying.

9. Men of passion desire food
that is pungent, sour, salty, too hot,
Sharp, astringent, or burning.
Such foods cause nausea, misery, sickness.

10. Men of sloth by nature turn to victuals
    that are spoiled, tasteless, stale, and rotten,
Even to polluted leftovers
    not sanctified by sacrifice.

11. Men who do not build upon the result of rituals
    perform sacrifices as they are ordained.
"It is our duty," they know, and they concentrate.
    Their sacrifice is one of integrity.

12. A sacrifice is in the order of passion
    when it is aimed at results,
Or when it is offered
    without honesty.

13. They say a sacrifice is of the nature of sloth
    when conducted outside the established liturgy,
When no food is distributed, no sacred verse recited,
    no priests rewarded, and when trust is forgotten.

14. To honour the gods, the highest class of men,
    spiritual guides, and sages,
To be pure, upright, chaste, and gentle –
    such is austerity of the body.

15. To speak, without irritating others,
    words that are true, pleasing, and beneficial,
And to recite and study sacred texts –
    that is austerity in speech.

16. To be austere in mind means
    inner peace and joy, a kind disposition,
Stillness, self-control,
    and purifying one's place in the world.

17. These three austerities together,
    performed with the utmost trust
By disciplined men not craving results –
    that is being austere in integrity.

18. When one contrives austerity
    to gain a favour, esteem, or honour,

Then it is austerity of passion.
It is neither steadfast nor dependable.

19. Obsessions lead some to perform austerity.
They torture themselves.
Or their purpose is to destroy someone else.
Such austerity is slothful.

20. A gift is a gift of integrity
when it is given at the right place and time to the proper
person,
To one who cannot be expected to return the gift –
and given merely because it should be given.

21. But what is given to get a gift in return,
or for the sake of some result,
Or unwillingly,
that is a gift in the sphere of passion.

22. A gift is called slothful when it is given
not at the right time and place,
Nor to a worthy person,
nor with proper ceremony, but with contempt.

23. We have the record of a concise instruction
concerning the Eternal: "OM TAT SAT".
This threefold instruction of
OM, THAT, GOOD and REAL
Established of old
the people entitled to sacrifice
And the Scriptures
and the sacrifices.

24. Therefore those who speak with knowledge of the Eternal
say "OM" and engage in acts of sacrifice,
Gift-giving and austerity
set forth in scriptural statutes.

25. Men aiming for release say "That!"
and they perform various acts
Of sacrifice, austerity, and giving
without concentrating on the results.

26. SAT – good and real – relates to both
     what exists and what is good.
   The word is also fitting
     for celebrated acts.

27. In sacrifice, austerity, and giving
     faithful observance is SAT – good –
   And all rites performed for those purposes
     are likewise called SAT.

28. Whatever deed is done
     in sacrifice, giving or austerity without trust
   Is called ASAT – not good or unreal.
     It is nothing here or in the next world.

Part Eighteen

ARJUNA:
   1. O warrior, I want to understand
        what renouncing means,
      And also what abandoning possessions means,
        Slayer of Keśin.

THE LORD:
   2. Some sages hold that abandoning rites performed
        for personal advantage is renunciation.
      Others speak of giving up the effects of all rituals
        as true abandonment.

   3. Some wise men say that ritual as such is wrong
        and therefore should be abandoned.
      But others hold that rites
        of sacrifice, gifts, and austerity should be kept.

   4. Hear my judgement, best of Bharatas,
        in this matter of abandonments,
      For renunciation is traditionally known
        to be threefold.

   5. The work of sacrifice, gifts, and austerity
        should not be given up, but done.

The wise are purified through
  sacrifice, giving required gifts, and austerity.

6. It is my definitive, supreme judgement
    that these works must be performed,
  But only after giving up attachment
    to them and their effects.

7. It is not right to abandon
    the regular, required sacrifice.
  Giving it up out of delusion
    is known as an act of sloth.

8. A man will not reap good of any abandonment
    that occurs in the sphere of passion.
  For then he thinks of the sacrifice as bothersome
    and omits it for fear of physical discomfort.

9. Abandonment abides in the sphere of integrity
    when a regular, required ritual is done
  Merely because it should be done,
    without attachment or desire for its effects.

10. The man of integrity practising abandonment,
    who is wise and has vanquished doubt,
  Has no loathing for improper ritual
    nor has a special love for proper rites.

11. For as long as a man has a body,
    he cannot relinquish action altogether,
  But he who can give up the effects of actions
    is a true renouncer.

12. People unable to renounce have their
    triple reward in the next world:
  Undesired, desired, or a mixture of both;
    but for renouncers there is nothing like that.

13. Learn from me, warrior,
    that there are five moments,
  Distinguished in the Philosophy of Reason
    as the basis of all successful acts:

14. The physical body; the individual self;
    the various means by which an act is done;
  Various kinds of activities;
    and, lastly, providence.

15. These five are the grounds of whatever act
    a man engages in
  With body, speech, or mind,
    whether the act is enjoined or forbidden.

16. A fool cannot see this, because
    of the imperfection of his intelligence.
  In the whole matter, he regards instead
    the self alone as the agent.

17. A man who is not ego-centred
    and whose understanding is not muddled
  Does not kill even if he kills these men here,
    and he is not imprisoned by his acts.

18. Our knowledge, what we know, and we the knowers –
    these three together impel us to ritual acts.
  A sacrifice consists in three: that which is offered,
    the action, and the performer of the sacrifice.

19. The theory of the three states of being says that
    knowledge, act, and performer are of three kinds,
  Each according to the three states.
    Listen also to these three kinds.

20. That knowledge, that wisdom, is of integrity
    whereby one sees in all realities
  One changeless reality
    undivided in diverseness.

21. But that knowledge which perceives
    many realities, each of a different kind,
  In all existing beings –
    that knowledge is in the sphere of passion.

22. If one's knowledge attaches itself to one task only,
    as if this task were all-comprehensive,

While in fact it is groundless, unreal, worthless,
the knowledge is of sloth.

23. When one does the regular rituals without clinging to them,
neither with passion nor aversion,
Without anticipating their effects –
that is acting with integrity.

24. But it is acting in the sphere of passion
when a man makes strenuous efforts
And performs the rites to gain his desires
or out of selfishness.

25. It is an act of sloth when one engages in ritual
out of delusion, without considering
What is involved, payments, hurting living beings,
and one's own ability.

26. He who acts demonstrates integrity
when he is freed from attachments,
Does not speak of himself, is steady and energetic,
and is not changed by success or failure.

27. He clearly belongs in the sphere of passion
when he is excitable,
Eager for results, greedy, cruel, impure,
and affected by joy and grief.

28. He who acts is a man of sloth when he is
undisciplined, uneducated, arrogant,
Deceitful, dishonest, inert,
despondent, and boring.

29. Let me set forth fully and distinctly,
Winner of Wealth,
The variety in understanding and in persistence,
in accordance with the three states.

30. That understanding shows integrity
which grasps action and its cessation,
Duty and transgression, fear and peace,
bondage and freedom.

31. That understanding flawed in judging
     what is right, what is prohibited,
   What should be done, what not,
     that understanding is in the sphere of passion.

32. When understanding, enveloped by darkness,
     upholds what is wrong as right,
   And sees all things perverted,
     it is slothful.

33. The persistence whereby one controls
     the activities of mind, breath, and senses,
   With unswerving discipline –
     that is persistence of integrity.

34. But the persistence whereby a man,
     with attachment, eager for results,
   Holds on to religion, desires, and gains,
     is in the sphere of passion.

35. The stubbornness with which a foolish man
     does not let go of sleep, fear, sorrow,
   Despondency, and pride –
     that is persistence of sloth.

36. And now, Strongest of Bharatas, hear from me
     what the threefold happiness is,
   In which a man delights through training
     and where he reaches the end of unpleasantness.

37. Happiness of integrity springs
     from clearly understanding the reality of the self.
   This happiness seems like poison in the beginning;
     in the end it is like ambrosia.

38. That which comes from the confusion
     of senses and sense-objects and tastes first like nectar
   But like poison in the end,
     is happiness in the sphere of passion.

39. That happiness which at its beginning
     and in its wake is a delusion

And which arises from sleep, idleness, or negligence,
  that is happiness of sloth.

40. There is no being on earth or
      among the gods in heaven
    That can be free from these
      three states of matter.

41. Spiritual guides, warriors, producers of wealth,
      and the servant class, O Conqueror,
    Have tasks and rites which differ
      according to the state natural to each class.

42. The acts of spiritual leaders by nature express
      serenity, self-control, austerity,
    Purity, forbearance, uprightness,
      wisdom, discernment, the proper teachings.

43. Valour, majesty, perseverance, skill,
      and endurance in battle,
    Generosity, and authority are inherent
      in the acts of warriors.

44. The work of those who produce wealth is by nature
      agricultural, pastoral, and commercial.
    The servant class by nature has work
      consisting in service.

45. If a man is engaged in his proper work,
      he attains the highest end.
    Hear how this engagement to his own work
      is crowned with success.

46. He reaches success when he worships
      with his own work him
    From whom all beings emanate
      and who stretched forth the world.

47. One's own duty in its imperfection
      is better than someone else's duty well performed.
    A man doing work proper to his own station
      does not incur demerit.

48. Man should not give up work natural to him,
     even though it is imperfect;
   Imperfection mars *all* undertakings,
     as smoke beclouds the fire.

49. In the end, he does reach perfection beyond acts
     through renunciation,
   When his meditation is not tied down to anything,
     he has conquered himself, and is free from desires.

50. Learn from me, concisely,
     how upon this success he can reach the Divine.
   It is the absolute
     culmination of wisdom.

51–53. Man is qualified for reaching the Divine
     when his meditation is pure and properly directed,
   When he controls himself steadily, when he has done away
     with sound and other nourishment of the senses, cast off
   Desire and aversion, learned to observe solitude,
     eat moderately, control speech, body, and mind;
   When he is always intent on the practice of meditation,
     devoted to equanimity,
   No longer centred in his ego,
     freed from reliance on force; from pride,
   Desire, anger, attachment to possessions;
     when he is unselfish, at peace.

54. Having reached the Divine, and perfectly peaceful,
     he knows no sadness and has no cravings.
   Equal-minded to all creatures,
     he reaches the supreme devotion to me.

55. Through love and worship he recognizes me,
     how great I am and who I am.
   Then, knowing me as I am,
     at once he enters into me.

56. Still he performs all actions, all rites,
     but, relying on me,
   He attains by my grace
     the eternal, changeless abode.

57. Having turned to training in meditation,
    making me your goal,
Keep your thoughts directed to me, always,
    while inwardly resigning all you do to me.

58. Directing your thought to me, by my grace, you will
    overcome all obstacles.
But if you are centred in yourself and hence unable to listen,
    you will perish.

59. If you decide not to fight
    out of sheer self-centredness,
Your decision will be worthless.
    Nature herself will compel you.

60. Whatever you do not wish to do
    because of your delusions,
You will do even against your will,
    bound by your natural duty.

61. The Lord, Arjuna, is present
    inside all beings,
Moving all of them like puppets
    by his magic power.

62. Seek refuge with him alone
    with your whole being, Bhārata.
By His grace, you will reach
    supreme peace, an everlasting estate.

63. Thus have I made known to you the wisdom
    of ultimate secrecy.
Reflect on it in full.
    Then, as you will, so act.

64. Listen again to my supreme word,
    to the highest of mysteries.
I truly love you.
    Therefore I shall tell you what is best for you.

65. Turn your mind to me, devoted to me.
    Doing your rituals for me, bow to me.

You will come to me.
    I promise it to you surely. I love you.

66. Passing beyond appearances,
    come for refuge to me alone.
I shall set you free from evil.
    Do not be anxious.

67. You must never tell this to a man who is
    devoid of religious zeal, or love,
Or to one who cannot listen to instruction,
    or one who shows indignation.

68. Whoever in supreme love and worship for me
    makes this highest mystery known
Among my worshippers
    shall certainly come to me.

69. No one renders me service
    more precious than this man's,
Nor will there ever be anyone
    whom I love more on earth.

70. I also hold that whoever recites
    this discourse of ours about the way to be followed
Sacrifices to me
    by his thirst for wisdom.

71. The man who merely listens to it,
    trustful and with an open mind,
He also, set free, will reach
    the fair worlds of the meritorious.

72. Have you truly heard this, son of Pṛthā,
    with singleness of heart?
Has the delusion of your ignorance
    come to an end, Winner of Wealth?

ARJUNA:
73. My delusion is cast out; I have gained understanding
    by your grace, Unshakeable One.
I stand firm; my doubts are dispelled.
    I shall act according to your word.

SAMJAYA:

74. This is the exciting and wonderful
    discourse I heard
  Between the son of Vasudeva
    and that great man, the son of Pṛthā.

75. Through Vyāsa's favour I heard
    this supreme mystery
  From Kṛṣṇa, the Lord of mystic powers,
    who revealed his discipline himself.

76. O King, as often as I recall
    this wonderful and holy discourse
  Between Keśava and Arjuna,
    I rejoice, every time again.

77. And as often as I recall
    that marvellous form of Hari,
  I am filled with astonishment
    and delight, every time.

78. Wherever the Lord of mystic power, Kṛṣṇa,
    and the Bowman, the son of Pṛthā, are present,
  There happiness, victory, prosperity,
    and unswerving morality are found, I am certain.

II

BUDDHISM

Dhammapada
Awakening of Faith
(Mayahana Shraddhotpada Shastra)

The Buddha started from the opposite point of view to the Hindu. He was concerned not with the mystery of being but with the fact of change and becoming. Like Heraclitus compared with Parmenides in the Greek tradition, he saw everything as impermanent, insubstantial, subject to change and decay. Not only the outer world of sense appearance but also the inner world of consciousness was seen to be in perpetual flux. But as he meditated beneath the Bo-Tree, the tree of enlightenment, he realized that beyond this flux of change and becoming, there was something permanent and unchanging. But he did not want to give it a name, as this would imply a substance, a being, and so he called it *nirvana*, "the blowing out", the cessation of change and becoming. This remains today the supreme insight of Buddhism, the perception that beyond all the changes of sense and thought, behind all phenomena, there is an unchanging reality, which cannot be named but which gives meaning to all names and forms.

In the early tradition of Buddhism, which became known as Hinayana, the Lesser Way, the emphasis was on the "eightfold noble path", the way for the individual to be released from the suffering of this world and to obtain the peace of nirvana. But at a later date a new way was opened, the Mahayana, or Great Way, in which the *bodhisattva*, the person who had attained enlightenment, made a vow not to enter nirvana until all living beings had been saved. This opened the way to a new sense of compassion (*Karuna*) not only for human beings but for all creatures. At the same time the Buddha came to be seen not simply as the enlightened one who had found the way to liberation but as the Saviour, who could open the way of liberation for all humanity and for the whole universe. In the course of its development the Mahayana initiated a philosophical movement of immense complexity and a refinement of thought which is more subtle than that of Kant or of any modern philosopher, but still it always retains a sense of the transcendent mystery, the unfathomable ground of consciousness, in which all truth is to be found.

DHAMMAPADA

DHAMMAPADA

Translated by Nārada Thera

Part One

The Twin Verses

1. Mind foreruns all evil conditions, mind is chief, mind-made are they; if one speaks or acts with wicked mind, because of that, pain pursues him, even as the wheel follows the hoof of the draught-ox.

2. Mind foreruns all good conditions, mind is chief, mind-made are they; if one speaks or acts with pure mind, because of that, happiness follows him, even as the shadow that never leaves.

3. "He abused me, he beat me, he defeated me, he robbed me", the hatred of those who harbour such thoughts is not appeased.

4. "He abused me, he beat me, he defeated me, he robbed me", the hatred of those who do not harbour such thoughts is appeased.

5. Hatreds never cease by hatred in this world; by love alone they cease. This is an ancient law.

6. The others know not that in this quarrel we perish; those of them who realize it have their quarrels calmed thereby.

7. Whoever lives contemplating pleasant things, with senses unrestrained, in food immoderate, indolent, inactive, him verily Māra overthrows, as wind a weak tree.

8. Whoever lives contemplating unpleasant things, with senses well-restrained, in food moderate, replete with confidence and sustained effort, him Māra* overthrows not, as wind a rocky mountain.

9. Whoever, unstainless, without self-control and truthfulness, should don the yellow robe, is not worthy of it.

10. He who has vomited all impurities, in morals is well-established and endowed with self-control and truthfulness, is indeed worthy of the yellow robe.

11. In the unreal they imagine the real, in the real they see the unreal; they who feed on wrong thoughts never achieve the real.

12. Seeing the real as real, the unreal as unreal, they who feed on right thoughts achieve the real.

---

* The passions

13. Even as rain penetrates an ill-thatched house, so does lust penetrate an undeveloped mind.

14. Even as rain does not penetrate a well-thatched house, so does lust not penetrate a well-developed mind.

15. Here he grieves, hereafter he grieves; in both states the evil-doer grieves; he grieves, he perishes, seeing his own impure deeds.

16. Here he rejoices, hereafter he rejoices; in both states the well-doer rejoices; he rejoices, exceedingly rejoices, seeing the purity of his own deeds.

17. Here he laments, hereafter he laments; in both states the evil-doer laments; thinking, "evil have I done", thus he laments. Furthermore he laments, having gone to a state of woe.

18. Here he is happy, hereafter he is happy; in both states the well-doer is happy. Thinking, "good have I done", thus he is happy. Furthermore is he happy, having gone to a state of bliss.

19. Though much he recites the Sacred texts, but acts not accordingly, that heedless man is like a cow-herd who counts others' kine; he has no share in the blessings of a recluse.

20. Though little he recites the Sacred texts, but acts in accordance with the teaching, forsaking lust, hatred, and ignorance, truly knowing, with mind well freed, clinging for naught here and hereafter, he shares in the blessings of a recluse.

Part Two

Heedfulness

21. Heedfulness is the path to the deathless; heedlessness is the path to death. The heedful do not die; the heedless are like unto the dead.

22. Distinctly understanding this difference, the wise in heedfulness rejoice in heedfulness, delighting in the realm of the Ariyas.

23. The constantly meditative, the ever earnestly striving ones, realize the bond-free, supreme Nirvāna.*

24. The reputation of him who is energetic, mindful, pure in deed, considerate, self-controlled, right-living, and heedful steadily increases.

25. By sustained effort, earnestness, discipline, and self-control let the wise man make for himself an island which no flood overwhelms.

26. The ignorant, foolish folk indulge in heedlessness; the wise man guards earnestness as the greatest treasure.

---

* departure from craving

27. Indulge not in heedlessness, have no intimacy with sensuous delights; for the earnest, meditative person obtains abundant bliss.

28. When the sagacious one discards heedlessness by heedfulness, this sorrowless wise one ascends the palace of wisdom and surveys the ignorant sorrowing folk as one standing on a mountain the groundlings.

29. Heedful amongst the heedless, wide awake amongst the slumbering, the wise man advances like a swift horse, leaving a weak jade behind.

30. By earnestness Maghavā* rose to the lordship of the gods. Earnestness is ever praised; carelessness is ever despised.

31. The bhikkhu† who delights in earnestness, and looks with fear on negligence, advances like fire, burning all fetters, great and small.

32. The bhikkhu who delights in earnestness, and looks with fear on negligence, is not liable to fall; he is in the presence of Nirvāna.

Part Three
The Mind

33. The flickering, fickle mind, difficult to guard, difficult to control, the wise person straightens, as a fletcher an arrow.

34. Like a fish that is drawn from its watery abode and thrown upon land, even so does this mind flutter. Hence should the realm of the passions be shunned.

35. The mind is hard to check, swift, flits wherever it listeth, the control of which is good; a controlled mind is conducive to happiness.

36. The mind is very hard to perceive, extremely subtle, flits wherever it listeth; let the wise person guard it; a guarded mind is conducive to happiness.

37. Faring far, wandering alone, bodiless, lying in the cave is the mind; those who subdue it are freed from the bond of Māra.

38. He whose mind is not steadfast, he who knows not the true Doctrine, he whose confidence wavers – the wisdom of such a one will never be perfect.

39. He whose mind is not whetted by lust, he who is not affected by hatred, he who has discarded both good and evil – for such a vigilant one there is no fear.

40. Realizing that this body is as fragile as a jar, establishing his mind as firm as a fortified city, he should attack Māra with the weapon of wisdom; he should guard his conquest, and be without attachment.

* Another name of Sakka, the king of the gods.
† a mendicant monk

41. Before long, alas! this body will lie upon the ground; cast aside, devoid of consciousness, even as a useless log.

42. Whatever harm a foe may do to a foe, or a hater to a hater, an ill-directed mind can do one far greater harm.

43. What neither mother, nor father, nor any other relative can do, a well-directed mind does and thereby elevates one.

Part Four
Flowers

44. Who will conquer this earth self, and this realm of *Yama*,* and this world together with the gods? Who will investigate the well-taught Path of Virtue, even as an expert garland-maker will pluck flowers?

45. A disciple in training *sekha* will conquer this earth, and this realm of *Yama* together with the realm of the gods; a disciple in training will investigate the well-taught Path of Virtue, even as an expert garland-maker will pluck flowers.

46. Knowing that this body is like foam, and comprehending its mirage-nature, one should destroy the flower-shafts of sensual passions *Māra* and pass beyond the sight of the King of death.

47. The man who gathers flowers of sensual pleasures, whose mind is distracted, death carries off as a great flood a sleeping village.

48. The man who gathers flowers of sensual pleasures, whose mind is distracted, and who is insatiate in desires, the Destroyer brings under his sway.

49. As a bee without harming the flower, its colour or scent, flies away, collecting only the honey, even so should the sage wander in the village.

50. One should not pry into the faults of others, things left done and undone by others, but one's own deeds done and undone.

51. As a flower that is lovely and beautiful, but is scentless, even so fruitless is the well-spoken word of one who does not practise it.

52. As a flower that is lovely, beautiful, and scent-laden, even so fruitful is the well-spoken word of one who practises it.

53. As from a heap of flowers many a garland is made, even so many good deeds should be done by one born a mortal.

54. The perfume of flowers blows not against the wind, nor does the fragrance of sandal-wood, *tagara* and jasmine; but the fragrance of the virtuous blows against the wind; the virtuous man pervades every direction.

---

* the vale of tears

55. Sandal-wood, *tagara*, lotus, jasmine, above all these kinds of fragrance, the perfume of virtue is by far the best.

56. Of little account is the fragrance of *tagara* or sandal; the fragrance of the virtuous that blows even amongst the gods is supreme.

57. *Māra* finds not the path of those who are virtuous, careful in living, and freed by right knowledge.

58, 59. As upon a heap of rubbish thrown on the highway, a sweet-smelling, lovely lotus there may grow, even so amongst the rubbish of beings, a disciple of the Fully Enlightened One outshines the blind worldlings with wisdom.

Part Five
Fools

60. Long is the night to the wakeful; long is the league to the weary; long is *saṃsāra** to the foolish who know not the Sublime Truth.

61. If, as he fares, he meets no companion who is better or equal, let him firmly pursue his solitary career; there is no fellowship with the foolish.

62. "Sons have I; wealth have I": Thus is the fool worried; verily, he himself is not his own. Whence sons? Whence wealth?

63. A fool who thinks that he is a fool is for that very reason a wise man; the fool who thinks that he is wise is called a fool indeed.

64. Though a fool through all his life associates with a wise man, he no more understands the Dhamma than a spoon the flavour of soup.

65. Though an intelligent person only for a moment associates with a wise man, quickly he understands the Dhamma as the tongue the flavour of soup.

66. Fools of little wit move about with the very self as their own foe, doing evil deeds, the fruit of which is bitter.

67. That deed is not well done when after having done it one repents, and when one weeping and with tearful face reaps the fruit thereof.

68. That deed is well done when after having done it one repents not, and when one with joy and pleasure reaps the fruit thereof.

69. As sweet as honey the fool thinks an evil deed, so long as it ripens not; but, when it ripens, then he comes to grief.

70. Month after month, with a kusa-grass blade, a fool may eat his food; but he is not worth a sixteenth part of them who have comprehended the Truth.

---

* the river of life

71. Verily, an evil deed committed does not immediately bear fruit, just as milk curdles not at once; smouldering, it follows the fool like fire covered with ashes.

72. To his ruin, indeed, the fool gains knowledge and fame; they destroy his bright lot and cleave his head.

73. The fool will desire undue reputation, precedence among monks, authority in the monasteries, honour among other families.

74. Let both laymen and monks think, "by myself was this done; in every work, great or small, let them refer to me". Such is the ambition of the fool; his desires and pride increase.

75. Surely, the path that leads to worldly gain is one, and the path that leads to Nirvāna is another; thus understanding this the bhikkhu, the disciple of the Buddha, should not rejoice in worldly favours, but cultivate detachment.

Part Six

The Wise

76. Should one see a wise man, who, like a revealer of treasures, points out faults and reproves, let one associate with such a wise person; it will be better, not worse, for him who associates with such a one.

77. Let him advise, instruct, and dissuade one from evil; truly pleasing is he to the good, displeasing is he to the bad.

78. Associate not with evil friends, associate not with mean men; associate with good friends, associate with noble men.

79. He who imbibes the Dhamma abides in happiness with mind pacified; the wise man ever delights in the Dhamma revealed by the Ariyas.*

80. Irrigators lead the waters; fletchers bend the shafts; carpenters bend the wood; the wise control themselves.

81. As a solid rock is not shaken by the wind, even so the wise are not ruffled by praise or blame.

82. Just as a lake, deep, clear, and still, even so on hearing the teachings the wise become exceedingly peaceful.

83. The good give up attachment for everything; the saintly prattle not with thoughts of craving: whether affected by happiness or by pain, the wise show neither elation nor depression.

84. Neither for the sake of oneself nor for the sake of another a wise person does any wrong; he should not desire sons, wealth, or kingdom

---

* those far removed from passions

by doing wrong; by unjust means he should not desire his own success. Then only such a one is indeed virtuous, wise, and righteous.

85. Few are there amongst men who go to the Further Shore; the rest of this mankind only run about on the bank.

86. But those who rightly act according to the teaching, which is well expounded, those are they who will reach the Further Shore crossing the realm of passions, so hard to cross.

87, 88. Coming from home to the homeless, the wise man should abandon dark states and cultivate the bright. He should seek great delight in detachment Nirvāna, so hard to enjoy. Giving up sensual pleasures, with no impediments, the wise man should cleanse himself of the impurities of the mind.

89. Whose minds are well perfected in the factors of Enlightenment, – who, without clinging, delight in "the giving up of grasping" (i.e. Nirvāna), they, the corruption-free, shining ones, have attained Nirvāna even in this world.

Part Seven
The Worthy One

90. For him who has completed the journey, for him who is sorrowless, for him who from everything is wholly free, for him who has destroyed all Ties, the fever of passion exists not.

91. The mindful exert themselves; to no abode are they attached; like swans that quit their pools, home after home they abandon and go.

92. They for whom there is no accumulation, who reflect well over their food, whose object is the Void, the Signless, Deliverance – their course cannot be traced, like that of birds in air.

93. He whose corruptions are destroyed, he who is not attached to food, he whose object is the Void, the Signless, Deliverance, his path cannot be traced, like that of birds in air.

94. He whose senses are subdued, like steeds well trained by a charioteer; he whose pride is destroyed and is free from the corruptions, such steadfast ones even the gods hold dear.

95. Like the earth, like an *indakhīla*, a balanced and well-conducted person is not resentful; like a pool unsullied by mud is he; to such a stable one life's wanderings are no more.

96. Calm is his mind, calm is his speech, calm is his action, who, rightly knowing, is wholly freed, perfectly peaceful, and equipoised.

97. The man who is not credulous, who understands the uncreate Nirvāna, who has cut off the links, who has put an end to occasion of good

and evil, who has vomited all desires, he, indeed, is a supreme man.

98. Whether in village or in forest, in vale or on hill, wherever arahats dwell, delightful, indeed, is that spot.

99. Delightful are the forests where worldlings delight not; the passionless will rejoice therein, for they seek no sensual pleasures.

Part Eight

Thousands

100. Better than a thousand utterances with useless words is one single beneficial word, by hearing which one is pacified.

101. Better than a thousand verses with useless words is one beneficial single line, by hearing which one is pacified.

102. Should one recite a hundred verses with useless words, better is one single word of the Dhamma, by hearing which one is pacified.

103. Though he should conquer a thousand thousand men in the battlefield, yet he, indeed, is the noblest victor who should conquer himself.

104, 105. Self-conquest is, indeed, far greater than the conquest of all other folk; neither a god nor a *gandhabba*,* nor *Māra* with *Brahmā*, can win back the victory of such a person who is self-subdued and ever lives in restraint.

106. Though month after month with a thousand, one should make an offering for a hundred years, yet, if only for a moment, one should honour one whose self has been well trained, that honour is, indeed, better than a century of sacrifice.

107. Though a man for a century should tend the sacred fire in the forest, yet, if only for a moment, he should honour one whose self has been well trained, that honour is, indeed, better than a century of sacrifice.

108. In this world whatever gift or alms a person seeking merit should offer for a year, all that is not worth a single quarter. Better is homage towards the Upright.

109. For one who frequently honours and respects elders, four things increase: age, beauty, bliss, and strength.

110. Though he should live a hundred years, immoral and uncontrolled, yet better, indeed, is it to live one single day, virtuous and meditative.

111. Though one should live a hundred years, without wisdom and control, yet better, indeed, is the single day's life of one who is moral and meditative.

112. Though one should live a hundred years, idle and inactive, yet

* heavenly musician

better, indeed, is the single day's life of one who makes an intense effort.

113. Though one should live a hundred years, without comprehending rising and passing away, yet better, indeed, is the single day's life of one who comprehends rising and passing away.

114. Though one should live a hundred years, without seeing the deathless state, yet better, indeed, is the single day's life of one who sees the deathless state.

115. Though one should live a hundred years, not seeing the Truth sublime; yet better, indeed, is the single day's life of one who sees the Truth sublime.

Part Nine
Evil

116. Make haste in doing good; check your mind from evil; for the mind of him who is slow in doing merit delights in evil.

117. Should a person commit evil, he should not do it again and again; he should not find pleasure therein: painful is the accumulation of evil.

118. Should a person perform merit, he should do it again and again; he should find pleasure therein: blissful is the accumulation of merit.

119. Even an evil-doer sees good so long as evil ripens not; but when it bears fruit, then he sees the evil results.

120. Even a good person sees evil so long as good ripens not; but when it bears fruit, then the good one sees the good results.

121. Despise not evil, saying, "It will not come nigh unto me"; by the falling of drops even a water-jar is filled; likewise the fool, gathering little by little, fills himself with evil.

122. Despise not merit, saying, "It will not come nigh unto me"; even by the falling of drops a water-jar is filled; likewise the wise man, gathering little by little, fills himself with good.

123. Just as a merchant, with a small escort and great wealth, avoids a perilous way, just as one desiring to live avoids poison, even so should one shun evil things.

124. If no wound there be in the hand, one may carry poison in it; poison does not affect one who has no wound; there is no ill for him who does no wrong.

125. Whoever offends a harmless person, one pure and guiltless, upon that very fool the evil recoils like fine dust thrown against the wind.

126. Some are born in a womb; evil-doers in hell; the pious go to Heaven; Undefiled Ones pass away into Nirvāna.

127. Not in the sky, nor in mid-ocean, nor on entering a mountain cave,

is found that place on earth, where abiding one may escape from the consequences of an evil deed.

128. Not in the sky, nor in mid-ocean, nor on entering a mountain cave, is found that place on earth where abiding one will not be overcome by death.

Part Ten
Punishment or the Rod

129. All tremble at punishment. All fear death; comparing others with oneself, one should neither kill nor cause to kill.

130. All tremble at punishment. Life is dear to all; comparing others with oneself, one should neither kill nor cause to kill.

131. Whoever seeking his own happiness, harms with rod pleasure-loving beings gets no happiness hereafter.

132. Whoever seeking his own happiness, harms not with rod pleasure-loving beings gets happiness hereafter.

133. Speak not harshly to anyone; those thus addressed will retort; painful, indeed, is vindictive speech; blows in exchange may bruise you.

134. If, like a broken gong, you silence yourself, you have already attained Nirvāna; no vindictiveness will be found in you.

135. As with a staff the herdsman drives kine to pasture, even so do old age and death drive out the lives of beings.

136. So when a fool does wrong deeds, he does not realize their evil nature; by his own deeds the stupid man is tormented, like one burnt by fire.

137. He who with rod harms the rodless and harmless, soon will come to one of these states:

138–140. He will be subject to acute pain, disaster, bodily injury, or even grievous sickness, or loss of mind, or oppression by the king, or heavy accusation, or loss of relatives, or destruction of wealth, or ravaging fire that will burn his houses. Upon the dissolution of the body this unwise man will be born in hell.

141. Not wandering naked, nor matted locks, nor filth, nor fasting, nor lying on the ground, nor dust, nor ashes, nor squatting on the heels, purify a mortal who has not overcome doubts.

142. Though gaily decked, if he should live in peace, with passions subdued and senses controlled, certain of the four Paths of Saintship, perfectly pure, laying aside the rod towards all living beings, a Brahman indeed is he, an ascetic is he, a bhikkhu is he.

143. Rarely is found in this world anyone who, restrained by modesty, avoids reproach, as a thorough-bred horse the whip.

144. Like a thorough-bred horse, touched by the whip, even so be strenuous and zealous. By confidence, by virtue, by effort, by concentration, by the investigation of the Truth, by being endowed with knowledge and conduct, and by being mindful, get rid of this great suffering.

145. Irrigators lead the waters; fletchers bend the shafts; carpenters bend the wood; the virtuous control themselves.

Part Eleven
Old Age

146. What is laughter, what is joy, when the world is ever burning? Shrouded by darkness, do you not seek a light?

147. Behold this beautiful body, a mass of sores, a heaped-up lump, diseased, much thought of, in which nothing lasts, nothing persists.

148. Thoroughly worn out is this body, a nest of diseases, perishable; this putrid mass breaks up; truly, life ends in death.

149. Like gourds cast away in autumn are these dove-hued bones. What pleasure is there in looking at them?

150. Of bones is this city made, plastered with flesh and blood. Herein are stored decay, death, conceit, and detraction.

151. Even ornamented royal chariots wear out; so too the body reaches old age; but the Dhamma of the Good grows not old; thus do the Good reveal it among the Good.

152. The man of little learning grows old like the bull: his muscles grow, his wisdom grows not.

153, 154. Through many a birth I wandered in saṃsāra, Seeking, but not finding, the builder of the house.

Sorrowful is birth again and again.

O House-builder! Thou art seen. Thou shalt build no house again. All thy rafters are broken, thy ridge-pole is shattered.

My mind has attained the unconditioned, achieved is the end of cravings.

155. They who have not led the Holy Life, who in youth have not acquired wealth, pine away like old herons on a pond without fish.

156. They who have not led the Holy Life, who in youth have not acquired wealth, lie like worn-out bows, sighing after the past.

Part Twelve
The Self

157. If one hold one's self dear, one should protect oneself well; during any of the three watches the wise man should keep vigil.

158. Let one first establish one's self in what is proper, and then instruct others. Such a wise man will not get defiled

159. As he instructs others so should he himself act; himself fully controlled, he should control others; for the self indeed is difficult to control.

160. The self is lord of the self: for what other lord would there be? For with self well controlled one obtains a lord difficult to gain.

161. By one's self alone is evil done; it is self-born, it is self-caused; evil grinds the unwise as a diamond a hard gem.

162. He who is exceedingly corrupt, like a māluvā creeper strangling a sal tree, does to himself what even an enemy would wish for him.

163. Easy to do are things that are bad and not beneficial to oneself, but very, very difficult indeed to do is that which is beneficial and good.

164. The stupid man, who on account of false views scorns the teaching of the arahats, the noble ones, and the Righteous, ripens like the fruits of the kashta reed, only for his own destruction.

164. By oneself, indeed, is evil done; by oneself is one defiled; by oneself is evil left undone; by oneself, indeed, is one purified. Purity and impurity depend on oneself. No one purifies another.

166. Because of others' well-being, howsoever great, let not one neglect his own welfare; clearly perceiving his own welfare, let him be intent on his own goal.

Part Thirteen
The World

167. Do not serve mean ends; do not live in heedlessness; do not embrace false views; do not be a world-upholder.

168. Be not heedless in standing at doors for alms; observe scrupulously this practice; he who observes this practice lives happily both in this world and the next.

169. Observe scrupulously this practice; do not observe it unscrupulously; he who observes this practice lives happily both in this world and the next.

170. Just as one would view a bubble, just as one would view a mirage; if a person thus looks upon the world, the King of Death sees him not.

171. Come, behold this world, like an ornamented royal chariot, wherein fools flounder, but for the wise there is no attachment.

172. Whoever was heedless before and afterwards is not, such a one illumines this world like the moon freed from clouds.

173. Whoever, by good deed, covers the evil done, such a one illumines the world like the moon freed from clouds.

174. Blind is this world; few are there who clearly see; as birds that escape from a net few go to heaven.

175. Swans go on the path of the sun; men go through air by psychic powers. The wise are led away from the world, having conquered Māra and his host.

176. There is no evil that cannot be done by a lying person, who has transgressed the one law of truthfulness and who is indifferent to a world beyond.

177. Verily, the misers go not to celestial realms. Fools do not indeed praise liberality; the wise man rejoices in giving and thereby becomes happy thereafter.

178. Better than sole sovereignty over the earth, better than going to heaven, better than even lordship over all the worlds is the Fruit of a Stream-winner.

Part Fourteen
The Buddha

179. Whose conquest of passion is not turned into defeat, no conquered passion of his in this world follows him that trackless Buddha of infinite range, by what way will you lead him?

180. Him in whom there is not that entangling, embroiling craving to lead to any life, him the trackless Buddha of infinite range – by what way will you lead him?

181. Those wise ones who are absorbed in meditation, who delight in the stillness of renunciation i.e. Nirvāna, such mindful perfect Buddhas even the gods hold most dear.

182. Rare is birth as a human being, hard is the life of mortals; hard is the hearing of the Sublime Truth, rare is the appearance of Buddhas.

183. Not to do any evil, to cultivate good, to purify one's mind – this is the teaching of the Buddhas.

184. Forbearing patience is the highest austerity, Nirvāna is supreme say the Buddhas; he, verily, is not a recluse who harms another; nor is he an ascetic who oppresses others.

185. Not insulting, not harming, restraint according to the Fundamental

Moral Code, moderation in food, secluded abode, intent on the higher consciousness, this is the teaching of the Buddhas.

186, 187. Not by a shower of gold coins does contentment arise in sensual pleasures. Of little sweetness, but painful, are sensual pleasures. Knowing thus, the wise man finds no delight even in heavenly pleasures. The disciple of the Fully Enlightened One delights in the destruction of craving.

188. To many a refuge fear-stricken men betake themselves, to hills, woods, gardens, trees, and shrines.

189. Nay, no such refuge is safe, no such refuge is supreme; not by resorting to such a refuge is one freed from all ill.

190–192. He who has gone for refuge to the Buddha, the Dhamma, and the Sangha, sees with right knowledge the four Noble Truths, Sorrow, the Cause of Sorrow, the Transcending of Sorrow, and the Noble Eight-fold Path which leads to the Cessation of Sorrow.

This indeed is refuge secure; this indeed is refuge supreme. By reaching such refuge one is released from all sorrow.

193. Hard to find is a personage of great wisdom: he is not born everywhere; where such a man is born that family thrives happily.

194. Happy is the birth of Buddhas; happy is the teaching of the Sublime Dhamma; happy is the unity of the Sangha; happy is the devotion of the united ones.

195, 196. He who reverences those worthy of reverence, whether the Buddhas or disciples; those who have overcome passions and have got rid of grief and lamentation; the merit of him who reverences such peaceful and fearless Ones cannot be measured by anyone as such and such.

Part Fifteen

Happiness

197. Ah, happily do we live without hate amongst the hateful; amidst hateful men we dwell unhating.

198. Ah, happily do we live in good health among the ailing; amidst ailing men we dwell in good health.

199. Ah, happily do we live without yearning for sensual pleasures amongst those who yearn for them; amidst those who yearn for them we dwell without yearning.

200. Ah, happily do we live, we who have no impediments; feeders of joy shall we be even as the gods of the Radiant Realm.

201. Victory breeds hatred; the defeated live in pain. Happily the peaceful live, giving up victory and defeat.

202. There is no fire like lust, no crime like hate; there is no ill like the body, no bliss higher than Peace Nirvana.

203. Hunger is the greatest disease, compound things the greatest ill; knowing this as it really is the wise realize Nirvana, the bliss supreme.

204. Health is the highest gain; contentment is the greatest wealth; trustful are the best kinsmen; Nirvāna is the highest bliss.

205. Having tasted the flavour of seclusion and the flavour of Nirvāna's Peace, woeless and stainless becomes he, drinking the taste of the joy of the Dhamma.

206. Good is the sight of Ariyas: their company is ever happy; by not seeing fools one may ever be happy.

207. Truly he who moves in company with fools grieves for a long time; association with fools is ever painful as with a foe. Happy is association with the wise, even like meeting with kinsfolk.

208. With the intelligent, the wise, the learned, the devout, the dutiful and the Ariya – with such a virtuous, intellectual man should one associate, as the moon follows its course among the stars.

Part Sixteen
Affections

209. Applying oneself to that which should be avoided, not attaching oneself to that which should be pursued, giving up the quest, one who goes after pleasure envies him who exerts himself.

210. Consort not with those that are dear, nor ever with those that are not dear; not seeing those that are dear and the sight of those that are not dear, are both painful.

211. Hence hold nothing dear, for separation from those that are dear is bad: bonds do not exist for those to whom nought is dear or not dear.

212. From endearment springs grief, from endearment springs fear; for him who is wholly free from endearment there is no grief, much less fear.

213. From affection springs grief, from affection springs fear; for him who is wholly free from affection there is no grief, much less fear.

214. From attachment springs grief, from attachment springs fear; for him who is wholly free from attachment there is no grief, much less fear.

215. From lust springs grief, from lust springs fear; for him who is wholly free from lust there is no grief, much less fear.

216. From craving springs grief, from craving springs fear; for him who is wholly free from craving there is no grief, much less fear.

217. Whoso is perfect in virtue and insight, is established in the Dhamma, has realized the Truths, and fulfils his own duties, him do folk hold dear.

218. He who has developed a wish for the Undeclared (Nirvāna), he whose mind is thrilled with the three Fruits, he whose mind is not bound by material pleasures, such a person is called an "Upstream-bound One".

219. A man long absent and returned safe from afar, kinsmen, friends, and well-wishers welcome on his arrival.

220. Likewise, his good deeds too will receive the doer who has gone from this world to the next, as kinsmen will receive a dear one on his return.

Part Seventeen
Anger

221. One should give up anger; one should abandon pride; one should overcome all fetters. Ills never befall him who clings not to mind and body and is passionless.

222. Whoso, as a rolling chariot, checks his uprisen anger, him I call a charioteer; other folk merely hold the reins.

223. Conquer anger by love; conquer evil by good; conquer the stingy one by giving; conquer the liar by truth.

224. One should utter the truth; one should not be angry; one should give even from a scanty store to him who asks; by these three things one may go to the presence of the gods.

225. Those sages who are harmless, and are ever restrained in body, go to the deathless state, where gone they never grieve.

226. The Defilements of those who are ever vigilant, who train themselves day and night, who are wholly intent on Nirvāna, fade away.

227. This O Atula, is an old saying, it is not only of today: they blame those who sit silent, they blame those who speak too much; those speaking little too they blame; in this world no one is there unblamed.

228. There never was, there never will be, nor does there exist now, a person who is wholly blamed or wholly praised.

229. The intelligent examining day by day, praise him who is of flawless life, wise, and endowed with knowledge and virtue.

230. Who deigns to blame him who is like refined gold? Even the gods praise him; by Brahmā too is he praised.

231. One should guard against misdeeds caused by body, and one should be restrained in body; giving up evil conduct in body, one should be of good bodily conduct.

232. One should guard against misdeeds caused by speech, and one should be restrained in speech; giving up evil conduct in speech, one should be of good conduct in speech.

233. One should guard against misdeeds caused by mind, and one should be restrained in mind; giving up evil conduct in mind, one should be of good conduct in mind.

234. The wise are restrained in deed; in speech, too, they are restrained; they are restrained in mind as well; yea, they are fully restrained.

Part Eighteen
Taints

235. Like a withered leaf are you now; the messengers of death wait on you. On the threshold of decay you stand. Provision too there is none for you.

236. Make an island unto yourself; strive quickly; become wise; purged of stain and passionless, you shall enter the heavenly stage of the Ariyas.

237. Your life has come to an end now; to the presence of death you are setting out. No halting place is there for you by the way. Provision too there is none for you.

238. Make an island unto yourself. Strive without delay; fast; become wise. Purged of stain and passionless, you will not come again to birth and old age.

239. By degrees a wise man, little by little, from time to time, should remove his own impurities, as a smith removes the dross of silver.

240. As rust sprung from iron, eats itself away when arisen; even so his own deeds lead the transgressor to states of woe.

241. Non-recitation is the rust of doctrines; non-exertion is the rust of homes; sloth is the taint of beauty; carelessness is the flaw of a watcher.

242. Misconduct is the taint of a woman; stinginess is the taint of a donor. Taints, indeed, are all evil things both in this world and in the next.

243. A worse taint that these is Ignorance, the greatest taint. Abandoning this taint be taintless, O bhikkhus!

244. Easy is the life of a shameless one who, with the boldness of a crow, is back-biting, forward, arrogant, and corrupt.

245. Hard is the life of a modest one who ever seeks purity, is detached, humble, clean in life, and reflective.

246, 247. Whoso in this world destroys life, tells lies, takes what is not given, goes to others' wives, and the man who is addicted to intoxicating drinks, such a one digs up his own root in this very world.

248. Know thus, O good man! "Not easy of restraint are evil things." Let not greed and wickedness drag you to protracted misery.

249. People give according to their faith and as they are pleased. Whoever therein is envious of others' food and drink, gains no peace either by day or by night.

250. But he who has this feeling fully cut off, uprooted and destroyed, gains peace by day and by night.

251. There is no fire like lust, no grip like hate; there is no net like delusion, no river like craving.

252. Easily seen are others' faults, hard indeed to see are one's own; like chaff one winnows others' faults, but one's own one hides, as a crafty fowler covers himself.

253. He who sees others' faults, and is ever irritable, the corruptions of such a one grow. He is far from the destruction of the corruptions.

254. In the sky there is no track. Outside there is no Saint. Mankind delights in obstacles. The *Tathāgatas* are free from obstacles.

255. In the sky there is no track. Outside there is no Saint. There is no compound thing that is eternal. There is no instability in the Buddhas.

Part Nineteen
The Just or the Righteous

256. He is not thereby "just" because he hastily arbitrates. The wise man should investigate both right and wrong.

257. The intelligent man who leads others not falsely but lawfully and impartially, and is guarded by the law, is called "one who abides by the law (*dhammaṭṭha*)".

258. He is not thereby a learned man merely because he speaks much; he who is secure, without hate, and fearless, is called learned.

259. He is not versed in the Dhamma because he speaks much; he who hears little and sees the Dhamma mentally, and who does not neglect the Dhamma, is, indeed, versed in the Dhamma.

260. He is not therefore an "elder" merely because his head is grey; ripe is he in age, "old-in-vain" is he called.

261. In whom are truth, virtue, harmlessness, restraint, and control, that wise man who has cast out impurities is indeed called an elder.

262. Not by mere eloquence, nor by beautiful appearance does a man become "good-natured", should he be jealous, selfish, and deceitful.

263. But in whom these are wholly cut off, uprooted, and extinct, that wise man who has cast out hatred is indeed called "good-natured".

264. Not by a shaven head does an undisciplined man, who utters lies,

become an ascetic. How will one be an ascetic who is full of desire and greed?

265. He who wholly subdues evil deeds both small and great, is called an ascetic because he has overcome all evil.

266. He is not therefore a bhikkhu merely because he begs from others; by following ill-smelling actions one certainly does not become a bhikkhu.

267. Herein he who has abandoned both merit and demerit, he who is holy, he who lives with understanding in this world, he indeed is called a bhikkhu.

268. Not by silence alone does he become a sage who is dull and ignorant, but he who, as if holding a pair of scales, embraces the best and shuns evil, is indeed a wise man.

269. The sage avoids evils: for that reason he is a sage; he that understands both worlds is therefore called a sage.

270. He is not therefore an Ariya in that he harms living beings; through his harmlessness towards all living beings is he called an Ariya.

271, 272. . Not only by mere morality, nor again by much learning, nor even by gaining concentration, nor by lonely lodging, thinking "I enjoy the bliss of renunciation not resorted to by the worldling", not with these should you, O bhikkhu, rest content without reaching the extinction of the corruptions.

Part Twenty
The Way

273. Of paths the Eightfold is the best, of truths the four Sayings are the best; non-attachment is the best of states and of bipeds the Seeing One.

274. This is the only Way, there is none other for the purity of vision; do you follow this Path. This is the bewilderment of Māra.

275. Entering upon that Path you will make an end of pain; having learned have I taught you the Path that removes the thorns.

276. You yourselves must make an effort; the Tathāgatas are only teachers. The meditative ones who enter the way are delivered from the bonds of Māra.

277. "Transient are all compound things": when this one discerns with wisdom, then is one disgusted with Ill; this is the Path to Purity.

278. "Sorrowful are all compound things": when this one discerns with Ill; this is the Path to Purity.

279. "All Dhammas are soulless"; when this one discerns with wisdom, then is one disgusted with Ill; this is the Path to Purity.

280. The idler who strives not when he should strive, who though young and strong is slothful, with mind and purpose depressed, the lazy one does not by wisdom realize the Path.

281. Watchful of speech, well restrained in mind, let him do naught unskilful through his body; let him purify these three ways of action, and win the Path realized by the sages.

282. Indeed from meditation wisdom arises, without meditation wisdom wanes; knowing this twofold path of gain and loss, so let him conduct himself that wisdom grows.

283. Cut down the forest of passions, but not real trees; from the forest of passions springs fear; cutting down both forest and brushwood of passions, be forestless, O bhikkhus.

284. For as long as the brushwood of passions of man towards women is not cut down even a jot, so long is his mind in bondage, like the milch calf to its mother-cow.

285. Cut off your affection as an autumn lily with the hand; cultivate the very path of Peace. Nirvāna has been expounded by the Auspicious One.

286. Here will I live in the rains, here in the autumn and the summer: thus the fool muses. He realizes not the danger of death.

287. The doting man with mind set on children and herds, death seizes and carries away, as a great flood a slumbering village.

288. No sons are there to give protection, neither father nor even kinsmen; for him who is overcome by death no protection is to be found among kinsmen.

289. Understanding this fact, let the virtuous and wise person swiftly clear the way that leads to Nirvāna.

Part Twenty-one
Miscellaneous

290. If by giving up a slight happiness one may behold a larger one, let the wise persons give up the lesser happiness in consideration for the greater happiness.

291. He who wishes his own happiness by causing pain to others is not released from hatred, being himself entangled in the tangles of hatred.

292. What should be done is left undone; what should not be done is done; of those who are puffed up and heedless the corruptions increase.

293. They who always practise well "mindfulness of the body", who follow not what should not be done and constantly do what should be done, of those mindful and reflective ones the corruptions come to an end.

294. Having slain mother craving and father conceit, and two warrior kings views of eternalism and nihilism, and having destroyed a country sense-avenues and sense-objects together with its revenue officer attachment, ungrieving goes the brāhmaṇa arahat.

295. Having slain mother and father and two brahmin kings, and having destroyed the perilous path hindrances, ungrieving goes the brāhmaṇa.

296. Well awakened ever the disciples of Gautama arise; they who by day and by night always contemplate the Buddha.

297. Well awakened ever the disciples of Gautama arise; they who by day and by night always contemplate the Dhamma.

298. Well awakened ever the disciples of Gautama arise; they who by day and by night always contemplate the Sangha.

299. Well awakened ever the disciples of Gautama arise; they who by day and by night always contemplate the body.

300. Well awakened ever the disciples of Gautama arise; they who by day and by night delight in harmlessness.

301. Well awakened ever the disciples of Gautama arise; they who by day and by night delight in meditation.

302. Difficult is renunciation, difficult is it to delight therein, difficult and painful is household life, painful is association with unequals; ill befalls a wayfarer in *saṃsāra*; therefore be not a wayfarer, be not a pursuer of ill.

303. He who is full of confidence and virtue, possessed of repute and wealth, everywhere, in whatever land he sojourns, he is honoured.

304. Even from afar the good reveal themselves like the Himalaya mountain; the wicked though near are invisible like arrows shot by night.

305. He who sits alone, rests alone, walks alone unwearied, who alone controls oneself, will find delight in the forest.

Part Twenty-Two
Hell

306. The speaker of untruth goes to hell; and also he who having done it says, "I did not"; both after death become equal, men of base actions in the other world.

307. Many on whose neck is the yellow robe are of evil disposition and uncontrolled; evil ones by their evil deeds are born in hell.

308. Better to eat an iron ball red-hot, like a flame of fire, than as an immoral, uncontrolled person to eat the alms of people.

309. Four misfortunes befall a careless man who commits adultery:

acquisition of demerit, disturbed sleep, blame the third, and hell the fourth.

310. There is also acquisition of demerit as well as evil destiny; brief is the joy of the frightened man and woman; the king imposes a heavy punishment; hence no man should frequent another's wife.

311. Just as kusa grass wrongly grasped cuts the hand indeed; even so the ascetic life wrongly handled drags one to hell.

312. Any loose act, any corrupt vow, a dubious holy life, none of this is of great fruit.

313. If aught should be done, let one do it; let one promote it steadily, for slack asceticism scatters dust all the more.

314. An evil deed is better not done; a misdeed hereafter torments one; better it is to do a good deed, after doing which one does not grieve.

315. Like a border city, guarded within and without, so guard yourself; surely, do not let slip this opportunity, for they who let slip the opportunity grieve when born in hell.

316. Beings who are ashamed of what is not shameful, and are not ashamed of what is shameful, embrace false views and go to a woeful state.

317. Beings who see fear in what is not to be feared, and see no fear in the fearsome, embrace false views and go to a woeful state.

318. Beings who imagine wrong in the faultless and view no wrong in what is wrong, embrace false views and go to a woeful state.

319. Beings knowing wrong as wrong and what is right as right, embrace right views and go to a blissful state.

Part Twenty-Three
The Elephant

320. As an elephant in the battlefield withstands the arrows shot from a bow, even so will I endure abuse; verily most people are undisciplined.

321. They lead the trained horses or elephants to an assembly. The king mounts the trained; best among men are the trained who endure abuse.

322. Excellent are trained mules, so are thoroughbreds of Sindh and noble elephants, the tuskers; but far more excellent is he that trains himself.

323. Surely never by those vehicles would one go to the untrodden land Nirvāna, as does one who is controlled through his subdued and well-trained self.

324. The uncontrollable, captive tusker, named Dhanapālaka, with

pungent rut flowing, eats no morsel; the tusker calls to mind the elephant forest.

325. The stupid one, when he is torpid, gluttonous, sleepy, rolls about as he lies like a great hog nourished on pig-wash, again and again goes to rebirth.

326. Formerly this mind went wandering where it liked, as it wished, as it listed; today with attentiveness I shall completely hold it in check, as a mahout a rut-elephant.

327. Take delight in heedfulness; guard your mind well. Draw yourself out of the evil way like an elephant sunk in the mire.

328. If you get a prudent companion who is fit to live with you, who behaves well and is wise, you should live with him, joyfully and mindfully overcoming all dangers.

329. If you do not get a prudent companion who is fit to live with you, who behaves well, and is wise, then like a king who leaves a conquered kingdom, you should live alone as an elephant in the elephant forest.

330. Better it is to live alone. There is no fellowship with a fool; let one live alone doing no evil, being care-free, like an elephant in the elephant forest.

331. When need arises, happy is it to have friends; happy is contentment with just this and that; merit is happy, when life is at an end; happy is the shunning of all ill.

332. Happy in this world is ministering to mother; ministering to father too is happy; happy in this world is ministering to ascetics; happy too is ministering to the Noble Ones.

333. Happy is virtue till old age; happy is steadfast confidence; happy is the attainment of wisdom; happy is it to do no evil.

Part Twenty-Four

Craving

334. The craving of the person addicted to careless living grows like a creeper; he jumps from life to life like a fruit-loving monkey in the forest.

335. Whomsoever in this world this base clinging thirst overcomes, his sorrows flourish like well-watered bīraṇa grass.

336. Whoso in the world overcomes this base unruly craving, from him sorrows fall away, like waterdrops from a lotus leaf.

337. This I say to you, Good luck to you all who have assembled here; dig up the root of craving, as one in quest of bīraṇa's sweet root. Let not Māra crush you again and again, as the flood a reed.

338. Just as a tree, with roots undamaged and firm, though hewn down,

sprouts again; even so, while latent craving is not rooted out, this sorrow springs up again and again.

339. In whom the thirty-six streams of craving that rush towards pleasurable objects are strong, then powerful, lustful thoughts carry off that misunderstanding person.

340. The streams (cravings) flow everywhere. The creeper sprouts and stands; seeing the creeper that has sprung up, with wisdom cut off the root.

341. To beings there arise pleasures that rush towards sense-objects and are moistened with craving; bent on pleasure they seek happiness. Verily, those men come to birth and decay.

342. Folk enwrapt in craving are terrified like a captive hare; held fast by fetters and bonds, for long they come to sorrow again and again.

343. Folk enwrapt in craving are terrified like a captive hare; therefore a bhikkhu, who wishes his own passionlessness Nirvāna, should discard craving.

344. Whoever with no desire for the household finds pleasure in the forest of asceticism, and though freed from desire for the household, yet runs back to that very home, behold that very man! Freed he runs back to that very bondage.

345. That which is made of iron, wood, or hemp is not a strong bond, say the wise; but that longing for jewels, ornaments, children, and wives is far greater an attachment.

346. That bond is strong, say the wise, it hurls down, yields, and is hard to loosen; this too they cut off, and leave the world, with no longing renouncing sensual pleasures.

347. They who are infatuated with lust fall back into the stream as a spider on its self-spun web; this too the wise cut off and wander, with no longing, giving up all sorrow.

348. Let go the past, let go the future, let go the present front, back and middle; crossing to the farther shore of existence, with mind released from everything, do not again undergo birth and decay.

349. For the person who is perturbed by evil thoughts, who is of strong passions, who sees but the pleasurable, craving steadily grows. Indeed, he makes the bond strong.

350. He who delights in subduing evil thoughts, he who meditates on Impurity, he who is ever mindful, it is he who will make an end of craving, he will cut Māra's bond.

351. He who has reached the goal, is fearless, is without craving, is passionless, has cut the thorns of life; this is his final body.

352. He who is without craving and grasping, he who is skilled in etymology and terms, he who knows the grouping of letters and their

sequence, it is he who is called the bearer of the final body, one of profound wisdom, a great man.

353. All have I overcome, all do I know; from all am I detached, all have I renounced; wholly absorbed am I in the "Destruction of Craving". Having comprehended all by myself whom shall I call my teacher?

354. The gift of Truth excels all gifts; the flavour of Truth excels all flavours; the pleasure in Truth excels all pleasures; he who has destroyed craving overcomes all sorrow.

355. Riches ruin the foolish, but not those in quest of the Beyond Nirvāna; through craving for riches, the foolish one ruins himself as if he were ruining others.

356. Weeds are the bane of fields, lust is the bane of this mankind; hence what is given to the lustless yields abundant fruit.

357. Weeds are the bane of fields, hatred is the bane of this mankind; hence what is given to those rid of hatred yields abundant fruit.

358. Weeds are the bane of fields, delusion is the bane of this mankind; hence what is given to those rid of delusion yields abundant fruit.

359. Weeds are the bane of fields, desire is the bane of this mankind; hence what is given to the desireless yields abundant fruit.

Part Twenty-Five

The Bhikkhu or Mendicant Monk

360. Good is restraint in the eye; good is restraint in the ear; good is restraint in the nose; good is restraint in the tongue.

361. Good is restraint in deed; good is restraint in speech; good is restraint in mind; good is restraint in everything. The bhikkhu restrained everywhere is freed from all sorrow.

362. He who is controlled in hand, foot, speech, and in the highest head, he who delights in meditation, and is composed, he who is alone and contented, him they call a bhikkhu.

363. That bhikkhu who is controlled in tongue, who speaks wisely, who is not puffed up, who explains the meaning and the text, sweet, indeed, is his speech.

364. That bhikkhu who dwells in the Dhamma, who delights in the Dhamma, who meditates on the Dhamma, who well remembers the Dhamma, does not fall away from the sublime Dhamma.

365. Let him not despise what he has received, nor fare envying the gains of others. The bhikkhu who envies the gains of others does not attain concentration.

366. Though a recipient of little, if a bhikkhu does not despise what he has received, even the gods praise him who is pure in livelihood and is not slothful.

367. He who has no thought of "I and mine" whatever towards mind and body, he who grieves not for that which he has not, he is indeed called a bhikkhu.

368. The bhikkhu who abides in loving-kindness, who is pleased with the Buddha's teaching, attains to that state of peace and happiness, the stilling of conditioned things.

369. Empty this boat, O bhikkhu! Emptied by you it will move swiftly; cutting off lust and hatred, to Nirvāna you will thereby go.

370. Five cut off, five give up, five further cultivate. The bhikkhu who has gone beyond the five bonds is called a "Flood-Crosser".

371. Meditate, O bhikkhu! Be not heedless. Do not let your mind whirl on sensual pleasures. Do not be careless and swallow a lead-ball. As you burn cry not "This is sorrow".

372. There is no concentration to one who lacks wisdom, nor is there wisdom to him who lacks concentration. In whom are both concentration and wisdom, he, indeed, is in the presence of Nirvāna.

373. The bhikkhu who has retired to a lonely abode, who has calmed his mind, who clearly perceives the Doctrine, experiences a joy transcending that of men.

374. Whenever he reflects on the rise and fall of the aggregates, he experiences joy and happiness. To the knowing ones that reflection is Deathless.

375. And this becomes the beginning here for a wise bhikkhu: sense-control, contentment, restraint with regard to the fundamental Moral Code *Pātimokkha*, association with beneficent and energetic friends whose livelihood is pure.

376. Let him be cordial in his ways and refined in conduct; thereby full of joy he will make an end of ill.

377. As the jasmine creeper sheds its withered flowers, even so, O bhikkhus, should you totally cast off lust and hatred.

378. The bhikkhu who is calm in body, calm in speech, calm in mind, who is well-composed, who has spewed out worldly things, is truly called a "peaceful one".

379. By self do you censure yourself, by self do you examine yourself. Self-guarded and mindful, O bhikkhu, you will live happily.

380. Self, indeed, is the protector of self; self, indeed, is one's refuge; control therefore your own self as a merchant, a noble steed.

381. Full of joy, full of confidence in the Buddha's Teaching, the bhikkhu will attain the Peaceful State, the stilling of conditioned things, the bliss supreme.

382. The bhikkhu who, while still young, devotes himself to the Buddha's teaching, illumines this world like the moon freed from a cloud.

Part Twenty-Six
The Brāhmaṇa

383. Strive and cleave the stream; discard, O brāhmaṇa, sense-desires, knowing the destruction of life's constituents, thou art, O brāhmaṇa, a knower of the Uncreate Nirvāna.

384. When in two states, a brāhmaṇa goes to the farther shore, then all the fetters of that knowing one pass away.

385. For whom there exists neither the hither nor the farther shore, nor both the hither and the farther shore, he who is undistressed and unbound, him I call a brāhmaṇa.

386. He that is meditative, stainless, and settled; he that has done his duty and is free from the Corruptions; he that has attained the Highest Goal, him I call a brāhmaṇa.

387. The sun shines by day, the moon is bright by night; armoured shines the warrior, meditating the brāhmaṇa shines; but all day and night the Buddha shines in glory.

388. Because he has discarded evil, he is called a *brāhmaṇa*; because he lives in quietude, he is called a *samaṇa*; because he gives up the impurities, he is called a *pabbajita* recluse.

389. One should not strike a brāhmaṇa; a brāhmaṇa should not vent his wrath on him. Shame on him who strikes a brāhmaṇa! More shame on him who gives vent to his wrath.

390. Unto a brāhmaṇa that non-retaliation is of no small advantage. When the mind is weaned from things dear, whenever the intent to harm ceases, then and then only sorrow subsides.

391. He that does no evil through body, speech, or mind, who is restrained in these three respects, him I call a brāhmaṇa.

392. If from anybody one should understand the Doctrine preached by the Fully Enlightened One, devoutly should one reverence him, as a brāhmaṇa reveres the sacrificial fire.

393. Not by matted hair, nor by family, nor by birth does one become a brāhmaṇa; but in whom there exist both truth and righteousness, pure is he, a brāhmaṇa is he.

394. What is the use of your matted hair, O witless man! What is the use of your antelope garment? Within you are full of passions, without you embellish.

395. The person who wears dust-heap robes, who is lean, who is over-

spread with veins, who meditates alone in the forest, him I call a brāhmaṇa.

396. I do not call him a brāhmaṇa merely because he is born of a womb or sprung from a brāhmaṇa mother. He is merely a "Dear addresser" if he is with impediments. He who is free from impediments, free from clinging, him I call a brāhmaṇa.

397. He who has cut off all fetters, who trembles not, who has gone beyond ties, who is unbound, him I call a brāhmaṇa.

398. He who has cut the strap hatred, the thong craving, and the rope heresies, together with the appendages latent tendencies, who has thrown up the cross-bar ignorance, who is enlightened buddha, him I call a brāhmaṇa.

399. He who, without anger, endures reproach, flogging and punishments, whose power, the potent army, is patience, him I call a brāhmaṇa.

400. He who is not wrathful, but is dutiful, virtuous, not moistened with craving, controlled, and bears his final body, him I call a brāhmaṇa.

401. Like water on a lotus leaf, like a mustard seed on the point of a needle, he clings not to sensual pleasures, him I call a brāhmaṇa.

402. He who realizes here in this world the destruction of his sorrow, who has laid the burden aside and is emancipated, him I call a brāhmaṇa.

403. He whose knowledge is deep, who is wise, who is skilled in the right and wrong way, who has reached the highest goal, him I call a brāhmaṇa.

404. He who is not intimate with both householders and homeless ones, who wanders without an abode, who is without desires, him I call a brāhmaṇa.

405. He who has laid aside the cudgel towards beings, whether feeble or strong, who neither kills nor causes to kill, him I call a brāhmaṇa.

406. He who is friendly amongst the hostile, who is peaceful amongst the violent, who is unattached amongst the attached, him I call a brāhmaṇa.

407. In whom lust, hatred, pride, detraction are fallen off like a mustard seed from the point of a needle, him I call a brāhmaṇa.

408. He who utters gentle, instructive, true words, who gives offence to none, him I call a brāhmaṇa.

409. He who in this world takes nothing that is not given, be it long or short, small or great, fair or foul, him I call a brāhmaṇa.

410. He who has no desires, whether of this world or of the next, who is desireless and emancipated, him I call a brāhmaṇa.

411. He who has no longings, who through knowledge is free from doubts, who has plunged into the Deathless Nirvāna, him I call a brāhmaṇa.

412. Herein he who has transcended both good and bad and the ties as well, who is sorrowless, stainless, and pure, him I call a brāhmaṇa.

413. He who is spotless as the moon, who is pure, serene, and still, who has destroyed craving for becoming, him I call a brāhmaṇa.

414. He who has passed beyond this quagmire, this difficult path, the ocean of life saṃsāra, and delusion, who has crossed and gone beyond, who is meditative, free from craving and doubts, who, clinging to nought, has attained Nirvāna, him I call a brāhmaṇa.

415. He who in this world giving up sensual pleasures, would renounce and become a homeless one, who has destroyed sense-desires and becoming, him I call a brāhmaṇa.

416. He who in this world giving up craving, would renounce and become a homeless one, who has destroyed craving and becoming, him I call a brāhmaṇa.

417. He who, discarding human ties and transcending celestial ties, is completely delivered from all ties, him I call a brāhmaṇa.

418. He who has given up likes and dislikes, who is cooled and is without substrata, who has conquered the world, and is strenuous, him I call a brāhmaṇa.

419. He who, in every way, knows the death and rebirth of beings, who is detached, well-gone, and enlightened, him I call a brāhmaṇa.

420. He whose destiny neither gods nor gandhabbas nor men know, who has destroyed all Defilements, and is an arahat, him I call a brāhmaṇa.

421. He who has no clinging to aggregates that are past, future, or present, who is without clinging and grasping, him I call a brāhmaṇa.

422. The fearless, the noble, the hero, the great sage, the conqueror, the desireless, the enlightened, him I call a brāhmaṇa.

423. That sage who knows his former abodes, who sees heaven and hell, who has reached the end of births, who, with superior wisdom, has perfected himself, who has completed the holy life the end of all passions, him I call a brāhmaṇa.

AWAKENING OF FAITH
(MAHAYANA SHRADDHOTPADA SHASTRA)

AWAKENING OF FAITH
(MAHAYANA SHRADDHOTPADA SHASTRA)

Translated by Dwight Goddard

Preface

This commentary upon the Mahayana Shradhotpadda Shastra is one of the most profound and wonderful books that has ever been written. It elucidates the significance of the Mahayana which is the Noble Path to Enlightenment and Nirvana, and by so doing it unveils the development of the Truth of Mind-Essence under the conditions of this *Saha* world. Its meaning is wide and profound, being as tranquil and peaceful as open space, and its potentialities as limitless and varied and vast as the boundless ocean. In its scope it includes divinities as well as humans, indeed, it reveals the origin of all individualized concepts. Because of its succinctness and profundity only a few are able to understand it.

In India, at the time of its writing some six hundred years after the Nirvana of our Lord Tathagata, the philosophic and religious culture of the times had developed and become segregated into many different schools and cults, so that all kinds of heresies and fallacies were flourishing everywhere. In only one thing did they agree and that was in a common attack and slanders about the True Teaching of Buddhism. At this crisis there came into prominence in India a scholar of outstanding virtue by the name of Ashvaghosha, who rose to be the greatest controversialist of his time and who was able to subdue all opponents of Buddhism. As a Brahmin scholar he had studied all philosophies, but had become convinced that in the Truth of Mahayana he had found the ultimate ground of Truth and Faith, and he cherished a deep and abiding faith in it. Although in the beginning a proud and egoistic Brahmin pedant, under the influence of his new faith he awakened a great heart of compassion and resolved that whenever opportunity came he would willingly interpret it to others. It was in this spirit of compassion for all the world, seeing them suffering under delusion, that he wrote this commentary that by so doing he might broadcast the Three Treasures of Buddhism (Buddha, Dharma, Sangha, that is, Buddha, His Teaching, His Brotherhood) and revive their appeal. Any one who by reading it awakened a pure faith would be quickly turned away from his heretical preconceptions and enter upon the true Path. Since the time of the Lord Tathagata this Mahayana

Teaching had only imperfectly been understood because its time of maturity had not yet fully come. In China it had not even been heard of. It was not until the times of the Later Liang Dynasty (505–552) that the Emperor Liang Wu-ti, becoming interested in this Indian Teaching, sent envoys to the Magadha country of India to secure copies of its Sanskrit Scriptures and to invite learned Masters to return with them to China. There these envoys met a great Sanskrit Master by the name of Kulnanda, who afterwards became better known as Paramartha. He had been a great student of Indian philosophies and religions during his academic life, but had later become wholly interested in the Teachings of the Mahayana and had become a Master of great insight into its Truths. He was eminently the Master the envoys were looking for, and they invited him to return with them to be under the patronage of the Emperor. At first he refused to go, but under the urgent appeal of his own King, he at last consented and sailed for China with suitable attendants and a store of images and books.

He was received with great respect by the Emperor, but unfortunately within ten days a rebellion broke out, surrounded the palace and in less than eighty days the Emperor had died of starvation, leaving the Indian Master unprotected, but not without friends. At first he prepared to return to his native country, but certain of us, including Lord Shaube of the Privy Council and the Generalissimo's office, advised him to remain and provided him with a safe retreat in the Kien-shing Temple in Hengchow, Hunan Province.

In the Third Year of Shen-Seng (557) The Master began the translation of this Shastra and completed it in two years in one volume, elucidating the Mahayana very vividly and clearly. Besides this he translated many other Scriptures, notably, Metaphysical Buddhism in twenty volumes, the Metaphysics of the Mahavagga in four volumes, and An Interpretation of the Nine Kinds of Consciousness in two volumes. Besides the Grand Master Paramartha, he was assisted by the Indo-Scythian Master Surnam and others, and I was one of the Chinese writers to put their interpretations into classical Chinese characters. From the commencement of the work to its ending, the task lasted two years. Since then this elucidation of the principle and practice of the Mahayana written by the Venerable Patriarch Ashvaghosha has prevailed in the scholarly world, and most of the heretical scholars have submitted to the orthodox.

It was a cause of great regret to me that I was never able to meet the Venerable Patriarch personally, but I count it a good fortune to have had the chance to study his wonderful teaching and witness and praise its profound wisdom. I reverenced this Principle so much that I could hardly give up its study. In spite of my unlearnedness, I presumptuously accepted the honour of writing down the oral interpretations of my colleagues. If there ever should be greater scholars who by chance should read it, I would count it a great indebtedness if they would correct any errors.

Written by BHIKSHU CHIH-CHI *of the* LIANG DYNASTY

Introduction

ADORATION to our Great Compassionate Saviour, Omnipresent, Omniscient, Omnipotent!

ADORATION to his Potentiality and unmanifested Universality!

ADORATION to his Activity, perfectly balanced and accommodating!

ADORATION to the pure Essence of Mind, wide and deep as the sea!

ADORATION to its Store of infinite Virtues and Merit, that may be fully developed by earnest and true practising!

IN THY NAME I interpret the Mahayana for the sake of dispelling the suspicions and heretical prejudices of all sentient beings!

By the Awakening of their Faith in the Mahayana may I scatter Buddha seeds for an unending harvest!

This commentary is written wholly on the ground that there is a way in which faith in the Mahayana can be developed. It was for this reason and no other that I was impelled to the writing of this interpretation of the Mahayana Principle. The interpretation is divided into five parts: 1) The introduction. 2) Terms used in the Mahayana. 3) The interpretation of the Mahayana. 4) The practising of the Mahayana. 5) The advantages of practising the Mahayana.

Part One

Someone may enquire why I was led to write this Commentary. The reply is that there are eight kinds of causes and affinities that led me to undertake this task. My first and main purpose was to save all sentient beings from suffering and to bring them to eternal happiness: I had no desire to gain by it worldly fame, riches or honour. The second reason was a desire to present the true meaning of the Lord Tathagata's teachings so that all sentient beings might have the advantage of a true understanding of it at the very beginning. The third reason was to enable those who have made some advance on the Path to enlightenment to conserve their gain and not to later lose it. The fourth reason was to awaken and strengthen the faith of beginners on the path and to encourage them to a more earnest practice. The fifth reason was to show all those who are following the path expedient means for getting rid of the hindrances of bad karma, for keeping their minds free from the cravings and infatuations of egoism, and to keep free from the net of evil influences. The sixth reason was the wish to help all seekers to practise right methods for practising "stopping and reflecting" so as to guard them against the false viewpoints of both worldly minded people and Hinayana disciples. The seventh reason was to explain the expedient means of reciting the Divine Name of Amitabha Buddha and to prove to them that if they should recite the name of Amitabha with one-pointed mind they would be sure to be reborn in Buddha's pure land, and once reborn there that they would never suffer retrogression. The eighth reason was to show to those whose faith was awakened by the reading of this treatise the inestimable advantages of the practice of Dhyana and to persuade them to an earnest perseverance in it. These are the reasons that led me to the writing of this commentary.

Again, someone may enquire why, so long as the Dharma was presented in the Sutras, a commentary was called for. My reply is this. It is true that the Buddha teachings are fully presented in the Sutras, but as the karmas and inherited tendencies of sentient beings vary widely, and their experiences and practices are different from one another, so the conditions of their awakening faith and their realization of its fruits will be different. During the presence of the Lord Tathagata in this world those sentient beings who were endowed with competent and intelligent minds as they listened to the Lord Buddha, whose words were transcendental both in their form and meaning, and which were interpreted with perfect accommodation, understood them, and there was no need at that time for such a treatise as this. But after the Nirvana of the Lord Tathagata conditions were different. The teachings had been reduced to written words, and men's minds were less acute and more varied. Some were able to acquire an understanding of the teaching by their own study of them after a long time, and some after a short time. Some who lacked intellectual power would acquire an understanding after the study of long and erudite commentaries, and some becoming confused by long and tiresome commentaries were helped by brief and concise ones. Because of these conditions I felt that a new and different commentary was called for and I felt impelled to present the Lord's Teachings in all their profound wisdom but to explain them briefly, succinctly, but clearly and adequately.

Part Two
Terms used in the Mahayana

Generally speaking the Mahayana employs two sets of terms. One set is used when speaking of the Dharma as Essence, the other when speaking of the Dharma as Principle. The Dharma is the mind of all sentient beings. This mind embraces all conceptions both relating to the phenomenal world and those relating to the mind world and leading to the purity and freedom of eternity. It is by means of the concepts of this mind that the principle of the Mahayana is being unfolded and comprehended. In one aspect it manifests the true essence of the Mahayana; in the other aspect it reflects the appearing and disappearing, because of causes and conditions, and unfolds the potentialities and activities of the principle of the Mahayana.

The concept of the principle of the Mahayana is capable of three kinds of interpretation. The first is its immensity, its all-embracing wholeness, in which all concepts are intrinsic but undifferentiated and of the same suchness neither decreasing nor increasing in quantity, but abiding in perfect purity and unity. The second is its immensity of potentiality; as the womb of Tathagata it is the fountain of all dharmas, of all natures and merits, even to infinities of infinity. The third is the immensity of its manifesting activities, giving rise to all manner of good causes and effects belonging both to this terrestrial world and to the mind world leading to the perfect purity and freedom of eternity. It is the path by which all the Buddhas have attained Nirvana, and by it the Bodhisattva-Mahasattvas will attain the sure ground of Tathagatahood.

Part Three
The interpretation of the Mahayana

The interpretation of the Mahayana is divided into three sections. The first section treats of the unfolding of the true principle. The second is a refutation of false doctrines and prejudices. The third, relates to right practices leading to enlightenment.

1

First as to the unfolding of the true principle. The mind has two doors from which issue its activities. One leads to a realization of the mind's Pure Essence, the other leads to the differentiations of appearing and disappearing, of life and death. Through each door passes all the mind's conceptions so interrelated that they never have been separated and never will be.

What is meant by the Pure Essence of Mind? It is the ultimate purity and unity, the all-embracing wholeness, the quintessence of Truth. Essence of Mind belongs to neither death nor rebirth, it is uncreated and eternal. The concepts of the conscious mind are being individualized and discriminated by false imaginations. If the mind could be kept free from discriminative thinking there would be no more arbitrary thoughts to give rise to appearances of form, existencies and conditions. Therefore from the beginning, all concepts have been independent of individuation, of names and mental moods and conditions. They are in their essential nature of an equal sameness, neither variable nor breakable nor destructible. As they are of one suchness, of one purity, it is spoken of as Mind-essence.

For the differentiations of words are but false notions with no basis in reality. They have in their falsity only a relative existence as false imaginations and thoughts arise and pass away. Even as applying to Mind-essence words have no value, for in Mind-essence there is nothing to be grasped nor named. But we use words to get free from words until we reach the pure wordless Essence. In Essence of Mind there is nothing that can be taken away and nothing that can be added. All concepts are an undivided part of Reality; they are not artificial but are unchangeable and ineffable and unthinkable. They are the Essence of Mind itself. Someone may ask that if all concepts are to be thus regarded, how are sentient beings to make use of them to abstract their minds into the Mind's pure Essence? The reply is that whenever any sentient being uses words in relation to the mind's pure Essence he should remember their falsity and cherish no arbitrary conceptions, nor distinctions between themselves and the spoken words and the thing spoken about. As they use words to express their thoughts they should remember that words are wholly independent of the speaker and are not to be grasped as their own. If any sentient being should be able to thus keep free from all arbitrary conceptions, it would mean that they had attained oneness with the pure Essence of all concepts.

Again, if we are to distinguish different aspects of Mind-Essence, there is an emptiness aspect of its invariable Essence for it can unfold its primal reality. And there is a non-emptiness aspect, for it has its own substantiality possessing all sorts of merits of a non-intoxicant nature, that is, that it exists in its own right. The first is an aspect of negation, the second an aspect of affirmation. From the very beginning Mind-Essence has never given any mutual response to any contaminated conceptions of differentiations, it has ever been free from discriminations among thoughts or phenomena, for it is perfect unity, perfect purity. It should be clearly understood that the true nature of Mind-Essence does not belong to any individualized conception of phenomena or of non-phenomena; nor of the absence of phenomena; nor of the absence of non-phenomena; nor of unity or of disunity; nor of the absence of unity or of disunity; in other words, it has no particularizing consciousness, it does not belong to any kind of describable nature. Individuations and the consciousness of them come into being only as sentient beings cherish false imaginations of differences and the mind makes discriminations among them, thought after thought rising with no mutual response among them, resulting in confusion and conflict and suffering. This is what is meant when speaking of Mind-Essence as being empty. But if the Truth is fully understood it will be seen that the conception of emptiness as it relates to Mind-Essence is itself, "empty". If the mind can be kept free from false imaginations there can be no conceivable meaning to the term, "emptiness".

On the other hand, Mind-Essence is by no means to be thought of as being empty of its own perfectly universalized nature; it is only empty in the sense that it includes in its true nature no elements of falsity, namely, it is the pure Dharmakaya, the very suchness of Truth. Since it has ever been permanent and invariable in its nature, and possessing the whole body of conceptions in perfectly undifferentiated purity, it is the very acme of non-emptiness. At the same time, it must by no means be considered that Mind-Essence has its own transcendental phenomena; not at all, it has no conceivable or inconceivable phenomena of its own, it is perfect Emptiness, and can only be apprehended as the mind transcending its discriminating processes of thought and all imagery of selfness, becomes itself unified with the pure Suchness of Mind-Essence.

Then there is the appearing and disappearing aspect of Mind-Essence, that we think of as birth and death. In this connection we think of Mind-Essence as the Womb of Tathagata, but in fact nothing comes forth and nothing returns and there is no Womb of Tathagata, for the nature of appearing and disappearing coincides with the nature of non-appearing and non-disappearing. The pure Essence of Mind is neither unity nor plurality and yet we conceive it as the inconceivable Alaya-vijnana, the "storage" or Universal Mind. This Alaya consciousness embraces two significant aspects which can both receive and give forth all definitive concepts. The one aspect is that of Enlightenment, the other that of Ignorance.

In its aspect of Enlightenment, Mind-Essence is free from all manner of individuation and discriminative thinking; it is all-embracing, extending to all immensities as vast as open space, as pure, as unchanging, as indefinable. It is the Dharmakaya of Tathagatahood. It is innate Enlightenment, but because it is Enlightenment, it foreshadows the appearing of Enlightenment, but innate Enlightenment and the appearing of

Enlightenment are of one sameness; because there is the conception of Enlightenment, there is the conception of non-Enlightenment, and because of the conception of non-Enlightenment there is the conception of Enlightenment. Because of the conception of Enlightenment, and of non-Enlightenment, there is the conception of attaining Enlightenment, but Enlightenment, non-Enlightenment, attaining of Enlightenment are all of one sameness and unity. When the mind becomes conscious of its ultimate nature of Enlightenment, it speaks of it as Enlightenment; when it is not enlightened as to its ultimate nature, we think of it as Ignorance, but truly in the Alaya-vijnana there is no difference between them, there is only the perfect purity of the Dharmakaya.

Among human beings, Enlightenment appears in varying degrees of purity. Just as soon as a common person is conscious of a difference between right thoughts and false thoughts, between good thoughts and evil thoughts, it can be said that he has become enlightened, but it is a very rudimentary form of Enlightenment. Hinayana disciples as they begin their practice of Dhyana are conscious of their discriminating thoughts and at the same time are conscious that they have no validity; they are said to have attained Enlightenment, but it is a very crude form of Enlightenment. As they restrain their discriminative concepts, being conscious of their falsity their enlightenment becomes more refined. As they become Bodhisattvas, becoming more conscious of the grasping nature of discriminative thoughts and yet reminding themselves that even discriminative thoughts have no grasping quality in their self-nature, their Enlightenment has become partly accommodating. As Bodhisattvas advance along the stages, they more and more become sensitive to the arising of these false discriminations and more and more quickly react against them, and become more and more skilful in employing expedient means for checking their arising and ignoring them if they arise. Until at last they come to a state of awareness in which they are able to keep far away from even the most refined conceptions, knowing that Essential Mind is permanent and abiding in its purity. This is a state of perfect accommodation; it can be truly called Enlightenment. Therefore it is said in the Sutras, if any sentient being is able to keep free from all discriminative thinking, he has attained to the wisdom of a Buddha.

In the foregoing we have referred to the rising of conscious and discriminative thoughts, but speaking truly, there is no rising of thoughts of any kind, for conscious thinking is wholly subjective and imaginary. Most people are said to be lacking in Enlightenment. This is not because they have no thoughts, but because from the very beginning they have had a continuous stream of discriminations with no break in their succession. They are still abiding in a beginningless Ignorance. But when a Bodhisattva has completed the stages and has attained a state of no thinking, he is able to realize that all the phenomena of conscious mentation – its rising, growing, passing, disappearing – is the same as no thinking, that all the apparent changes are inherent but unmanifest in the Primal Enlightening Nature of Mind-Essence, and that the Primal state of Enlightenment is the Ultimate Enlightenment.

The question arises, how can these apparent differences arise out of the purity of Mind-Essence? The answer is, that it is because of the perfect accommodation of the Alaya-vijnana to its store of defilements that have been accumulated since beginningless time. These give rise to two classes of phenomena which are inseparable from its intrinsic nature of Enlightenment and yet are in mutual relationship with each other. In one class are phenomena relating to intellectual purity and moving towards Enlightenment, and in the other class are phenomena relating to karma and moving toward Ignorance.

By means of intellectual purity the Bodhisattva has been able to practise right methods and employ expedient means to transcend the influence of these defilements, to break away from their entanglements, destroy the enslaving power of conscious discriminations, and by intuition come into a realization of his pure Dharmakaya. Though all the phenomena of the mind, its perceptions, its discriminations, its consciousness, belong to the nature of non-enlightenment, yet because the nature of non-enlightenment is the same as the nature of Enlightenment, it is neither destructible nor indestructible. It is like the waves on the surface of the ocean raised by the passing wind, both are involved but water does not of itself possess the nature of movement, so when the wind ceases the waves subside and the water returns to its natural tranquillity. It is the same with sentient beings. Their pure Essential Mind has been disturbed by the supposed wind of Ignorance, but neither mind nor Ignorance has any substance or form or phenomena of its own, neither are they separated from each other. As disturbance does not belong to the nature of Mind, so when its Ignorance is discarded, the disturbing phenomena of false imaginations and discriminating thoughts will disappear also, for its power of intuition does not disturb its true nature in the least.

In the outward activities of the discriminating mind, karma is the record of its habit-energy urging it on to further differentiation, but in the inconceivable integrating activities of Intuitional Purity, karma is the record of its unifying attractions reducing multiplicities to unities and resulting in all manner of transcendental syntheses and mysterious wonders, and effecting within the minds of earnest disciples all manner of spiritual benefits and powers, all of which because of their vows are available to all sentient beings.

Likening Enlightenment to space or a clear mirror, a fourfold significance relating to its greatness is revealed. The first significance to be revealed is when by reason of removing all objects to a distance from a mirror there is no reflection, so when all disturbing mental conditions and all mental spheres in contact with objects through the sense organs are done away with there is no disturbance of the Mind's tranquillity. This first significance, therefore, is a revelation of the greatness of the Mind's Emptiness. The second significance is one of greatness of its affirmation of trueness. No matter what the phenomena or the conditions may be in the Saha world they are reflected in the mirror of the Mind's pure Essence with perfect trueness and impartiality. There is nothing that enters and nothing that departs, there is nothing that is lost or destroyed, for in the true Essential Mind all conceptions are of one sameness that in its such-ness abides unchanged and permanent. For true Essential Mind yields to no contaminations that can possibly contaminate it, and even its reflected contaminated conceptions have no effect upon it. Its intuitional nature is never disturbing and, on the contrary, is in possession of boundless non-intoxicant virtues that influence all sentient beings to draw them into the unity and purity of its pure Essence.

The third significance of Mind-Essence considered as a mirror, is an affirmation of the greatness of its freedom. Just as a mirror reflects freely all objects brought before it, so Essential Mind reflects all concepts freely without being contaminated by them. They go forth freely just as they are, separated from all hindrances and annoyances of knowledge, and all the phenomena of composition and conformity, for in Essential Mind all is pure and bright and free.

The fourth significance is an affirmation of compassionate helpfulness, for being free from all limitations of selfness, it draws all alike into its all-embracing purity and unity and peacefulness, illumining their minds with equal brightness so that all sentient beings have an equal right to Enlightenment, an equal chance to practise the ultimate principle of kindness, an equal surety that ultimately all sentient beings will attain Enlightenment, mature their root of merit and realize their inherent Buddha-nature.

Let us now consider further the real nature of non-Enlightenment. In the foregoing pages we have said that non-Enlightenment is related to Ignorance. This is true in the sense that the thinking mind, being confused by its false imaginations and discriminations, does not see clearly its own Mind-Essence, and the real sameness of all its conceptions. Just as soon as the mind notes differences because of its different sensations and sense perceptions, it immediately begins to unite them into conceptions, to name them, to discriminate them, to think about them, from which arises all manner of false judgements and self-consciousness. These discriminated thoughts have no substance of their own; they are not at all different from thought in its wholeness that by his Essential Nature is pure and enlightening. An ignorant man, one controlled by his discriminating mind, is like a man who has lost his way. When we speak of a man losing his way, we mean that he has a prior conception of a right way from which he has gone astray. Apart from this prior conception of a right way, of a place to which he wishes to reach, going astray has no meaning. It is just the same with sentient beings said to be un-enlightened. They have an innate affinity for Enlightenment, but because of their false imaginations and discriminations they go astray. Thus Ignor-ance and Enlightenment have only a relative meaning. If a man had no conception of Enlightenment, he would have no conception of Ignorance; and if he can get rid of his ignorance, he will have no conception of Enlightenment. It is by means of his discriminating mind that leads a man astray that he can also gain Enlightenment, therefore we can truly speak of the true and Enlightening Nature of a man's mind, but if he can free himself from all consciousness of his Enlightening Nature, then the significance of Enlightenment would vanish also.

Because of discriminating Ignorance, the mind gives rise to three kinds of conceptions which are in close mutuality and are inseparable from discriminations. The first is a conception of activity; the second is a conception of an actor; the third is a conception of a world of action. The first is called karma. If there was only a state of pure Enlightenment, the mind would remain undisturbed and in tranquillity, but because of discriminating Ignorance the mind becomes disturbed, and this disturb-ance and its habit-energy we speak of as karma. As soon as the mind becomes disturbed by its discriminating differences, desire arises to be followed by suffering, all of which is embraced in the conception of Karma.

The second is called egoism. As soon as the mind perceives differences, it awakens desire, grasping and following suffering, and then the mind notes that some relate to himself and some to not-self, from which arises a conception of an actor, an ego-self. If the mind could remain undis-turbed by differences and discriminations the conception of an ego-self would die away.

The third is a conception of a surrounding world that is not-self. Independent of an actor there is no meaning to an external world of things produced, acted upon and reacting. As one gets rid of the conception of self, the conception of an external world vanishes with it.

Again, because of discriminating Ignorance and the intimate relations of the conceptions of thinking, thinker and things thought about, there rise six kinds of mental phenomena. First, there are feelings of liking and disliking. Second, these feelings following in quick succession are fixed in memory and become intensified by a kind of habit-energy. Third, because of this habit-energy, there is a grasping after the agreeable and a shrinking from the disagreeable, thus abiding in either happiness or suffering. Fourth, because of the foregoing, there is a continuity or clinging that reacts on the thinker himself to condition his thoughts and he gives names and false meanings to things. Fifth, these false names and discriminating thoughts react upon his conception of an external world to condition his surroundings and build up a conditioning karma. Sixth, this karma going on accumulating from beginningless time develops a strong and stronger tendency to action that enslaves the thinker until he more and more loses his freedom. Thus we see that defiling thoughts and suffering do not exist in their own right but arise from the non-enlightenment of discriminating Ignorance.

Again, these two conceptions of Enlightenment and non-Enlightenment have a twofold relation. The first is a relation of similarity, the other a relation of dissimilarity. Just as different pieces of pottery made by a potter are similar in the sense that they are all made of clay, so with the different kinds of karma and karmaic illusions, the defiling as well as the purifying, they all have their only reality in the pure Essence of Mind. In this sense they are similar, as the Sutras say: all sentient beings are ever abiding in Nirvana. Nevertheless, the thing called Enlightenment is nothing that can be attained by practising, nor can it be created by human hands; it is intangible and ungraspable, having no form that can be seen or nature that can be described. The reason that Enlightenment can take on different manifestations of form and explicability is wholly because of the conditioning power of karma in correspondence with the defilements of the mind. Enlightenment and Wisdom in their true Nature have nothing to do with material forms or phenomena that it can become an object of sensation.

The relation of dissimilarity is this. Just as different objects made by the potter are infinitely diversified, so the manifestations of the mind's discriminating thoughts, both enlightening and defiling are infinitely varied. Just as karmas and karmaic conditions are varied, so the manifestations of their conditioning power are varied and dissimilar.

Again, what has been said in the foregoing about the appearing and disappearing, or what is known as birth and death, has its particular causes and conditions. We mean by this that sentient beings with their ever-active discriminating and thinking minds are for ever accumulating a body of false imaginations and notions which become defilements on the face of the Alaya-vijnana and give rise to self-consciousness and its propensity for desires and habits of grasping and clinging, all of which are dependent on the thinking mind without any self-nature of their own. This body of false notions having its dependence on the thinking mind and providing the causes and conditions for the evolution of mind is Ignorance. By it there arises the intuitive mind (*manas*), the intellectual mind (*mano-vijnana*) and the six sense-minds (*the vijnanas*). *Manas* having relations with both the Alaya-vijnana and the *mano-vijnana* mediates between them and gives rise to the conceptions of consciousness and the faculties of both intellection and intuition which lead respectively to Ignorance and Enlightenment. As soon as the non-enlightening nature begins to rise there develops perceptibility, the manifesting power of discriminating thoughts, grasping upon conditions and causing a continuous evolution of changes and transformations, from which arises the consciousness of an ego-self and an external world of causes and conditions. This false notion of an ego-self is in possession of five aspects or names. The first is its activity-consciousness (*karma*-consciousness), which means that owing to the particularizing power of Ignorance, the non-enlightening potentialities of the mind are awakened and brought into activity. The second is the evolving-consciousness or power of transforming sensations into perceptions. The third is the reflecting-consciousness which reflects all kinds of perceptions originating in the contact of objects with the sense-organs and unites them into unities, spontaneously and without prejudice. The fourth is the discriminating-consciousness that classifies these unified perceptions as they are in relation to itself, into favourable or unfavourable, pure or defiled. The fifth is the memory-consciousness that retains all conceptions in mind and in mutual relations and synthetic response without any cessation. It keeps all the elements of karma accumulated from a beginningless past in activity and registering their full value. It compels the mind to endure the reactions of karma whether they be painful or pleasant to their full maturity; it brings past experiences into sudden remembrance and projects its false imaginations into the future. It is the cause of all the illusions of the triple-world, not one of which has any cause apart from the discriminating and thinking mind. Separated from the mind there are no objects of sense, all conceptions of them arise in the mind and are developed and manifested by the false activities of the mind. Not one of them has any self-substance of its own, they are all alike brought into manifestation and kept in continuity of relation by the false imaginations of Ignorance of sentient beings. They are, indeed, like reflections in a mirror which if grasped lead to hallucinations of a self and an external world, but which if allowed to pass, if the discriminating and thinking mind stops its thinking, leave the mind in tranquillity.

This memory consciousness because of the desiring and grasping nature of the mind becomes more and more ingrained in the mind. It develops and intensifies the false notion of an ego-self and exaggerates the supposed importance of its interests. This is the reason why the memory-consciousness is also thought of as the egoistic-consciousness, the separating-consciousness, because by reason of its activities the mind becomes more and more separated by its egoistic desires, prejudices and imaginary annoyances, from its true oneness in the pure Essence of Mind.

The relation of the conceptual, discriminating, thinking and conscious mind to Essential Mind, how it arises, develops and becomes established, is very difficult to understand. It is quite impossible for ordinary human beings, and even Hinayana disciples misunderstand it. Bodhisattvas who begin their practice of stopping thought and realizing truth in pure faith as they gain a degree of insight acquire a small degree of its understanding. Even those Bodhisattvas who have attained to the stage of immovability and constancy cannot understand it thoroughly, only Buddhas can understand it perfectly. Essential Mind is pure and immaculate by nature, it possesses Ignorance only as a superficial and transient defilement, but by reason of the defiling nature of Ignorance, it gives rise to all varieties and degrees of mental illusions and conceptions and discriminated appearances. But in spite of its relation to defiled minds, in its own Essentiality, it ever abides in unchanging and unchangeable purity. It is this profound relation of unchanging Purity to evolving impurities that is only understood by the highest perfect Wisdom of Buddhas. Because the mind does not realize the perfect purity of the all-embracing wholeness it falls into the habit of imagining differences where there are no differences, and thus the mind, being inharmonious with itself, becomes the puppet of Ignorance.

There are six different kinds of mental contaminations. The first is defilement by attachment by consent, from which disciples, Pratyekabuddhas, and Bodhisattvas of the early stages, can be liberated, and Bodhisattvas as they attain the stage of "self-mastery" are kept far away. The second is defilement by attachments in spite of disapproval and resistance. This can be partially controlled as the Bodhisattva by his earnest practice gradually advances along the stages to the stage of "realization", when although still in touch with the discriminations and passions of outer things, realizes their emptiness. And as he further advances to the stage of "far-going" and leaves behind all thoughts and remembrances of discriminations, truly abiding in the inner world, can be wholly controlled. The third kind is defilement by attachment with consent to discriminations of the intellectual mind, the clinging to ideas and definitions. This can be gradually cleared away by the Bodhisattva's perfect and selfless keeping of the Precepts, and can be completely discarded after attaining a great heart of compassion and command of skilful and efficient means, which come to him as he gets rid of all arbitrary conceptions of phenomena, and passes from outward morality, to inner Wisdom and finally to perfect spirituality. The fourth kind is defilement of the intellectual mind in spite of disapproval and resistance. It can be purified as the Bodhisattva attains to the intrinsic ground of transcendental mental freedom. The fifth kind is defilement by the Bodhisattva still clinging to the notion of a perceiving and discriminating mind although no longer in bondage to it. This can be got rid of as he advances in transcendental mental freedom where there is no further thought of self or not-self, of self and otherness, as he passes beyond all duality, all incompleteness, and attains perfect equanimity. The sixth kind is the mental contamination that a Bodhisattva must accept of the general and universal karma until he passes into the Great Truth Cloud of Tathagatahood.

To review these paragraphs let us add the following observations. The common non-realization of the Essential purity and unity of the all-embracing Wholeness, can be partially discarded by the awakening of a pure faith, and then as the Bodhisattva ascends the stages by his earnest practice of Dhyana can be progressively discarded, until he attains to the highest stage of Tathagatahood when it will be perfectly discarded. The reference to the principle of mutuality of response or lack of it, means that the mind is always in contact with the various conceptions arising from the senses and which are being differentiated by means of contaminated or pure thoughts, and that the mind is sensitive to their relations of likeness and affinity. In regard to the principle of resistance, it means that the mind having the faculty of intuition that transcends all states of consciousness, all unconscious of their mutual resemblances and affinities, never makes any distinctions nor discriminations but reflects spontaneously their true nature. In regard to the reference to the principle of intellectual contaminations, it refers to the hindrances that obscure the forth-shining of the intrinsic Wisdom of the Mind's pure Essence. As regards the principle of Ignorance, it means the intellectual hindrance that obscures the free illumination of the general karma by the Light of Transcendental Intelligence. What is meant by this? It means that by means of mental contaminations and false imaginations the mind becomes disturbed and moved to different forms of manifesting activity which is contrary to its true nature of Equanimity. Pure concepts undefiled by the mind's discriminating judgements come and go unnoticed, but when disturbed by Ignorance they lose their quietness and enlightening nature and add to the world's karma.

Further, mind in its manifestation as birth and death has two appearances. First there is a crude state as seen in the minds of common people, and there a refined state as manifested in the minds of Buddhas. The mental state of a novice Bodhisattva may be said to be in a refined state of crudeness, and the mental state of an advanced Bodhisattva, in a crude state of refinement. But these two states of crudeness and refinement both exist because of the defiling power of Ignorance. As the thoughts of the mind appear and disappear the mind variously cherishes them and there develop causes and conditions of affinities. The causes are the unenlightened nature of Ignorance, and because of there being affinities among the causes there develop varying conditions. If the cause should disappear, the affinities would disappear, and moreover, if the cause should disappear those parts of the mental attributes that are not in mutual response will disappear also. And because of the disappearing of the affinities, those parts of the mental attributes that are in mutual response will disappear, too.

It may then be asked, if all mental attributes should disappear what would become of the unceasing continuity of the mind? Or, if there should be some continuity of mind after its attributes had disappeared, how could we speak of the disappearing of the mental attributes? The reply is, as regards the disappearing of the mental attributes, it means the disappearing of the mind's arbitrary conceptions, not the disappearing of the mind's substantiality in Essential Mind. It is just the same as the relation of the wind and water and waves. Wind has the power to disturb water and by it to create waves, but if there is no water, the power remains potential and there are no waves. But so long as there is water and wind there will be waves. Again, if the wind loses its potential power of motion, there will be no waves even if the water remains. That is, it takes both wind and water to make waves. It is just the same with Ignorance and mind and discriminating thoughts. The reason that Ignorance is the cause of disturbing thoughts is because of the mind's Essential stability. If the mind should lose its stability, all sentient beings would disappear because there would be nothing for Ignorance to play upon. However, as the substantiality of the mind never disappears so the mind retains its continuity. But if Ignorance some day should disappear, then all arbitrary conceptions of form and phenomena would disappear with it, but it would not be the disappearing of the Mind's pure Wisdom.

There is a constant succession of thoughts both pure and defiled that is taking place because of the interaction of four elements. First, there is the Ultimate Principle of the Mind's pure Essence; the second is the cause of all the mind's contaminations, namely Ignorance; the third is the discriminating mind, or the karma-consciousness; the fourth are the false conditions of the external world, that is, the six objects of sense.

We may think of the interaction of these four elements as a process of fumigation. Just as clothing that is perfectly clean has no odour, yet if it is packed away with fragrant herbs for a long time the clothing becomes fumigated with the same fragrance. It is the same with these four elements, each tends to fumigate the other as they come into relation with each other. Pure Mind-Essence is by nature free of any contamination, but by association with Ignorance its pure concepts become defiled. Conversely, the impure concepts of Ignorance are in their nature free of any purity of karma, but having their substantiality in the purity of Mind-Essence they come to partake of its purity.

How can impure concepts continually arise by reason of the habitual fumigation of Ignorance? It is because the Mind's pure Essence has the potentiality for giving rise to all conceptual ideas and it follows from this that there develops the principle of individuation and discrimination that we name Ignorance, and it is because of Ignorance giving rise to impure concepts that there is the habitual fumigation of Mind-Essence. By means of this habitual fumigation there develops the appearance of a false mind, and it is by reason of this false mind that there is the habitual fumigation of Ignorance. Since Ignorance does not realize the pure Concepts of Mind-Essence, by its non-enlightening nature it gives rise continually to manifestations of false conditions. By means of there being these false conditions affinities appear between them and the false mind, continually reminding the mind of their existence and thus fumigating it, and continually giving rise to grasping and activities and the laying up of all kinds of karma and all kinds of suffering both mental and physical.

There are two ways by which the false conditions of an external world fumigate the mind; first, by continually increasing its thinking faculty, and second, by continually strengthening its desires and graspings. The false mind has, also, two kinds of habitual ways for fumigating false conditions of the external world; first, to quicken the fundamental activity-consciousness by reason of which disciples, Pratyekabuddhas, Arhats and Bodhisattvas can endure all kinds of suffering and deaths and rebirths; second, continually to increase the discriminating-consciousness by reason of which common human beings suffer under their karma all manner of suffering. Again, the habitual fumigation of Ignorance has two other kinds of manifestation, first, a primary habitual fumigation by reason of which one's karma, or activity-consciousness, is being developed; second, an accompanying development of the desiring, or fondness for the agreeable objects of sense, consciousness. The first, by reason of its sufferings, awakens a dislike for the experiences of birth and death, the second, by its delights, urges it on to the grasping for more.

How are pure concepts constantly produced by the perfuming of Ignorance? It is because of there being the potentiality for pure concepts which reacts upon Ignorance, awakening in the false minds a feeling of abhorrence of the sufferings of birth and death, and prompts it to seek Nirvana with willingness and earnestness. This abhorrence for the suffering of birth and death and the seeking for Nirvana with earnestness, in turn reacts upon Mind-Essence. By reason of this, the thinking mind attains a conception of its Essential Nature and discriminates it from the changing and pain-producing nature of the experiential mind, to convince him of the latter's unreality and to enable him to practise right means for keeping away from its dissatisfying experiences and disturbances. Having become convinced that all external conditions and all the discriminations of the conscious mind have no true existence, it is led to make use of skilful means and appropriate activities to treat these false conditions and thoughts with indifference, neither fearing nor grasping nor desiring nor even thinking about them. Thus by means of the long continued fumigation of Ignorance by Mind-Essence, the state of Ignorance is got rid of altogether. As Ignorance is discarded the rising of all thoughts of individuation and discrimination are brought to an end. Because of the ceasing of all such thoughts there are no more conceptions of external things and conditions to appeal to one through the senses. Accordingly as conditions and discriminations come to an end, all the mental phenomena cease to disturb the mind and it becomes empty and tranquil. The dying down of all disturbance is the attainment of Nirvana, the state of perfect freedom.

Let us now further consider the reactions of the false mind and the pure concepts of the Mind's Essence. The habitual fumigation of the false mind by the Pure Concepts of Mind-Essence are of two kinds: first, there is the fumigation of the discriminating-consciousness by reason of which, disciples, Pratyekabuddhas and Arhats abhorring the suffering of life and death are supported according to their individual needs and possibilities in their purpose and effort to attain Perfect Enlightenment. Second, there is the habitual fumigation of the mind's states by reason of which the Bodhisattvas advance along the stages with zeal and courage and perfect faith until their goal of Nirvana is attained.

The habitual fumigation of Mind-Essence by the false mind is also of two kinds: first, there is the habitual fumigation of the potentialities of one's own true nature; second, there is the habitual fumigation of the mind's true activities, which are no activity but are the spontaneous drawing-togetherness of the mind's disturbances and tensions. Since beginningless time, the mind has been fully possessed of its rightful non-intoxicating pure concepts which have been defiled and covered up by an inconceivable Karma to appear in all manner of forms and conditions. By means of the interaction of these two kinds of reaction, sentient beings are led to abhor the suffering of birth and death and to be willing to seek for the attainment of Nirvana, thus it awakens faith in their true Essence of Mind and enables them to begin, and to continue the practice of devotion, and to endure the necessary restraints.

If the foregoing is true, that all sentient beings are possessed of their pure Mind-Essence and have been equally exposed to the habitual fumigation of its pure concepts, how is it that some of them awaken a pure faith and some do not. And how is it that there are so many and so great inequalities among sentient beings, and why is it that some continue in the dreary round of death and rebirth and only a few awaken a pure faith, practise expedient means with earnest diligence and attain to Nirvana? The reply is that while Essence of Mind in all alike is of one pure sameness, because of the fumigating power of Ignorance it has become differently defiled and therefore manifests its defilement in different ways and different degrees, so that their number is incalculable. So great is the variety of their personalities, their experiences, hindrances and suffering that only Buddha can comprehend them and embrace them all in perfect compassion.

As all sentient beings in spite of their common Buddha Nature are subject to the fumigation of Ignorance they would, except for the like constant fumigation of their pure Mind-Essence, fall deep and deeper into the defilements of Ignorance, but by reason of Buddha's compassion, they sooner or later meet causes and affinities that enable them to awaken a pure faith and attain emancipation from their bondage to Ignorance. Possessed of suitable causes and affinities any attainment is possible. It is the nature of wood to burn, but wood will not burn unless suitable conditions are present and there is some exciting cause. Wood will not ignite itself or burn itself. Therefore, if sentient beings are to become emancipated and enlightened there must be present suitable causes and affinities. By nature sentient beings have affinity for emancipation and enlightenment, but without suitable causes and conditions they cannot attain them. Even if they have a Buddha Nature but do not chance to meet a Buddha, or a good learned Master, or a Bodhisattva, they could not of themselves attain Nirvana. In like manner, no matter how suitable external conditions may be, if they were immune to the fumigation of the Mind's pure Concepts, so that there was no awakening of faith, how could they come to abhor the suffering of rebirths and deaths and willingly and earnestly seek the attainment of Nirvana? But if both causes and affinities are present, their Buddha Nature, the fumigating power of Mind-Essence, the kind teaching and sympathy of Bodhisattvas, then there will come an abhorrence of the suffering of birth and death, the awakening of faith, the purpose to practise kindness and to press on towards Nirvana. Then after their karma has become matured, they will, all of a sudden, meet a Buddha or a Bodhisattva who will show them the benefits and joy of following the Path toward Englightenment and Buddhahood.

There is an unceasing fumigation of the external activities of sentient beings, by the pure Concepts of the fundamental Essence of Mind. By means of this fumigation these external activities take on a power of affinity for similar activities drawing them together into closer synthesis and harmony. This power of affinity is manifested in innumerable ways, but for convenience in considering it, we may think of it as of two kinds. The first is affinity drawing dissimilar things together; the second is affinity drawing likenesses together.

The affinity between dissimilar things is seen in the compassion which disciples upheld by the transcendental powers of Buddhas and Bodhisattvas, from the very beginning of their devotion to seeking Enlightenment, have had for all sentient beings, wishing to develop and strengthen their better nature. This compassion reveals itself whenever they meet or think of their families, their parents, their relatives or servants or familiar friends, or even their bitter enemies. This compassion reveals itself in the awakening of aspirations to teach them and to influence them by the four ways of charity, kind words, self-forgetting kindnesses and sympathy. Such deeds of kindness react upon their own natures to strengthen and deepen their own faith and their own aspiration to benefit all sentient beings, and to draw them together in bonds of affectionate fellowship. This kind of affinity is of two kinds, one kind is immediate in the sense that its effects are seen in the present time; the other kind is more remote in the sense that its effects continue and come to fruition long after in later rebirths. These affinities may be further divided into two aspects, namely, an increasing and developing affinity, and an unchanging affinity as Enlightenment is attained and mutually enjoyed.

The affinity between similarities is seen in the Buddha's recognition of their oneness's with all sentient beings in the purity of Mind-Essence; it is seen in the self-lessness of the Buddha's compassion and self-yielding; it is seen in the Buddha's constant spontaneity in responding to human needs; and because of it, human beings, by their potentiality for intuitive Samadhi may realize Buddhahood even as Buddhas realize their sufferings.

These interacting fumigations of Essence of Mind and activities may be considered as being divided into two aspects as they are ready or unready for the reactions of habitual fumigation. The unready are those common disciples, Pratyekabuddhas and Arhats who, having had sufficient faith to begin their practice as they continued to receive the habitual fumigation under relations with their discriminated ideas and their consciousness dependent upon those ideas, could neither discard those ideas nor attain a state of mutual responsiveness with their Mind-Essence, nor continue their practice with spontaneity, nor be in mutual response with their activities. Such disciples and Bodhisattvas are to be classed as unready for Enlightenment.

Those who are ready for Enlightenment are those advanced Bodhisattvas who have discarded all discriminated ideas and consciousness dependent upon them, and are in mutual response with the Buddha's inconceivable activities which are no activity, and prosecute their devotional practices with spontaneity, and are relying sincerely and wholly on the fumigating power of their Mind's pure Essence to annihilate their Ignorance and bring them to Buddhahood. Such Dharmakaya Bodhisattvas are ready for Enlightenment.

This difference between the ready and the unready is explained as we understand that the impure concepts of the human mind have become defiled by the habitual fumigation of Ignorance since beginningless time which fumigation will continue until they attain to Buddhahood, when it will be totally discarded. On the contrary, the pure concepts of Mind-Essence having the power of fumigation within their own nature, while the impure concepts of the false mind are slowly being discarded, their pure conceptual Dharmakaya is being brought into manifestation in unceasing continuity.

The Threefold Nature of Mind-Essence

The self-substance of Mind-Essence is inconceivably pure and, therefore, all sentient beings, common people, disciples, Pratyekabuddhas, Arhats, Bodhisattvas and Buddhas are, in their essential nature, of the same purity. In not one is it deficient, in not one is it in excess; nor has it any source of arising, nor time of disappearing; it is ever abiding, a permanent, unchangeable Reality. From its beginningless beginning it has been in full possession of all virtue and merit. It is in full possession of radiant Wisdom and luminosity, penetrating everywhere by the purity of its Concepts; seeing everything adequately and truly, its mind innately free and unprejudiced, ever abiding in blissful peace, pure, fresh, unchangeable, ever abounding, never segregating, never ceasing, never conceivable, an illimitable Fountain, a Womb of exuberant fertility, a Mind of perfect clarity and universality – the Tathagata's Truth-body, the all-embracing Dharmakaya.

The question might be raised: If Mind-Essence is free from all conceptions of phenomena, how can it be said to possess all kinds of merits and virtues? The reply is, that although it really possesses all kinds of merits and virtues, it does not possess them in the sense of grasping them.

Mind-Essence in its nature of Purity is free from all individuation and discrimination and dualisms of any kind. All objects have but one flavour, the flavour of reality, but depending upon the principle of appearing and disappearing, by reason of its activity-consciousness, there are signs of individuation, discrimination and opposing dualisms. It is true that the Mind embraces all Pure Concepts, and yet in reality it possesses no discriminative thoughts, but by means of its false defilements discriminative thoughts are developed, causing the mind to lose its Enlightenment, and to be given over to false imaginations and thus to become enslaved by all kinds of conditions and the puppet of Ignorance. If there should be no rising of discriminating thoughts, the mind, because of its Essence of Mind, would manifest Wisdom and Brightness. But if the mind gives rise to discriminations and prejudices, it soon becomes darkened and the prey of imaginary phenomena. So when one's Essence of Mind is kept away from all discrimination and prejudices, it radiates its inherent Brightness to all parts of the conceptual world. But if the mind becomes disturbed by its false imaginations, it would lose its true intuitional insight and understanding, and would become changing, unhappy, lacking self-control, impure, entangled, and the victim of innumerable vexations and hindrances. When the mind is not disturbed it reflects its potentiality for all pure merits and virtues. Thus it is seen that the possession of all pure merits and virtues is the natural and simple state of Mind-Essence, undefiled by any thoughts of individuation or discrimination. It is the true Dharmakaya, the true Tathagata Womb.

Reference has been made to the Activity-Consciousness of Mind-Essence; what is the nature of its activity? The activity of the false mind is an outer activity bringing about changes and increased complexity and confusion, but the activity of the Mind's pure Essence is an inner activity that brings about harmony, simplicity and unity. All Buddhas and Tathagatas from their very beginnings have developed hearts of compassion and have spontaneously manifested the Paramitar of charity, unselfish kindness, humility and patience, zeal and perseverance, tranquillity and Wisdom, not for any gain to themselves but for the sake of all sentient beings. They have made great vows, dedicating themselves to emancipating all sentient beings from their bondage in the world of sense. Yet the deliverance is effected not by outer acts but by an inner drawing of spirit that is not limited by time or conditions, but is ceaseless even to infinite ages of the future. The activity of Buddhas and Tathagatas is eternal because it is the opposite of outer activities of the false mind which are subject to weariness and inertia. Its activities release and store up energy, restoring the original purity and unity and peacefulness.

Tathagatas and Buddhas look upon sentient beings as being their own sameness not cherishing any conceptions of separation and individuation.

To them all sentient beings together with themselves come from one and the same Mind-Essence in which there are no differences to be distinguished. As they possess such great Wisdom and command of skilful means all the defilements of Ignorance have been discarded. They have realized their oneness with the pure Dharmakaya in the possession of an ever-renewing and inconceivable potentiality for activity and karma that is ceaselessly being irradiated to all parts of the universes, and just as ceaselessly returning to its primal unity and purity and peacefulness. They do not grasp upon any arbitrary conceptions of their harmonizing and integrating activities, for why should they grasp after that which they already possess, the whole body of the potentialities of the Dharmakaya. Their activities are unconditioned by causes and circumstances, they flow out spontaneously as the imaginary needs of sentient beings arise.

These harmonizing activities of the Tathagatas, that are no activity in a worldly sense, are of two kinds. The first kind can be perceived by the minds of common people, disciples and Pratyekabuddhas and is known as Nirmanakaya, the appearance body of Buddha and his inscrutable activities. But common people, disciples and Pratyekabuddhas do not realize that the Nirmanakaya are being manifested by reason of their own consciousness and its false imaginations. They imagine that all sights arise from prior causes and conditions, and they grasp them and seek to profit by them, and thus fail to understand their true significance. The second kind can only be perceived by the purified minds of the highest Bodhisattvas; they have no form that can be differentiated and described; it is the Dharmakaya in its aspect of Spirit and Principle. It is the Recompense Body of all the Buddhas, it is the abiding Bliss-body of Buddhahood, the inconceivable and inscrutable Sambhogakaya. This Sambhogakaya possesses a vast and boundless Potentiality, and the Blissful Peace in which it abides is adorned with inconceivably beautiful adornments, which are shadowed forth as its potential wisdom and compassion is manifested in spontaneously meeting the needs of human beings. It has no limitations of boundaries or quantity, it has no spheres nor points. Though it is responsive at any time of need, yet it ever abides in its permanent unchanging peacefulness, undiminished and unchanged. All its merits and virtues are being verified by means of such things as the Paramitas and other non-intoxicating perfumes. And, moreover, it is in full possession of boundless potentialities of joy and blissful peace. That is the reason it is called the Sambhogakaya.

That of the Dharmakaya which can be perceived by the minds of common people is only a shadow of it, and takes on different aspects according as it is considered from the different viewpoints of the six realms of existence. Their crude perception of it does not include any conception of its possibilities for happiness and enjoyment; they see only its reflection in the Nirmanakaya. Again, the conception of it which novice Bodhisattvas get is also only partial and unsatisfactory, but is true as far as it goes because of their sincere faith in their pure Mind-Essence. At least, they realize that its potentialities and embellishments are neither coming nor going, are free of all limitations, and are manifestations of, not parts of, the Pure Dharmakaya. But as the Bodhisattvas advance along the stages their minds become purified, their conceptions of it more profound and mysterious, their harmonizing activities more transcendental, until, when they have attained to the highest stage, they will be able to realize intuitively its true Reality. In that final realization all traces of their individual selfness and of the selfness of their brother Bodhisattvas will have faded away, and only a realization of one undifferentiated Buddhahood will remain.

It may be asked then: If the Buddha's Dharmakaya is free from any perceptions or conceptions of form, how can they manifest themselves as sights and forms? The reply is that the Dharmakaya is the very Essence of all sights and forms, and therefore can manifest itself in sights and form. Both the mind and the sights that it perceives are in one and the same unity since beginningless time, because the essential nature of sights and forms is nothing but Mind-only. As the essence of sights possesses no physical form, it is the same as the Dharmakaya, formless and yet pervading all parts of the universes. The particular sights which Mind-Essence manifests are in their essential nature devoid of any limitations or points of definition. If conditions are suitable, appearances may be manifested in any part of the universes, being solely dependent upon the mind for their appearing. Thus, there are vast Bodhisattvas, vast Sambhogakayas, vast embellishments, all of which are different from one another and yet are devoid of any spheres of limitation or points of definition, for Tathagatas are able to manifest themselves in bodily forms anywhere and at the same moment that other Tathagatas are manifesting themselves, without any conflict or hindrance. This marvellous interpenetration is inconceivable by any consciousness dependent upon sense-mind, but is a commonplace of the inconceivable, spontaneous activities of Mind-Essence.

2

Refutation of False Doctrines and Prejudices

Again, in order to awaken faith in the minds of sentient beings that they may turn from the cycle of deaths and rebirths and enter the path that leads to Enlightenment and Nirvana, it is necessary to show the falsity of the common conception of an ego-self and its aggregates of sensation, perception, discrimination and consciousness. If one is to become free from the bondage of these grasping aggregates then one must understand clearly their unreality. This obsession of an ego-personality may be considered in two ways. First, the aspects of it that arise from the physical organism; and second, the aspects of it that arise in the intellectual mind.

First let us consider the aspects of it that arise from the physical organism. These may be considered, as common minds think about them, under five heads. The first is the aspect of it as perceived by the sense-mind. According to the Sutras, Tathagatas are represented as existing in a state of emptiness and tranquillity. Common minds interpret this to mean that Tathagatas' minds are empty and tranquil, a physical analogy. They do not understand that it refers to the immaterial perceptions of the thinking mind, a metaphysical analogy, so they mistakenly consider that "emptiness" is a characteristic of Tathagatas. To disabuse their minds of this false conception, it is necessary to show that "emptiness" is a false conception arising in their own minds, existing only in relation to their senses and discriminating mind, and having no substantiality of its own. Its visible manifestation is to be recognized in the tendency of human beings to turn to the cycle of births and deaths and to continue therein. All these physical sights and mental perceptions and discriminations of them belong to the mind and have no existence apart from the mind. As soon as the mind understands this, even the conception of pure space is seen to be a false and arbitrary conception. And the same is true, also, of all sorts of physical conditions and conceptions about them, that common minds take for granted are in a state of existence, they are all simply the false arisings of the experiential mind, and when the mind understands the falsity of the conceptions, the objects themselves vanish into nothingness. Then, nothing would remain but the purity of Essential Mind radiantly present in all the ten quarters of the universes. This is the true significance of the Tathagata's intrinsic and all-embracing Wisdom.

The second aspect of egoism as perceived by the sense-minds relates to the conception of substantiality. In the Sutras it is stated that all conceptions of the world are in a state of emptiness. This is interpreted by common minds as meaning that it is in a state of physical emptiness but, in truth, it refers to a state of mental emptiness, a mental analogy. Common minds apply it to all their conceptions – their conceptions of Mind-Essence and Nirvana – and therefore think of them as empty of all "substantiality". To disabuse their minds of this false conception it is necessary to show that the Dharmakaya of Mind-Essence is not empty of its own true substantiality. Mind-Essence is replete with its own merits and virtues, all-embracing, boundlessly potential, inconceivably vast and beautiful.

The third aspect arises from the saying in the Sutras that the Tathagata's Womb is neither in a state of increasing nor in a state of decreasing, that its substantiality is embodied in an exhaustless store of Pure Concepts of merits and virtues. Common minds fail to understand the true significance of this, and understand that it refers to some definite possession that is separate from the merits and virtues possessed by human beings. To disabuse their minds of this false conception, it is necessary to show that the true significance of Mind-Essence is its undifferentiated purity from all the differentiated conceptual defilements such as the false concept of birth and death.

The fourth aspect arises from the sayings in the Sutras that all the inipure, contaminated concepts of deaths and rebirths belonging to the world exist because they come from Tathagata's Womb, a physical analogy, and that all concepts are not independent of Mind-Essence. However, as common people they do not understand the true significance of the sayings in the Sutras, and imagine that the self-nature of Tathagata's Womb is fully embodied in such concepts as deaths and rebirths belonging to the world. To disabuse their minds of this false understanding, it is necessary to show that Tathagata's Womb from beginningless time has only embraced the pure concepts of undifferentiated merit and virtue, all of which are neither independent of nor differentiated from the true significance of Mind-Essence. For all the contaminated concepts and vexatious differences and annoying discriminations, which are beyond all estimation, only exist as the false illusions of the thinking mind, not in its true essential Nature. More than this, they have never been in any kind of mutual response with Tathagata's Womb. Or, if it should be granted that the substantiality of Mind-Essence is embodied in the false concepts of birth and death, but that it could be discarded by intuitive realization, this would be, indeed, an absurdity.

The fifth aspect of egoism arises from statements in the Sutras that births and deaths arise from Tathagata's Womb and that the attainment of Nirvana, also, arises from the same source. However, as common people they do not understand the true significance of these sayings in the Sutras, and they imagine that sentient beings have their beginnings and endings, and that the Nirvana attained by Tathagatas, also, has its beginnings and endings, and renewed births in this Saha world. To disabuse their minds of this false assumption, we have only to call attention to the fact that Tathagata's Womb is devoid of any beginnings or endings or relations of succession. And the same is true of Ignorance, also. Or, if it should be asserted that there are beings independent of this Saha world that have transcendental qualities, our reply would be, that the only basis for such assertions are the unprovable teachings of heretical books. Moreover, there are no endings to be conceived of as having relation to Tathagata's Womb, for the Nirvana attained by the Buddhas being in mutual sameness with Tathagata's Womb, has likewise no beginning and no ending.

Second, let us consider the aspects of it arising from the immaterial, mental faculties. This refers to the clinging to the notions of personalities such as the immature disciples of the Hinayana reveal when they think the Tathagata has simply taught the non-existence of and ego-self as it relates to personalities, but who still cherish the notion of selfness as it relates to their attainment of Enlightenment and Nirvana. Just as common people are fearful of the physical suffering of life, so these disciples fear the notions of failure in their effort to attain Enlightenment and Nirvana, and they cling to the conception of a Nirvana for themselves. To disabuse their minds of these erroneous conceptions, be it known that just as the nature of physical concepts arising from the sense reactions are devoid of any rebirths, so these metaphysical concepts derived from the intellectual mind are also devoid of any deaths for in their essence they are from the beginning in Nirvana.

If one is to become free from the grasping nature of these aspects of ego-selfness, one must clearly understand that all mental concepts, both the pure and the impure, exist only in a state of relativity, they have no self-hood in their own right. From their very beginnings they are neither matter nor mind, neither intelligence nor consciousness, neither existence nor nonexistence, they are wholly imaginary. But still having a kind of relative existence they are used by the Lord Tathagata as expedient means to guide sentient beings by means of words, into the path that leads to Enlightenment. The purpose of the Lord Tathagata is to emancipate sentient beings from the bondage of their thinking by means of their thinking, and to bring them back to their origin in Mind-Essence. But to let the mind dwell upon and grasp words and concepts only entangles the mind the more in the cycle of deaths and rebirths, and hinders it from merging into its true nature of Wisdom.

3

Right Practices Leading to Enlightenment

At the beginning, we must define what is meant by right practices leading to Enlightenment and distinguish between the spontaneous activities attained by Buddhas and the crude practices laboriously undertaken by the Bodhisattvas at the beginning of their devotions. There are three motives that lead a novice to the beginning of his practices. The first is the awakening of faith in the Dharma. The second is some understanding as to what will be required of him if he is to attain a realization of the

Dharma. The third is the unfolding insight that comes to him as he progressively attains a realization of Dharma.

First, let us consider the awakening and maturing of a pure faith in the Dharma. Every sentient being, no matter how unconcentrated his mind may be, has certain instinctive reactions of mind that make him sensitive to kindness, shrink from suffering, fear evil, dread retribution, be confident in self-effort and attainment, and hopeful of something better. If by chance they should come in contact with a Buddha, give offerings to him, worship him or his image, they would develop their germ of faith and after ten thousand kalpas would have so far matured their faith that all Buddhas and Bodhisattvas would teach them how to start their devotions.

Or, because of a natural compassionate disposition, they may awaken faith in a conception of a Supernatural Compassionate One and start their devotional practices. Or, because of the absence of the Dharma, or fear that it might become lost, their faith may awaken and they begin devotional practices for the sake of preserving the true Dharma. All of these ways of beginning devotional practices are a manifestation of true faith. It will not be in vain nor will it suffer retrogression, but will develop, under proper conditions, into right aspiration and right ways of practice until it merges into the true Samadhi of Buddhahood.

There may be others who, having a less developed kindness of disposition, but having suffered extremes of vexations and sufferings for many kalpas, by chance meet Buddhas and make offerings to them and worship them, and who awaken faith, also, and start their devotions for the purposes of attaining a happy rebirth in this world, or among devas in some super-realm of heaven, or as an Arhat, or as a Pratyekabuddha in some Nirvana of their own.

There may be some even who wish to seek the true Mahayana attainment of Buddhahood but whose root of merit is deficient of stability, now earnest now heedless, now advancing now receding. These start devotional practices more or less on impulse, and lacking stability, when they meet difficulties or hindrances within their own minds, they turn aside from the true Mahayana path into the path of Hinayana disciples and Pratyekabuddhas.

From the foregoing we see that there are many reasons that move disciples to begin their practices of devotion, but they all are based on the awakening of faith. Let us now consider right reasons for beginning devotional practices. These are of three kinds; first, reasons based upon an intellectual understanding of the truth of Mind-Essence. This is the most straightforward reason. Second, reasons based upon an earnest purpose to keep the precepts and develop a good life. Third, reasons based upon a heart of compassion, that seeing the suffering among all sentient beings wishes out of the kindness of his heart to deliver them.

It may be inferred from what has been said that if a disciple has the true understanding of Mind-Essence and concentrates his mind on that, he needs to do nothing further but to wait quietly for the unfolding of Enlightenment and Nirvana. The answer to this is that a disciple is like a precious gem whose brilliance is hidden by a coating of impurities. If we are to enjoy the pure brilliance of the gem we must first resort to polishing. The true nature of Mind-Essence is immaculately pure but in the disciple it is hidden by accumulations of defilement that must be removed by expedient means if he is to attain Enlightenment. Therefore, besides having a true understanding of the Dharma, he must also keep the precepts and cherish a great heart of compassion.

There are four kinds of expedient means for beginning and continuing devotional practices if one is to be confident of attaining Enlightenment. The first is to understand and cherish certain fundamental intellectual convictions. He should practise recollective mindfulness of the true nature of all concepts, that they are empty of any self-nature of their own, that they are devoid of any rebirth and free from all false prejudices and do not abide in the cycle of deaths and rebirths. He should practise recollective mindfulness upon the fact that concepts are purely relative being altered, united or destroyed by causes and affinities. He should practise recollective mindfulness as to the fact of karma and its inevitable maturing, and purpose to lay up a good karma by keeping with sincerity and faithfulness all the precepts and practising all the Paramitas, and to have all their practising of recollective mindfulness and outward keeping of the precepts and inward keeping of the Paramitas motivated by a great heart of compassion. He should try to develop all merits and virtues; he should sympathize with all sentient beings and seek to awaken faith and aspiration in their minds. He must not think over-much of Nirvana nor seek to grasp it for himself, for in the Pure Concepts of Mind-Essence there are no desires, no graspings, no clingings.

The second kind of expedient means for practising is to develop feelings of shame and repentence after giving place to evil thoughts or doing evil acts, as a means for restraining one from yielding to them again, for Mind-Essence must be kept free from all evil defilements. The third kind is to develop one's root of kindness by the spontaneous and willing doing of all kinds of charity in cases of need, by making willing offerings to Buddha, Dharma and the Brotherhood. It is to praise Buddha and to beseech him to emancipate and enlighten all sentient beings. It is to practise expressing adoration and affection and dependence upon Buddha, Dharma and the Brotherhood, with perfect sincerity so as to increase one's faith and earnestness of practice in seeking for highest perfect Enlightenment, for it is only by the protecting and supporting power of Buddha, Dharma, Sangha, that he will be able to attain it. For to integrate oneself with the Pure Concepts of Mind-Essence one must be free from all hindrances, both from without and within.

The fourth expedient means is the practising of compassion, the uttering of earnest wishes that all sentient beings may be taught and delivered, not a single one omitted even to infinite future, all to be brought to Nirvana, and that his merits may be devoted to that end. And to be in harmony with the pure concepts of Mind-Essence there must be no cessation or intermissions of his compassionate wishes and vows.

The essential nature of the Pure Concepts of Mind-Essence are its all-embracing inclusiveness, embracing all sentient beings in its perfect purity and unity with no shadow of individuation in either mind or the substance of compassion. Any Bodhisattva having made this solemn pranadana will attain to some measure of intuitive insight into the pure Dharmakaya of his Mind-Essence. As they by their intuition enter into pure Dharmakaya, they are enabled to make transcendental manifestations of eight kinds that will benefit all sentient beings. First, according to the purity and earnestness of their pranadana, after the example of Buddhas, they can descend from the heavenly palaces of the Tusita Realm, they can enter into a human womb, undergo a period of gestation, be born as a human, become a Bhikshu, attain Enlightenment, turn the wheel of the Dharma, pass into Nirvana. However, such Bodhisattvas cannot be said to have attained to Dharmakaya, because they have not yet fully matured their karmas that had been inherited from infinite periods of past ages, so they still remain in mutual response with light sufferings in following rebirths, but enduring these light sufferings they are not in bondage to them because of their transcendental freedom and power belonging to their great pranadana. Some of these Bodhisattvas, it is said in the Sutras, must descend into the evil realms for a period, but this does not mean that they have retrograded, it only means that for the maturing of their remaining karma they must experience the suffering of those lower realms to cure them of any remaining shadow of indolence lest they fall short of attaining true Bodhisattvahood, so that their courage and boldness may be adequate. Such Bodhisattvas by reason of this experience in the lower realms will start their devotional practices with renewed earnestness and will never again become timid or indolent, or have any fear of retrograding. Or if they should learn that in order to attain Nirvana they must endure hardship for immense kalpas, they would never slacken their zeal in practice or become cowardly and timid, for they have attained a pure faith in the teaching that all pure concepts, since beginning less time, are in their self-nature Nirvana itself.

Understanding and Practice

As Bodhisattvas advance along the stages they attain a clearer understanding of the Dharma and of how to practise it more perfectly. As the first Asamkya Kalpa of their practice draws to a close, these advanced Bodhisattvas attain a transcendental understanding of the self-nature of the Pure Concepts of Mind-Essence and conform their practices to it. As they see that the essential nature of the Pure Concepts is free from all acquisitiveness, all stinginess and greediness, all covetousness, they bring their practising into conformity with it by practising the paramita of charity. As they see that the essential nature of the Pure Concepts of Mind-Essence are free from the defilement of all sensual desires, they bring their practising into conformity with it by practising the paramita of keeping the Precepts. As they see that the essential nature of the Pure Concepts is free from all resentment, all malice, all anger, they try to conform to it by practising the paramita of patience and humility. As they see that the essential nature of the Pure Concepts is free from all slothfulness and idleness and indifference, they try to conform to it by practising the paramita of zeal and perseverance. As they see that the essential nature of the Pure Concepts is free from all disturbance and confusion, the very perfection of permanence and peacefulness, they try to conform to it by practising the paramita of tranquillity. As they see that the essential nature of the Pure Concepts is free from all obscurity caused by segregation and individuation, and the darkness caused by Ignorance, and is luminous with the Brightness of Truth, they try to conform to it by practising the paramita of Wisdom.

Realization and Attainment

Let us now consider the unfolding insight that comes to a Bodhisattva as he attains the object of his faith and earnest practices. From the first awakening of his faith and beginning of his practice to his full realization and attainment there has been but one object in mind, enlightenment and Buddhahood for the sake of all sentient beings. But can this truly be called "an object"? If we think of it as a state or condition, that he as an ego-personality is to attain, it might be, but we have already found that the conception of an ego-personality is a false conception that the highest Bodhisattvas have already discarded. In the Pure Concepts of Mind-Essence there is no object and no subject, there is only the nature of Wisdom, the Pure Dharmakaya. It is this that highest Bodhisattvas realize and attain. In an instant of true realization they are offering gifts

and worship to all the Buddhas in all the Buddha-lands of all the universes, they are beseeching the Buddhas to turn the wheel of the Dharma
for the sake of all sentient beings, they are awakening faith in the minds
of all beginners, they are supporting them and bestowing upon them all
pure merits and virtue, and at long last they are present when the realization comes to welcome them into the pure suchness of Enlightenment,
the pure Dharmakaya. And all this not as a glorified personality but as
Buddhahood itself. However, on account of the timid and cowardly disciples, sometimes they will encourage them by such words as, "You will
attain Enlightenment and Buddhahood after infinite ages", or on account
of the indolent and sluggish disciples, they may urge them forward by
many skillful devices, but in all cases the awakening of faith and the
beginning of practice is equal, so their realization and attainment of
Enlightenment is always on an equality. There are no Dharmas to bring
one disciple quickly and another slowly to enlightenment, all Dharmas
are of an equal potency, and all disciples must practise through many
asamkyas of kalpas, and no Bodhisattva-Mahasattva has ever attained it
in any less. It is only because of differences in the dispositions and
environments of sentient beings that different skilful means are used
and different advancements seem to be made, but in truth, in the pure
Dharmakaya everything is in perfect balance and purity.

The Potential Merit and Virtue of
Bodhisattva-Mahasattvas

Again, when Bodhisattva-Mahasattvas awaken faith and make up their
minds to begin spiritual devotions and discipline for the sake of al sentient
beings, there come into potentiality great merits and virtues, which we
will now consider under three heads. The first is the True Mind, for it
embraces and cherishes no individuation nor discriminations nor partial-
ities nor prejudices. The second is the Mind of Perfect Wisdom, for it
unfolds all manner of skilful and expedient principles and means. The
third is the Mind of Perfect Compassion, for it unfolds an activity or
karma-consciousness that is sympathetic towards all sentient beings, cherishing good-will towards them and spontaneously willing to satisfy their
needs and benefit them in innumerable and inconceivable ways, appearing
and disappearing with no thought of self. Furthermore, this kind of
Bodhisattva-Mahasattva, having matured their merits and virtues, attain
the ultimate perfection of Purity and Unity and Peacefulness, unimagin-
ably supernal and harmonious and blissful, the Pure Dharmakaya. By the
inscrutable integrancy of this Ultimate Purity, spontaneous and constant
and ceaseless, Ignorance disappears. This is Ultimate, All-embracing

Wisdom, the immaculate Womb of all Pure Dharmas, and the awakening faith and beginning spiritual devotions and practices of all sentient beings. It is the Ultimate and Universal Breathing going forth in radiantly creative activity, drawing inward by intuitive sympathy and boundless good-will to the perfect purity and unity and peacefulness of the Pure Dharmakaya, and all for the benefit of all sentient beings, that they may be One and fully realize their perfect Oneness.

It may be asked at this point: If the principle of individuation and discrimination is transcended by the vanishing of Ignorance, how can omniscience of Perfect Wisdom be attained by Bodhisattva-Mahasattvas? If an infinity of universes arises because of infinite space, and if because of an infinity of universes there is an infinity of sentient beings, and if because of infinite beings there are an infinitude of mentalities and predispositions and conditions and circumstances and differentiated activities, how can even a Bodhisattva-Mahasattva attain perfect understanding, or command of adequate skilful means, or highest perfect Wisdom? The explanation is that all these infinity of infinities are fully embraced in the perfect self-awareness of the Bliss-body of Buddhahood which is the ineffable Dharmakaya, which is free of all differentiation or premonition of differentiation. But as sentient beings have falsely imagined illusions of objects and conditions and self-ness, and because of it discriminative thinking has arisen and egoism and grasping and clinging and karma. But all these false imaginations are not to be regarded as of the intrinsic self-nature of the Pure Dharmakaya, and provide no ground for infallibly understanding or perfectly realizing Truth itself. But by intuitively becoming identified with Truth, Highest Bodhisattva-Mahasattvas become free of all such differentiated thinking and prejudices and are free to react to the undifferentiated purity of their Mind-Essence. Their minds can reflect all false concepts but without stain or desire, by reason of which they attain perfect wisdom and command of expedient means and harmonizing activities. By entering intuitively and with sympathy and good will into the minds and desires and limitations of all sentient beings, they can elucidate the Dharmas and deliver all sentient beings. This is the reply to the question how purified Bodhisattva-Mahasattvas can attain highest perfect Wisdom: It is because they understand and sympathize with the false imaginations of sentient beings and at the same time enter intuitively into the purity and unity of their Mind-Essence, not as standing apart and judging, but one with all sentient beings, themselves, the Buddhas, Mind-Essence, Dharmakaya itself, one and inseparable.

Still another question may arise: If all the Buddhas from remotest beginnings have had these transcendental powers of Wisdom, Compassion and command of unlimited expedient means for benefiting all sentient beings, how is it that sentient beings do not recognize and appreciate their good-will and beneficent activities and respond to them by awakening faith and beginning devotional practices and, in due course, attain enlightenment and Buddhahood? Instead, most sentient beings are indifferent and seem to prefer their own illusions to embracing the sufferings that follow Ignorance? The reply is that all Buddhas and Tathagatas and Bodhisattva-Mahasattvas having become identified with the pure Dharmakaya pervade all the universes equally and potently and spontaneously, but embracing in their pure Essence all sentient beings, also, and being in eternal relations with them and being of the same self-nature, they await the willing and inevitable response that is a necessary part of the perfect purity and unity of the Dharmakaya. The minds of sentient beings are truly like a mirror, reflecting all Dharmas, but if the mirror is stained or defiled there will be no clear reflection. Not until the mirror of human minds and hearts is purified by the awakening of faith and the beginnings of spiritual practices, can they hope to see Buddhas, attain Enlightenment, and realize their own identity with Dharmakaya.

Part Four
Practice of the Mahayana

Thus far we have been elucidating the principles of the Mahayana. Now we will explain the practice of the Mahayana, and to do so effectively we must begin by showing the part that faith plays in the Practice, especially in the beginning when the minds of the novice Bodhisattvas have not yet attained to right Samadhi. We will then proceed to explain what kind of faith a disciple should have and how to apply his faith in practice. There are four kinds of faith. First, the novice disciple must have faith in the fundamental, ultimate Principle of things, that it is perfect Wisdom and perfect Compassion, and perfect Oneness. He should think joyfully of his own identity with its pure Mind-Essence. Second, the disciple should have abounding faith in Buddhahood. This means that he should cherish a sincere faith in the merits and virtues of the Buddhas, that he should constantly remember them, to feel his fellowship with them, to make offerings to them of adoration and gifts, to seek instruction and guidance from them. Third, the disciple should have an unshakeable faith in the wisdom, the compassion, the power of the Dharma. This means that he should look to it and rely upon it as an infallible guide in his practice of its Paramita ideals. Fourth, the disciple should have an unfeigned, affectionate and abounding faith in the Brotherhood of Homeless-

Bhikshus, caring for them, supplying their few needs, looking to them for instruction and sympathy in their own practice, that they may perfect their faith and move toward Buddhahood together.

There are six ways of practising faith. First, there is the way of Charity. Second, the way of unselfish kindness in Keeping the Precepts. Third, the way of Patience and Humility. Fourth, the way of Zeal and Perseverance. Fifth, the way of Tranquillity, stopping all discriminating thoughts and quietly realizing Truth itself. Sixth, the way of Wisdom.

First, the Way of Charity. The purpose of this practice is to eradicate one's own stinginess and cupidity. To effect this one should train oneself to be generous. If anyone comes to him begging, he should give him money or things as he has particular need, with discretion and kindness, as much as he can, up to his ability and the other's need, so that the begging ones may be relieved and go away cheerful. Or, if the disciple comes upon one in danger or hardship or an extremity of any kind, he should encourage him and help him as much as he can. Or, if one should come seeking instruction in the Dharma, he should humbly and patiently interpret it to him, using expedient means, as much as he can interpret with clearness according to his ability. The disciple should practise Charity simply and unostentatiously, with no ulterior motive of ambition, self-interest, reward, or praise, keeping in mind only this, that the giving and receiving shall both tend in the direction of Enlightenment from them both alike and equally.

Second, the way of Keeping the Precepts. The purpose of this practice is to get rid of all selfish grasping after comforts, delights, and self-interests. It means not to kill any sentient being, not to steal, not to commit adultery, not to deceive nor slander nor to utter malicious words nor to flatter. If he is a layman, it means keeping away from all greedy actions, envy, cheating, mischief, injustice, hatred, anger, and all heretical views. If he is a Bhikshu, it means he should avoid all vexatious and annoying acts, he should keep away from the turmoil and activities of the worldly life and live in solitude and quietness, practising begging and disciplining himself to be content with least desires. He should feel regret over any slight fault and should always act with prudence and attentiveness. He should not neglect any of the Lord Tathagata's instructions, and should be always ready to defend anyone suffering under suspicion or slander so as to restrain them from falling into further evil.

Third, the Way of Patience. This means to practise patience when vexed or annoyed by others, and to restrain any rising thoughts of ill-will or vengeance. It means being patient when overtaken by any affront to one's pride, personal losses, criticisms, or praise, or flattery; it means being patient and undisturbed by either happiness or suffering, comfort or discomfort.

Fourth, the Way of Zeal. The purpose of this discipline is to restrain oneself from yielding to temptations to laziness and weariness. It disciplines one not to relax one's effort when he meets success and praise, but ever to renew one's resolution to seek enlightenment. It should strengthen one to keep far away from temptations to timidity or false modesty. One should ever remember past sufferings borne because of evil committed carelessly and to no benefit to himself, and by these recollections to renew his zeal and perseverance to make diligent practising of all kinds of meritorious and virtuous deeds that will benefit both others and himself and keep himself free from suffering in the future. In spite of his being a Bhikshu he may be suffering from unmatured karma of previous lives and thus still be open to the attacks of evil influences, or still be entangled in worldly affairs, or the responsibilities of a family life, or under some chronic illness or disability. In the face of all such burdensome hindrances, he should be courageous and zealous and ceaselessly diligent in his practisings during the day, and in the six watches of the night should be on his guard against idle thoughts by constantly repeating adorations to all the Buddhas with zeal and sincerity, beseeching the Buddhas to abide in the world to turn the Dharma wheel, to support all right efforts to practise, to encourage all kind acts, to awaken faith in the faithless, to encourage right vows and to return all merit for the Enlightenment of all sentient beings. Unless one is zealous and persevering in his practice he will not be able to keep himself from increasing hindrances to cultivating his root of devotion.

Fifth, the Way of Tranquillity. The purpose of this discipline is twofold, to bring to a standstill all disturbing thoughts, and all discriminating thoughts are disturbing, to quiet all engrossing moods and emotions so that it will be possible to concentrate the mind for the practice of meditation and realization, and thus to be able to follow the practice willingly and gladly. Secondly, when the mind is tranquillized by stopping all thought, to practise "reflection" or meditation not in a discriminating way but in a more intellectual way of realizing the meaning and significance of one's thoughts and experiences, and also to follow this part of the practice willingly and gladly. By this twofold practice of "stopping and realizing", one's faith, that is already awakened, will become developed and gradually the two aspects of this practice will merge into one another – the mind perfectly tranquil but most active in realization. In the past, one naturally has had confidence in his faculty of discrimination, but this is now to be eradicated and ended.

For those who are practising "stopping", they should retire to some quiet place, or better live in some quiet place, sitting erect and with earnest and zestful purpose seek to quiet and concentrate the mind. While one may at first think of his breathing, it is not wise to continue it very long, nor to let the mind rest on any particular appearances or sights, or conceptions arising from the senses, such as the primal elements of earth, water, fire and ether, nor to let it rest on any of the lower mind's perceptions, particularizations, discriminations, moods or emotions. All kinds of ideation are to be discarded as fast as they arise, even the notions of controlling and discarding are to be got rid of. One's mind should become like a mirror, reflecting things but not judging them nor retaining them. Conceptions of themselves have no substance, let them rise and pass away unheeded. Conceptions arising from the senses and lower mind will not take form of themselves, unless they are grasped by the attention, but if they are ignored there will be no appearing and no disappearing. The same is true of conditions outside the mind: they should not be permitted to engross one's attention nor hinder one's practice. As the mind cannot be absolutely vacant, as thoughts rising from the senses and discriminating mind are discarded and ignored, one must supply their place by right mentation. The question then arises; What is right mentation? The reply is: right mentation is the realization of the mind itself, of its pure undifferentiated Essence. Even when we sit quietly with the mind fixed on its pure Essence, there should be no lingering notions of self, of self-realizing, or any phenomena of realization. Pure Mind-Essence is ungraspable of any rising or appearing of individuation.

Sixth, the Way of Wisdom. The purpose of this discipline is to bring one into the habit of applying the insight that has come to him by the preceding ways of discipline. Even when one is rising, standing, walking, doing something, stopping, one should constantly concentrate his mind on the act and the doing of it, not on his relation to it or its character or its value. One should think: there is walking, there is doing, there is stopping, there is realizing; not, I am walking, I am doing this, it is a good thing, it is disagreeable, it is I who am gaining merit, it is I who am realizing how wonderful it is. Then come vagrant thoughts, feelings of elation or defeat and failure and unhappiness. Instead of all this, one should simply practise concentration of the mind on the act itself, under-standing it to be an expedient means for attaining tranquillity of mind, realization, insight and Wisdom, and to follow the practice in faith, will-ingness and gladness. After long practice the bondage of old habits becomes weakened and disappears, and in its place appears confidence, satisfaction, awareness and tranquillity.

What is this practice of Wisdom designed to accomplish? There are three classes of conditions that hinder one from advancing along the path to Enlightenment: first, the allurements arising from the senses and external conditions and the discriminating mind; second, the inner conditions of the mind, its thoughts, desires and moods; these the earlier practices are designed to eliminate. The third class is the instinctive and fundamental, insidious and persistent, urgings, the will-to-live and enjoy, the will-to-protect one's life and personality, the will-to-propagate, which give rise to greed and lust, fear and anger, infatuation and pride of egoism. The practice of the Wisdom Paramita is designed to control and eliminate these fundamental and instinctive hindrances. By means of it the mind gradually becomes clearer, more luminous, more peaceful. Insight clears, faith deepens and broadens, until they merge into the inconceivable Samadhi of the Mind's Pure Essence. As one continues the practice of Wisdom, one less and less yields to thoughts of comfort or discomfort, faith becomes surer, more pervasive, beneficent, joyous, and fear of retrogression vanishes.

But do not think that these consummations are to be attained easily or quickly; many rebirths may be necessary, many asamkyas of kalpas may have to elapse. So long as doubt, unbelief, slanders, evil conduct, hindrances of karma, weakness of faith, pride, laziness, a disturbed mind, persist, or their shadows linger, there can be no attainment of the Samadhi of the Buddhas. But once attained, in the luminous brightness of highest Samadhi, one will be able to realize with all the Buddhas, the perfect unity of all sentient beings with Buddhahood's Dharmakaya. In the pure Dharmakaya, there is no dualism, neither shadow of differences. All sentient beings, if they are able to realize it, are already in Nirvana. The Mind's pure Essence is Highest Samadhi. The Mind's Pure Essence is *anuttara-samyak-sambodhi*, is Prajna Paramita, Highest Perfect Wisdom.

Part Five
The Advantages of Practising the Mahayana

There may be some disciples whose root of merit is not yet matured, whose control of mind is weak and whose power of application is limited, and yet who are sincere in their purpose to seek Enlightenment; these, for a time, may be beset and bewildered by maras, and evil influences who are seeking to break down their good purpose. Such disciples, seeing seductive sights, attractive girls, strong young men, must constantly remind themselves that all such tempting and alluring things are mind-made, and if they do this, their tempting power will disappear and they will no longer be annoyed. Or, if they have visions of heavenly gods and Bodhisattvas and Tathagatas surrounded by celestial glories, they should remind themselves that they, too, are mind-made and unreal. Or if they should be uplifted and excited by listening to mysterious Dharanis, to lectures upon the Paramitas, to elucidations of the great principles of the Mahayana, they must remind themselves that these also are emptiness and mind-made, that in their Essence they are Nirvana itself. Or, if they should have intimations within that they have attained transcendental powers, recalling past lives, or foreseeing future lives, or reading others' thoughts, or freedom to visit other Buddha-lands, or great powers of eloquence, all of which may tempt them to become covetous for worldly power and riches and fame. Or, they may be tempted by extremes of emotion, at times angry, at other times joyous, or, at times very kind-hearted and compassionate, at other times the very opposite, or, at times alert and purposeful, at other times indolent and stupid, at times full of faith and zealous in their practice, at other times engrossed in other affairs and negligent. All of which will keep them vacillating, at times experiencing a kind of fictitious samadhi, such as the heretics boast of, but not the True Samadhi. Or later, when they are quite advanced and become absorbed in trance for a day, or two, or even seven, not partaking of any food but upheld by inward food of their spirit, being admired by their friends and feeling very comfortable and proud and complacent, and then later becoming very erratic, sometimes eating little, sometimes greedily, and the expression of their face constantly changing.

Because of all such queer manifestations and developments in the course of their practisings, disciples should be on their guard to keep the mind under constant control. They should neither grasp after nor become attached to the passing and unsubstantial things of the senses or concepts and moods of the mind. If they do this they will be able to keep far away from the hindrances of karma. They should constantly remind themselves that the false samadhis and raptures of the heretics always have some imperfections about them and affinities with the triple world which lead the heretics to grasp after worldly fame, self-interest and self-pride, and becoming defiled by these graspings and prejudices and defilements, and becoming separated from their good Buddhist friends and learned masters, they miss the path of the Buddhas and quickly fall away into the path of the heretics.

The true Samadhi of Mind-Essence is free from all arbitrary conceptions, all prejudices, all attainments. There is only purity and blissful tranquillity. As the advanced Bodhisattva passes into true Samadhi all individualized concepts of body or mind vanish, and only the pure awareness of truth in its undifferentiated wholeness remains, and the mind realizes its true freedom and peace, with no notions of egoism or individuality beclouding it.

As advanced Bodhisattvas practise this true Samadhi of Mind-Essence they will acquire in this present life ten great advantages. First, they will at all times be under the protection and support of all the Buddhas and Bodhisattvas who constitute the Eternal Sanga. Second, they will never fear evil. Third, they will attain clearing insight and intuitive understanding, and will cease to be confused or disturbed by false teachings. Fourth, they will no longer doubt the profound Dharma teaching, their predispositions and karma hindrances will gradually disappear. Fifth, the rising of instinctive desires, suspicious and malicious feelings, will cease. Sixth, their faith in the purposive good-will of the Tathagatas and of the wisdom and compassion of Buddhahood will increase. Seventh, they will become courageous and serene in the face of the issues of life and death, escaping grief, and all feelings of contrition and despondency. Eighth, they will unfold a great heart of compassion themselves, their spirit will become gentle and mild, discarding all pride of egoism and untroubled by the acts of others. Ninth, they will cease to find pleasure in worldly things, and though they may not have attained samadhi, they will remain tranquil under ordinary conditions. Tenth, after they have attained Samadhi, they never again will be in bondage to sense-originating concepts.

Here ends this treatise interpreting the principles and practice of Mahayana Buddhism and designed to awaken faith in it. It is by means of these principles and practices that the Bodhisattvas are able to advance along the stages to the perfect attainment of Enlightenment and Buddhahood. All Bodhisattva-Mahasattvas of the past have by means of this Dharma awakened faith, undertaken devotional practices, continued them earnestly and perseveringly, and attained the goal of faith in Buddhahood. The same is true of all the Bodhisattvas of the present and the future, they are awakening faith and continuing the practices and will surely attain the consummation of their faith. Therefore, all sentient beings ought to awaken a like faith, and be diligent and faithful in studying and practising it.

I have now finished this interpretation of the Dharma. May any merit that arises from it benefit all sentient beings and bring them to Buddhahood.

III

CHINESE TRADITION

Lao Tsu: Tao Te Ching

While the genius of India has always been for metaphysical thought, the genius of China is for practical life. Confucius, the typical Chinese sage, whose thought dominated China for two thousand years before it was supplanted by the crudity of Marxism, constructed a system of philosophy which regulated the life both of the individual and of the social order. The basic principal of Confucian philosophy was *jen*, which has been translated as "human heartedness". It is, in fact, a profound system of humanism, but of humanism of a special kind. It was based on veneration for the "ancestors" which made "filial piety" the supreme principle, and it was organized by a system of ritual. Ritual, which has practically lost its meaning today, is essentially the art of giving transcendent significance to the ordinary actions of life. In modern society all normal activity is regarded as profane (literally "outside the temple"), but for Confucius, as for most ancient societies, every action had to be given significance by relating it to a transcendent source. Human beings are part of a cosmic whole, and every human activity of eating and drinking, walking and talking, marrying and caring for a family, sowing and harvesting, caring for the sick and dying, has to be related to the universe to which we all belong and to the power, by whatever name it is known, which rules the universe. It was this that Confucius attempted to do, and he was so successful that Chinese society was governed by the principles of his philosophy until modern times.

But though Confucius believed in piety, he was not a mystic and it was left to Lao Tzu, or whoever composed the Tao Te Ching, to reveal the deeper reality behind the social order. Lao Tzu's philosophy had two basic principles. The first was *wu-wei* or active inactivity. Lao Tzu realized that all human action has its source in a power which is inactive. He called it the "Uncarved Block". Before any action comes into being it is conceived in a "still point", a level of consciousness which is not perceived and is unconscious from that point of view. This led Lao Tzu to his other great principle of humility, of keeping low, like water which always seeks the lowest place. These two principles led to the discovery of the feminine as the moving power in human existence. The Chinese see the universe as a play between two forces, the yin and the yang. The yin is feminine and the yang masculine, and all human happiness depends on the right relation between the yin and yang. Thus the Chinese were able to escape from the dualism which has divided western consciousness and to see life in terms of harmony and relationship, of a mutual interdependence, of the coincidence of opposites of which Nicholas of Cusa spoke, which alone can preserve human life from the violence and domination of male over female which have marked the western world.

LAO TSU: TAO TE CHING

LAO TSU: TAO TE CHING

translated by Gia-Fu Feng and Jane English

1

The Tao that can be told is not the eternal Tao.
The name that can be named is not the eternal name.
The nameless is the beginning of heaven and earth.
The named is the mother of ten thousand things.
Ever desireless, one can see the mystery.
Ever desiring, one can see the manifestations.
These two spring from the same source but differ in name; this appears
    as darkness.
Darkness within darkness.
The gate to all mystery.

2

Under heaven all can see beauty only because there is ugliness.
All can know good as good only because there is evil.

Therefore having and not having arise together.
Difficult and easy complement each other.
Long and short contrast each other;
High and low rest upon each other;
Voice and sound harmonize each other;
Front and back follow one another.
Therefore the sage goes about doing nothing, teaching no-talking.
The ten thousand things rise and fall without cease,
Creating, yet not possessing,
Working, yet not taking credit.
Work is done, then forgotten.
Therefore it lasts forever.

3

Not exalting the gifted prevents quarrelling.
Not collecting treasures prevents stealing.
Not seeing desirable things prevents confusion of the heart.

The wise therefore rule by emptying hearts and stuffing bellies, by
    weakening ambitions and strengthening bones,
If people lack knowledge and desire, then intellectuals will not try to
    interfere.
If nothing is done, then all will be well.

4

The Tao is an empty vessel; it is used, but never filled.
Oh, unfathomable source of ten thousand things!
Blunt the sharpness,
Untangle the knot,
Soften the glare,
Merge with dust.
Oh, hidden deep but ever present!
I do not know from whence it comes.
It is the forefather of the emperors.

5

Heaven and earth are ruthless;
They see the ten thousand things as dummies.
The wise are ruthless;
They see the people as dummies.

The space between heaven and earth is like a bellows.
The shape changes but not the form;
The more it moves, the more it yields.
More words count less.
Hold fast to the centre.

6

The valley spirit never dies;
It is the woman, primal mother.
Her gateway is the root of heaven and earth.
It is like a veil barely seen.
Use it; it will never fail.

7

Heaven and earth last forever.
Why do heaven and earth last forever?
They are unborn.
So ever living.
The sage stays behind, thus he is ahead.
He is detached, thus at one with all.
Through selfless action, he attains fulfilment.

8

The highest good is like water.
Water gives life to the ten thousand things and does not strive.
It flows in places men reject and so is like the Tao.

In dwelling, be close to the land.
In meditation, go deep in the heart.
In dealing with others, be gentle and kind.
In speech, be true.
In ruling, be just.
In business, be competent.
In action, watch the timing.

No fight: No blame.

9

Better stop short than fill to the brim.
Oversharpen the blade, and the edge will soon blunt.
Amass a store of gold and jade, and no one can protect it.
Claim wealth and titles, and disaster will follow.
Retire when the work is done.
This is the way of heaven.

10

Carrying body and soul and embracing the one,
Can you avoid separation?
Attending fully and becoming supple,
Can you be as a newborn babe?
Washing and cleansing the primal vision,
Can you be without stain?
Loving all men and ruling the country,
Can you be without cleverness?
Opening and closing the gates of heaven,
Can you play the role of woman?

Understanding and being open to all things,
Are you able to do nothing?
Giving birth and nourishing,
Bearing yet not possessing,
Working yet not taking credit,
Leading yet not dominating,
This is the Primal Virtue.

11

Thirty spokes share the wheel's hub;
It is the centre hole that makes it useful.
Shape clay into a vessel;
It is the space within that makes it useful.
Cut doors and windows for a room;
It is the holes which make it useful.
Therefore profit comes from what is there;
Usefulness from what is not there.

12

The five colours blind the eye.
The five tones deafen the ear.
The five flavours dull the taste.
Racing and hunting madden the mind.
Precious things lead one astray.

Therefore the sage is guided by what he feels and not by what he sees.
He lets go of that and chooses this.

13

Accept disgrace willingly.
Accept misfortune as the human condition.

What do you mean by "Accept disgrace willingly"?
Accept being unimportant.
Do not be concerned with loss or gain.
This is called "accepting disgrace willingly".

What do you mean by "Accept misfortune as the human condition"?
Misfortune comes from having a body.
Without a body, how could there be misfortune?

Surrender yourself humbly; then you can be trusted to care for all
    things.
Love the world as your own self; then you can truly care for all things.

14
Look, it cannot be seen – it is beyond form.
Listen, it cannot be heard – it is beyond sound.
Grasp, it cannot be held – it is intangible.
These three are indefinable;
Therefore they are joined in one.

From above it is not bright;
From below it is not dark:
An unbroken thread beyond description.
It returns to nothingness.
The form of the formless,
The image of the imageless,
It is called indefinable and beyond imagination.
Stand before it and there is no beginning.
Follow it and there is no end.
Stay with the ancient Tao,
Move with the present.

Knowing the ancient beginning is the essence of Tao.

15
The ancient masters were subtle, mysterious, profound, responsive.
The depth of their knowledge is unfathomable.
Because it is unfathomable,
All we can do is describe their appearance.
Watchful, like men crossing a winter stream.
Alert, like men aware of danger.
Courteous, like visiting guests.
Yielding, like ice about to melt.
Simple, like uncarved blocks of wood.
Hollow, like caves.
Opaque, like muddy pools.

Who can wait quietly while the mud settles?
Who can remain still until the moment of action?
Observers of the Tao do not seek fulfilment.
Not seeking fulfilment, they are not swayed by desire for change.

16
Empty yourself of everything.
Let the mind rest at peace.
The ten thousand things rise and fall while the Self watches their return.
They grow and flourish and then return to the source.
Returning to the source is stillness, which is the way of nature.
The way of nature is unchanging.
Knowing constancy is insight.
Not knowing constancy leads to disaster.
Knowing constancy, the mind is open.
With an open mind, you will be openhearted.
Being openhearted, you will act royally.
Being royal, you will attain the divine.
Being divine, you will be at one with the Tao.
Being at one with the Tao is eternal.
And though the body dies, the Tao will never pass away.

17
The very highest is barely known by men.
Then comes that which they know and love.
Then that which is feared.
Then that which is despised.

He who does not trust enough will not be trusted.

When actions are performed
Without unnecessary speech.
People say, "We did it!"

18
When the great Tao is forgotten,
Kindness and morality arise.
When wisdom and intelligence are born,
The great pretence begins.

When there is no peace within the family,
Filial piety and devotion arise.
When the country is confused and in chaos,
Loyal ministers appear.

19

Give up sainthood, renounce wisdom,
And it will be a hundred times better for everyone.

Give up kindness, renounce morality,
And men will rediscover filial piety and love.

Give up ingenuity, renounce profit,
And bandits and thieves will disappear.

These three are outward forms alone; they are not sufficient in
    themselves.
It is more important
To see the simplicity,
To realize one's true nature,
To cast off selfishness
And temper desire.

20

Give up learning, and put an end to your troubles.

Is there a difference between yes and no?
Is there a difference between good and evil?
Must I fear what others fear? What nonsense!
Other people are contented, enjoying the sacrificial feast of the ox.
In spring some go to the park, and climb the terrace,
But I alone am drifting, not knowing where I am.
Like a newborn babe before it learns to smile,
I am alone, without a place to go.

Others have more than they need, but I alone have nothing.
I am a fool. Oh, yes! I am confused.
Other men are clear and bright,
But I alone am dim and weak.
Other men are sharp and clever,
But I alone am dull and stupid.
Oh, I drift like the waves of the sea,
Without direction, like the restless wind.

Everyone else is busy,
But I alone am aimless and depressed.
I am different.
I am nourished by the great mother.

21

The greatest Virtue is to follow Tao and Tao alone.
The Tao is elusive and intangible.
Oh, it is intangible and elusive, and yet within is image.
Oh, it is elusive and intangible, and yet within is form.
Oh, it is dim and dark, and yet within is essence.
This essence is very real, and therein lies faith.
From the very beginning until now its name has never been forgotten.
Thus I perceive the creation.
How do I know the ways of creation?
Because of this.

22

Yield and overcome;
Bend and be straight;
Empty and be full;
Wear out and be new;
Have little and gain;
Have much and be confused.

Therefore wise men embrace the one
And set an example to all.
Not putting on a display,
They shine forth.
Not justifying themselves,
They are distinguished.
Not boasting,
They receive recognition.
Not bragging,
They never falter.
They do not quarrel,
So no one quarrels with them.
Therefore the ancients say, "Yield and overcome".
Is that an empty saying?
Be really whole,
And all things will come to you.

23

To talk little is natural.
High winds do not last all morning.
Heavy rain does not last all day.
Why is this? Heaven and earth!
If heaven and earth cannot make things eternal,
How is it possible for man?

He who follows the Tao
Is at one with the Tao.
He who is virtuous
Experiences Virtue.
He who loses the way
Feels lost.
When you are at one with the Tao,
The Tao welcomes you.
When you are at one with Virtue,
The Virtue is always there.
When you are at one with loss,
The loss is experienced willingly.

He who does not trust enough
Will not be trusted.

24

He who stands on tiptoe is not steady.
He who strides cannot maintain the pace.
He who makes a show is not enlightened.
He who is self-righteous is not respected.
He who boasts achieves nothing.
He who brags will not endure.
According to followers of the Tao,
    "These are extra food and unnecessary luggage."
They do not bring happiness.
Therefore followers of the Tao avoid them.

25

Something mysteriously formed,
Born before heaven and earth.
In the silence and the void,
Standing alone and unchanging,
Ever present and in motion.
Perhaps it is the mother of ten thousand things.
I do not know its name.
Call it Tao.
For lack of a better word, I call it great.

Being great, it flows.
It flows far away.
Having gone far, it returns.

Therefore, "Tao is great;
Heaven is great;
Earth is great;
The king is also great."
These are the four great powers of the universe,
And the king is one of them.

Man follows the earth.
Earth follows heaven.
Heaven followed the Tao.
Tao follows what is natural.

26

The heavy is the root of the light;
The still is the master of unrest.

Therefore the sage, travelling all day,
Does not lose sight of his baggage.
Though there are beautiful things to be seen,
He remains unattached and calm.

Why should the lord of ten thousand chariots act lightly in public?
To be light is to lose one's root.
To be restless is to lose one's control.

27

A good walker leaves no tracks;
A good speaker makes no slips;
A good reckoner needs no tally.
A good door needs no lock,
Yet no one can open it.
Good binding requires no knots,
Yet no one can loosen it.

Therefore the sage takes care of all men
And abandons no one.
He takes care of all things
And abandons nothing.

This is called "following the light".

What is a good man?
A teacher of a bad man.
What is a bad man?
A good man's charge.
If the teacher is not respected,
And the student not cared for,
Confusion will arise, however clever one is.
This is the crux of mystery.

28

Know the strength of man,
But keep a woman's care!
Be the stream of the universe!
Being the stream of the universe,
Ever true and unswerving,
Become as a little child once more.

Know the white,
But keep the black!
Be an example to the world!
Being an example to the world,
Ever true and unwavering,
Return to the infinite.

Know honour,
Yet keep humility.
Be the valley of the universe!
Being the valley of the universe,
Ever true and resourceful,
Return to the state of the uncarved block.

When the block is carved, it becomes useful.
When the sage uses it, he becomes the ruler.
Thus, "A great tailor cuts little".

29
Do you think you can take over the universe and improve it?
I do not believe it can be done.

The universe is sacred.
You cannot improve it.
If you try to change it, you will ruin it.
If you try to hold it, you will lose it.

So sometimes things are ahead and sometimes they are behind;
Sometimes breathing is hard, sometimes it comes easily;
Sometimes there is strength and sometimes weakness;
Sometimes one is up and sometimes down.

Therefore the sage avoids extremes, excesses and complacency.

30
Whenever you advise a ruler in the way of Tao,
Counsel him not to use force to conquer the universe.
For this would only cause resistance.
Thorn bushes spring up wherever the army has passed.
Lean years follow in the wake of a great war.
Just do what needs to be done.
Never take advantage of power.

Achieve results,
But never glory in them.
Achieve results,
But never boast.
Achieve results,
But never be proud.
Achieve results,
Because this is the natural way.
Achieve results,
But not through violence.

Force is followed by loss of strength.
This is not the way of Tao.
That which goes against the Tao comes to an early end.

31
Good weapons are instruments of fear; all creatures hate them.
Therefore followers of Tao never use them.
The wise man prefers the left.
The man of war prefers the right.

Weapons are instruments of fear; they are not a wise man's tools.
He uses them only when he has no choice.
Peace and quiet are dear to his heart,
And victory no cause for rejoicing.
If you rejoice in victory, then you delight in killing;
If you delight in killing, you cannot fulfil yourself.

On happy occasions precedence is given to the left,
On sad occasions to the right.
In the army the general stands on the left,
The commander-in-chief on the right.
This means that war is conducted like a funeral.
When many people are being killed,
They should be mourned in heartfelt sorrow.
That is why a victory must be observed like a funeral.

32
The Tao is forever undefined.
Small though it is in the unformed state, it cannot be grasped.
If kings and lords could harness it,
The ten thousand things would naturally obey.
Heaven and earth would come together
And gentle rain fall.
Men would need no more instruction and all things would take their
    course.

Once the whole is divided, the parts need names.
There are already enough names.
One must know when to stop.
Knowing when to stop averts trouble.
Tao in the world is like a river flowing home to the sea.

33
Knowing others is wisdom;
Knowing the self is enlightenment.
Mastering others requires force;
Mastering the self needs strength.

He who knows he has enough is rich.
Perseverance is a sign of will-power.
He who stays where he is endures.
To die but not to perish is to be eternally present.

34
The great Tao flows everywhere, both to the left and to the right.
The ten thousand things depend upon it; it holds nothing back.
It fulfils its purpose silently and makes no claim.

It nourishes the ten thousand things,
And yet is not their lord.
It has no aim; it is very small.

The ten thousand things return to it,
Yet it is not their lord.
It is very great.

It does not show greatness,
And is therefore truly great.

35

All men will come to him who keeps to the one,
For there lie rest and happiness and peace.

Passersby may stop for music and good food,
But a description of the Tao
Seems without substance or flavour.
It cannot be seen, it cannot be heard,
And yet it cannot be exhausted.

36

That which shrinks
Must first expand.
That which fails
Must first be strong.
That which is cast down
Must first be raised.
Before receiving
There must be giving.

This is called perception of the nature of things.
Soft and weak overcome hard and strong.

Fish cannot leave deep waters,
And a country's weapons should not be displayed.

37

Tao abides in non-action,
Yet nothing is left undone.
If kings and lords observed this,
The ten thousand things would develop naturally.
If they still desired to act,
They would return to the simplicity of formless substance.
Without form there is no desire.
Without desire there is tranquillity.
And in this way all things would be at peace.

38

A truly good man is not aware of his goodness,
And is therefore good.
A foolish man tries to be good,
And is therefore not good.

A truly good man does nothing,
Yet leaves nothing undone.
A foolish man is always doing,
Yet much remains to be done.

When a truly kind man does something, he leaves nothing undone.
When a just man does something, he leaves a great deal to be done.
When a disciplinarian does something and no one responds,
He rolls up his sleeves in an attempt to enforce order.

Therefore when Tao is lost, there is goodness.
When goodness is lost, there is kindness.
When kindness is lost, there is justice.
When justice is lost, there is ritual.
Now ritual is the husk of faith and loyalty, the beginning of confusion.
Knowledge of the future is only a flowery trapping of Tao.
It is the beginning of folly.

Therefore the truly great man dwells on what is real and not what is
    on the surface,
On the fruit and not the flower.
Therefore accept the one and reject the other.

39
These things from ancient times arise from one:
The sky is whole and clear.
The earth is whole and firm.
The spirit is whole and strong.
The valley is whole and full.
The ten thousand things are whole and alive.
Kings and lords are whole, and the country is upright.
All these are in virtue of wholeness.

The clarity of the sky prevents its falling.
The firmness of the earth prevents its splitting.
The strength of the spirit prevents its being used up.
The fullness of the valley prevents its running dry.
The growth of the ten thousand things prevents their dying out.
The leadership of kings and lords prevents the downfall of the country.

Therefore the humble is the root of the noble.
The low is the foundation of the high.
Princes and lords consider themselves "orphaned", "widowed", and
   "worthless".
Do they not depend on being humble?

Too much success is not an advantage.
Do not tinkle like jade
Or clatter like stone chimes.

40
Returning is the motion of the Tao.
Yielding is the way of the Tao.
The ten thousand things are born of being.
Being is born of not being.

41
The wise student hears of the Tao and practises it diligently.
The average student hears of the Tao and gives it thought now and
   again.
The foolish student hears of the Tao and laughs aloud.
If there were no laughter, the Tao would not be what it is.

Hence it is said:
The bright path seems dim;
Going forward seems like retreat;
The easy way seems hard;
The highest Virtue seems empty;
Great purity seems sullied;
A wealth of Virtue seems inadequate;
The strength of Virtue seems frail;
Real Virtue seems unreal;
The perfect square has no corners;
Great talents ripen late;
The highest notes are hard to hear;
The greatest form has no shape.
The Tao is hidden and without name.
The Tao alone nourishes and brings everything to fulfilment.

42
The Tao begot one.
One begot two.
Two begot three.
And three begot the ten thousand things.

The ten thousand things carry yin and embrace yang.
They achieve harmony by combining these forces.

Men hate to be "orphaned", "widowed", or "worthless",
But this is how kings and lords describe themselves.

For one gains by losing
And loses by gaining.

What others teach, I also teach; that is:
"A violent man will die a violent death!"
This will be the essence of my teaching.

43
The softest thing in the universe
Overcomes the hardest thing in the universe.
That without substance can enter where there is no room.
Hence I know the value of non-action.

Teaching without words and work without doing
Are understood by very few.

44
Fame or self: Which matters more?
Self or wealth: Which is more precious?
Gain or loss: Which is more painful?

He who is attached to things will suffer much.
He who saves will suffer heavy loss.
A contented man is never disappointed.
He who knows when to stop does not find himself in trouble.
He will stay forever safe.

45

Great accomplishments seems imperfect,
Yet it does not outlive its usefulness.
Great fullness seems empty,
Yet it cannot be exhausted.

Great straightness seems twisted.
Great intelligence seems stupid.
Great eloquence seems awkward.

Movement overcomes cold.
Stillness overcomes heat.
Stillness and tranquillity set things in order in the universe.

46

When the Tao is present in the universe,
The horses haul manure.
When the Tao is absent from the universe,
War horses are bred outside the city.
There is no greater sin than desire,
No greater curse than discontent,
No greater misfortune than wanting something for oneself.
Therefore he who knows that enough is enough will always have enough.

47

Without going outside, you may know the whole world.
Without looking through the window, you may see the ways of heaven.
The farther you go, the less you know.

Thus the sage knows without travelling;
He sees without looking;
He works without doing.

48

In the pursuit of learning, every day something is acquired.
In the pursuit of Tao, every day something is dropped.

Less and less is done
Until non-action is achieved.
When nothing is done, nothing is left undone.

The world is ruled by letting things take their course.
It cannot be ruled by interfering.

49

The sage has no mind of his own.
He is aware of the needs of others.

I am good to people who are good.
I am also good to people who are not good.
Because Virtue is goodness.
I have faith in people who are faithful.
I also have faith in people who are not faithful.
Because Virtue is faithlessness.

The sage is shy and humble – to the world he seems confusing.
Men look to him and listen.
He behaves like a little child.

50

Between birth and death,
Three in ten are followers of life,
Three in ten are followers of death,
And men just passing from birth to death also number three in ten.
Why is this so?
Because they live their lives on the gross level.

He who knows how to live can walk abroad
Without fear of rhinoceros or tiger.
He will not be wounded in battle.
For in him rhinoceroses can find no place to thrust their horn,
Tigers no place to use their claws,
And weapons no place to pierce.
Why is this so?
Because he has no place for death to enter.

51

All things arise from Tao.
They are nourished by Virtue.
They are formed from matter.
They are shaped by environment.
Thus the ten thousand things all respect Tao and honour Virtue.
Respect of Tao and honour of Virtue are not demanded,
But they are in the nature of things.

Therefore all things arise from Tao.
By Virtue they are nourished,
Developed, cared for,
Sheltered, comforted,
Grown, and protected.
Creating without claiming,
Doing without taking credit,
Guiding without interfering,
This is Primal Virtue.

52

The beginning of the universe
Is the mother of all things.
Knowing the mother, one also knows the sons.
Knowing the sons, yet remaining in touch with the mother,
Brings freedom from the fear of death.

Keep your mouth shut,
Guard the senses,
And life is ever full.
Open your mouth,
Always be busy,
And life is beyond hope.
Seeing the small is insight;
Yielding to force is strength.
Using the outer light, return to insight,
And in this way be saved from harm.
This is learning constancy.

53

If I have even just a little sense,
I will walk on the main road and my only fear will be of straying from it.
Keeping to the main road is easy,
But people love to be sidetracked.

When the court is arrayed in splendour,
The fields are full of weeds,
And the granaries are bare.
Some wear gorgeous clothes,
Carry sharp swords,
And indulge themselves with food and drink;
They have more possessions than they can use.
They are robber barons.
This is certainly not the way of Tao.

54

What is firmly established cannot be uprooted.
What is firmly grasped cannot slip away.
It will be honoured from generation to generation.

Cultivate Virtue in your self,
And Virtue will be real.
Cultivate it in the family,
And Virtue will abound.
Cultivate it in the village,
And Virtue will grow.
Cultivate it in the nation,
And Virtue will be abundant.
Cultivate it in the universe,
And Virtue will be everywhere.

Therefore look at the body as body;
Look at the family as family;
Look at the village as village;
Look at the nation as nation;
Look at the universe as universe.

How do I know the universe is like this?
By looking!

55
He who is filled with Virtue is like a newborn child.
Wasps and serpents will not sting him;
Wild beasts will not pounce upon him;
He will not be attacked by birds of prey.
His bones are soft, his muscles weak,
But his grip is firm.
He has not experienced the union of man and woman, but is whole.
His manhood is strong.
He screams all day without becoming hoarse.
This is perfect harmony.

Knowing harmony is constancy.
Knowing constancy is enlightenment.

It is not wise to rush about.
Controlling the breath causes strain.
If too much energy is used, exhaustion follows.
This is not the way of Tao.
Whatever is contrary to Tao will not last long.

56
Those who know do not talk.
Those who talk do not know.

Keep your mouth closed.
Guard your senses.
Temper your sharpness.
Simplify your problems.
Mask your brightness.
Be at one with the dust of the earth.
This is primal union.

He who has achieved this state
Is unconcerned with friends and enemies,
With good and harm, with honour and disgrace.
This therefore is the highest state of man.

57
Rule a nation with justice.
Wage war with surprise moves.
Become master of the universe without striving.
How do I know that this is so?
Because of this!

The more laws and restrictions there are,
The poorer people become.
The sharper men's weapons,
The more trouble in the land.
The more ingenious and clever men are,
The more strange things happen.
The more rules and regulations,
The more thieves and robbers.

Therefore the sage says:
   I take no action and people are reformed.
   I enjoy peace and people become honest.
   I do nothing and people become rich.
   I have no desires and people return to the good and simple life.

58
When the country is ruled with a light hand
The people are simple.
When the country is ruled with severity,
The people are cunning.

Happiness is rooted in misery.
Misery lurks beneath happiness.
Who knows what the future holds?
There is no honesty.
Honesty becomes dishonest
Goodness becomes witchcraft.
Man's bewitchment lasts for a long time.

Therefore the sage is sharp but not cutting,
Pointed but not piercing,
Straightforward but not unrestrained,
Brilliant but not blinding.

59

In caring for others and serving heaven,
There is nothing like using restraint.
Restraint begins with giving up one's own ideas.
This depends on Virtue gathered in the past.
If there is a good store of Virtue, then nothing is impossible.
If nothing is impossible, then there are no limits.
If a man knows no limits, then he is fit to be a ruler.
The mother principle of ruling holds good for a long time.
This is called having deep roots and a firm foundation,
The Tao of long life and eternal vision.

60

Ruling the country is like cooking a small fish.
Approach the universe with Tao,
And evil will have no power.
Not that evil is not powerful,
But its power will not be used to harm others.
Not only will it do no harm to others,
But the sage himself will also be protected.
They do not hurt each other,
And the Virtue in each one refreshes both.

61

A great country is like low land.
It is the meeting ground of the universe,
The mother of the universe.

The female overcomes the male with stillness,
Lying low in stillness.

Therefore if a great country gives way to a smaller country,
It will conquer the smaller country.
And if a small country submits to a great country,
It can conquer the great country.
Therefore those who would conquer must yield,
And those who conquer do so because they yield.

A great nation needs more people;
A small country needs to serve.
Each gets what it wants.
It is fitting for a great nation to yield.

62

Tao is the source of the ten thousand things.
It is the treasure of the good man, and the refuge of the bad.
Sweet words can buy honour;
Good deeds can gain respect.
If a man is bad, do not abandon him.
Therefore on the day the emperor is crowned,
Or the three officers of state installed,
Do not send a gift of jade and a team of four horses,
But remain still and offer the Tao.
Why does everyone like the Tao so much at first?
Isn't it because you find what you seek and are forgiven when you sin?
Therefore this is the greatest treasure of the universe.

63

Practise non-action.
Work without doing.
Taste the tasteless.
Magnify the small, increase the few.
Reward bitterness with care.

See simplicity in the complicated.
Achieve greatness in little things.

In the universe the difficult things are done as if they are easy.
In the universe great acts are made up of small deeds.
The sage does not attempt anything very big,
And thus achieves greatness.

Easy promises make for little trust.
Taking things lightly results in great difficulty.
Because the sage always confronts difficulties,
He never experiences them.

64

Peace is easily maintained;
Trouble is easily overcome before it starts.
The brittle is easily shattered;
The small is easily scattered.
Deal with it before it happens.
Set things in order before there is confusion.

A tree as great as a man's embrace springs from a small shoot;
A terrace nine storeys high begins with a pile of earth;
A journey of a thousand miles starts under one's feet.

He who acts defeats his own purpose;
He who grasps loses.
The sage does not act, and so is not defeated.
He does not grasp and therefore does not lose.

People usually fail when they are on the verge of success.
So give as much care to the end as to the beginning;
Then there will be no failure.

Therefore the sage seeks freedom from desire.
He does not collect precious things.
He learns not to hold on to ideas.
He brings men back to what they have lost.
He helps the ten thousand things find their own nature,
But refrains from action.

65

In the beginning those who knew the Tao did not try to enlighten
     others,
But kept them in the dark.
Why is it so hard to rule?
Because people are so clever.
Rulers who try to use cleverness
Cheat the country.
Those who rule without cleverness
Are a blessing to the land.
These are the two alternatives.
Understanding these is Primal Virtue.
Primal Virtue is deep and far.
It leads all things back
Toward the great oneness.

66

Why is the sea king of a hundred streams?
Because it lies below them.
Therefore it is the king of a hundred streams.

If the sage would guide the people, he must serve with humility.
If he would lead them, he must follow behind.
In this way when the sage rules, the people will not feel oppressed;
When he stands before them, they will not be harmed.
The whole world will support him and will not tire of him.

Because he does not compete,
He does not meet competition.

67

Everyone under heaven says that my Tao is great and beyond compare.
Because it is great, it seems different.
If it were not different, it would have vanished long ago.

I have three treasures which I hold and keep.
The first is mercy; the second is economy;
The third is daring not to be ahead of others.
From mercy comes courage; from economy comes generosity;
From humility comes leadership.
Nowadays men shun mercy, but try to be brave;
They abandon economy, but try to be generous;
They do not believe in humility, but always try to be first.
This is certain death.

Mercy brings victory in battle and strength in defence.
It is the means by which heaven saves and guards.

68

A good soldier is not violent.
A good fighter is not angry.
A good winner is not vengeful.
A good employer is humble.
This is known as the Virtue of not striving.
This is known as ability to deal with people
This since ancient times has been known as the ultimate unity with
  heaven.

69

There is a saying among soldiers:
  I dare not make the first move but would rather play the guest;
  I dare not advance an inch but would rather withdraw a foot.

This is called marching without appearing to move,
Rolling up your sleeves without showing your arm,
Capturing the enemy without attacking,
Being armed without weapons.

There is no greater catastrophe than underestimating the enemy.
By underestimating the enemy, I almost lose what I value.
Therefore when the battle is joined,
The underdog will win.

70

My words are easy to understand and easy to perform,
Yet no man under heaven knows them or practises them.

My words have ancient beginnings.
My actions are disciplined.
Because men do not understand, they have no knowledge of me.

Those that know me are few;
Those that abuse me are honoured.
Therefore the sage wears rough clothing and holds the jewel in his
    heart.

71

Knowing ignorance is strength.
Ignoring knowledge is sickness.

If one is sick of sickness, then one is not sick.
The sage is not sick because he is sick of sickness.
Therefore he is not sick.

72

When men lack a sense of awe, there will be disaster.

Do not intrude in their homes.
Do not harass them at work.
If you do not interfere, they will not weary of you.
Therefore the sage knows himself but makes no show,
Has self-respect but is not arrogant.
He lets go of that and chooses this.

73

A brave and passionate man will kill or be killed.
A brave and calm man will always preserve life.
Of these two which is good and which is harmful?
Some things are not favoured by heaven. Who knows why?
Even the sage is unsure of this.

The Tao of heaven does not strive, and yet it overcomes.
It does not speak, and yet is answered.
It does not ask, yet is supplied with all its needs.
It seems at ease, and yet it follows a plan.

Heaven's net casts wide.
Though its meshes are coarse, nothing slips through.

74

If men are not afraid to die,
It is of no avail to threaten them with death.

If men live in constant fear of dying,
And if breaking the law means that a man will be killed,
Who will dare to break the law?

There is always an official executioner.
If you try to take his place,
It is like trying to be a master carpenter and cutting wood.
If you try to cut wood like a master carpenter, you will only hurt your
    hand.

75

Why are the people starving?
Because the rulers eat up the money in taxes.
Therefore the people are starving.

Why are the people rebellious?
Because the rulers interfere too much.
Therefore they are rebellious.

Why do the people think so little of death?
Because the rulers demand too much of life.
Therefore the people take death lightly.

Having little to live on, one knows better than to value life too much.

76

A man is born gentle and weak.
At his death he is hard and stiff.
Green plants are tender and filled with sap.
At their death they are withered and dry.

Therefore the stiff and unbending is the disciple of death.
The gentle and yielding is the disciple of life.

Thus an army without flexibility never wins a battle.
A tree that is unbending is easily broken.

The hard and strong will fall.
The soft and weak will overcome.

77

The Tao of heaven is like the bending of a bow.
The high is lowered, and the low is raised.
If the string is too long, it is shortened;
If there is not enough, it is made longer.

The Tao of heaven is to take from those who have too much and give
    to those who do not have enough.
Man's way is different.
He takes from those who do not have enough to give to those who
    already have too much.
What man has more than enough and gives it to the world?
Only the man of Tao.

Therefore the sage works without recognition.
He achieves what has to be done without dwelling on it.
He does not try to show his knowledge.

78

Under heaven nothing is more soft and yielding than water.
Yet for attacking the solid and strong, nothing is better;
It has no equal.
The weak can overcome the strong;
The supple can overcome the stiff.
Under heaven everyone knows this,
Yet no one puts it into practice.
Therefore the sage says:
  He who takes upon himself the humiliation of the people is fit to rule
    them.
  He who takes upon himself the country's disasters deserves to be
    king of the universe.
The truth often sound paradoxical.

79

After a bitter quarrel, some resentment must remain.
What can one do about it?
Therefore the sage keeps his half of the bargain
But does not exact his due.
A man of Virtue performs his part,
But a man without Virtue requires others to fulfil their obligations.
The Tao of heaven is impartial.
It stays with good men all the time.

80

A small country has fewer people.
Though there are machines that can work ten to a hundred times faster
    than man, they are not needed.
The people take death seriously and do not travel far.
Though they have boats and carriages, no one uses them.
Though they have armour and weapons, no one displays them.
Men return to the knotting of rope in place of writing.
Their food is plain and good, their clothes fine but simple, their homes
    secure;
They are happy in their ways.
Though they live within sight of their neighbours,
And crowing cocks and barking dogs are heard across the way,
Yet they leave each other in peace while they grow old and die.

81

Truthful words are not beautiful.
Beautiful words are not truthful.
Good men do not argue.
Those who argue are not good.
Those who know are not learned.
The learned do not know.

The sage never tries to store things up.
The more he does for others, the more he has.
The more he gives to others, the greater his abundance.
The Tao of heaven is pointed but does no harm.
The Tao of the sage is work without effort.

IV

SIKHISM

Morning Prayer
Evening Prayer
Bed-Time Prayer

Though there have been always many gods and goddesses in India, many names and forms of God, there has been in India from the beginning a tendency towards monotheism. The Rig Veda itself speaks of the "one being" (*ekam sat*), "of whom the wise speak in many ways". This one Being came to be known in the Upanishads as Brahman and Atman; but as the spirit of *bhakti*, of personal devotion to God, grew, the one Being came to receive a more personal character. This was clearly revealed in the Bhagavadgita, where Krishna as the *avatara*, the incarnation, of Vishnu was recognized as the "name and form" of the one God. But in India, unlike in the Semitic religions, it was understood that the one God, eternal and omnipresent could be worshipped under different names and forms. Vishnu, Siva, Rama, Krishna and also the Mother Goddess, the Devi, were all recognized as different names and forms of the one, infinite, eternal, unchanging Reality, the Ground and origin of all creation. There are obvious dangers in this that it can lead back to polytheism, to the belief in many gods, many sources of creation and therefore to no ultimate unity or truth in the universe. But the opposite danger which has affected the Semitic religions, is that God, the ultimate Reality, is identified with one particular name and form, Yahweh or Allah, and all who refuse to accept that particular name and form of God are condemned. In the Sikh religion, however, a form of monotheism was found which could accept other names and forms of the one God while retaining a strict monotheism, a devotion to the one, absolute, eternal, unchanging Being and Truth in whom the fullness of all personal being, of all wisdom and goodness is found. This was the great achievement of Guru Nanak, that he was able to reconcile both Hindu and Muslim in faith in the one God. "I belong, both body and soul", he could say, "to the one God, who is both Allah and Ram." The reason why Guru Nanak could reconcile different names and forms of God with faith in the one God is that for him God was not projected outside himself but recognized as dwelling within. For him God was Truth, immanent in the heart of man, the Word, the Light, the Name beyond all names. There has never been such a pure monotheism as that of Guru Nanak. As soon as God is projected outside, a division is made between man and God, and from this spring all other divisions between man and man, and still more between man and woman. In the

Semitic religions God is always conceived in masculine terms. Yahweh and Allah are always "He". But in the Sikh tradition God is both Father and Mother, "You are my Father, You are my Mother, You are my Brother, You are my Kin". So sings Guru Arjan. When the feminine is rejected in God, it is also rejected or suppressed in human society, and we are slowly realizing today that we live in a patriarchal culture in which the feminine has been rejected in God and woman subjected to man.

MORNING PRAYER

MORNING PRAYER

Translated by Khushwant Singh and others

There is one God,
Eternal Truth is His Name;
Maker of all things,
Fearing nothing and at enmity with nothing,
Timeless is His Image;
Not begotten, being of His own Being:
By the grace of the Guru, made known to men.

The Meditation

AS HE WAS IN THE BEGINNING: THE TRUTH,
SO THROUGHOUT THE AGES,
HE EVER HAS BEEN: THE TRUTH,
SO EVEN NOW HE IS TRUTH IMMANENT,
SO FOR EVER AND EVER HE SHALL BE TRUTH ETERNAL.

1

It is not through thought that He is to be comprehended
Though we strive to grasp Him a hundred thousand times;
Nor by outer silence and long deep meditation
Can the inner silence be reached;
Nor is man's hunger for God appeasable
By piling up world-loads of wealth.
All the innumerable devices of worldly wisdom
Leave a man disappointed; not one avails.
How then shall we know the Truth?
How shall we rend the veils of untruth away?
Abide thou by His Will, and make thine own,
His will, O Nānak, that is written in thine heart.

2
Through His Will He creates all forms of things,
But what the form of His Will is, who can express?
All life is shaped by His ordering,
By His ordering some are high, some of low estate,
Pleasure and pain are bestowed as His Writ ordaineth.

Some through His Will are graciously rewarded,
Others must grope through births and deaths;
Nothing at all, outside His Will, is abiding.
O Nānak, he who is aware of the Supreme Will
Never in his selfhood utters the boast: "It is I."

3
Those who believe in power,
Sing of His power;
Others chants of His gifts
As His messages and emblems;
Some sing of His greatness,
And His gracious acts;
Some sing of His wisdom
Hard to understand;
Some sing of Him as the fashioner of the body.
Destroying what He has fashioned;
Others praise Him for taking away life
And restoring it anew.
Some proclaim His Existence
To be far, desperately far, from us;
Others sing of Him
As here and there a Presence
Meeting us face to face.

To sing truly of the transcendent Lord
Would exhaust all vocabularies, all human powers of expression,
Myriads have sung of Him in innumerable strains.
His gifts to us flow in such plentitude
That man wearies of receiving what God bestows;
Age on unending age, man lives on His bounty;
Carefree, O Nānak, the Glorious Lord smiles.

4

The Lord is the Truth Absolute,
True is His Name.
His language is love infinite;
His creatures ever cry to Him;
"Give us more, O Lord, give more";
The Bounteous One gives unwearyingly.
What then should we offer
That we might see His Kingdom?
With what language
Might we His love attain?

In the ambrosial hours of fragrant dawn
Think upon and glorify
His Name and greatness.
Our own past actions
Have put this garment on us,
But salvation comes only through His Grace.

O Nānak, this alone need we know,
That God, being Truth, is the one Light of all.

5

He cannot be installed like an idol,
Nor can man shape His likeness.
He made Himself and maintains Himself
On His heights unstained for ever;
Honoured are they in His shrine
Who meditate upon Him.

Sing thou, O Nānak, the psalms
Of God as the treasury
Of sublime virtues.
If a man sings of God and hears of Him,
And lets love of God sprout within him,
All sorrow shall depart;
In the soul, God will create abiding peace.

The Word of the Guru is the inner Music;
The Word of the Guru is the highest Scripture;
The Word of the Guru is all pervading.
The Guru is Śiva, the Guru is Visbnu and Brahma,
The Guru is the Mother goddess.
If I knew Him as He truly is
What words could utter my knowledge?
Enlightened by God, the Guru has unravelled one mystery
"There is but one Truth, one Bestower of life;
May I never forget Him."

6

I would bathe in the holy rivers
If so I could win His love and grace;
But of what use is the pilgrimage
If it pleaseth Him not that way?

What creature obtains anything here
Except through previous good acts?
Yet hearken to the Word of the Guru
And his counsel within thy spirit
Shall shine like precious stone.

The Guru's divine illumination
Has unravelled one mystery;
There is but one Bestower of life
May I forget Him never.

7

Were a man to live through the four ages,
Or even ten times longer,
Though his reputation were to spread over the nine shores,
Though the whole world were to follow in his train,
Though he were to be universally famous,
Yet lacking God's grace, in God's presence
Such a man would be disowned;
Such a man would be merely a worm among vermin
And his sins will be laid at his door.
On the imperfect who repent, O Nānak, God bestows virtue,
On the striving virtuous He bestows increasing blessedness.
But I cannot think there is any man so virtuous
Who can bestow any goodness on God.

8

By hearkening to the Name
The disciple becomes a Master,
A guide, a saint, a seraph;
By hearkening to the Name
The earth, the bull that bears it
And the heavens are unveiled.

By hearkening to the Name
Man's vision may explore
Planets, continents, nether regions.
Death vexes not in the least
Those that hearken to the Name;
They are beyond Death's reach.
Saith Nānak, the saints are always happy;
By hearkening to the Name
Sorrow and sin are destroyed.

9

By hearkening to the Name
Mortals obtain the godliness
Of Śiva, Brahma and Indra;
By hearkening to the Name
The lips of the lowly
Are filled with His praise.
By hearkening to the Name
The art of Yoga and all the secrets
Of body and mind are unveiled.
By hearkening to the Name
The Vedic wisdom comes,
And also the knowledge of the shastras and smritis.

Saith Nānak, the saints are always happy;
By hearkening to the Name
Sorrow and sin are destroyed.

10
Hearkening to the Name bestows
Truth, divine wisdom, contentment.
To bathe in the joy of the Name
Is to bathe in the holy places.
By hearing the Name and reading it
A man attains to honour;
By hearkening, the mind may reach
The highest blissful poise
Of meditation on God.

Saith Nānak, the saints are always happy;
By hearkening to the Name
Sorrow and sin are destroyed.

11
By hearkening to the Name,
Man dives deep in an ocean of virtues;
By hearkening to the Name
The disciple becomes an apostle,
A prelate, a sovereign of souls.
By hearkening to the Name
The blind man sees the way;
By hearkening to the Name
Impassable streams are forded.

Saith Nānak, the saints are always happy;
By hearkening to the Name
Sorrow and sin are destroyed.

12
Of him who truly believes in the Name
Words cannot express the condition;
He himself will later repent
Should he ever try to describe it;
No pen, no paper, no writer's skill
Can get anywhere really near it.

Such is the power of His stainless Name,
He who truly believes in it, knows it.

13

Through belief in the Name
The mind soars high into enlightenment.
The whole universe stands self-revealed.
Through inner belief in the Name
One avoids ignorant stumbling;
In the light of such a faith
The fear of death is broken.

Such is the power of His stainless Name,
He who truly believes in it, knows it.

14

Nothing can bar or mar the paths
Of those who truly believe in the Name,
They depart from here with honour;
They do not lose the proper path.
The spirit of those imbued with faith
Is wedded to realization of truth.

Such is the power of His stainless Name,
He who truly believes in it, knows it.

15

Those who have inner belief in the Name,
Always achieve their own liberation,
Their kith and kin are also saved.
Guided by the light of the Guru
The disciple steers safe himself,
And many more he saves;
Those enriched with inner belief
Do not wander begging.

Such is the power of His stainless Name,
He who truly believes in it, knows it.

16

His chosen are His saints, and great are they,
Honoured are the saints in the court of God;
The saints add lustre to the courts of the Lord.
Their minds are fixed upon the Guru alone.
All that they say is wisdom, but by what wisdom
Can we number the works of the Lord?
The mythical bull is *dharma*: the offspring of compassion
That holds the thread on which the world is strung.

Even a little common sense makes one understand this:
How could a bull's shoulders uphold the earth?
There are so many earths, planets on planet.
What is that bears these burdens?

One ever-flowing pen inscribed the names
Of all the creatures, in their kinds and colours;
But which of us would seek to pen that record?
Of if we could, how great the scroll would be.

How can one describe Thy beauty and might of Thy Works?
And Who has power to estimate Thy Bounty, O Lord?
All creation emerging from Thy One Word,
Flowing out like a multitude of rivers.

How can an insignificant creature like myself
Express the vastness and wonder of Thy creation?
I am too petty to have anything to offer Thee;
I cannot, even once, be sacrifice unto Thee.

To abide by Thy Will, O Formless One, is man's best offering;
Thou who art Eternal, abiding in Thy Peace.

17

There is no counting of men's prayers,
There is no counting their ways of adoration.
Thy lovers, O Lord, are numberless;
Numberless those who read aloud from the Vedas;
Numberless those Yogis who are detached from the world;

Numberless are Thy Saints contemplating,
Thy virtues and Thy wisdom;
Numberless are the benevolent, the lovers of their kind.
Numberless Thy heroes and martyrs
Facing the steel of their enemies;
Numberless those who in silence
Fix their deepest thoughts upon Thee;

How can an insignificant creature like myself
Express the vastness and wonder of Thy creation?
I am too petty to have anything to offer Thee;
I cannot, even once, be a sacrifice unto Thee.
To abide by Thy Will, O Lord, is man's best offering;
Thou who art Eternal, abiding in Thy Peace.

18
There is no counting fools, the morally blind;
No counting thieves and the crooked,
No counting the shedders of the innocent blood;
No counting the sinners who go on sinning;
No counting the liars who take pleasure in lies;
No counting the dirty wretches who live on filth;
No counting the calumniators
Who carry about on their heads their loads of sin.

Thus saith Nānak, lowliest of the lowly:
I am too petty to have anything to offer Thee;
I cannot, even once, be a sacrifice unto Thee.
To abide by Thy Will, O Lord, is man's best offering;
Thou who art Eternal, abiding in Thy Peace.

19
Countless are Thy Names, countless Thine abodes;
Completely beyond the grasp of the imagination
Are Thy myriad realms;
Even to call them myriad is foolish.
Yet through words and through letters
Is Thy Name uttered and Thy praise expressed;
In words we praise Thee,
In words we sing of Thy virtues.

It is in the words that we write and speak about Thee,
In words on man's forehead
Is written man's destiny,
But God who writes that destiny
Is free from the bondage of words.

As God ordaineth, so man receiveth.
All creation is His Word made manifest;
Except in the Light of His Word
There is no way.
How can an insignificant creature like myself
Express the vastness and wonder of Thy creation?
I am too petty to have anything to offer Thee;
I cannot, even once, be a sacrifice unto Thee.
To abide by Thy Will, O Lord, is man's best offering;
Thou who art Eternal, abiding in Thy Peace.

20
When the hands, feet and other parts
Of the body are besmeared with filth,
They are cleansed with water;
When a garment is defiled
It is rinsed with soapsuds;
So when the mind is polluted with sin,
We must scrub it in love of the Name.

We do not become sinners or saints,
By merely saying we are;
It is actions that are recorded;
According to the seed we sow, is the fruit we reap.
By God's Will, O Nānak,
Man must either be saved or endure new births.

21

Pilgrimages, penances, compassion and almsgiving
Bring a little merit, the size of sesame seed.
But he who hears and believes and loves the Name
Shall bathe and be made clean
In a place of pilgrimage within him.
All goodness is Thine, O Lord, I have none;
Though without performing good deeds
None can aspire to adore Thee.
Blessed Thou the Creator and the Manifestation,
Thou art the word, Thou art the primal Truth and Beauty,
And Thou the heart's joy and desire.

When in time, in what age, in what day of the month or week
In what season and in what month didst Thou create the world?
The Pundits do not know or they would have written it in the Purāṇas;
The Qazis do not know, or they would have recorded it in the Koran;
Nor do the Yogis know the moment of the day,
Nor the day of the month or the week, nor the month nor the season.
Only God Who made the world knows when He made it.

Then how shall I approach Thee, Lord?
In what words shall I praise Thee?
In what words shall I speak of Thee?
How shall I know Thee?
O Nānak, all men speak of Him, and each would be wiser than the next
    man;
Great is the Lord, great is His Name,
What He ordaineth, that cometh to pass,
Nānak, the man puffed up with his own wisdom
Will get no honour from God in the life to come.

22

There are hundreds of thousands of worlds below and above ours,
And scholars grow weary of seeking for God's bounds.
The Vedas proclaim with one voice that He is boundless.
The Semitic Books mention eighteen hundred worlds;
But the Reality behind all is the One Principle.

If it could be written, it would have been,
But men have exhausted themselves in the effort;
O Nānak, call the Lord Great;
None but He knoweth how great He is.

23

Thy praisers praise Thee,
And know not Thy greatness;
As rivers and streams flow into the sea,
But know not its vastness.

Kings who possess dominions vast as the sea,
With wealth heaped high as the mountain,
Are not equal to the little worm
That forgetteth not God in its heart.

24

Infinite in His Goodness, and infinite its praise;
Infinite are His Works and infinite His gifts;
Where are the bounds of His seeing or His hearing?
Unfathomable in the infinity of His Mind;
There are no bounds even to His creation.
How many vex their hearts to know His limits
But seeking to explore Infinity, can find no bounds;
The more we say, the more there is left to say;
High is our Lord and very High is His throne;
His holy Name is higher than the highest.

He that would know His height, must be of the same height;
Only the Lord knoweth the greatness of the Lord.
Saith Nānak, only be God's grace and bounty
Are God's gifts bestowed on man.

25

Of His bounty one cannot write enough;
He is the great Giver, Who covets nothing;
How many mighty warriors beg at His door;
How many others, in numbers beyond reckoning.

Many waste His gifts in idle pleasure,
Many receive His gifts and yet deny Him;
Many are the fools who merely eat,
Many are always sorrowing and hungering;
Sorrow and hunger are also Thy gifts.

Liberation from bondage depends upon Thy Will;
There is no one to gainsay it;
Should a fool wish to,
Suffering will teach him wisdom.

The Lord knoweth what to give and He giveth;
Few acknowledge this. Those on whom He bestows,
O Nānak, the gift of praising Him and adoring Him
Are the true Kings of Kings.

26
Priceless are His attributes,
Priceless His dealings;
Priceless the stores of His virtues,
Priceless the dealers in them;
Priceless those who seek these gifts,
Priceless those who take these gifts.

Pricelessly precious is devotion to Thee,
Pricelessly precious is absorption in Thee;
Priceless His Law and spirit of righteousness,
Priceless His Mansions of dispensation;
Priceless His scales of judgement,
Priceless His weights for judging.

Priceless His gifts,
Priceless His marks upon them;
Priceless His Mercy and priceless His Will;
How beyond price He is cannot be expressed.
Those who try to express it,
Are mute in adoration.

The Vedas proclaim Him,
So do the readers of the Purāṇas;
The learned speak of Him in many discourses;
Brahma and Indra speak of Him,
Śivas speak of Him, Siddhas speak of Him,
The Buddhas He has created, proclaim Him.

The demons and the gods speak of Him,
Demigods, men, sages and devotees
All try to describe Him;
Many have tried and still try to describe Him;
Many have spoken of Him and departed.
If as many people as lived in all the past
Were now to describe Him each in His own way,
Even then He would not be adequately described.
The Lord becometh as great as He wishes to be.
If anyone dares to claim that he can describe Him,
Write him down as the greatest fool on earth.

27
Where is the gate, where the mansion
From whence Thou watchest all creation,
Where sounds of musical melodies,
Of instruments playing, minstrel singing,
Are joined in divine harmony?
In various measures celestial musicians sing of Thee.

There the breezes blow, the waters run and the fires burn,
There Dharmrāj, the king of death, sits in state;
There the recording angels Chitra and Gupta write
For Dharmrāj to read and adjudicate;
There are the gods Īśvara and Brahma,
The goddess Pārvatī adorned in beauty,
There Indra sits on his celestial throne
And lesser gods, each in his place;
One and all sing of Thee.

There ascetics in deep meditation,
Holy men in contemplation,
The pure of heart, the continent,
Men of peace and contentment,
Doughty warriors never yielding
Thy praises ever singing.
From age to age, the pundit and the sage
Do Thee exalt in their studies;
There maidens fair, heart bewitching,
Who inhabit the earth, the upper and the lower regions,
Thy praises chant in their singing.

By the gems that Thou didst create,
In the sixty-eight places of pilgrimage
Is Thy Name exalted;
By warriors strong and brave in strife,
By the sources four from whence came life,
Of egg or womb, of sweat or seed,
Is Thy Name magnified.

The regions of the earth, the heavens and the Universe
That Thou didst make and dost sustain,
Sing to Thee and praise Thy Name.
Only those Thou lovest and have Thy grace
Can give Thee praise and in Thy love be steeped.

Others too there must be who Thee acclaim,
I have no memory of knowing them
Nor of knowledge, O Nānak, make a claim.
He alone is the Master true, Lord of the Word, ever the same.
He who made creation, is, shall be and shall ever remain;
He who made things of diverse species, shapes and hues,
Beholds that His handiwork His greatness proves.

What He Wills He ordains,
To Him no one can an order give,
For He, O Nānak, is the King of Kings,
As He Wills so we must live.

28
Going forth a begging,
Let contentment be thine earings,
Modesty thy begging bowl,
Smear thy body with ashes of meditation,
Let contemplation of death be thy beggar's rags;

Let thy body be chaste, virginal, clean,
Let faith in God be the staff on which thou leanest;
Let brotherhood with every man on earth
Be the highest aspiration of your Yogic Order.
Know that to subdue the mind
Is to subdue the world.
Hail, all hail unto Him,
Let your greetings be to the Primal God;
Pure and without beginning, changeless,
The same from age to age.

29

Let knowledge of God be thy food,
Let mercy keep thy store,
And listen to the Divine Music
That beats in every heart.

He is the supreme Master,
He holdeth the nosestring of creation;
In the secret powers and magics,
There is no true saviour.

Union with God and separation from Him
Are according to His Will,
What each gets is his meed.
Hail, all hail unto Him,
Let your greetings be to the Primal Lord;
Pure and without beginning, changeless,
The same from age to age.

30

Māyā, the mythical goddess,
Sprang from the One, and her womb brought forth
Three acceptable disciples of the One:
Brahma, Viṣṇu and Śiva.
Brahma, it is said bodies forth the world,
Viṣṇu it is who sustains it;
Śiva the destroyer who absorbs,
He controls death and judgement.
God makes them to work as He wills,
He sees them ever, they see Him not:
That of all is the greatest wonder.

Hail, all hail unto Him,
Let your greetings be to the Primal Lord;
Pure and without beginning, changeless,
The same from age to age.

31

God has His seat everywhere,
His treasure houses are in all places.
Whatever a man's portion is
God at the creation
Apportioned him that share once and for all.
What He has created
The Lord for ever contemplates.
O Nānak, true are His works
As He Himself is the True.

Hail, all hail unto Him,
Let your greetings be to the Primal Lord;
Pure and without beginning, changeless,
The same from age to age.

32

Let my tongue become a hundred thousand tongues,
Let the hundred thousand be multiplied twenty-fold,
With each tongue many hundred thousands of times
I would repeat the holy Name of the Lord;
Thus let the soul step by step
Mount the stairs to the Bridegroom
And become one with Him.
On hearing of heavenly things,
He who can only crawl also longs to fly.
By God's grace alone, saith Nānak, is God to be grasped.
All else is false, all else is vanity.

33

Ye have no power to speak or in silence listen,
To ask or to give away;
Ye have no power to live or die,
Ye have no power to acquire wealth and dominion and be vain,
Ye have no power to compel the mind to thought or reason,
He who hath the power, He creates and sees;
O Nānak, before the Lord there is no low or high degree.

34

God made the night and the day,
The days of the week and the months,
And He made the seasons;
He made winds to blow and water to run,
He made fire, He made the lower regions;
In the midst of all this He set the earth as a temple,
On it He set a diversity of creatures,
Various in kind and colour
Endless the number of their names.

All these lives are judged by their actions.
God is True and in His Court is truth dispensed;
There the elects are acceptable to Him,
And by His grace and His mercy
Honoured in His presence.
In that Court the bad shall be sifted from the good
When we reach His Court, O Nānak
We shall know this to be true.

35

I have described the realm of *dharma*,
Now I shall describe the realm of Knowledge;

How many are the winds, the fires, the waters,
How many are the Krishṇas and Śivas,
How many are the Brahmas fashioning the worlds,
Of many kinds and shapes and colours;
How many worlds, like our own there are,
Where action produces the consequences.

How many holy mountains to be climbed,
With how many sages, like Dhruva's teacher, Nārada
On the top of them.
How many adepts, Buddhas and Yogis are there,
How many goddesses and how many the images of the goddesses;
How many gods and demons and how many sages;

How many hidden jewels in how many oceans,
How many the sources of life;
How many the modes and diversities of speech,
How many are the kings, the rulers and the guides of men;
How many the devoted there are, who pursue this divine knowledge,
His worshippers are numberless, saith Nānak.

36

As in the realm of Knowledge wisdom shines forth,
And Music is heard from which myriad joys proceed;
So in the realm of Spiritual endeavour
The presiding deity is Beauty.
All things are shaped there incomparably,
The beauty of the place is beyond description;
And whoever even attempts to describe it,
Will certainly afterwards feel deep remorse:
Understanding, discernment, the deepest wisdom is fashioned there.
There are created the gifts of the sages and the seers.

37

In the realm of Grace, spiritual power is supreme,
Nothing else avails;
There dwell doughty warriors brave and strong,
In whom is the Lord's Spirit,
And who by His praise are blended in Him.
Their beauty is beyond telling,
In their hearts the Lord dwelleth,
They do not die and they are not deceived.

There dwell also the congregations of the blessed,
In bliss they dwell, with the true one in their hearts.

In the realm of Truth,
Dwelleth the Formless One
Who, having created, watcheth His creation
And where He looks upon them with Grace;
And His creatures are happy.
All continents, worlds and universes
Are contained in this supreme realm;
Were one to strive to make an account of them all,
There would be no end to the count.

World there is on world there, form upon form there,
And all have their functions as God's will ordaineth;
The Lord seeth His creation and seeing it He rejoiceth.
O Nānak, the telling is hard, as iron is hard to hand.

38

In the forge of continence,
Let patience be the goldsmith,
On the anvil of understanding
Let him strike with the hammer of knowledge.

Let the fear of God be the bellows,
Let austerities be the fire,
Let the love of God be the crucible,
Let the nectar of life be melted in it;

Thus in the mint of Truth,
A man may coin the Word,
This is the practice of those
On whom God looks with favour.
Nānak, our gracious Lord
With a glance makes us happy.

Epilogue

Air like the Guru's Word gives us the breath of life,
Water sires us, earth is our mother.
Day and night are the two nurses
That watch over the world,
And in whose lap we all play.

On good as well as our bad deeds
Shall be read His judgement;
As we have acted,
Some of us shall be near to God
Some of us far away.

Those that have meditated
On the Holy Name,
And have departed, their task completed,
Their faces are those of shining ones and, O Nānak,
How many they bring to liberty in their train.

EVENING PRAYER

EVENING PRAYER

Translated by Khushwant Singh
and others

1

(This, the First Hymn of the Evening Prayer is the same as the Twenty-Seventh Hymn of the Morning Prayer.)

2

On hearing of the Lord,
All men speak of His greatness;
Only he that hath seen Him
Can know how great is He.
Who can conceive of His worth
Or who can describe Him?
Those who seek to describe Thee
Are lost in Thy depths.

O Great Lord, of depth unfathomable,
Ocean of virtues!
Who knoweth the bounds of Thy shores?
All the contemplatives
Have met and sought to contemplate Thee;
All the weighers of worth
Have met and sought to weigh Thy worth;
All the theologians and the mystics,
All the preachers and their teachers
Have not been able to grasp
One jot of Thy greatness.
All truths, all fervent austerities, every excellent act,
Every sublime achievement of the adepts,
Are Thy gifts, O Lord: without Thee
No man could attain perfection;
But where Thou hast granted Thy grace to a man,
Nothing can stand in his way.

How vain are the words of those that seek to praise Thee,
Thy treasuries are already filled with Thy praises;
He to whom Thou givest freely,
What should he do but praise Thee?

Saith Nānak: The True One is He
From whom all perfection springs.

3

If I remember Him I live,
If I forget Him I die;
Hard very hard indeed it is
To contemplate His Name;
If a man hungers after His Name
In that holy hunger
He consumeth all His pains.
True is the Lord
True is His Name.
O Mother, how can He be forgotten?

Even in praising a tiny part of His Name
Men grow weary but His true worth is not weighed;
If all men were to meet, and begin to try to exalt Him,
He would grow neither greater nor lesser by their praise.
He does not die, He does not suffer sorrow;
Ever He giveth, and never His store faileth.
This is the greatest wonder in Him,
That there never was nor there ever will be,
Another like to the Lord.
As great as Thou Thyself art, O my Lord,
So great are Thy gifts; as Thou madest the day,
So Thou madest the night also.
He who forgets Thee is low born
O Nānak: without His Name
Man is like the lowest of the outcasts.

4

O Servant of God, True Guru, Truth's true embodiment:
We that are low worms, seek our refuge in thee;
Mercifully bestow on us the light of the True Name.

O my friend, my divine Guru! set alight His Name within me;
The Name taught by my Guru is the help of my soul;
The praise of the Lord is my vocation;
Happy, most happy are the Lord's people,
Who have faith in the Lord, who thirst for Him,
And with the gift of His Name their thirst is slaked.
Then in the company of the blessed: they exalt His virtues.

Unhappy, most unhappy are those,
To whom is not granted the sweet savour of His Name;
Death is their portion
Who have not sought their refuge
With the True Guru;
Nor have come to the congregation of the saints;
Accursed be their lives,
Accursed be the hopes they set on living.
The blessed who have entered into the companionship
Of the True Guru,
Are those on whose foreheads from the very beginning
This blessed fate was written.
Hail, hail to the holy congregation
In whose midst is the sweet savour of the Lord;
In the company of the saints, O Nānak,
The Lord sheddeth the true Light of His Name.

5
O my soul, why art thou busy and troubled
When thou knowest the Lord will provide?
In the rocks and stones He hath set living creatures,
He putteth their food before them.

Beloved Lord, they who fall in with the company of the blessed,
Shall obtain their liberation.
By the grace of the Guru
They shall attain the state supreme;
Yea, though they were as the dry tree
They shall again be green.

Not on thy father or mother,
Not on the friends of thy household,
Not on thy wife nor on thy son,
Darest thou lean for thy daily bread:
The Lord provideth all
Why have fear in the mind.

The migrating cranes fly hundreds of miles,
They leave their young behind them.
Think, O Man: Who feedeth the young birds?
God holdeth as in His palm
All the treasures of the world
And all the eighteen occult powers;
O Nānak, for ever and ever
Make thy heart a sacrifice unto Him.
There is no end or limit to His Being.

6
That Being is Pure; He is without stain;
He is Infinite and beyond comprehension;
All worship Thee, all bow to Thee:
Thou who art Truth and the Creator.
All creatures are Thine, for all of them Thou provideth;
O saint, meditate on the Lord: who makes sorrow to be forgotten;
He Himself is the Lord, He Himself is the worshipper;
O Nānak, how insignificant is man.

Thou, O Lord, O One Supreme Being!
Thou art in every heart and soul,
Thou pervadest all things:
Some men beg for alms, some bestow them,
All this is the great game Thou playest.
It is Thou who givest and enjoyest the gifts,
I know of none other beside Thee.
Thou art the utterly Transcendent:
Infinite art Thou! Infinite art Thou!
How can I describe Thy attributes?
Unto those who serve and worship Thee truly
Nānak is a humble sacrifice.
They who think on Thee, they who meditate on Thee,
In this dark age have their peace.
They who think on Thee: they are saved, they are liberated;
For them death's noose is broken.

Those who meditate on the Fearless One
Will lose all their fear;
Those who have worshipped the Lord,
In the Lord they are now mingled.
Blest and blest again are those
That have set their thoughts on the Lord.
The humble Nānak is a sacrifice unto them.
O Lord, Thy inexhaustible treasure
Is filled and refilled with Thy worship;
O many and innumerable are the saints who adore Thee,
Manifold are their devotions;
They practise austerities and endlessly repeat Thy Name,
How many read the Smrities and Shastras, perform the six Hindu
   Observances.
But only those are truly saints
Who have won the love of my Lord.
Thou art the Primal Being, the Creator:
None setteth bounds on Thee, there is none other so great;
From age to age one and the same:
Ever and ever art Thou the same: Immovable Creator.
Whatever Thou willest, it is,
As Thou actest, so Thy acts prevaileth.
It is Thou who createst all things
And by whose command all things pass away.
Nānak singeth the praises of the Maker: the All-knowing.

7

Lord, Creator and Truth,
As Thy Will is, it is done; as Thou givest I receive;
All that is, is Thine: all men adore Thee;
Those whom Thou favourest have gotten the jewel of Thy Name.
The enlightened have sought it; the self-willed have lost it;
It is Thou who settest apart and Thou who unitest.

Thou art the Ocean: all things are within Thee,
There is none other beside Thee,
All the living are merely the game Thou playest;
By Thee, having fallen apart, one is set apart;
By Thee, being in union, one is united.

He whom Thou makest to know Thee, he knoweth Thee
And his mouth shall be for ever full of Thy praises;
He who has truly served the Lord is happy
And with ease is absorbed into the Divine Name.

Thou art the Creator: all that is, is Thy handiwork;
There is none other beside Thee.
What Thou createst, that Thou seest and knowest.
Through the Guru, saith Nānak,
Thou art revealed in Thy Truth.

8

Man, thou dwellest in the world that is as a pool,
Whose waters God hath made as hot as fire.
Stuck in the mire of worldly love, thy feet cannot move forward,
I have seen people drowning in this swamp.
O heart, O foolish heart, why thinkest thou not on the One?
Through forgetting thy Lord, thy virtues have melted away.

I am not chaste nor honest, I am not even a scholar;
Foolish and ignorant I came into the world,
O Lord, Nānak prayeth ever to seek
The sanctuary of their gathering
Who have not forgotten Thee.

9

Thou hast acquired this human frame,
This is thy opportunity to be one with God;
All other labours are unprofitable.
Seek the company of the holy and glorify His Name.
Strenuously prepare to cross this terrible ocean.
Thy life is being wasted
In love of the world's illusions.
I have not repeated His Name,
Nor made penance, practised austerities, nor been pious;
I have not served my Lord's saints nor thought of Him.
Nānak saith, my acts have been low;
Preserve me from shame O Lord,
Since I take my shelter in Thee.

BED-TIME PRAYER

BED-TIME PRAYER

Translated by Khushwant Singh
and others

1

In the house in which men sing the Lord's praises
And meditate upon Him,
In that house sing the songs of praise
And remember the Creator;
Sing the song of praise of thy fearless Lord,
Let me be a sacrifice unto that song,
By which we attain everlasting solace.

Day by day, ever and ever,
He watcheth over His living creatures;
The Bountiful Giver looks after one and all.
Who can set a price on His gifts,
Or say how great is He.

The year and the sacred day for the wedding is fixed,
Comrades! pour oil at the door to welcome the bride;
Give me your blessings, O friends,
I depart for my union with God.

The summons is sent to every house,
To every soul, every day, it is issued;
Remember, O Nānak, Him who sends the summons,
The day is not far when you also may hear it.

2

Six the systems, six their teachers,*
And six their different teachings:
The Lord of them all is the One Lord
However various His aspects are;
O brother, follow that system
That sings the Lord's praises:
There thy true glory lies.

Seconds, minutes, hours, quarters of a day;
Lunar and solar days make up a month,
Yet there are many times and many seasons;
One single sun runs through them all.
O Nānak, Thy Lord is likewise One,
However various His aspects are.

3

The firmament is Thy salver,
The sun and the moon Thy lamps;
The galaxy of stars are as pearls scattered,
The woods of sandal are Thine incense.
The breezes blow Thy royal fan;
The flowers of the forests,
Lie as offerings at Thy feet.
What wonderful worship with lamps is this
O Thou destroyer of fear!
Unstruck Music is the sound of Thy temple drums.
Thousands are Thine eyes,
And yet Thou hast no eyes;
Thousands are Thy shapes,
And yet Thou hast no shape;
Thousands are Thy pure feet,
And yet Thou hast not one foot;
Thousands are Thy noses
And yet Thou hast no nose.

* Guru Nānak says that Divine Wisdom is like the Sun and the six Hindu systems
are like the seasons.

All this is Thy play and bewitches me.
In every heart there is light:
That light art Thou.
By the Light that is of God Himself
Is every soul illumined:
But this divine Light becomes manifest
Only by the Guru's teachings.
What is pleasing to Thee, O Lord
Is the best *arti*: worship with the lamps.

O Lord, my mind yearns for Thy lotus feet,
As the honey-bee for the nectar of the flowers.
Night and day Lord, I am athirst for Thee,
Give water of Thy mercy to Nānak:
He is like the sārang: the hawk-cuckoo that drinks only rain drops
So that he may dwell ever in the peace of Thy Name.

4

With lust and with anger,
The city, that is thy body
Is full to the brim.
Meet as saint and destroy
That lust and that anger.
By God's decree
I have found my Guru
And my soul is absorbed
In the love of My Lord.
Bow humbly to the saint
That is a pious act.
Bow to the ground before him
That is devotion, indeed.

The faithless know not,
The joy of the love of the Lord;
In their hearts
Is the thorn of self-love,
And each step they take,
It pierces deeper and deeper
And they feel pain and sorrow
Till they bring death on their heads.

The Lord's chosen are absorbed in the Lord's Name.
The pain of birth and the fear of death are broken.
They have attained the Imperishable Lord;
Great honour is theirs in all regions.

I am poor and wretched,
But I am Thine, O Lord:
Save me, O save me
Thou greatest of the great.
Thy Name, to Thy slave Nānak
Is as his staff and his shield.
Only in the Name of the Lord
I have found my comfort.

5
I supplicate thee, my friend, to listen to me,
Here and now is the time to serve the saints;
Here, in this world, acquire the gain of godliness;
Thou shalt have ease enough in the world to come.
By day and by night the sum of the days decreaseth:
Seek the True Guru and balance thine accounts.

The world is awry, is illusionary. The man
Who knoweth God, the Brahm-jñani, is saved.
Whom God awakeneth to drink of His Name's essence,
He knowest the Unknowable, whose story can never be told.

Strive to seek that
For which thou hast come into the world,
And through the grace of the Guru
God will dwell in thy heart.
Thou shalt abide in His Presence,
In comfort and in peace
And not return ever
To be born and to die once more.

O God, Searcher of hearts,
O God, who dispensest to each of us
The fruits of our acts,
Fulfil one wish of my heart:
Nānak, thy slave, craveth
The boon that he may be made
The dust that clings to the soles
Of the feet, O Lord, of the saints.

V

ISLAM

Quran
The Deliverance from Error
– Al Ghazali
Poems – Rumi

When we turn to the two great traditions of Semitic mono-theism, Judaism and Islam, we have to recognize that they were both born and bred in violence and conflict. Israel emerged as a separate nation with the massacre of the first-born of the Egyptians and the conquest of Palestine, and Islam emerged as a separate religion with the battle with the people of Mecca. Violence and conflict have accompanied each religion until the present day. In each religion a profound faith in one God, opposed to every form of polytheism, became the vital principle, which distinguished them from all other religions and united people of different races and cultures and customs and languages in faith in one God and in a revelation contained in one sacred Book. One cannot deny the power of this faith or question of depth of its understanding of God as "the merciful, the compassionate", holy and just, creator and saviour, Lord of the world. Yet one cannot also ignore the negative aspect of this monotheism. Though God is merciful and compassionate to all believers, he is relentless in his animosity towards unbelievers. All the worst characteristics of a dominating warlike people are projected on to their God. He is depicted as angry, vengeful, jealous, vindictive and merciless towards his enemies and those who do not believe in him. It is not surprising that these religions have left a trail of blood behind them and that they continue to divide the world at the present day.

Yet when we have said this, we must not be thought to condemn the Jew or the Muslim today. Jews and Muslims today are challenged to transcend the cultural limitations of their religions, as are Christians and Hindus. We cannot deny that the divine wisdom and the divine goodness are revealed in the Bible and the Quran in a unique way. But the divine revelation always comes through a human medium, and it is in the psychological and social dimensions of religion that its limitations become clear. It is religion itself which is being challenged today. No religion which projects an unworthy image of God can hope to survive much longer; Christianity no less than any other religion comes under this judgement. We are being challenged to purify our religion from all traces of its primitive origin, to see it in the context of other religions and of the scientific world today. The world is looking for a religion which will unify humanity and give ultimate meaning and purpose to the world in which we live. Science today has undergone a "paradigm" shift, as the old Newtonian, mechanistic system has collapsed and relativity and quantum physics have taken its place. Religion today is called to undergo a similar paradigm shift, as it faces the new vision of the world which is emerging, as we see this world, this planet, this cosmos, to which we belong, in the light of our present understanding of science and of the universal wisdom which underlies all religion.

QURAN

SURA 24:35

QURAN

SURA 24:35

Translated by N. J. Darwood

Light (24:35)

Allah is the light of the heavens and the earth.
His light may be compared to a niche that enshrines
a lamp, the lamp within a crystal of star-like brilliance.
It is lit from a blessed Olive tree . . .

. . . Allah gives without measure to whom He will.

DELIVERANCE FROM ERROR

by Al Ghazali

SELECTED EXTRACTS

Translated by Montgomery Watt

DELIVERANCE FROM ERROR

AND ATTACHMENT TO THE LORD OF
MIGHT AND MAJESTY

In the name of God, the Merciful and Compassionate

Part One
Introduction

Praise be to Him with Whose praise every message and every discourse
commences. And blessings be upon Muhammad the Chosen, the Prophet
and Messenger, and on his house and his Companions, who guide men
away from error.

You have asked me, my brother in religion, to show you the aims and
inmost nature of the sciences and the perplexing depths of the religious
systems. You have begged me to relate to you the difficulties I encountered in my attempt to extricate the truth from the confusion of contending sects and to distinguish the different ways and methods, and the
venture I made in climbing from the plain of naïve and second-half belief
(*taqlīd*) to the peak of direct vision. You want me to describe, firstly, what
profit I derived from the science of theology (*kalām*), secondly, what I
disapprove of in the methods of the party of *ta'līm* (authoritative instruction), who restrict the apprehension of truth to the blind following (*taqlīd*)
of the Imam, thirdly, what I rejected of the methods of philosophy, and
lastly, what I approved in the Sufi way of life. You would know, too, what
essential truths became clear to me in my manifold investigations into
the doctrines held by men, why I gave up teaching in Baghdad although
I had many students, and why I returned to it at Naysābūr (Nīshāpūr)
after a long interval. I am proceeding to answer your request, for I recognize that your desire is genuine. In this I seek the help of God and trust
in Him; I ask His succour and take refuge with Him.

You must know – and may God most high perfect you in the right way
and soften your hearts to receive the truth – that the different religious
observances and religious communities of the human race and likewise
the different theological systems of the religious leaders, with all the
multiplicity of sects and variety of practices, constitute ocean depths in
which the majority drown and only a minority reach safety. Each separate
group thinks that it alone is saved, and "each party is rejoicing in what
they have" (Q. 23, 55; 30, 31). This is what was foretold by the prince
of the Messengers (God bless him), who is true and trustworthy, when

he said, "My community will be split up into seventy-three sects, and but one of them is saved"; and what he foretold has indeed almost come about.

From my early youth, since I attained the age of puberty before I was twenty, until the present time when I am over fifty, I have ever recklessly launched out into the midst of these ocean depths, I have ever bravely embarked on this open sea, throwing aside all craven caution; I have poked into every dark recess, I have made an assault on every problem, I have plunged into every abyss, I have scrutinized the creed of every sect, I have tried to lay bare the inmost doctrines of every community. All this have I done that I might distinguish between true and false, between sound tradition and heretical innovation. Whenever I meet one of the Bāṭinīyah, I like to study his creed; whenever I meet one of the Zāhirīyah, I want to know the essentials of his belief. If it is a philosopher, I try to become acquainted with the essence of his philosophy; if a scholastic theologian I busy myself in examining his theological reasoning; if a Sufi, I yearn to fathom the secret of his mysticism; if an ascetic (*muta'ab-bid*), I investigate the basis of his ascetic practices; if one of the Zanādiqah or Mu'aṭṭilah, I look beneath the surface to discover the reasons for his bold adoption of such a creed.

To thirst after a comprehension of things as they really are was my habit and custom from a very early age. It was instinctive with me, a part of my God-given nature, a matter of temperament and not of my choice or contriving. Consequently as I drew near the age of adolescence the bonds of mere authority (*taqlīd*) ceased to hold me and inherited beliefs lost their grip upon me, for I saw that Christian youths always grew up to be Christians, Jewish youths to be Jews and Muslim youths to be Muslims. I heard, too, the Tradition related of the Prophet of God according to which he said: "Everyone who is born is born with a sound nature; it is his parents who make him a Jew or a Christian or a Magian." My inmost being was moved to discover what this original nature really was and what the beliefs derived from the authority of parents and teachers really were. The attempt to distinguish between these authority-based opinions and their principles developed the mind, for in distinguishing the true in them from the false differences appeared.

I therefore said within myself: "To begin with, what I am looking for is knowledge of what things really are, so I must undoubtedly try to find what knowledge really is." It was plain to me that sure and certain knowledge is that knowledge in which the object is disclosed in such a fashion that no doubt remains along with it, that no possibility of error or illusion accompanies it, and that the mind cannot even entertain such a supposition. Certain knowledge must also be infallible; and this infallibility or security from error is such that no attempt to show the falsity of the knowledge can occasion doubt or denial, even though the attempt is made by someone who turns stones into gold or a rod into a serpent. Thus, I know that ten is more than three. Let us suppose that someone says to me: "No, three is more than ten, and in proof of that I shall change this rod into a serpent"; and let us suppose that he actually changes the rod into a serpent and that I witness him doing so. No doubts about what I know are raised in me because of this. The only result is that I wonder precisely how he is able to produce this change. Of doubt about my knowledge there is no trace.

After these reflections I knew that whatever I do not know in this fashion and with this mode of certainty is not reliable and infallible knowledge; and knowledge that is not infallible is not certain knowledge.

Part Two
Preliminaries:
Scepticism and the Denial of all Knowledge

Thereupon I investigated the various kinds of knowledge I had, and found myself destitute of all knowledge with this characteristic of infallibility except in the case of sense-perception and necessary truths. So I said: "Now that despair has come over me, there is no point in studying any problems except on the basis of what is self-evident, namely, necessary truths and the affirmations of the senses. I must first bring these to be judged in order that I may be certain on this matter. Is my reliance on sense-perception and my trust in the soundness of necessary truths of the same kind as my previous trust in the beliefs I had merely taken over from others and as the trust most men have in the result of thinking? Or is it a justified trust that is in no danger of being betrayed or destroyed?"

I proceeded therefore with extreme earnestness to reflect on sense-perception and on necessary truths, to see whether I could make myself doubt them. The outcome of this protracted effort to induce doubt was that I could no longer trust sense-perception either. Doubt began to spread here and say: "From where does this reliance on sense-perception come? The most powerful sense is that of sight. Yet when it looks at the shadow (*sc.* of a stick or the gnomon of a sundial), it sees it standing still, and judges that there is no motion. Then by experiment and observation after an hour it knows that the shadow is moving and, moreover, that it is moving not by fits and starts but gradually and steadily by infinitely small distances in such a way that it is never in a state of rest. Again, it looks at the heavenly body (*sc.* the sun) and sees it small, the size of a shilling; yet geometrical computations show that it is greater than the earth in size."

In this and similar cases of sense-perception the sense as judge forms his judgements, but another judge, the intellect, shows him repeatedly to be wrong; and the charge of falsity cannot be rebutted.

To this I said: "My reliance on sense-perception also has been destroyed. Perhaps only those intellectual truths which are first principles (or derived from first principles) are to be relied upon, such as the assertion that ten are more than three, that the same thing cannot be both affirmed and denied at one time, that one thing is not both generated in time and eternal, nor both existence and non-existence, nor both necessary and impossible."

Sense-perception replied: "Do you not expect that your reliance on intellectual truths will fare like your reliance on sense-perception? You used to trust in me; then along came the intellect-judge and proved me wrong; if it were not for the intellect-judge you would have continued to regard me as true. Perhaps behind intellectual apprehension there is another judge who, if he manifests himself, will show the falsity of intellect in its judging, just as, when intellect manifested itself, it showed the falsity of sense in its judging. The fact that such a supra-intellectual apprehension has not manifested itself is no proof that it is impossible."

My ego hesitated a little about the reply to that, and sense-perception heightened the difficulty by referring to dreams. "Do you not see", it said, "how, when you are asleep, you believe things and imagine circumstances, holding them to be stable and enduring, and, so long as you are in that dream-condition, have no doubts about them? And is it not the case that when you awake you know that all you have imagined and believed is unfounded and ineffectual? They are true in respect of your present state; but it is possible that a state will come upon you whose relation to your waking consciousness is analogous to the relation of the latter to dreaming. In comparison with this state your waking consciousness would be like dreaming! When you have entered into this state, you will be certain that all the suppositions of your intellect are empty imaginings. It may be that that state is what the Sufis claim as their special 'state' (*sc.* mystic union or ecstasy), which occur when they have withdrawn into themselves and are absent from their senses, they witness states (or circumstances) which do not tally with these principles of the intellect. Perhaps that 'state' is death; for the Messenger of God (God bless and preserve him) says: 'The people are dreaming; when they die, they become awake'. So perhaps life in this world is a dream by comparison with the world to come; and when a man dies, things come to appear differently to him from what he now beholds, and at the same time the words are addressed to him: 'We have taken off thee thy covering, and thy sight today is sharp'" (Q. 50, 21).

When these thoughts had occurred to me and penetrated my being, I tried to find some way of treating my unhealthy condition; but it was not easy. Such ideas can only be repelled by demonstration; but a demonstration requires a knowledge of first principles; since this is not admitted, however, it is impossible to make the demonstration. The disease was baffling, and lasted almost two months, during which I was a sceptic in fact though not in theory nor in outward expression. At length God cured me of the malady; my being was restored to health and an even balance; the necessary truths of the intellect became once more accepted, as I regained confidence in their certain and trustworthy character.

This did not come about by systematic demonstration or marshalled argument, but by a light which God most high cast into my breast. That light is the key to the greater part of knowledge. Whoever thinks that the understanding of things Divine rests upon strict proofs has in his thought narrowed down the wideness of God's mercy. When the Messenger of God (peace be upon him) was asked about "enlarging" (*sharḥ*) and its meaning in the verse, "Whenever God wills to guide a man, He enlarges his breast for *islām* [i.e. surrender to God]" (Q. 6, 125), he said, "It is a light which God most high casts into the heart." When asked, "What is the sign of it?", he said, "Withdrawal from the mansion of deception and return to the mansion of eternity." It was about this light that Muhammad (peace be upon him) said, "God created the creatures in darkness, and then sprinkled upon them some of His light." From that light must be sought an intuitive understanding of things Divine. That light at certain times gushes from the spring of Divine generosity, and for it one must watch and wait – as Muhammad (peace be upon him) said: "In the days of your age your Lord has gusts of favour; then place yourselves in the way of them."

The point of these accounts is that the task is perfectly fulfilled when the quest is prosecuted up to the stage of seeking what is not sought (but stops short of that). For first principles are not sought, since they are present and to hand; and if what is present is sought for, it becomes hidden and lost. When, however, a man seeks what is sought (and that only), he is not accused of falling short in the seeking of what is sought.

Part Three
The Classes of Seekers

When God by His grace and abundant generosity cured me of this disease, I came to regard the various seekers (*sc.* after truth) as comprising four groups:

1 the **Theologians** (*mutakallimūn*), who claim that they are the exponents of thought and intellectual speculation;

2 the **Bāṭinīyah**, who consider that they, as the party of "authoritative instruction" (*ta'līm*), alone derive truth from the infallible *imam*;

3 the **Philosophers**, who regard themselves as the exponents of logic and demonstration;

4 the **Sufis** or **Mystics**, who claim that they alone enter into the "presence" (*sc.* of God), and possess vision and intuitive understanding.

I said within myself: "The truth cannot lie outside these four classes. These are the people who treat the paths of the quest for truth. If the truth is not with them, no point remains in trying to apprehend the truth. There is certainly no point in trying to return to the level of naïve and derivative belief (*taqlīd*) once it has been left, since a condition of being at such a level is that one should not know one is there; when a man comes to know that, the glass of his naïve beliefs is broken. This is a breakage which cannot be mended, a breakage not to be repaired by patching or by assembling of fragments. The glass must be melted once again in the furnace for a new start, and out of it another fresh vessel formed."

I now hastened to follow out these four ways and investigate what these groups had achieved, commencing with the science of theology and then taking the way of philosophy, the "authoritative instruction" of the Bāṭinī-yah, and the way of mysticism, in that order.

1
The Science of Theology: its Aims and Achievements

I commenced, then, with the science of Theology (*'ilm al-kalām*), and obtained a thorough grasp of it. I read the books of sound theologians and myself wrote some books on the subject. But it was a science, I found, which, though attaining its own aim, did not attain mine. Its aim was merely to preserve the creed of orthodoxy and to defend it against the deviations of heretics.

Now God sent to His servants by the mouth of His messenger, in the

Qur'an and Traditions, a creed which is the truth and those contents are the basis of man's welfare in both religious and secular affairs. But Satan too sent, in the suggestions of heretics, things contrary to orthodoxy; men tended to accept his suggestions and almost corrupted the true creed for its adherents. So God brought into being the class of theologians, and moved them to support traditional orthodoxy with the weapon of systematic argument by laying bare the confused doctrines invented by the heretics at variance with traditional orthodoxy. This is the origin of theology and theologians.

In due course a group of theologians performed the task to which God invited them; they successfully preserved orthodoxy, defended the creed received from the prophetic source and rectified heretical innovations. Nevertheless in so doing they based their arguments on premises which they took from their opponents and which they were compelled to admit by naïve belief (*taqlīd*), or the consensus of the community, or bare acceptance of Qur'an and Traditions. For the most part their efforts were devoted to making explicit the contradictions of their opponents and criticizing them in respect of the logical consequences of what they admitted.

This was of little use in the case of one who admitted nothing at all save logically necessary truths. Theology was not adequate to my case and was unable to cure the malady of which I complained. It is true that, when theology appeared as a recognized discipline and much effort had been expended in it over a considerable period of time, the theologians, becoming very earnest in their endeavours to defend orthodoxy by the study of what things really are, embarked on a study of substances and accidents with their nature and properties. But, since that was not the aim of their science, they did not deal with the question thoroughly in their thinking and consequently did not arrive at results sufficient to dispel universally the darkness of confusion due to the different views of men. I do not exclude the possibility that for others than myself these results have been sufficient; indeed, I do not doubt that this has been so for quite a number. But these results were mingled with naïve belief in certain matters which are not included among first principles.

My purpose here, however, is to describe my own case, not to disparage those who sought a remedy thereby, for the healing drugs vary with the disease. How often one sick man's medicine proves to be another's poison!

2
Philosophy

After I had done with theology I started on philosophy. I was convinced that a man cannot grasp what is defective in any of the sciences unless he has so complete a grasp of the science in question that he equals its most learned exponents in the appreciation of its fundamental principles, and even goes beyond and surpasses them, probing into some of the tangles and profundities which the very professors of the science have neglected. Then and only then is it possible that what he has to assert about its defects is true.

So far as I could see none of the doctors of Islam had devoted thought and attention to philosophy. In their writings none of the theologians engaged in polemic against the philosophers, apart from obscure and scattered utterances so plainly erroneous and inconsistent that no person of ordinary intelligence would be likely to be deceived, far less one versed in the sciences.

I realized that to refute a system before understanding it and becoming acquainted with its depths is to act blindly. I therefore set out in all earnestness to acquire a knowledge of philosophy from books, by private study without the help of an instructor. I made progress towards this aim during my hours of free time after teaching in the religious sciences and writing, for at this period I was burdened with the teaching and instruction of three hundred students in Baghdad. By my solitary reading during the hours thus snatched God brought me in less than two years to a complete understanding of the sciences of the philosophers. Thereafter I continued to reflect assiduously for nearly a year on what I had assimilated, going over it in my mind again and again and probing its tangled depths, until I comprehended surely and certainly how far it was deceitful and confusing and how far true and a representation of reality.

3
The Ways of Mysticism

When I had finished with these sciences, I next turned with set purpose to the method of mysticism (or Sufism). I knew that the complete mystic "way" includes both intellectual belief and practical activity; the latter consists in getting rid of the obstacles in the self and in stripping off its base characteristics and vicious morals, so that the heart may attain to freedom from what is not God and to constant recollection of Him.

The intellectual belief was easier to me than the practical activity. I began to acquaint myself with their belief by reading their books, such as *The Food of the Hearts* by Abū Ṭālib al-Makki (God have mercy upon him), the works of al-Ḥārith al-Muḥāsibī, the various anecdotes about al-Junayd, ash-Shiblī and Abū Yazīd al-Bisṭāmī (may God sanctify their spirits), and other discourses of their leading men. I this comprehended their fundamental teachings on the intellectual side, and progressed, as far as is possible by study and oral instruction, in the knowledge of mysticism. It became clear to me, however, that what is most distinctive of mysticism is something which cannot be apprehended by study, but only by immediate experience (*dhawq* – literally "tasting"), by ecstasy and by a moral change. What a difference there is between *knowing* the definition of health and satiety, together with their causes and presuppositions, and *being* healthy and satisfied! What a difference between being acquainted with the definition of drunkenness – namely, that it designates a state arising from the domination of the seat of the intellect by vapours arising from the stomach – and being drunk! Indeed, the drunken man while in that condition does not know the definition of drunkenness nor the scientific account of it; he has not the very least scientific knowledge of it. The sober man, on the other hand, knows the definition of drunkenness and its basis, yet he is not drunk in the very least. Again the doctor, when he is himself ill, knows the definition and causes of health and the remedies which restore it, and yet is lacking in health. Similarly there is a difference between knowing the true nature and causes and conditions of the ascetic life, and actually leading such a life and forsaking the world.

I apprehended clearly that the mystics were men who had real experiences, not men of words, and that I had already progressed as far as was possible by way of intellectual apprehension. What remains for me was not to be attained by oral instruction and study but only by immediate experience and by walking in the mystic way.

Now from the sciences I had laboured at and the paths I had traversed in my investigation of the revelational and rational sciences (that is, presumably, theology and philosophy), there had come to me a sure faith in God most high, in prophethood (or revelation), and in the Last Day. These three credal principles were firmly rooted in my being, not through any carefully argued proofs, but by reason of various causes, coincidences and experiences which are not capable of being stated in detail.

It had already become clear to me that I had no hope of the bliss of the world to come save through a God-fearing life and the withdrawal of myself from vain desire. It was clear to me too that the key to all this was to sever the attachment of the heart to worldly things by leaving the mansion of deception and returning to that of eternity, and to advance towards God most high with all earnestness. It was also clear that this was only to be achieved by turning away from wealth and position and fleeing from all time-consuming entanglements.

Next I considered the circumstances of my life, and realized that I was caught in a veritable thicket of attachments. I also considered my activities, of which the best was my teaching and lecturing, and realized that in them I was dealing with sciences that were unimportant and contributed nothing to the attainment of eternal life.

After that I examined my motive in my work of teaching, and realized that it was not a pure desire for the things of God, but that the impulse moving me was the desire for an influential position and public recognition. I saw for certain that I was on the brink of a crumbling bank of sand and in imminent danger of hell-fire unless I set about to mend my ways.

I reflected on this continuously for a time, while the choice still remained open to me. One day I would form the resolution to quit Baghdad and get rid of these adverse circumstances; the next day I would abandon my resolution. I put one foot forward and drew the other back. If in the morning I had a genuine longing to seek eternal life, by the evening the attack of a whole host of desires had reduced it to impotence. Worldly desires were striving to keep me by their chains just where I was, while the voice of faith was calling, "To the road! To the road! What is left of life is but little and the journey before you is long. All that keeps you busy, both intellectually and practically, is but hypocrisy and delusion. If you do not prepare *now* for eternal life, when will you prepare? If you do not now sever these attachments, when will you sever them?" On hearing that, the impulse would be stirred and the resolution made to take to flight.

Soon, however, Satan would return. "This is a passing mood", he would say; "do not yield to it, for it will quickly disappear; if you comply with it and leave this influential position, these comfortable and dignified circumstances where you are free from troubles and disturbances, this state of safety and security where you are untouched by the contentions of your adversaries, then you will probably come to yourself again and will not find it easy to return to all this."

For nearly six months beginning with Rajab 488 A.H. (=July 1095 A.D.), I was continuously tossed about between the attractions of worldly desires and the impulses towards eternal life. In that month the matter ceased to be one of choice and became one of compulsion. God caused my tongue to dry up so that I was prevented from lecturing. One particular day I would make an effort to lecture in order to gratify the hearts of my following, but my tongue would not utter a single word nor could I accomplish anything at all.

This impediment in my speech produced grief in my heart, and at the same time my power to digest and assimilate food and drink was impaired; I could hardly swallow or digest a single mouthful of food. My powers became so weakened that the doctors gave up all hope of successful treatment. "This trouble arises from the heart", they said, "and from there it has spread through the constitution; the only method of treatment is that the anxiety which has come over the heart should be allayed."

Thereupon, perceiving my impotence and having altogether lost my power of choice, I sought refuge with God most high as one who is driven to Him, because he is without further resources of his own. He answered me, He who "answers him who is driven (to Him by affliction) when he calls upon Him" (Qur'an 27, 63).He made it easy for my heart to turn away from position and wealth, from children and friends. I openly professed that I had resolved to set out for Mecca, while privately I made arrangements to travel to Syria. I took this precaution in case the Caliph and all my friends should oppose my resolve to make my residence in Syria. This stratagem for my departure from Baghdad I gracefully executed, and had it in my mind never to return there. There was much talk about me among all the religious leaders of 'Iraq, since none of them would allow that withdrawal from such a state of life as I was in could have a religious cause, for they looked upon that as the culmination of a religious career; that was the sum of their knowledge.

Much confusion now came into people's minds as they tried to account for my conduct. Those at a distance from 'Iraq supposed that it was due to some apprehension I had of action by the government. On the other hand those who were close to the governing circles and had witnessed how eagerly and assiduously they sought me and how I withdrew from them and showed no great regard for what they said, would say, "This is a supernatural affair; it must be an evil influence which has befallen the people of Islam and especially the circle of the learned."

I left Baghdad, then. I distributed what wealth I had, retaining only as much as would suffice myself and provide sustenance for my children. This I could easily manage, as the wealth of 'Iraq was available for good works, since it constitutes a trust fund for the benefit of the Muslims. Nowhere in the world have I seen better financial arrangements to assist a scholar to provide for his children.

In due course I entered Damascus, and there I remained for nearly two years with no other occupation than the cultivation of retirement and solitude, together with religious and ascetic exercises, as I busied myself purifying my soul, improving my character and cleansing my heart for the constant recollection of God most high, as I had learned from my study of mysticism. I used to go into retreat for a period in the mosque of Damascus, going up the minaret of the mosque for the whole day and shutting myself in so as to be alone.

At length I made my way from Damascus to the Holy House (that is, Jerusalem). There I used to enter into the precinct of the Rock every day and shut myself in.

Next there arose in me a prompting to fulfil the duty of the Pilgrimage, gain the blessings of Mecca and Medina, and perform the visitation of the Messenger of God most high (peace be upon him), after first performing the visitation of al-Khalīl, the Friend of God (God bless him).* I therefore made the journey to the Hijaz. Before long, however, various concerns, together with the entreaties of my children, drew me back to my home (country); and so I came to it again, though at one time no one had seemed less likely than myself to return to it. Here, too, I sought retirement, still longing for solitude and the purification of the heart for the recollection (of God). The events of the interval, the anxieties about my family, and the necessities of my livelihood altered the aspect of my purpose and impaired the quality of my solitude, for I experienced pure ecstasy only occasionally, although I did not cease to hope for that; obstacles would hold me back, yet I always returned to it.

I continued at this stage for the space of ten years, and during these periods of solitude there were revealed to me things innumerable and unfathomable. This much I shall say about that in order that others may be helped: I learned with certainty that it is above all the mystics who walk on the road of God; their life is the best life, their method the soundest method, their character the purest character; indeed, were the intellect of the intellectuals and the learning of the learned and the scholarship of the scholars, who are versed in the profundities of revealed truth, brought together in the attempt to improve the life and character of the mystics, they would find no way of doing so; for to the mystics all movement and all rest, whether external or internal, brings illumination from the light of the lamp of prophetic revelation; and behind the light of prophetic revelation there is no other light on the face of the earth from which illumination may be received.

In general, then, how is a mystic "way" (*tarīqah*) described? The purity which is the first condition of it (*sc.* as bodily purity is the prior condition of formal Worship for Muslims) is the purification of the heart completely from what is other than God most high; the key to it, which corresponds to the opening act of adoration in prayer, is the sinking of the heart completely in the recollection of God; and the end of it is complete absorption (*fanā'*) in God. At least this is its end relatively to those first steps which almost come within the sphere of choice and personal

---

* That is, Abraham, who is buried in the cave of Machpelah under the mosque at Hebron, which is called 'al-Khalīl' in Arabic; similarly the visitation of the Messenger is the formal visit to his tomb at Medina.

responsibility; but in reality in the actual mystic "way" it is the first step, what comes before it being, as it were, the ante-chamber for those who are journeying towards it.

With this first stage of the "way" there begin the revelations and visions. The mystics in their waking state now behold angels and the spirits of the prophets; they hear these speaking to them and are instructed by them. Later, a higher state is reached; instead of beholding forms and figures, they come to stages in the "way" which it is hard to describe in language; if a man attempts to express these, his words inevi- tably contain what is clearly erroneous.

In general what they manage to achieve is nearness to God; some, however, would conceive of this as "inherence" (*ḥulūl*), some as "union" (*ittiḥād*), and some as "connection" (*wuṣūl*). All that is erroneous. In my book, *The Noblest Aim*, I have explained the nature of the error here. Yet he who has attained the mystic "state" need do no more than say:

> Of the things I do not remember, what was, was;
> Think it good; do not ask an account of it.
>   (Ibn al-Muʻtazz).

In general the man to whom He has granted no immediate experience at all, apprehends no more of what prophetic revelation really is than the name. The miraculous graces given to the saints are in truth the begin- nings of the prophets; and that was the first "state" of the Messenger of God (peace be upon him) when he went out to Mount Ḥirāʾ, and was given up entirely to his Lord, and worshipped, so that the bedouin said, "Muhammad loves his Lord passionately".

Now this is a mystical "state" which is realized in immediate experience by those who walk in the way leading to it. Those to whom it is not granted to have immediate experience can become assured of it by trial (*sc.* contact with mystics or observation of them) and by hearsay, if they have sufficiently numerous opportunities of associating with mystics to understand that (*sc.* ecstasy) with certainty by means of what accompanies the "states". Whoever sits in their company derives from them this faith; and none who sits in their company is pained.

Those to whom it is not even granted to have contacts with mystics may know with certainty the possibility of ecstasy by the evidence of demonstration, as I have remarked in the section entitled "The Wonders of the Heart" of my *Revival of the Religious Sciences*.

Certainty reached by demonstration is *knowledge* (*ʻilm*); actual acquaint- ance with that "state" is *immediate experience* (*dhawq*); the acceptance of it as probable from hearsay and trial (or observation) is *faith* (*imān*). These are three degrees. "God will raise those of you who have faith and those who have been given knowledge in degrees (*sc.* of honour)" (Q. 58, 12).

Behind the mystics, however, there is a crowd of ignorant people. They deny this fundamentally, they are astonished at this line of thought, they listen and mock. "Amazing", they say. "What nonsense they talk!" About such people God most high has said: "Some of them listen to you, until, upon going out from you, they say to those to whom knowledge has been given, 'What did he say just now?' These are the people on whose hearts God sets a seal and they follow their passions" (Q. 47, 18). He makes them deaf, and blinds their sight.

Among the things that necessarily became clear to me from my practice of the mystic "way" was the true nature and special characteristics of prophetic revelation. The basis of that must undoubtedly be indicated in view of the urgent need for it.

Part Four

The True Nature of Prophecy and the Compelling Need of all Creation for it

You must know that the substance of man in his original condition was created in bareness and simplicity without any information about the worlds of God most high. These worlds are many, not to be reckoned save by God most high Himself. As He said, "None knows the hosts of thy Lord save He" (Q. 74, 34). Man's information about the world is by means of perception; and every perception of perceptibles is created so that thereby man may have some acquaintance with a world (or sphere) from among existents. By "worlds (or spheres)" we simply mean "classes of existents".

The first thing created in man was the sense of *touch*, and by it he perceives certain classes of existents, such as heat and cold, moisture and dryness, smoothness and roughness. Touch is completely unable to apprehend colours and noises. These might be non-existent so far as concerns touch.

Next there is created in him the sense of *sight*, and by it he apprehends colours and shapes. This is the most extensive of the worlds of sensibles. Next *hearing* is implanted in him, so that he hears sounds of various kinds. After that *taste* is created in him; and so on until he has completed the world of sensibles.

Next, when he is about seven years old, there is created in him *discernment* (or the power of distinguishing – *tamyiz*). This is a fresh stage in his development. He now apprehends more than the world of sensibles; and none of these additional factors (*sc.* relations, etc.) exists in the world of sense.

From this he ascends to another stage, and *intellect* (or reason) (*'aql*) is created in him. He apprehends things necessary, possible, impossible, things which do not occur in the previous stages.

Beyond intellect there is yet another stage. In this another eye is opened, by which he beholds the unseen, what is to be in the future, and other things which are beyond the ken of intellect in the same way as the objects of intellect are beyond the ken of the faculty of discernment and the objects of discernment are beyond the ken of sense. Moreover, just as the man at the stage of discernment would reject and disregard the objects of intellect were these to be presented to him, so some intellectuals reject and disregard the objects of prophetic revelation. That is sheer ignorance. They have no ground for their view except that this is a stage which they have not reached and which for them does not exist; yet they suppose that it is non-existent in itself. When a man blind from birth, who has not learned about colours and shapes by listening to people's talk, is told about these things for the first time, he does not understand them nor admit their existence.

God most high, however, has favoured His creatures by giving them something analogous to the special faculty of prophecy, namely dreams. In the dream-state a man apprehends what is to be in the future, which is something of the unseen; he does so either explicitly or else clothed in a symbolic form whose interpretation is disclosed.

Suppose a man has not experienced this himself, and suppose that he is told how some people fall into a dead faint, in which hearing, sight and the other senses no longer function, and in this condition perceive the unseen. He would deny that this is so and demonstrate its impossibility. "The sensible powers", he would say, "are the causes of perception (or apprehension); if a man does not perceive things (*sc.* the unseen) when these powers are actively present, much less will he do so when the senses are not functioning." This is a form of analogy which is shown to be false by what actually occurs and is observed. Just as intellect is one of the stages of human development in which there is an "eye" which sees the various types of intelligible objects, which are beyond the ken of the senses, so prophecy also is the description of a stage in which there is an eye endowed with light such that in that light the unseen and other supra-intellectual objects become visible.

Doubt about prophetic revelation is either (a) doubt of its possibility in general, or (b) doubt of its actual occurrence, or (c) doubt of the attainment of it by a specific individual.

The proof of the possibility of there being prophecy and the proof that there has been prophecy is that there is knowledge in the world the attainment of which by reason is inconceivable; for example, in medical science and astronomy. Whoever researches in such matters knows of necessity that this knowledge is attained only by Divine inspiration and by assistance from God most high. It cannot be reached by observation. For instance, there are some astronomical laws based on phenomena which occur only once in a thousand years; how can these be arrived at by personal observation? It is the same with the properties of drugs.

This argument shows that it is possible for there to be a way of apprehending these matters which are not apprehended by the intellect. This is the meaning of prophetic revelation. That is not to say that prophecy is merely an expression for such knowledge. Rather, the apprehending of this class of extra-intellectual objects is *one* of the properties of prophecy; but it has many other properties as well. The said property is but a drop in the ocean of prophecy. It has been singled out for mention because you have something analogous to it in what you apprehend in dreaming, and because you have medical and astronomical knowledge belonging to the same class, namely, the miracles of the prophets,* for the intellectuals cannot arrive at these at all by any intellectual efforts.

The other properties of prophetic revelation are apprehended only by immediate experience (*dhawq*) from the practice of the mystic way, but this property of prophecy you can understand by an analogy granted you, namely, the dream-state. If it were not for the latter you would not believe in that. If the prophet possessed a faculty to which you had nothing analogous and which you did not understand, how could you believe in it? Believing presupposes understanding. Now that analogous experience comes to a man in the early stages of the mystic way. Thereby he attains to a kind of immediate experience, extending as far as that to which he has attained, and by analogy to a kind of belief (or assent) in respect to that to which he has not attained. Thus this single property is a sufficient basis for one's faith in the principle of prophecy.

If you come to doubt whether a specific person is a prophet or not, certainty can only be reached by acquaintance with his conduct, either by personal observation, or by hearsay as a matter of common knowledge. For example, if you are familiar with medicine and law, you can recognize lawyers and doctors by observing what they are, or, where observation is impossible, by hearing what they have to say. Thus you are not unable to recognize the al-Shāfiʿī (God have mercy upon him) is a lawyer and Galen a doctor; and your recognition is based on the facts and not on the judgement of someone else. Indeed, just because you have some knowledge of law and medicine, and examine their books and writings, you arrive at a necessary knowledge of what these men are.

---

* This is a little obscure; al-Ghazāli appears to regard certain miraculous signs as belonging to the spheres of medicine and astronomy; perhaps he was thinking of this when he spoke of events occurring once in a thousand years.

Similarly, if you understand what it is to be a prophet, and have devoted much time to the study of the Qur'an and the Traditions, you will arrive at a necessary knowledge of the fact that Muhammad (God bless and preserve him) is in the highest grades of the prophetic calling. Convince yourself of that by trying out what he said about the influence of devotional practices on the purification of the heart – how truly he asserted that "whoever lives out what he knows will receive from God what he does not know"; how truly he asserted that "if anyone aids an evildoer, God will give that man power over him"; how truly he asserted that "if anyone aids an evildoer, God will give that man power over him"; how truly he asserted that "if a man rise up in the morning with but a single care (*sc.* to please God), God most high will preserve him from all cares in this world and the next." When you have made trial of these in a thousand or several thousand instances, you will arrive at a necessary knowledge beyond all doubt.

By this method, then, seek certainty about the prophetic office, and not from the transformation of a rod into a serpent or the cleaving of the moon. For if you consider such an event by itself, without taking account of the numerous circumstances accompanying it – circumstances readily eluding the grasp of the intellect – then you might perhaps suppose that it was magic and deception and that it came from God to lead men astray; for "He leads astray whom He will, and guides whom He will". Thus the topic of miracles will be thrown back upon you; for it your faith is based on a reasoned argument involving the probative force of the miracle, then your faith is destroyed by an ordered argument showing the difficulty and ambiguity of the miracle.

Admit, then, that wonders of this sort are one of the proofs and accompanying circumstances out of the totality of your thought on the matter; and that you attain necessary knowledge and yet are unable to say specifically on what it is based. The case is similar to that of a man who receives from a multitude of people a piece of information which is a matter of common belief . . . He is unable to say that the certainty is derived from the remark of a single specific person; rather, its source is unknown to him; it is neither from outside the whole, nor is it from specific individuals. This is strong, intellectual faith. Immediate experience, on the other hand, is like actually witnessing a thing and taking it in one's hand. It is only found in the way of mysticism.

We pray God Almighty that He will number us among those whom He has chosen and elected, whom He has led to the truth and guided, whom He has inspired to recollect Him and not to forget Him, whom He has preserved from the evil in themselves so that they do not prefer ought to Him, and whom He has made His own so that they serve only Him.

POEMS OF RUMI

NUMBERS 1–11, 14, 15, 31, 37
50, 51, 52(1–8), 61, 106, 118, 119

POEMS OF RUMI

Translated by Reynold A. Nicholson

1
The Song of the Reed

Hearken to this Reed forlorn,
Breathing, even since 'twas torn
From its rushy bed, a strain
Of impassioned love and pain.

"The secret of my song, though near,
None can see and none can hear.
Oh, for a friend to know the sign
And mingle all his soul with mine!

'Tis the flame of Love that fired me,
'Tis the wine of Love inspired me.
Wouldst thou learn how lovers bleed,
Hearken, hearken to the Reed!"

2
Remembered Music

'Tis said, the pipe and lute that charm our ears
Derive their melody from rolling spheres;
But Faith, o'erpassing speculation's bound,
Can see what sweetens every jangled sound.

We, who are parts of Adam, heard with him
The song of angels and of seraphim.
Our memory, though dull and sad, retains
Some echo still of those unearthly strains.
Oh, music is the meat of all who love,
Music uplifts the soul to realms above.
The ashes glow, the latent fires increase:
We listen and are fed with joy and peace.

3   *Love in Absence*

How should not I mourn, like night, without His day and the favour of
    His day-illuming countenance?
His unsweetness is sweet to my soul: may my soul be sacrificed to the
    Beloved who grieves my heart!
I am in love with grief and pain for the sake of pleasing my peerless
    King.
Tears shed for His sake are pearls, though people think they are tears.
I complain of the Soul of my soul, but in truth I am not complaining:
    I am only telling.
My heart says it is tormented by Him, and I have long been laughing at
    its poor pretence.
Do me right, O Glory of the righteous, O Thou Who art the dais, and
    I the threshold of Thy door!
Where are threshold and dais in reality? Where the Beloved is, where
    are "we" and "I"?
O Thou Whose soul is free from "we" and "I", O Thou Who art the
    essence of the spirit in men and women,
Where men and women become one, Thou art that One; when the
    units are wiped out, lo, Thou art that Unity.
Thou didst contrive this "I" and "we" in order to play the game of
    worship with Thyself,
That all "I's" and "thou's" might become one soul and at last be
    submerged in the Beloved.

4   *"The Marriage of True Minds"*

Happy the moment when we are seated in the palace, thou
    and I,
With two forms and with two figures but with one soul, thou and I.
The colours of the grove and the voices of the birds will bestow
    immortality
At the time when we shall come into the garden, thou and I.
The stars of Heaven will come to gaze upon us:
We shall show them the moon herself, thou and I.
Thou and I, individuals no more, shall be mingled in ecstasy,
Joyful and secure from foolish babble, thou and I.
All the bright-plumed birds of Heaven will devour their hearts with
    envy

In the place where we shall laugh in such a fashion, thou
   and I.
This is the greatest wonder, that thou and I, sitting here in the same
   nook,
Are at this moment both in 'Irāq and Khorāsān, thou and I.

5   *"A Sleep and a Forgetting"*

One who has lived many years in a city, so soon as he goes to sleep,
Beholds another city full of good and evil, and his own city vanishes
   from his mind.
He does not say to himself, "This is a new city: I am a stranger here";
Nay, he thinks he has always lived in this city and was born and bred
   in it.
What wonder, then, if the soul does not remember her ancient abode
   and birth-place,
Since she is wrapt in the slumber of this world, like a star covered by
   clouds? –
Especially as she has trodden so many cities and the dust that darkens
   her vision is not yet swept away.

6   *The Grief of the Dead*

The Prince of mankind (Muhammad) said truly that no one who has
   passed away from this world
Feels sorrow and regret for having died; nay, but he feels a hundred
   regrets for having missed the opportunity,
Saying to himself, "Why did I not make death my object – death which
   is the store-house of all fortunes and riches,
And why, through seeing double, did I fasten my lifelong gaze upon
   those phantoms than vanished at the fated hour?"
The grief of the dead is not on account of death; it is because they
   dwelt on the phenomenal forms of existence
And never perceived that all this foam is moved and fed by the Sea.
When the Sea has cast the foam-flakes on the shore, go to the graveyard
   and behold them!
Say to them, "Where is your swirling onrush now?" and hear them
   answer mutely, "Ask this question of the Sea, not of us."
How should the foam fly without the wave? How should the dust rise
   to the zenith without the wind?

Since you have seen the dust, see the Wind; since you have seen the
   foam, see the Ocean of Creative Energy.
Come, see it, for insight is the only thing in you that avails: the rest of
   you is a piece of fat and flesh, a woof and warp (of bones and sinews).
Dissolve your whole body into Vision: become seeing, seeing, seeing!
One sight discerns but a yard or two of the road; another surveys
   the temporal and spiritual worlds and beholds the Face of their
   King.

7   *The Unregenerate*

If any one were to say to the embryo in the womb, "Outside is a world
   well-ordered,
A pleasant earth, broad and long, wherein are a thousand delights and
   many things to eat;
Mountains and seas and plains, fragrant orchards, gardens and sown
   fields,
A sky very lofty and full of light, sunshine and moonbeams and
   innumerable stars;
Its wonders are beyond description: why dost thou stay, drinking blood,
   in this dungeon of filth and pain?" –
The embryo, being what it is, would turn away in utter disbelief; for
   the blind have no imagination.
So, in this world, when the saints tell of a world without scent
   and hue,
None of the vulgar hearkens to them: sensual desire is a barrier huge
   and stout –
Even as the embryo's craving for the blood that nourishes it in its low
   abodes
Debarred it from the perception of the external world, since it knows
   no food but blood.

8   *The Burden of Existence*

From Thee first came this ebb and flow from within me; else, O
   Glorious One, my sea was still.
Now, from the same source whence Thou broughtest this trouble on
   me, graciously send me comfort!
O Thou Whose affliction makes men weak as women, show me the one
   path, do not let me follow ten!

I am like a jaded camel: the saddle of free-will has sorely bruised my
    back
With its heavy panniers sagging from this side to that in turn.
Let the ill-balanced load drop from me, so that I may browse in the
    Meadow of Thy Bounty.
Hundreds of thousands of years I was flying to and fro involuntarily,
    like a mote in the air.
If I have forgotten that time and state, yet the migration in sleep recalls
    it to my memory.
At night I escape from this four-branched cross into the spacious
    pastures of the spirit.
From the nurse, Sleep, I suck the milk of those bygone days of mine,
    O Lord.
All mortals are fleeing from their free-will and self-existence to their
    unconscious selves.
They lay upon themselves the opprobrium of wine and minstrelsy in
    order that for awhile they may be delivered from self-consciousness.
All know that this existence is a snare, that will and thought and memory
    are a hell.

9   *The Spirit of the Saints*

There is a Water that flows down from Heaven
To cleanse the world of sin by grace Divine.
At last, its whole stock spent, its virtue gone,
Dark with pollution not its own, it speeds
Back to the Fountain of all purities;
Whence, freshly bathed, earthward it sweeps again,
Trailing a robe of glory bright and pure.

This Water is the Spirit of the Saints,
Which ever sheds, until itself is beggared,
God's balm on the sick soul; and then returns
To Him who made the purest light of Heaven.

10   *The Children of Light*

Beyond the stars are Stars in which there is no combust nor sinister
    aspect,
Stars moving in other Heavens, not the seven heavens known to all,
Stars immanent in the radiance of the Light of God, neither joined to
    each other nor separate.
Whoso hath his fortune from these Stars, his soul drives off and
    consumes the unbelievers.
God sprinkled His Light over all spirits, but only the blest held up their
    skirts to receive it;
And, having gained that largesse of light, they turned their faces away
    from all but God.
That which is of the sea is going to the sea: it is going to the place
    whence it came –
From the mountain the swift-rushing torrent, and from our body the
    soul whose motion is inspired by love.

11   *Love, the Hierophant*

'Tis heart-ache lays the lover's passion bare:
No sickness with heart-sickness may compare.
Love is a malady apart, the sign
And astrolabe of mysteries Divine.
Whether of heavenly mould or earthly cast,
Love still doth lead us Yonder at the last.
Reason, explaining Love, can naught but flounder
Like ass in mire: Love is Love's own expounder.
Does not the sun himself the sun declare?
Behold him! All the proof thou seek'st is there.

14   *"I Turn Toward Thee"*

O Thou Who art my soul's comfort in the season of sorrow,
O Thou Who art my spirit's treasure in the bitterness of death!
That which the imagination hath not conceived, that which the
    understanding hath not seen,
Visiteth my soul from Thee; hence in worship I turn toward Thee.
By Thy Grace I keep fixed on eternity my amorous gaze,
Except, O King, the pomps that perish lead me astray.

The favour of him who brings glad tidings of Thee,
Even without Thy summons, is sweeter in mine ear than songs.
If the never-ceasing Bounty should offer kingdoms,
If the Hidden Treasure should set before me all that is,
I would bow down with my soul, I would lay my face in the dust,
I would cry, "Of all these the love of such an One for me!"

15 *The Truth within Us*

'Twas a fair orchard, full of trees and fruit
And vines and greenery. A Ṣūfī there
Sat with eyes closed, his head upon his knee,
Sunk deep in meditation mystical.
"Why", asked another, "dost thou not behold
These Signs of God the Merciful displayed
Around thee, which He bids us contemplate?"
"The signs," he answered, "I behold within;
Without is naught but symbols of the Signs."

What is all beauty in the world? The image,
Like quivering boughs reflected in a stream,
Of that eternal Orchard which abides
Unwithered in the hearts of Perfect Men.

22 *The Man who Looked Back on his way to Hell*

The guardian angels, who used to walk unseen before and behind him,
  have now become visible like policemen.
They drag him along, prodding him with goads and crying, "Begone,
  O dog, to thy kennel!"
He looks back towards the Holy Presence: his tears fall like autumn
  rain. A mere hope – what has he but that?
Then from God in the realm of Light comes the command – "Say ye
  to him: 'O ne'er-do-well destitute of merit,
Thou hast seen the black scroll of thy misdeeds. What dost thou expect?
  Why art thou tarrying in vain?' "
He answers: "Lord, Thou knowest I am a hundred hundred times
  worse than Thou hast declared;
But beyond my exertion and action, beyond good and evil and faith and
  infidelity,

Beyond living righteously or behaving disobediently – I had a great hope
  of Thy Loving-kindness.
I turn again to that pure Grace, I am not regarding my own works.
Thou gavest me my being as a robe of honour: I have always relied on
  that munificence."
When he confesses his sins, God saith to the Angels, "Bring him back,
  for he never lost hope of Me.
Like one who recks of naught, I will deliver him and cancel all his
  trespasses.
I will kindle such a fire of Grace that the least spark thereof consumes
  all sin and necessity and free-will.
I will set fire to the tenement of Man and make its thorns a bower of
  roses."

31   *"Omnes Eodem Cogimur"*

Every blind wayfarer, be he righteous or wicked, God is dragging, bound
  in chains, into His Presence.
All are dragged along this Way reluctantly, save those who are
  acquainted with the mysteries of Divine action.
The command *Come against your will* is addressed to the blind follower;
  Come willingly is for the man moulded of truth.
While the former, like an infant, loves the Nurse for the sake of milk,
  the other has given his heart away to this Veiled One.
The "infant" hath no knowledge of Her beauty: he wants nothing of
  Her except milk;
The real lover of the Nurse is disinterested, single-minded in pure
  devotion.
Whether God's seeker love Him for something other than He, that he
  may continually partake of His good,
Or whether he love God for His Very Self, for naught besides Him,
  lest he be separated from Him,
In either case the quest and aspiration proceed from that Source: the
  heart is made captive by that Heart-ravisher.

37   *The Mystic Way*

> Plug thy low sensual ear, which stuffs like cotton
> Thy conscience and makes deaf thine inward ear.
> Be without ear, without sense, without thought,
> And hearken to the call of God, "*Return!*"
> Our speech and action is the outer journey,
> Our inner journey is above the sky
> The body travels on its dusty way;
> The spirit walks, like Jesus, on the sea.

50   *"Here Am I"*

One night a certain man cried "Allah!" till his lips grew sweet with
  praising Him.
The Devil said, "O man of many words, where is the response 'Here
  am I' (*labbayka*) to all this 'Allah'?
Not a single response is coming from the Throne: how long will you
  say 'Allah' with grim face?"
He was broken-hearted and lay down to sleep: in a dream he saw Khaḍir
  amidst the verdure,
Who said, "Hark, you have held back from praising God: why do you
  repent of calling unto Him?"
He answered. "No 'Here am I' is coming to me in response: I fear that
  I am turned away from the Door."
Said Khaḍir, "Nay; God saith: That 'Allah' of thine is My 'Here am
  I,' and that supplication and grief
And ardour of thine is My messenger to thee. They fear and love are
  the noose to catch My Favour:
Beneath ever 'O Lord' of thine is many a 'Here am I' from Me."

51   *The Soul of Prayer*

Jalalu'l-dīn was asked, "Is there any way to God nearer than the ritual
prayer?" "No," he replied; "but prayer does not consist in forms alone.
Formal prayer has a beginning and an end, like all forms and bodies and
everything that partakes of speech and sound; but the soul is unconditioned and infinite: it has neither beginning nor end. The prophets
have shown the true nature of prayer. . . . Prayer is the drowning and
unconsciousness of the soul, so that all these forms remain without. At

that time there is no room even for Gabriel, who is pure spirit. One may say that the man who prays in this fashion is exempt from all religious obligations, since he is deprived of his reason. Absorption in the Divine Unity is the soul of prayer."

52   *The Friend who said "I"*

A certain man knocked at his friend's door: his friend asked, "Who is
    there?"
He answered, "I." "Begone," said his friend, " 'tis too soon: at my table
    there is no place for the raw."
How shall the raw one be cooked but in the fire of absence? What else
    will deliver him from hypocrisy?
He turned sadly away, and for a whole year the flames of separation
    consumed him;
Then he came back and again paced to and from beside the house of
    his friend.
He knocked at the door with a hundred fears and reverences, lest any
    disrespectful word might escape from his lips.
"Who is there?" cried his friend. He answered, "Thou, O charmer of
    all hearts!"
"Now," said the friend, "since thou art I, come in: there is no room
    for two I's in this house."

61   *The Ascending Soul*

I died as mineral and became a plant,
I died as plant and rose to animal,
I died as animal and I was Man.
Why should I fear? When was I less by dying?
Yet once more I shall die as Man, to soar
With angels blest; but even from angelhood
I must pass on: *all except God doth perish*.
When I have sacrificed my angel-soul,
I shall become what no mind e'er conceived.
Oh, let me not exist! for Non-existence
Proclaims in organ tones. "To him we shall return."

106   *The Shepherd's Prayer*

Moses saw a shepherd on the way, crying, "O Lord Who choosest as
   Thou wilt,
Where art Thou, that I may serve Thee and sew Thy shoon and comb
   Thy hair?
That I may wash Thy clothes and kill Thy lice and bring milk to Thee,
   O worshipful One;
That I may kiss Thy little hand and rub Thy little feet and sweep Thy
   little room at bed-time."
On hearing these foolish words, Moses said, "Man, to whom are you
   speaking?
What babble! What blasphemy and raving! Stuff some cotton into your
   mouth!
Truly the friendship of a fool is enmity: the High God is not in want
   of suchlike service."
The shepherd rent his garment, heaved a sigh, and took his way to the
   wilderness.
Then came to Moses a Revelation: "Thou hast parted My servant from
   Me.
Wert thou sent as a prophet to unite, or wert thou sent to sever?
I have bestowed on every one a particular mode of worship, I have given
   every one a peculiar form of expression.
The idiom of Hindustānh is excellent for Hindūs; the idiom of Sind is
   excellent for the people of Sind.
I look not at tongue and speech, I look at the spirit and the inward
   feeling.
I look into the heart to see whether it be lowly, though the words uttered
   be not lowly.
Enough of phrases and conceits and metaphors! I want burning,
   burning: become familiar with that burning!
Light up a fire of love in thy soul, burn all thought and expression away!
O Moses, they that know the conventions are of one sort, they whose
   souls burn are of another."

The religion of love is apart from all religions. The lovers of God have
   no religion but God alone.

118   *The Progress of Man*

> First he appeared in the realm inanimate;
> Thence came into the world of plants and lived
> The plant-life many a year, nor called to mind
> What he had been; then took the onward way
> To animal existence, and once more
> Remembers naught of that life vegetive.
> Save when he feels himself moved with desire
> Towards it in the season of sweet flowers,
> As babes that seek the breast and know not why.

119   *"Ripeness is All"*

Since thou canst not bear the unveiled Light, drink the Word of
  Wisdom, for its light is veiled,
To the end that thou mayst become able to receive the Light, and
  behold without veils that which now is hidden,
And traverse the sky like a star; nay, journey unconditioned, without a
  sky.
'Twas thus thou camest into being from non-existence. How didst thou
  come? Thou camest insensibly.
The ways of thy coming thou rememberest not, but I will give thee an
  indication.
Let thy mind go, then be mindful! Close thine ear, then listen!
Nay, I will not tell, for thou art still unripe: thou art in thy springtime,
  thou hast not seen the summer.
This world is as the tree: we are like the half-ripened fruit upon it.
The unripe fruits cling fast to the bough, because they are not fit for
  the palace;
But when they have ripened and become sweet and delicious – after
  that, they lose hold of the bough.
Even so does the kingdom of the world lose its savour for him whose
  mouth has been sweetened by the great felicity.
Something remains untold, but the Holy Spirit will tell thee without
  me as the medium.
Nay, thou wilt tell it to thine own ear – neither I nor another, O thou
  who art one with me –
Just as, when thou fallest asleep, thou goest from the presence of thyself
  into the presence of thyself
And hearest from thyself that which thou thinkest is told thee secretly
  by someone in the dream.

O good friend, thou art not a single "thou": thou art the sky and the deep sea.

Thy mighty infinite "Thou" is the ocean wherein myriads of "thou's" are sunken.

Do not speak, so that thou mayst hear from the Speakers what cannot be uttered or described.

Do not speak, so that the Spirit may speak for thee: in the ark of Noah leave off swimming!

VI

JUDAISM
FROM THE WISDOM BOOKS:

The Proverbs
Sirach
The Wisdom of Solomon

THE PROVERBS

CHAPTERS 1–9

THE PROVERBS

*The translation is taken from
the Revised Standard Version of the Bible*

CHAPTER ONE

1 The proverbs of Solomon, son of David, king of Israel:

2 That men may know wisdom and instruction,
   understand words of insight,
3 receive instruction in wise dealing,
   righteousness, justice, and equity;
4 that prudence may be given to the simple,
   knowledge and discretion to the youth—
5 the wise man also may hear and increase in learning,
   and the man of understanding acquire skill,
6 to understand a proverb and a figure,
   the words of the wise and their riddles.

7 The fear of the LORD is the beginning of knowledge;
   fools despise wisdom and instruction.

8 Hear, my son, your father's instruction,
   and reject not your mother's teaching;
9 for they are a fair garland for your head,
   and pendants for your neck.
10 My son, if sinners entice you,
   do not consent.
11 If they say, "Come with us, let us lie in wait for blood,
   let us wantonly ambush the innocent;
12 like Sheol let us swallow them alive
   and whole, like those who go down to the Pit;
13 we shall find all precious goods,
   we shall fill our houses with spoil;
14 throw in your lot among us,
   we will all have one purse"—
15 my son, do not walk in the way with them,
   hold back your foot from their paths;

16 for their feet run to evil,
    and they make haste to shed blood.
17 For in vain is a net spread
    in the sight of any bird;
18 but these men lie in wait for their own blood,
    they set an ambush for their own lives.
19 Such are the ways of all who get gain by violence;
    it takes away the life of its possessors.

20 Wisdom cries aloud in the street;
    in the markets she raises her voice;
21 on the top of the walls she cries out;
    at the entrance of the city gates she speaks:
22 "How long, O simple ones, will you love being simple?
    How long will scoffers delight in their scoffing
    and fools hate knowledge?
23 Give heed to my reproof; behold, I will pour out my thoughts to
    you;
    I will make my words known to you.
24 Because I have called and you refused to listen,
    have stretched out my hand and no one has heeded,
25 and you have ignored all my counsel
    and would have none of my reproof,
26 I also will laugh at your calamity;
    I will mock when panic strikes you,
27 when panic strikes you like a storm,
    and your calamity comes like a whirlwind,
    when distress and anguish come upon you.
28 Then they will call upon me, but I will not answer;
    they will seek me diligently but will not find me.
29 Because they hated knowledge
    and did not choose the fear of the LORD,
30 would have none of my counsel,
    and despised all my reproof,
31 therefore they shall eat the fruit of their way
    and be sated with their own devices.
32 For the simple are killed by their turning away,
    and the complacence of fools destroys them;
33 but he who listens to me will dwell secure
    and will be at ease, without dread of evil."

CHAPTER TWO

1 My son, if you receive my words and treasure up my commandments
   with you,
2 making your ear attentive to wisdom
   and inclining your heart to understanding;
3 yes, if you cry out for insight
   and raise your voice for understanding,
4 if you seek it like silver
   and search for it as for hidden treasures;
5 then you will understand the fear of the LORD
   and find the knowledge of God.
6 For the LORD gives wisdom;
   from his mouth come knowledge and understanding;
7 he stores up sound wisdom for the upright;
   he is a shield to those who walk in integrity,
8 guarding the paths of justice
   and preserving the way of his saints.
9 Then you will understand righteousness and justice
   and equity, every good path;
10 for wisdom will come into your heart,
   and knowledge will be pleasant to your soul;
11 discretion will watch over you;
   understanding will guard you;
12 delivering you from the way of evil,
   from men of perverted speech,
13 who forsake the paths of uprightness
   to walk in the ways of darkness,
14 who rejoice in doing evil
   and delight in the perverseness of evil;
15 men whose paths are crooked,
   and who are devious in their ways.

16 You will be saved from the loose woman,
   from the adventuress with her smooth words,
17 who forsakes the companion of her youth
   and forgets the covenant of her God;
18 for her house sinks down to death,
   and her paths to the shades;
19 none who go to her come back
   nor do they regain the paths of life.

20 So you will walk in the way of good men
  and keep to the paths of the righteous.
21 For the upright will inhabit the land,
  and men of integrity will remain in it;
22 but the wicked will be cut off from the land,
  and the treacherous will be rooted out of it.

CHAPTER THREE

1 My son, do not forget my teaching, but let your heart keep my
  commandments;
2 for length of days and years of life
  and abundant welfare will they give you.

3 Let not loyalty and faithfulness forsake you;
  bind them about your neck,
  write them on the tablet of your heart.
4 So you will find favour and good repute
  in the sight of God and man.

5 Trust in the LORD with all your heart,
  and do not rely on your own insight.
6 In all your ways acknowledge him,
  and he will make straight your paths.
7 Be not wise in your own eyes;
  fear the LORD, and turn away from evil.
8 It will be healing to your flesh
  and refreshment to your bones.

9 Honour the LORD with your substance
  and with the first fruits of all your produce;
10 then your barns will be filled with plenty,
  and your vats will be bursting with wine.

11 My son, do not despise the LORD's discipline
  or be weary of his reproof,
12 for the LORD reproves him whom he loves,
  as a father the son in whom he delights.

13 Happy is the man who finds wisdom,
  and the man who gets understanding,
14 for the gain from it is better than gain from silver
  and its profit better than gold.

15 She is more precious than jewels,
　　and nothing you desire can compare with her.
16 Long life is in her right hand;
　　in her left hand are riches and honour.
17 Her ways are ways of pleasantness,
　　and all her paths are peace.
18 She is a tree of life to those who lay hold of her;
　　those who hold her fast are called happy.

19 The LORD by wisdom founded the earth;
　　by understanding he established the heavens;
20 by his knowledge the deeps broke forth,
　　and the clouds drop down the dew.

21 My son, keep sound wisdom and discretion;
　　let them not escape from your sight,
22 and they will be life for your soul
　　and adornment for your neck.
23 Then you will walk on your way securely
　　and your foot will not stumble.
24 If you sit down, you will not be afraid;
　　when you lie down, your sleep will be sweet.
25 Do not be afraid of sudden panic,
　　or of the ruin of the wicked, when it comes;
26 for the LORD will be your confidence
　　and will keep your foot from being caught.
27 Do not withhold good from those to whom it is due,
　　when it is in your power to do it.

28 Do not say to your neighbour, "Go, and come again,
　　tomorrow I will give it" – when you have it with you.
29 Do not plan evil against your neighbour
　　who dwells trustingly beside you.
30 Do not contend with a man for no reason,
　　when he has done you no harm.
31 Do not envy a man of violence
　　and do not choose any of his ways;
32 for the perverse man is an abomination to the LORD,
　　but the upright are in his confidence.
33 The LORD's curse is on the house of the wicked,
　　but he blesses the abode of the righteous.
34 Toward the scorners he is scornful,
　　but to the humble he shows favour.

35 The wise will inherit honour,
   but fools get disgrace.

CHAPTER FOUR

1 Hear, O sons, a father's instruction,
   and be attentive, that you may gain insight;
2 for I give you good precepts:
   do not forsake my teaching.
3 When I was a son with my father,
   tender, the only one in the sight of my mother,
4 he taught me, and said to me,
   "Let your heart hold fast my words;
   keep my commandments, and live;
5 do not forget, and do not turn away from the words of my mouth.
   Get wisdom; get insight.
6 Do not forsake her, and she will keep you;
   love her, and she will guard you.
7 The beginning of wisdom is this: Get wisdom,
   and whatever you get, get insight.
8 Prize her highly, and she will exalt you;
   she will honour you if you embrace her.
9 She will place on your head a fair garland;
   she will bestow on you a beautiful crown."

10 Hear, my son, and accept my words,
   that the years of your life may be many.
11 I have taught you the way of wisdom;
   I have led you in the paths of uprightness.
12 When you walk, your step will not be hampered;
   and if you run, you will not stumble.
13 Keep hold of instruction, do not let go;
   guard her, for she is your life.
14 Do not enter the path of the wicked,
   and do not walk in the way of evil men.
15 Avoid it; do not go on it;
   turn away from it and pass on.
16 For they cannot sleep unless they have done wrong;
   they are robbed of sleep unless they have made some one stumble.
17 For they eat the bread of wickedness
   and drink the wine of violence.
18 But the path of the righteous is like the light of dawn,
   which shines brighter and brighter until full day.

19 The way of the wicked is like deep darkness;
    they do not know over what they stumble.

20 My son, be attentive to my words;
    incline your ear to my sayings.
21 Let them not escape from your sight;
    keep them within your heart.
22 For they are life to him who finds them,
    and healing to all his flesh.
23 Keep your heart with all vigilance;
    for from it flow the springs of life.
24 Put away from you crooked speech,
    and put devious talk far from you.
25 Let your eyes look directly forward,
    and your gaze be straight before you.
26 Take heed to the path of your feet,
    then all your ways will be sure.
27 Do not swerve to the right or to the left;
    turn your foot away from evil.

CHAPTER FIVE

1 My son, be attentive to my wisdom,
    incline your ear to my understanding;
2 that you may keep discretion,
    and your lips may guard knowledge.
3 For the lips of a loose woman drip honey,
    and her speech is smoother than oil;
4 but in the end she is bitter as wormwood,
    sharp as a two-edged sword.
5 Her feet go down to death;
    her steps follow the path to Sheol;
6 she does not take heed to the path of life;
    her ways wander, and she does not know it.

7 And now, O sons, listen to me,
    and do not depart from the words of my mouth.
8 Keep your way far from her,
    and do not go near the door of her house;
9 lest you give your honour to others
    and your years to the merciless;
10 lest strangers take their fill of your strength,
    and your labours go to the house of an alien;

11 and at the end of your life you groan,
    when your flesh and body are consumed,
12 and you say, "How I hated discipline,
    and my heart despised reproof!
13 I did not listen to the voice of my teachers
    or incline my ear to my instructors.
14 I was at the point of utter ruin
    in the assembled congregation."
15 Drink water from your own cistern,
    flowing water from your own well.
16 Should your springs be scattered abroad,
    streams of water in the streets?
17 Let them be for yourself alone,
    and not for strangers with you.
18 Let your fountain be blessed,
    and rejoice in the wife of your youth,
19 a lovely hind, a graceful doe.
    Let her affection fill you at all times with delight,
    be infatuated always with her love.
20 Why should you be infatuated, my son, with a loose
    woman
    and embrace the bosom of an adventuress?
21 For a man's ways are before the eyes of the LORD,
    and he watches all his paths.
22 The iniquities of the wicked ensnare him,
    and he is caught in the toils of his sin.
23 He dies for lack of discipline,
    and because of his great folly he is lost.

CHAPTER SIX

1 My son, if you have become surety for your neighbour,
    have given your pledge for a stranger;
2 if you are snared in the utterance of your lips,
    caught in the words of your mouth;
3 then do this, my son, and save yourself,
    for you have come into your neighbour's power:
    go, hasten, and importune your neighbour.
4 Give your eyes no sleep
    and your eyelids no slumber;
5 save yourself like a gazelle from the hunter,
    like a bird from the hand of the fowler.

6 Go to the ant, O sluggard;
  consider her ways, and be wise.
7 Without having any chief,
  officer or ruler,
8 she prepares her food in summer,
  and gathers her sustenance in harvest.
9 How long will you lie there, O sluggard?
  When will you arise from your sleep?
10 A little sleep, a little slumber,
  a little folding of the hands to rest,
11 and poverty will come upon you like a vagabond,
  and want like an armed man.

12 A worthless person, a wicked man,
  goes about with crooked speech,
13 winks with his eyes, scrapes with his feet,
  points with his finger,
14 with perverted heart devises evil,
  continually sowing discord;
15 therefore calamity will come upon him suddenly;
  in a moment he will be broken beyond healing.

16 There are six things which the LORD hates,
  seven which are an abomination to him:
17 haughty eyes, a lying tongue,
  and hands that shed innocent blood,
18 a heart that devises wicked plans,
  feet that make haste to run to evil,
19 a false witness who breathes out lies,
  and a man who sows discord among brothers.

20 My son, keep your father's commandment,
  and forsake not your mother's teaching.
21 Bind them upon your heart always;
  tie them about your neck.
22 When you walk, they will lead you;
  when you lie down, they will watch over you;
  and when you awake, they will talk with you.
23 For the commandment is a lamp and the teaching a light,
  and the reproofs of discipline are the way of life,
24 to preserve you from the evil woman,
  from the smooth tongue of the adventuress.

25 Do not desire her beauty in your heart,
  and do not let her capture you with her eyelashes;
26 for a harlot may be hired for a loaf of bread,
  but an adulteress stalks a man's very life.
27 Can a man carry fire in his bosom
  and his clothes not be burned?
28 Or can one walk upon hot coals
  and his feet not be scorched?
29 So is he who goes in to his neighbour's wife;
  none who touches her will go unpunished.
30 Do not men despise a thief if he steals
  to satisfy his appetite when he is hungry?
31 And if he is caught, he will pay sevenfold;
  he will give all the goods of his house.
32 He who commits adultery has no sense;
  he who does it destroys himself.
33 Wounds and dishonour will he get,
  and his disgrace will not be wiped away.
34 For jealousy makes a man furious,
  and he will not spare when he takes revenge.
35 He will accept no compensation,
  nor be appeased though you multiply gifts.

CHAPTER SEVEN

1 My son, keep my words
  and treasure up my commandments with you;
2 keep my commandments and live,
  keep my teachings as the apple of your eye;
3 bind them on your fingers,
  write them on the tablet of your heart.
4 Say to wisdom, "You are my sister,"
  and call insight your intimate friend;
5 to preserve you from the loose woman,
  from the adventuress with her smooth words.

6 For at the window of my house
  I have looked out through my lattice,
7 and I have seen among the simple,
  I have perceived among the youths,
  a young man without sense,
8 passing along the street near her corner,
  taking the road to her house

9 in the twilight, in the evening,
    at the time of night and darkness.

10 And lo, a woman meets him,
    dressed as a harlot, wily of heart.
11 She is loud and wayward,
    her feet do not stay at home;
12 now in the street, now in the market,
    and at every corner she lies in wait.
13 She seizes him and kisses him,
    and with impudent face she says to him:
14 "I had to offer sacrifices,
    and today I have paid my vows;
15 so now I have come out to meet you,
    to seek you eagerly, and I have found you.
16 I have decked my couch with coverings,
    coloured spreads of Egyptian linen;
17 I have perfumed my bed with myrrh,
    aloes, and cinnamon.
18 Come, let us take our fill of love till morning;
    let us delight ourselves with love.
19 For my husband is not at home;
    he has gone on a long journey;
20 he took a bag of money with him;
    at full moon he will come home."

21 With much seductive speech she persuades him;
    with her smooth talk she compels him.
22 All at once he follows her,
    as an ox goes to the slaughter,
    or as a stag is caught fast
23 till an arrow pierces its entrails;
    as a bird rushes into a snare;
    he does not know that it will cost him his life.

24 And now, O sons, listen to me,
    and be attentive to the words of my mouth.
25 Let not your heart turn aside to her ways,
    do not stray into her paths;
26 for many a victim has she laid low;
    yea, all her slain are a mighty host.
27 Her house is the way to Sheol,
    going down to the chambers of death.

CHAPTER EIGHT

1 Does not wisdom call,
　　does not understanding raise her voice?
2 On the heights beside the way,
　　in the paths she takes her stand;
3 beside the gates in front of the town,
　　at the entrance of the portals she cries aloud:
4 "To you, O men, I call,
　　and my cry is to the sons of men.
5 O simple ones, learn prudence;
　　O foolish men, pay attention.
6 Hear, for I will speak noble things,
　　and from my lips will come what is right;
7 for my mouth will utter truth;
　　wickedness is an abomination to my lips.
8 All the words of my mouth are righteous;
　　there is nothing twisted or crooked in them.
9 They are all straight to him who understands
　　and right to those who find knowledge.
10 Take my instruction instead of silver,
　　and knowledge rather than choice gold;
11 for wisdom is better than jewels,
　　and all that you may desire cannot compare with her.
12 I, wisdom, dwell in prudence,
　　and I find knowledge and discretion.
13 The fear of the Lord is hatred of evil.
　　Pride and arrogance and the way of evil
　　and perverted speech I hate.
14 I have counsel and sound wisdom,
　　I have insight, I have strength.
15 By me kings reign,
　　and rulers decree what is just;
16 By me princes rule,
　　and nobles govern the earth.
17 I love those who love me,
　　and those who seek me diligently find me.
18 Riches and honour are with me,
　　enduring wealth and prosperity.
19 My fruit is better than gold, even fine gold,
　　and my yield than choice silver.

20 I walk in the way of righteousness,
    in the paths of justice,
21 endowing with wealth those who love me,
    and filling their treasuries.

22 The LORD created me at the beginning of his work,
    the first of his acts of old.
23 Ages ago I was set up,
    at the first, before the beginning of the earth.
24 When there were no depths I was brought forth,
    when there were no springs abounding with water.
25 Before the mountains had been shaped,
    before the hills, I was brought forth;
26 before he had made the earth with its fields,
    or the first of the dust of the world.
27 When he established the heavens, I was there,
    when he drew a circle on the face of the deep,
28 when he made firm the skies above,
    when he established the fountains of the deep,
29 when he assigned to the sea its limit,
    so that the waters might not transgress his command,
    when he marked out the foundations of the earth,
30 then I was beside him, like a master workman;
    and I was daily his delight,
    rejoicing before him always,
31 rejoicing in his inhabited world
    and delighting in the sons of men.

32 And now, my sons, listen to me:
    happy are those who keep my ways.
33 Hear instruction and be wise,
    and do not neglect it.
34 Happy is the man who listens to me,
    watching daily at my gates,
    waiting beside my doors.
35 For he who finds me finds life
    and obtains favour from the LORD;
36 but he who misses me injures himself;
    all who hate me love death.''

CHAPTER NINE

1 Wisdom has built her house,
    she has set up her seven pillars.
2 She has slaughtered her beasts, she has mixed her wine,
    she has also set her table.
3 She has sent out her maids to call
    from the highest places in the town,
4 "Whoever is simple, let him turn in here!"
    To him who is without sense she says,
5 "Come, eat of my bread
    and drink of the wine I have mixed.
6 Leave simpleness, and live,
    and walk in the way of insight."

7 He who corrects a scoffer gets himself abuse,
    and he who reproves a wicked man incurs injury.
8 Do not reprove a scoffer, or he will hate you;
    reprove a wise man, and he will love you.
9 Give instruction to a wise man,
    and he will be still wiser;
    teach a righteous man and he will increase in learning.
10 The fear of the Lord is the beginning of wisdom,
    and the knowledge of the Holy One is insight.
11 For by me your days will be multiplied,
    and years will be added to your life.
12 If you are wise, you are wise for yourself;
    if you scoff, you alone will bear it.

13 A foolish woman is noisy;
    she is wanton and knows no shame.
14 She sits at the door of her house,
    she takes a seat on the high places of the town,
15 Calling to those who pass by,
    who are going straight on their way,
16 "Whoever is simple, let him turn in here!"
    And to him who is without sense she says,
17 "Stolen water is sweet,
    and bread eaten in secret is pleasant."
18 But he does not know that the dead are there,
    that her guests are in the depths of Sheol.

SIRACH

CHAPTERS 1–6, 24, 43 v. 13–50 v. 29

SIRACH

*The translation is taken from
the Revised Standard Version of the Bible*

THE PROLOGUE

Whereas many great teachings have been given to us through the law
and the prophets and the others that followed them, on account of which
we should praise Israel for instruction and wisdom; and since it is necessary not only that the readers themselves should acquire understanding
but also that those who love learning should be able to help the outsiders
by both speaking and writing, my grandfather Jesus, after devoting himself
especially to the reading of the law and the prophets and the other books
of our fathers, and after acquiring considerable proficiency in them, was
himself also led to write something pertaining to instruction and wisdom,
in order that, by becoming conversant with this also, those who love
learning should make even greater progress in living according to the
law.

You are urged therefore to read with good will and attention, and to
be indulgent in cases where, despite our diligent labour in translating,
we may seem to have rendered some phrases imperfectly. For what was
originally expressed in Hebrew does not have exactly the same sense
when translated into another language. Not only this work, but even the
law itself, the prophecies, and the rest of the books differ not a little as
originally expressed.

When I came to Egypt in the thirty-eighth year of the reign of
Eu-er'getes and stayed for some time, I found opportunity for no little
instruction. It seemed highly necessary that I should myself devote some
pains and labour to the translation of the following book, using in that
period of time great watchfulness and skill in order to complete and
publish the book for those living abroad who wished to gain learning,
being prepared in character to live according to the law.

CHAPTER ONE

1 All wisdom comes from the Lord and is with him for ever.
2 The sand of the sea, the drops of rain, and the days of eternity –
  who can count them?

3 The height of heaven, the breadth of the earth,
    the abyss, and wisdom – who can search them out?

4 Wisdom was created before all things,
    and prudent understanding from eternity.

6 The root of wisdom – to whom has it been revealed?
    Her clever devices – who knows them?

8 There is One who is wise, greatly to be feared,
    sitting upon his throne.

9 The Lord himself created wisdom;
    he saw her and apportioned her,
    he poured her out upon all his works.

10 She dwells with all flesh according to his gift,
    and he supplied her to those who love him.

11 The fear of the Lord is glory and exultation,
    and gladness and a crown of rejoicing.

12 The fear of the Lord delights the heart,
    and gives gladness and joy and long life.

13 With him who fears the Lord it will go well at the end;
    on the day of his death he will be blessed.

14 To fear the Lord is the beginning of wisdom;
    she is created with the faithful in the womb.

15 She made among men an eternal foundation,
    and among their descendants she will be trusted.

16 To fear the Lord is wisdom's full measure;
    she satisfies men with her fruits;

17 she fills their whole house with desirable goods,
    and their storehouses with her produce.

18 The fear of the Lord is the crown of wisdom,
    making peace and perfect health to flourish.

19 He saw her and apportioned her;
    he rained down knowledge and discerning
      comprehension,
    and he exalted the glory of those who held her fast.

20 To fear the Lord is the root of wisdom,
    and her branches are long life.

22 Unrighteous anger cannot be justified,
    for a man's anger tips the scale to his ruin.

23 A patient man will endure until the right moment,
    and then joy will burst forth for him.

24 He will hide his words until the right moment,
    and the lips of many will tell of his good sense.

25 In the treasuries of wisdom are wise sayings,
    but godliness is an abomination to a sinner.
26 If you desire wisdom, keep the commandments,
    and the Lord will supply it for you.
27 For the fear of the Lord is wisdom and instruction,
    and he delights in fidelity and meekness.
28 Do not disobey the fear of the Lord;
    do not approach him with a divided mind.
29 Be not a hypocrite in men's sight,
    and keep watch over your lips.
30 Do not exalt yourself lest you fall,
    and thus bring dishonour upon yourself.
    The Lord will reveal your secrets
    and cast you down in the midst of the congregation,
    because you did not come in the fear of the Lord,
    and your heart was full of deceit.

CHAPTER TWO

1 My son, if you come forward to serve the Lord,
    prepare yourself for temptation.
2 Set your heart right and be steadfast,
    and do not be hasty in time of calamity.
3 Cleave to him and do not depart,
    that you may be honoured at the end of your life.
4 Accept whatever is brought upon you,
    and in changes that humble you be patient.
5 For gold is tested in the fire,
    and acceptable men in the furnace of humiliation.
6 Trust in him, and he will help you;
    make your ways straight, and hope in him.

7 You who fear the Lord, wait for his mercy;
    and turn not aside, lest you fall.
8 You who fear the Lord, trust in him,
    and your reward will not fail;
9 you who fear the Lord, hope for good things,
    for everlasting joy and mercy.
10 Consider the ancient generations and see:
    who ever trusted in the Lord and was put to shame?
    Or who ever persevered in the fear of the Lord and was
      forsaken?
    Or who ever called upon him and was overlooked?

11 For the Lord is compassionate and merciful;
    he forgives sins and saves in time of affliction.

12 Woe to timid hearts and to slack hands,
    and to the sinner who walks along two ways!
13 Woe to the faint heart, for it has no trust!
    Therefore it will not be sheltered.
14 Woe to you who have lost your endurance!
    What will you do when the Lord punishes you?
15 Those who fear the Lord will not disobey his words,
    and those who love him will keep his ways.
16 Those who fear the Lord will seek his approval,
    and those who love him will be filled with the law.
17 Those who fear the Lord will prepare their hearts,
    and will humble themselves before him.
18 Let us fall into the hands of the Lord,
    but not into the hands of men;
    for as his majesty is,
    so also is his mercy.

CHAPTER THREE

1 Listen to me your father, O children;
    and act accordingly, that you may be kept in safety.
2 For the Lord honoured the father above the children,
    and he confirmed the right of the mother over her sons.
3 Whoever honours his father atones for sins,
4 and whoever glorifies his mother is like one who lays up treasure.
5 Whoever honours his father will be gladdened by his own
    children,
    and when he prays he will be heard.
6 Whoever glorifies his father will have long life,
    and whoever obeys the Lord will refresh his mother;
7 he will serve his parents as his masters.
8 Honour your father by word and deed,
    that a blessing from him may come upon you.
9 For a father's blessing strengthens the houses of the children,
    but a mother's curse uproots their foundations.

10 Do not glorify yourself by dishonouring your father,
    for your father's dishonour is no glory to you.
11 For a man's glory comes from honouring his father,
    and it is a disgrace for children not to respect their mother.

12 O son, help your father in his old age,
    and do not grieve him as long as he lives;
13 even if he is lacking in understanding, show forbearance;
    in all your strength do not despise him.
14 For kindness to a father will not be forgotten,
    and against your sins it will be credited to you;
15 in the day of your affliction it will be remembered in your favour;
    as frost in fair weather, your sins will melt away.
16 Whoever forsakes his father is like a blasphemer,
    and whoever angers his mother is cursed by the Lord.

17 My son, perform your tasks in meekness;
    then you will be loved by those whom God accepts.
18 The greater you are, the more you must humble yourself;
    so you will find favour in the sight of the Lord.
20 For great is the might of the Lord;
    he is glorified by the humble.
21 Seek not what is too difficult for you,
    nor investigate what is beyond your power.
22 Reflect upon what has been assigned to you,
    for you do not need what is hidden.
23 Do not meddle in what is beyond your tasks,
    for matters too great for human understanding have been shown
        you.
24 For their hasty judgment has led many astray,
    and wrong opinion has caused their thoughts to slip.

26 A stubborn mind will be afflicted at the end,
    and whoever loves danger will perish by it.
27 A stubborn mind will be burdened by troubles,
    and the sinner will heap sin upon sin.
28 The affliction of the proud has no healing,
    for a plant of wickedness has taken root in him.
29 The mind of the intelligent man will ponder a parable,
    and an attentive ear is the wise man's desire.
30 Water extinguishes a blazing fire:
    so almsgiving atones for sin.
31 Whoever requites favours gives thought to the future;
    at the moment of his falling he will find support.

CHAPTER FOUR

1 My son, deprive not the poor of his living,
    and do not keep needy eyes waiting.
2 Do not grieve the one who is hungry,
    nor anger a man in want.
3 Do not add to the troubles of an angry mind,
    nor delay your gift to a beggar.
4 Do not reject an afflicted suppliant,
    nor turn your face away from the poor.
5 Do not avert your eye from the need,
    nor give a man occasion to curse you;
6 for if in bitterness of soul he calls down a curse upon you,
    his Creator will hear his prayer.

7 Make yourself beloved in the congregation;
    bow your head low to a great man.
8 Incline your ear to the poor,
    and answer him peaceably and gently.
9 Deliver him who is wronged from the hand of the wrongdoer;
    and do not be fainthearted in judging a case.
10 Be like a father to orphans,
    and instead of a husband to their mother;
    you will then be like a son of the Most High,
    and he will love you more than does your mother.

11 Wisdom exalts her sons
    and gives help to those who seek her.
12 Whoever loves her loves life,
    and those who seek her early will be filled with joy.
13 Whoever holds her fast will obtain glory,
    and the Lord will bless the place she enters.
14 Those who serve her will minister to the Holy One;
    the Lord loves those who love her.
15 He who obeys her will judge the nations,
    and whoever gives heed to her will dwell secure.
16 If he has faith in her he will obtain her;
    and his descendants will remain in possession of her.
17 For at first she will walk with him on tortuous paths,
    she will bring fear and cowardice upon him,
    and will torment him by her discipline until she trusts him,
    and she will test him with her ordinances.

18 Then she will come straight back to him and gladden him,
  and will reveal her secrets to him.
19 If he goes astray she will forsake him,
  and hand him over to his ruin.

20 Observe the right time, and beware of evil;
  and do not bring shame on yourself.
21 For there is a shame which brings sin,
  and there is a shame which is glory and favour.
22 Do not show partiality, to your own harm,
  or deference, to your downfall.
23 Do not refrain from speaking at the crucial time,
  and do not hide your wisdom.
24 For wisdom is known through speech,
  and education through the words of the tongue.
25 Never speak against the truth,
  but be mindful of your ignorance.
26 Do not be ashamed to confess your sins,
  and do not try to stop the current of a river.
27 Do not subject yourself to a foolish fellow,
  nor show partiality to a ruler.
28 Strive even to death for the truth
  and the Lord God will fight for you.

29 Do not be reckless in your speech,
  or sluggish and remiss in your deeds.
30 Do not be like a lion in your home,
  nor be a faultfinder with your servants.
31 Let not your hand be extended to receive,
  but withdrawn when it is time to repay.

CHAPTER FIVE

1 Do not set your heart on your wealth,
  nor say, "I have enough."
2 Do not follow your inclination and strength,
  walking according to the desires of your heart.
3 Do not say, "Who will have power over me?"
  for the Lord will surely punish you.

4 Do not say, "I sinned, and what happened to me?"
  for the Lord is slow to anger.

5 Do not be so confident of atonement
    that you add sin to sin.
6 Do not say, "His mercy is great,
    he will forgive the multitude of my sins,"
    for both mercy and wrath are with him,
    and his anger rests on sinners.
7 Do not delay to turn to the Lord,
    nor postpone it from day to day;
    for suddenly the wrath of the Lord will go
      forth,
    and at the time of punishment you will perish.

8 Do not depend on dishonest wealth,
    for it will not benefit you in the day of calamity.
9 Do not winnow with every wind,
    nor follow every path:
    the double-tongued sinner does that.
10 Be steadfast in your understanding,
    and let your speech be consistent.
11 Be quick to hear,
    and be deliberate in answering.
12 If you have understanding, answer your neighbour;
    but if not, put your hand on your mouth.
13 Glory and dishonour come from speaking,
    and a man's tongue is his downfall.
14 Do not be called a slanderer,
    and do not lie in ambush with your tongue;
    for shame comes to the thief,
    and severe condemnation to the double-tongued.
15 In great or small matters do not act amiss,
    and do not become an enemy instead of a friend;

CHAPTER SIX

1 for a bad name incurs shame and reproach:
    so fares the double-tongued sinner.

2 Do not exalt yourself through your soul's counsel,
    lest your soul be torn in pieces like a bull.
3 You will devour your leaves and destroy your fruit,
    and will be left like a withered tree.
4 An evil soul will destroy him who has it,
    and make him the laughingstock of his enemies.

5 A pleasant voice multiplies friends,
   and a gracious tongue multiplies courtesies.
6 Let those that are at peace with you be many,
   but let your advisers be one in a thousand.
7 When you gain a friend, gain him through testing,
   and do not trust him hastily.
8 For there is a friend who is such at his own convenience,
   but will not stand by you in your day of trouble.
9 And there is a friend who changes into an enemy,
   and will disclose a quarrel to your disgrace.
10 And there is a friend who is a table companion,
   but will not stand by you in your day of trouble.
11 In your prosperity he will make himself your equal,
   and be bold with your servants;
12 but if you are brought low he will turn against you,
   and will hide himself from your presence.
13 Keep yourself far from your enemies
   and be on guard toward your friends.

14 A faithful friend is a sturdy shelter:
   he that has found one has found a treasure.
15 There is nothing so precious as a faithful friend,
   and no scales can measure his excellence.
16 A faithful friend is an elixir of life;
   and those who fear the Lord will find him.
17 Whoever fears the Lord directs his friendship aright,
   for as he is, so is his neighbour also.

18 My son, from your youth up choose instruction,
   and until you are old you will keep finding wisdom.
19 Come to her like one who ploughs and sows,
   and wait for her good harvest.
   For in her service you will toil a little while,
   and soon you will eat of her produce.
20 She seems very harsh to the uninstructed;
   a weakling will not remain with her.
21 She will weigh him down like a heavy testing stone,
   and he will not be slow to cast her off.
22 For wisdom is like her name,
   and is not manifest to many.

23 Listen, my son, and accept my judgement;
   do not reject my counsel.

24 Put your feet into her fetters,
    and your neck into her collar.
25 Put your shoulder under her and carry her,
    and do not fret under her bonds.
26 Come to her with all your soul,
    and keep her ways with all your might.
27 Search out and seek, and she will become known to you;
    and when you get hold of her, do not let her go.
28 For at last you will find the rest she gives,
    and she will be changed into joy for you.
29 Then her fetters will become for you a strong protection,
    and her collar a glorious robe.
30 Her yoke is a golden ornament,
    and her bonds are a cord of blue.
31 You will wear her like a glorious robe,
    and put her on like a crown of gladness.

32 If you are willing, my son, you will be taught,
    and if you apply yourself you will become clever.
33 If you love to listen you will gain knowledge,
    and if you incline your ear you will become wise.
34 Stand in the assembly of the elders.
    Who is wise? Cleave to him.
35 Be ready to listen to every narrative,
    and do not let wise proverbs escape you.
36 If you see an intelligent man, visit him early;
    let your foot wear out his doorstep.
37 Reflect on the statutes of the Lord, and meditate at all times on his
    commandments.
    It is he who will give insight to your mind,
    and your desire for wisdom will be granted.

CHAPTER TWENTY-FOUR

1 Wisdom will praise herself, and will glory in the midst of her
    people.
2 In the assembly of the Most High she will open her mouth,
    and in the presence of his host she will glory:
3 "I came forth from the mouth of the Most High,
    and covered the earth like a mist.
4 I dwelt in high places,
    and my throne was in a pillar of cloud.

5 Alone I have made the circuit of the vault of heaven
　　and have walked in the depths of the abyss.
6 In the waves of the sea, in the whole earth,
　　and in every people and nation I have gotten a
　　　possession.
7 Among all these I sought a resting place;
　　I sought in whose territory I might lodge.

8 "Then the Creator of all things gave me a commandment,
　　and the one who created me assigned a place for my tent.
　　And he said, 'Make your dwelling in Jacob,
　　and in Israel receive your inheritance.'
9 From eternity, in the beginning, he created me,
　　and for eternity I shall not cease to exist.
10 In the holy tabernacle I ministered before him,
　　and so I was established in Zion.
11 In the beloved city likewise he gave me a resting place,
　　and in Jerusalem was my dominion.
12 So I took root in an honoured people,
　　in the portion of the Lord, who is their inheritance.

13 "I grew tall like a cedar in Lebanon,
　　and like a cypress on the heights of Hermon.
14 I grew tall like a palm tree in Enged'i,
　　and like rose plants in Jericho;
　　like a beautiful olive tree in the field,
　　and like a plane tree I grew tall.
15 Like cassia and camel's thorn I gave forth the aroma of
　　　spices,
　　and like choice myrrh I spread a pleasant odour,
　　like galbanum, onycha, and stacte,
　　and like the fragrance of frankincense in the tabernacle.
16 Like a terebinth I spread out my branches,
　　and my branches are glorious and graceful.
17 Like a vine I caused loveliness to bud,
　　and my blossoms became glorious and abundant fruit.

19 "Come to me, you who desire me,
　　and eat your fill of my produce.
20 For the remembrance of me is sweeter than honey,
　　and my inheritance sweeter than the honeycomb.
21 Those who eat me will hunger for more,
　　and those who drink me will thirst for more.

22 Whoever obeys me will not be put to shame,
  and those who work with my help will not sin."

23 All this is the book of the covenant of the Most High God,
  the law which Moses commanded us
  as an inheritance for the congregations of Jacob.
25 It fills men with wisdom, like the Pishon,
  and like the Tigris at the time of the first fruits.
26 It makes them full of understanding, like the Euphra′tes,
  and like the Jordan at harvest time.
27 It makes instruction shine forth like light,
  like the Gihon at the time of vintage.
28 Just as the first man did not know her perfectly,
  the last one has not fathomed her;
29 for her thought is more abundant than the sea,
  and her counsel deeper than the great abyss.
30 I went forth like a canal from a river
  and like a water channel into a garden.
31 I said, "I will water my orchard and drench my garden plot";
  and lo, my canal became a river, and my river became a sea.
32 I will again make instruction shine forth like the dawn,
  and I will make it make it shine afar;
33 I will again pour out teaching like prophecy,
  and leave it to all future generations.
34 Observe that I have not laboured for myself alone,
  but for all who seek instruction.

CHAPTER FORTY-THREE

13 By his command he sends the driving snow
  and speeds the lightnings of his judgement.
14 Therefore the storehouses are opened,
  and the clouds fly forth like birds.
15 In his majesty he amasses the clouds,
  and the hailstones are broken in pieces.
16 At his appearing the mountains are shaken;
  at his will the south wind blows.
17 The voice of his thunder rebukes the earth;
  so do the tempest from the north and the whirlwind.
  He scatters the snow like birds flying down,
  and its descent is like locusts alighting.
18 The eye marvels at the beauty of its whiteness,
  and the mind is amazed at its falling.

19 He pours the hoarfrost upon the earth like salt,
    and when it freezes, it becomes pointed thorns.
20 The cold north wind blows,
    and ice freezes over the water;
    it rests upon every pool of water,
    and the water puts it on like a breastplate.
21 He consumes the mountains and burns up the wilderness,
    and withers the tender grass like fire.
22 A mist quickly heals all things;
    when the dew appears, it refreshes from the heat.

23 By his counsel he stilled the great deep
    and planted islands in it.
24 Those who sail the sea tell of its dangers,
    and we marvel at what we hear.
25 For in it are strange and marvellous works,
    all kinds of living things, and huge creatures of the sea.
26 Because of him his messenger finds the way,
    and by his word all things hold together.

27 Though we speak much we cannot reach the end,
    and the sum of our words is: "He is the all."
28 Where shall we find strength to praise him?
    For he is greater than all his works.
29 Terrible is the Lord and very great,
    and marvellous is his power.
30 When you praise the Lord, exalt him as much as you can;
    for he will surpass even that.
    When you exalt him, put forth all your strength,
    and do not grow weary, for you cannot praise him enough.
31 Who has seen him and can describe him?
    Or who can extol him as he is?
32 Many things greater than these lie hidden,
    for we have seen but few of his works.
33 For the Lord has made all things,
    and to the godly he has granted wisdom.

CHAPTER FORTY-FOUR

1 Let us now praise famous men, and our fathers in their
    generations.
2 The Lord apportioned to them great glory,
    his majesty from the beginning.
3 There were those who ruled in their kingdoms,
    and were men renowned for their power,
    giving counsel by their understanding,
    and proclaiming prophecies;
4 leaders of the people in their deliberations
    and in understanding of learning for the people,
    wise in their words of instruction;
5 those who composed musical tunes,
    and set forth verses in writing;
6 rich men furnished with resources,
    living peaceably in their habitations —
7 all these were honoured in their generations,
    and were the glory of their times.
8 There are some of them who have left a name,
    so that men declare their praise.
9 And there are some who have no memorial,
    who have perished as though they had not lived;
    they have become as though they had not been born,
    and so have their children after them.
10 But these were men of mercy,
    whose righteous deeds have not been forgotten;
11 their prosperity will remain with their descendants,
    and their inheritance to their children's children.
12 Their descendants stand by the covenants;
    their children also, for their sake.
13 Their posterity will continue for ever,
    and their glory will not be blotted out.
14 Their bodies were buried in peace,
    and their name lives to all generations.
15 Peoples will declare their wisdom,
    and the congregation proclaims their praise.
16 Enoch pleased the Lord, and was taken up;
    he was an example of repentance to all generations.

17 Noah was found perfect and righteous;
    in the time of wrath he was taken in exchange;

therefore a remnant was left to the earth
    when the flood came.
18 Everlasting covenants were made with him
    that all flesh should not be blotted out by a flood.

19 Abraham was the great father of a multitude of nations,
    and no one has been found like him in glory;
20 he kept the law of the Most High,
    and was taken into covenant with him;
    he established the covenant in his flesh,
    and when he was tested he was found faithful.
21 Therefore the Lord assured him by an oath
    that the nations would be blessed through his posterity;
    that he would multiply him like the dust of the earth,
    and exalt his posterity like the stars,
    and cause them to inherit from sea to sea
    and from the River to the ends of the earth.

22 To Isaac also he gave the same assurance
    for the sake of Abraham his father.

23 The blessing of all men and the covenant
    he made to rest upon the head of Jacob;
    he acknowledged him with his blessings,
    and gave him his inheritance;
    he determined his portions,
    and distributed them among twelve tribes.

CHAPTER FORTY-FIVE

1 From his descendants the Lord brought forth a man of
    mercy,
    who found favour in the sight of all flesh
    and was beloved by God and man,
    Moses, whose memory is blessed.
2 He made him equal in glory to the holy ones,
    and made him great in the fears of his enemies.
3 By his words he caused signs to cease;
    the Lord glorified him in the presence of kings.
    He gave him commands for his people,
    and showed him part of his glory.
4 He sanctified him through faithfulness and meekness;
    he chose him out of all mankind.

5 He made him hear his voice,
   and led him into the thick darkness,
   and gave him the commandments face to face,
   the law of life and knowledge,
   to teach Jacob the covenant,
   and Israel his judgements.

6 He exalted Aaron, the brother of Moses,
   a holy man like him, of the tribe of Levi.
7 He made an everlasting covenant with him,
   and gave him the priesthood of the people.
   He blessed him with splendid vestments,
   and put a glorious robe upon him.
8 He clothed him with superb perfection,
   and strengthened him with the symbols of authority,
   the linen breeches, the long robe, and the ephod.
9 And he encircled him with pomegranates,
   with very many golden bells round about,
   to send forth a sound as he walked,
   to make their ringing heard in the temple
   as a reminder to the sons of his people;
10 with a holy garment, of gold and blue
   and purple, the work of an embroiderer;
   with the oracle of judgement, Urim and Thummim;
11 with twisted scarlet, the work of a craftsman;
   with precious stones engraved like signets,
   in a setting of gold, the work of a jeweller,
   for a reminder, in engraved letters,
   according to the number of the tribes of Israel;
12 with a gold crown upon his turban,
   inscribed like a signet with "Holiness",
   a distinction to be prized, the work of an expert,
   the delight of the eyes, richly adorned.
13 Before his time there never were such beautiful things.
   No outsider ever put them on,
   but only his sons
   and his descendants perpetually.
14 His sacrifices shall be wholly burned
   twice every day continually.
15 Moses ordained him,
   and anointed him with holy oil;
   it was an everlasting covenant for him
   and for his descendants all the days of heaven,

to minister to the Lord and serve as priest
and bless his people in his name.

16 He chose him out of all the living
to offer sacrifice to the Lord,
incense and a pleasing odour as a memorial portion,
to make atonement for the people.

17 In his commandments he gave him
authority in statutes and judgements,
to teach Jacob the testimonies,
and to enlighten Israel with his law.

18 Outsiders conspired against him,
and envied him in the wilderness,
Dathan and Abi'ram and their men
and the company of Korah, in wrath and anger.

19 The Lord saw it and was not pleased,
and in the wrath of his anger they were destroyed;
he wrought wonders against them
to consume them in flaming fire.

20 He added glory to Aaron
and gave him a heritage;
he allotted to him the first of the first fruits,
he prepared bread of first fruits in abundance;

21 for they eat the sacrifices to the Lord,
which he gave to him and his descendants.

22 But in the land of the people he has no inheritance,
and he has no portion among the people;
for the Lord himself is his portion and inheritance.

23 Phin'ehas the son of Elea'zar is the third in glory,
for he was zealous in the fear of the Lord,
and stood fast, when the people turned away,
in the ready goodness of his soul,
and made atonement for Israel.

24 Therefore a covenant of peace was established with him,
that he should be leader of the sanctuary and of his people,
that he and his descendants should have
the dignity of the priesthood for ever.

25 A covenant was also established with David,
the son of Jesse, of the tribe of Judah:
the heritage of the king is from son to son only;
so the heritage of Aaron is for his descendants.

26 May the Lord grant you wisdom in your heart
to judge his people in righteousness,

so that their prosperity may not vanish,
and that their glory may endure throughout their
generations.

CHAPTER FORTY-SIX

1 Joshua the son of Nun was mighty in war,
and was the successor of Moses in prophesying.
He became, in accordance with his name,
a great saviour of God's elect,
to take vengeance on the enemies that rose against them,
so that he might give Israel its inheritance.
2 How glorious he was when he lifted his hands
and stretched out his sword against the cities!
3 Who before him ever stood so firm?
For he waged the wars of the Lord.
4 Was not the sun held back by his hand?
And did not one day become as long as two?
5 He called upon the Most High, the Mighty One,
when enemies pressed him on every side,
6 and the great Lord answered him
with hailstones of mighty power.
He hurled down war upon that nation,
and at the descent of Beth-horon
he destroyed those who resisted,
so that the nations might know his armament,
that he was fighting in the sight of the Lord;
for he wholly followed the Mighty One.
7 And in the days of Moses he did a loyal deed,
he and Caleb the son of Jephun'neh:
they withstood the congregation,
restrained the people from sin
and stilled their wicked murmuring.
8 And these two alone were preserved
out of six hundred thousand people on foot,
to bring them into their inheritance,
into a land flowing with milk and honey.
9 And the Lord gave Caleb strength,
which remained with him to old age,
so that he went up to the hill country,
and his children obtained it for an inheritance;
10 so that all the sons of Israel might see
that it is good to follow the Lord.

11 The judges also, with their respective names,
    those whose hearts did not fall into idolatry
    and who did not turn away from the Lord —
    may their memory be blessed!
12 May their bones revive from where they lie,
    and may the name of those who have been honoured
    live again in their sons!

13 Samuel, beloved by his Lord,
    a prophet of the Lord, established the kingdom
    and anointed rulers over his people.
14 By the law of the Lord he judged the congregation,
    and the Lord watched over Jacob.
15 By his faithfulness he was proved to be a prophet,
    and by his words he became known as a trustworthy seer.
16 He called upon the Lord, the Mighty One,
    when his enemies pressed him on every side,
    and he offered in sacrifice a sucking lamb.
17 Then the Lord thundered from heaven,
    and made his voice heard with a mighty sound;
18 and he wiped out the leaders of the people of Tyre
    and all the rulers of the Philistines.
19 Before the time of his eternal sleep,
    Samuel called men to witness before the Lord and his anointed:
    "I have not taken any one's property,
    not so much as a pair of shoes."
    And no man accused him.
20 Even after he had fallen asleep he prophesied
    and revealed to the king his death,
    and lifted up his voice out of the earth in prophecy,
    to blot out the wickedness of the people.

CHAPTER FORTY-SEVEN

1 And after him Nathan rose up to prophesy in the days of David.
2 As the fat is selected from the peace offering,
    so David was selected from the sons of Israel.
3 He played with lions as with young goats,
    and with bears as with lambs of the flock.
4 In his youth did he not kill a giant,
    and take away reproach from the people,
    when he lifted his hand with a stone in the sling
    and struck down the boasting of Goliath?

5 For he appealed to the Lord, the Most High,
 and he gave him strength in his right hand
 to slay a man mighty in war,
 to exalt the power of his people.
6 So they glorified him for his ten thousands,
 and praised him for the blessings of the Lord,
 when the glorious diadem was bestowed upon him.
7 For he wiped out his enemies on every side,
 and annihilated his adversaries the Philistines;
 he crushed their power even to this day.
8 In all that he did he gave thanks
 to the Holy One, the Most High, with ascriptions of glory;
 he sang praise with all his heart,
 and he loved his Maker.
9 He placed singers before the altar,
 to make sweet melody with their voices.
10 He gave beauty to the feasts,
 and arranged their times throughout the year,
 while they praised God's holy name,
 and the sanctuary resounded from early morning.
11 The Lord took away his sins,
 and exalted his power for ever;
 he gave him the covenant of kings
 and a throne of glory in Israel.

12 After him rose up a wise son
 who fared amply because of him;
13 Solomon reigned in days of peace,
 and God gave him rest on every side,
 that he might build a house for his name
 and prepare a sanctuary to stand for ever.
14 How wise you became in your youth!
 You overflowed like a river with understanding.
15 Your soul covered the earth,
 and you filled it with parables and riddles.
16 Your name reached to far-off islands,
 and you were loved for your peace.
17 For your songs and proverbs and parables,
 and for your interpretations, the countries marvelled at you.
18 In the name of the Lord God,
 who is called the God of Israel,
 you gathered gold like tin
 and amassed silver like lead.

19 But laid your loins beside women,
    and through your body you were brought into subjection.
20 You put a stain upon your honour,
    and defiled your posterity,
    so that you brought wrath upon your children
    and they were grieved at your folly,
21 so that the sovereignty was divided
    and a disobedient kingdom arose out of E'phraim.
22 But the Lord will never give up his mercy,
    nor cause any of his works to perish;
    he will never blot out the descendants of his chosen one,
    nor destroy the posterity of him who loved him;
    so he gave a remnant to Jacob,
    and to David a root of his stock.

23 Solomon rested with his fathers,
    and left behind him one of his sons,
    ample in folly and lacking in understanding,
    Rehobo'am, whose policy caused the people to revolt.
    Also Jerobo'am the son of Nebat, who caused Israel to sin
    and gave to E'phraim a sinful way.
24 Their sins became exceedingly many,
    so as to remove them from their land.
25 For they sought out every sort of wickedness,
    till vengeance came upon them.'

CHAPTER FORTY-EIGHT

1 Then the prophet Eli'jah arose like a fire,
    and his word burned like a torch.
2 He brought a famine upon them,
    and by his zeal he made them few in number.
3 By the word of the Lord he shut up the heavens,
    and also three times brought down fire.
4 How glorious you were, O Eli'jah, in your wondrous deeds!
    And who has the right to boast which you have?
5 You have raised a corpse from death
    and from Hades, by the word of the Most High;
6 who brought kings down to destruction,
    and famous men from their beds;
7 who heard rebuke at Sinai
    and judgements of vengeance at Horeb;

8 who anointed kings to inflict retribution,
    and prophets to succeed you.
9 You who were taken up by a whirlwind of fire,
    in a chariot with horses of fire;
10 you who are ready at the appointed time, it is written,
    to calm the wrath of God before it breaks out in fury,
    to turn the heart of the father to the son,
    and to restore the tribes of Jacob.
11 Blessed are those who saw you,
    and those who have been adorned in love;
    for we also shall surely live.

12 It was Eli'jah who was covered by the whirlwind,
    and Eli'sha was filled with his spirit;
    in all his days he did not tremble before any
      ruler,
    and no one brought him into subjection.
13 Nothing was too hard for him,
    and when he was dead his body prophesied.
14 As in his life he did wonders,
    so in death his deeds were marvellous.
15 For all this the people did not repent,
    and they did not forsake their sins,
    till they were carried away captive from their land
    and were scattered over all the earth;
    the people were left very few in number,
    but with rulers from the house of David.
16 Some of them did what was pleasing to God,
    but others multiplied sins.

17 Hezeki'ah fortified his city,
    and brought water into the midst of it;
    he tunnelled the sheer rock with iron
    and built pools for water.
18 In his days Sennach'erib came up,
    and sent the Rab'shakeh;
    he lifted up his hand against Zion
    and made great boasts in his arrogance.
19 Then their hearts were shaken and their hands
    trembled,
    and they were in anguish, like women in travail.
20 But they called upon the Lord who is merciful,
    spreading forth their hands toward him;

and the Holy One quickly heard them from heaven,
and delivered them by the hand of Isaiah.
21 The Lord smote the camp of the Assyrians,
and his angel wiped them out.
22 For Hezeki'ah did what was pleasing to the Lord,
and he held strongly to the ways of David his father,
which Isaiah the prophet commanded,
who was great and faithful in his vision.
23 In his days the sun went backward,
and he lengthened the life of the king.
24 By the spirit of might he saw the last things,
and comforted those who mourned in Zion.
25 He revealed what was to occur to the end of time,
and the hidden things before they came to pass.

CHAPTER FORTY-NINE

1 The memory of Josi'ah is like a blending of incense
prepared by the art of the perfumer;
it is sweet as honey to every mouth,
and like music at a banquet of wine.
2 He was led aright in converting the people,
and took away the abominations of iniquity.
3 He set his heart upon the Lord;
in the days of wicked men he strengthened godliness.

4 Except David and Hezeki'ah and Josi'ah
they all sinned greatly,
for they forsook the law of the Most High;
the kings of Judah came to an end;
5 for they gave their power to others,
and their glory to a foreign nation,
6 who set fire to the chosen city of the sanctuary,
and made her streets desolate,
according to the word of Jeremiah.
7 For they had afflicted him;
yet he had been consecrated in the womb as prophet,
to pluck up and afflict and destroy,
and likewise to build and to plant.

8 It was Ezekiel who saw the vision of glory
which God showed him above the chariot of the
cherubim.

9 For God remembered his enemies with storm,
    and did good to those who directed their ways aright.

10 May the bones of the twelve prophets revive from where
    they lie,
    for they comforted the people of Jacob
    and delivered them with confident hope.
11 How shall we magnify Zerub'babel?
    He was like a signet on the right hand,
12 and so was Jeshua the son of Jo'zadak;
    in their days they built the house
    and raised a temple holy to the Lord,
    prepared for everlasting glory.
13 The memory of Nehemi'ah also is lasting;
    he raised for us the walls that had fallen,
    and set up the gates and bars
    and rebuilt our ruined houses.

14 No one like Enoch has been created on earth,
    for he was taken up from the earth.
15 And no man like Joseph has been born,
    and his bones are cared for.
16 Shem and Seth were honoured among men,
    and Adam above every living being in the creation.

CHAPTER FIFTY

1 The leader of his brethren and the pride of his people
    was Simon the high priest, son of Oni'as,
    who in his life repaired the house,
    and in his time fortified the temple.
2 He laid the foundations for the high double walls,
    the high retaining walls for the temple enclosure.
3 In his days a cistern for water was quarried out,
    a reservoir like the sea in circumference.
4 He considered how to save his people from ruin,
    and fortified the city to withstand a siege.
5 How glorious he was when the people gathered round him
    as he came out of the inner sanctuary!
6 Like the morning star among the clouds,
    Like the moon when it is full;
7 like the sun shining upon the temple of the Most High,
    and like the rainbow gleaming in glorious clouds;

8 like roses in the days of the first fruits,
>   like lilies by a spring of water,
>   like a green shoot on Lebanon on a summer day;
9 Like fire and incense in the censer,
>   like a vessel of hammered gold
>   adorned with all kinds of precious stones;
10 like an olive tree putting forth its fruit,
>   and like a cypress towering in the clouds.
11 When he put on his glorious robe
>   and clothed himself with superb perfection
>   and went up to the holy altar,
>   he made the court of the sanctuary glorious.
12 And when he received the portions from the hands of the
>   priests,
>   as he stood by the hearth of the altar
>   with a garland of brethren around him,
>   he was like a young cedar on Lebanon;
>   and they surrounded him like the trunks of palm trees,
13 all the sons of Aaron in their splendour
>   with the Lord's offering in their hands,
>   before the whole congregation of Israel.
14 Finishing the service at the altars,
>   and arranging the offering to the Most High, the Almighty,
15 he reached out his hand to the cup
>   and poured a libation of the blood of the grape;
>   he poured it out at the foot of the altar,
>   a pleasing odour to the Most High, the King of all.
16 Then the sons of Aaron shouted,
>   they sounded the trumpets of hammered work,
>   they made a great noise to be heard
>   for remembrance before the Most High.
17 Then all the people together made haste
>   and fell to the ground upon their faces
>   to worship their Lord,
>   the Almighty, God Most High.
18 And the singers praised him with their voices
>   in sweet and full-toned melody.
19 And the people besought the Lord Most High
>   in prayer before him who is merciful,
>   till the order of worship of the Lord was ended;
>   so they completed his service.
20 Then Simon came down, and lifted up his hands
>   over the whole congregation of the sons of Israel,

to pronounce the blessing of the Lord with his lips,
    and to glory in his name;
21 and they bowed down in worship a second time,
    to receive the blessing from the Most High.

22 And now bless the God of all,
    who in every way does great things;
    who exalts our days from birth,
    and deals with us according to his mercy.
23 May he give us gladness of heart,
    and grant that peace may be in our days in Israel,
    as in the days of old.
24 May he entrust to us his mercy!
    And let him deliver us in our days!

25 With two nations my soul is vexed,
    and the third is no nation:
26 Those who live on Mount Se′ir, and the Philistines,
    and the foolish people that dwell in Shechem.

27 Instruction in understanding and knowledge
    I have written in this book,
    Jesus the son of Sirach, son of Elea′zar, of Jerusalem,
    who out of his heart poured forth wisdom.
28 Blessed is he who concerns himself with these things,
    and he who lays them to heart will become wise.
29 For if he does them, he will be strong for all things,
    for the light of the Lord is his path.

THE WISDOM OF SOLOMON

CHAPTERS 1–9

THE WISDOM OF SOLOMON

*This translation is taken from
the Revised Standard Version of the Bible*

CHAPTER ONE

1 Love righteousness, you rulers of the earth,
  think of the Lord with uprightness,
  and seek him with sincerity of heart;
2 because he is found by those who do not put him to the test,
  and manifests himself to those who do not distrust him.
3 For perverse thoughts separate men from God,
  and when his power is tested, it convicts the foolish;
4 because wisdom will not enter a deceitful soul,
  nor dwell in a body enslaved to sin.
5 For a holy and disciplined spirit will flee from deceit,
  and will rise and depart from foolish thoughts,
  and will be ashamed at the approach of unrighteousness.

6 For wisdom is a kindly spirit
  and will not free a blasphemer from the guilt of his words;
  because God is witness of his inmost feelings,
  and a true observer of his heart,
  and a hearer of his tongue.
7 Because the Spirit of the Lord has filled the world,
  and that which holds all things together knows what is said;
8 therefore no one who utters unrighteous things will escape notice,
  and justice, when it punishes, will not pass him by.
9 For inquiry will be made into the counsels of an ungodly man,
  and a report of his words will come to the Lord,
  to convict him of his lawless deeds;
10 because a jealous ear hears all things,
  and the sound of murmurings does not go unheard.
11 Beware then of useless murmuring,
  and keep your tongue from slander;
  because no secret word is without result,
  and a lying mouth destroys the soul.
12 Do not invite death by the error of your life,
  nor bring on destruction by the works of your hands;

13 because God did not make death,
　　and he does not delight in the death of the living.
14 For he created all things that they might exist,
　　and the generative forces of the world are wholesome,
　　and there is no destructive poison in them;
　　and the dominion of Hades is not on earth.
15 For righteousness is immortal.

16 But ungodly men by their words and deeds summoned death;
　　considering him a friend, they pined away,
　　and they made a covenant with him,
　　because they are fit to belong to his party.

CHAPTER TWO

1 For they reasoned unsoundly, saying to themselves,
　　"Short and sorrowful is our life,
　　and there is no remedy when a man comes to his end,
　　and no one has been known to return from Hades.
2 Because we were born by mere chance,
　　and hereafter we shall be as though we had never been;
　　because the breath in our nostrils is smoke,
　　and reason is a spark kindled by the beating of our hearts.
3 When it is extinguished, the body will turn to ashes,
　　and the spirit will dissolve like empty air.
4 Our name will be forgotten in time,
　　and no one will remember our works;
　　our life will pass away like the traces of a cloud,
　　and be scattered like mist
　　that is chased by the rays of the sun
　　and overcome by its heat.
5 For our allotted time is the passing of a shadow,
　　and there is no return from our death,
　　because it is sealed up and no one turns back.

6 "Come, therefore, let us enjoy the good things that exist,
　　and make use of the creation to the full as in youth.
7 Let us take our fill of costly wine and perfumes,
　　and let no flower of spring pass by us.
8 Let us crown ourselves with rosebuds before they wither.
9 Let none of us fail to share in our revelry,
　　everywhere let us leave signs of enjoyment,
　　because this is our portion, and this our lot.

10 Let us oppress the righteous poor man;
      let us not spare the widow
      nor regard the grey hairs of the aged.
11 But let our might be our law of right,
      for what is weak proves itself to be useless.

12 "Let us lie in wait for the righteous man,
      because he is inconvenient to us and opposes our actions;
      he reproaches us for sins against the law,
      and accuses us of sins against our training.
13 He professes to have knowledge of God,
      and calls himself a child of the Lord.
14 He became to us a reproof of our thoughts;
15 the very sight of him is a burden to us,
      because his manner of life is unlike that of others,
      and his ways are strange.
16 We are considered by him as something base,
      and he avoids our ways as unclean;
      he calls the last end of the righteous happy,
      and boasts that God is his father.
17 Let us see if his words are true,
      and let us test what will happen at the end of his life;
18 for if the righteous man is God's son, he will help him,
      and will deliver him from the hand of his adversaries.
19 Let us test him with insult and torture,
      that we may find out how gentle he is,
      and make trial of his forbearance.
20 Let us condemn him to a shameful death,
      for, according to what he says, he will be protected."

21 Thus they reasoned, but they were led astray,
      for their wickedness blinded them,
22 and they did not know the secret purposes of God,
      nor hope for the wages of holiness,
      nor discern the prize for blameless souls;
23 for God created man for incorruption,
      and made him in the image of his own eternity,
24 but through the devil's envy death entered the world,
      and those who belong to his party experience it.

CHAPTER THREE

1 But the souls of the righteous are in the hand of God,
   and no torment will ever touch them.
2 In the eyes of the foolish they seemed to have died,
   and their departure was thought to be an affliction,
3 and their going from us to be their destruction;
   but they are at peace.
4 For though in the sight of men they were punished,
   their hope is full of immortality.
5 Having been disciplined a little, they will receive great good,
   because God tested them and found them worthy of
      himself;
6 like gold in the furnace he tried them,
   and like a sacrificial burnt offering he accepted them.
7 In the time of their visitation they will shine forth,
   and will run like sparks through the stubble.
8 They will govern nations and rule over peoples,
   and the Lord will reign over them for ever.
9 Those who trust in him will understand truth,
   and the faithful will abide with him in love,
   because grace and mercy are upon his elect,
   and he watches over his holy ones.

10 But the ungodly will be punished as their reasoning deserves,
   who disregarded the righteous man and rebelled against
      the Lord;
11 for whoever despises wisdom and instruction is miserable.
   Their hope is vain, their labours are unprofitable,
   and their works are useless.
12 Their wives are foolish, and their children evil;
13 their offspring are accursed.
   For blessed is the barren woman who is undefiled,
   who has not entered into a sinful union;
   she will have fruit when God examines souls.
14 Blessed also is the eunuch whose hands have done no lawless
      deed,
   and who has not devised wicked things against the Lord;
   for special favour will be shown him for his faithfulness,
   and a place of great delight in the temple of the Lord.
15 For the fruit of good labours is renowned,
   and the root of understanding does not fail.

16 But children of adulterers will not come to maturity,
    and the offspring of an unlawful union will perish.
17 Even if they live long they will be held of no account,
    and finally their old age will be without honour.
18 If they die young, they will have no hope
    and no consolation in the day of decision.
19 For the end of an unrighteous generation is grievous.

CHAPTER FOUR

1 Better than this is childlessness with virtue,
    for in the memory of virtue is immortality,
    because it is known both by God and by men.
2 When it is present, men imitate it,
    and they long for it when it has gone;
    and throughout all time it marches crowned in triumph,
    victor in the contest for prizes that are undefiled.
3 But the prolific brood of the ungodly will be of no use,
    and none of their illegitimate seedlings will strike a deep root
    or take a firm hold.
4 For even if they put forth boughs for a while,
    standing insecurely they will be shaken by the wind,
    and by the violence of the winds they will be uprooted.
5 The branches will be broken off before they come to maturity,
    and their fruit will be useless,
    not ripe enough to eat, and good for nothing.
6 For children born of unlawful unions are witnesses of evil against
    their parents when God examines them.

7 But the righteous man, though he die early, will be at rest.
8 For old age is not honoured for length of time,
    nor measured by number of years;
9 but understanding is grey hair for men,
    and a blameless life is ripe old age.
10 There was one who pleased God and was loved by him,
    and while living among sinners he was taken up.
11 He was caught up lest evil change his understanding
    or guile deceive his soul.
12 For the fascination of wickedness obscures what is good,
    and roving desire perverts the innocent mind.
13 Being perfected in a short time, he fulfilled long years;
14 for his soul was pleasing to the Lord,
    therefore he took him quickly from the midst of wickedness.

15 Yet the peoples saw and did not understand,
    nor take such a thing to heart,
    that God's grace and mercy are with his elect,
    and he watches over his holy ones.

16 The righteous man who has died will condemn the ungodly who
    are living,
    and youth that is quickly perfected will condemn the prolonged
      old age of the unrighteous man.
17 For they will see the end of the wise man,
    and will not understand what the Lord purposed for him,
    and for what he kept him safe.
18 They will see, and will have contempt for him,
    but the Lord will laugh them to scorn.
    After this they will become dishonoured corpses,
    and an outrage among the dead for ever;
19 because he will dash them speechless to the ground,
    and shake them from the foundations;
    they will be left utterly dry and barren,
    and they will suffer anguish,
    and the memory of them will perish.

20 They will come with dread when their sins are reckoned up,
    and their lawless deeds will convict them to their face.

CHAPTER FIVE

1 Then the righteous man will stand with great confidence
    in the presence of those who have afflicted him,
    and those who make light of his labours.
2 When they see him, they will be shaken with dreadful fear,
    and they will be amazed at his unexpected salvation.
3 They will speak to one another in repentance,
    and in anguish of spirit they will groan, and say,
4 "This is the man whom we once held in derision
    and made a byword of reproach – we fools!
    We thought that his life was madness and that his end was without
      honour.
5 Why has he been numbered among the sons of God?
    And why is his lot among the saints?
6 So it was we who strayed from the way of truth,
    and the light of righteousness did not shine on us,
    and the sun did not rise upon us.

7 We took our fill of the paths of lawlessness and destruction,
  and we journeyed through trackless deserts,
  but the way of the Lord we have not known.

8 What has our arrogance profited us?
  And what good has our boasted wealth brought us?

9 "All those things have vanished like a shadow,
  and like a rumour that passes by;

10 like a ship that sails through the billowy water,
  and when it has passed no trace can be found,
  nor track of its keel in the waves;

11 or as, when a bird flies through the air,
  no evidence of its passage is found;
  the light air, lashed by the beat of its pinions
  and pierced by the force of its rushing flight,
  is traversed by the movement of its wings,
  and afterward no sign of its coming is found there;

12 or as, when an arrow is shot at a target, the air, thus divided, comes together at once,
  so that no one knows its pathway.

13 So we also, as soon as we were born, ceased to be,
  and we had no sign of virtue to show,
  but were consumed in our wickedness."

14 Because the hope of the ungodly man is like chaff carried by the wind,
  and like a light hoarfrost driven away by a storm;
  it is dispersed like smoke before the wind,
  and it passes like the remembrance of a guest who stays but a day.

15 But the righteous live for ever,
  and their reward is with the Lord;
  the Most High takes care of them.

16 Therefore they will receive a glorious crown
  and a beautiful diadem from the hand of the Lord,
  because with his right hand he will cover them,
  and with his arm he will shield them.

17 The Lord will take his zeal as his whole armour,
  and will arm all creation to repel his enemies;

18 he will put on righteousness as a breastplate,
  and wear impartial justice as a helmet;

19 he will take holiness as an invincible shield,

20 and sharpen stern wrath for a sword,
  and creation will join with him to fight against the madmen.

21 Shafts of lightning will fly with true aim,
    and will leap to the target as from a well-drawn bow of
      clouds,
22 and hailstones full of wrath will be hurled as from a catapult;
    the water of the sea will rage against them,
    and rivers will relentlessly overwhelm them;
23 a mighty wind will rise against them;
    and like a tempest it will winnow them away.
    Lawlessness will lay waste the whole earth,
    and evil-doing will overturn the thrones of rulers.

CHAPTER SIX

1 Listen therefore, O kings, and understand;
    learn, O judges of the ends of the earth.
2 Give ear, you that rule over multitudes,
    and boast of many nations.
3 For your dominion was given you from the Lord,
    and your sovereignty from the Most High,
    who will search out your works and inquire into your plans.
4 Because as servants of his kingdom you did not rule rightly,
    nor keep the law,
    nor walk according to the purpose of God,
5 he will come upon you terribly and swiftly,
    because severe judgement falls on those in high places.
6 For the lowliest man may be pardoned in mercy,
    but mighty men will be mightily tested.
7 For the Lord of all will not stand in awe of any one,
    nor show deference to greatness;
    because he himself made both small and great,
    and he takes thought for all alike.
8 But a strict inquiry is in store for the mighty.
9 To you then, O monarchs, my words are directed,
    that you may learn wisdom and not transgress.
10 For they will be made holy who observe holy things in holiness,
    and those who have been taught them will find a defence.
11 Therefore set your desire on my words;
    long for them, and you will be instructed.

12 Wisdom is radiant and unfading,
    and she is easily discerned by those who love her,
    and is found by those who seek her.
13 She hastens to make herself known to those who desire her.

14 He who rises early to seek her will have no difficulty,
    for he will find her sitting at his gates.
15 To fix one's thought on her is perfect understanding,
    and he who is vigilant on her account will soon be free from care,
16 because she goes about seeking those worthy of her,
    and she graciously appears to them in their paths,
    and meets them in every thought.

17 The beginning of wisdom is the most sincere desire for instruction,
    and concern for instruction is love of her,
18 and love of her is the keeping of her laws,
    and giving heed to her laws is assurance of immortality,
19 and immortality brings one near to God;
20 so the desire for wisdom leads to a kingdom.

21 Therefore if you delight in thrones and sceptres, O monarchs over
    the peoples,
    honour wisdom, that you may reign for ever.
22 I will tell you what wisdom is and how she came to be,
    and I will hide no secrets from you,
    but I will trace her course from the beginning of creation,
    and make the knowledge of her clear,
    and I will not pass by the truth;
23 neither will I travel in the company of sickly envy,
    for envy does not associate with wisdom.
24 A multitude of wise men is the salvation of the world,
    and a sensible king is the stability of his people.
25 Therefore be instructed by my words, and you will profit.

CHAPTER SEVEN

1 I also am mortal, like all men,
    a descendant of the first-formed child of earth;
    and in the womb of a mother I was moulded into flesh,
2 within the period of ten months, compacted with blood,
    from the seed of a man and the pleasure of marriage.
3 And when I was born, I began to breathe the common air,
    and fell upon the kindred earth,
    and my first sound was a cry, like that of all.
4 I was nursed with care in swaddling cloths.
5 For no king has had a different beginning of existence;
6 there is for all mankind one entrance into life, and a common
    departure.

7 Therefore I prayed, and understanding was given me;
    I called upon God, and the spirit of wisdom came to me.

8 I preferred her to sceptres and thrones,
    and I accounted wealth as nothing in comparison with her.

9 Neither did I liken to her any priceless gem,
    because all gold is but a little sand in her sight,
    and silver will be accounted as clay before her.

10 I loved her more than health and beauty,
    and I chose to have her rather than light,
    because her radiance never ceases.

11 All good things came to me along with her,
    and in her hands uncounted wealth.

12 I rejoiced in them all, because wisdom leads them;
    but I did not know that she was their mother.

13 I learned without guile and I impart without grudging;
    I do not hide her wealth,

14 for it is an unfailing treasure for men;
    those who get it obtain friendship with God,
    commended for the gifts that come from instruction.

15 May God grant that I speak with judgment
    and have thoughts worthy of what I have received,
    for he is the guide even of wisdom
    and the corrector of the wise.

16 For both we and our words are in his hand,
    as are all understanding and skill in crafts.

17 For it is he who gave me unerring knowledge of what exists,
    to know the structure of the world and the activity of the elements;

18 the beginning and end and middle of times,
    the alternations of the solstices and the changes of the seasons,

19 the cycles of the year and the constellations of the stars,

20 the natures of animals and the tempers of wild beasts,
    the powers of spirits and the reasonings of men,
    the varieties of plants and the virtues of roots;

21 I learned both what is secret and what is manifest,

22 for wisdom, the fashioner of all things, taught me.

    For in her there is a spirit that is intelligent, holy,
    unique, manifold, subtle,
    mobile, clear, unpolluted,
    distinct, invulnerable, loving the good, keen,
    irresistible,

23 beneficent, humane,
   steadfast, sure, free from anxiety,
   all-powerful, overseeing all,
   and penetrating through all spirits
   that are intelligent and pure and most subtle.
24 For wisdom is more mobile than any motion;
   because of her pureness she pervades and penetrates all things.
25 For she is a breath of the power of God,
   and a pure emanation of the glory of the Almighty;
   therefore nothing defiled gains entrance into her.
26 For she is a reflection of eternal light,
   a spotless mirror of the working of God,
   and an image of his goodness.
27 Though she is but one, she can do all things,
   and while remaining in herself, she renews all things;
   in every generation she passes into holy souls
   and makes them friends of God, and prophets;
28 for God loves nothing so much as the man who lives with wisdom.
29 For she is more beautiful than the sun,
   and excels every constellation of the stars.
   Compared with the light she is found to be superior,
30 for it is succeeded by the night,
   but against wisdom evil does not prevail.

CHAPTER EIGHT

1 She reaches mightily from one end of the earth to the other,
   and she orders all things well.

2 I loved her and sought her from my youth,
   and I desired to take her for my bride,
   and I became enamoured of her beauty.
3 She glorifies her noble birth by living with God,
   and the Lord of all loves her.
4 For she is an initiate in the knowledge of God,
   and an associate in his works.
5 If riches are a desirable possession in life,
   what is richer than wisdom who effects all things?
6 And if understanding is effective,
   who more than she is fashioner of what exists?
7 And if any one loves righteousness, her labours are virtues;
   for she teaches self-control and prudence,
   justice and courage;
   nothing in life is more profitable for men than these.

8 And if any one longs for wide experience,
    she knows the things of old, and infers the things to come;
    she understands turns of speech and the solutions of riddles;
    she has foreknowledge of signs, and wonders
    and of the outcome of seasons and times.

9 Therefore I determined to take her to live with me,
    knowing that she would give me good counsel
    and encouragement in cares and grief.

10 Because of her I shall have glory among the multitudes
    and honour in the presence of the elders, though I am young.

11 I shall be found keen in judgement,
    and in the sight of rulers I shall be admired.

12 When I am silent they will wait for me,
    and when I speak they will give heed;
    and when I speak at greater length
    they will put their hands on their mouths.

13 Because of her I shall have immortality,
    and leave an everlasting remembrance to those who come after
      me.

14 I shall govern peoples,
    and nations will be subject to me;

15 dread monarchs will be afraid of me when they hear of me;
    among the people I shall show myself capable, and courageous in
      war.

16 When I enter my house, I shall find rest with her,
    for companionship with her has no bitterness,
    and life with her has no pain, but gladness and joy.

17 When I considered these things inwardly,
    and thought upon them in my mind,
    that in kinship with wisdom there is immortality,

18 and in friendship with her, pure delight,
    and in the labours of her hands, unfailing wealth,
    and in the experience of her company, understanding,
    and renown in sharing her words,
    I went about seeking how to get her for myself.

19 As a child I was by nature well endowed,
    and a good soul fell to my lot;

20 or rather, being good, I entered an undefiled body.

21 But I perceived that I would not possess wisdom unless God gave
    her to me—
    and it was a mark of insight to know whose gift she was—
    so I appealed to the Lord and besought him,
    and with my whole heart I said:

CHAPTER NINE

1 "O God of my fathers and Lord of mercy,
 who hast made all things by thy word,
2 and by thy wisdom hast formed man,
 to have dominion over the creatures thou hast made,
3 and rule the world in holiness and righteousness,
 and pronounce judgement in uprightness of soul,
4 give me the wisdom that sits by thy throne,
 and do not reject me from among thy servants.
5 For I am thy slave and the son of thy maidservant,
 a man who is weak and short-lived,
 with little understanding of judgement and laws;
6 for even if one is perfect among the sons of men,
 yet without the wisdom that comes from thee he will be regarded
  as nothing.
7 Thou hast chosen me to be king of thy people
 and to be judge over thy sons and daughters.
8 Thou hast given command to build a temple on thy holy mountain,
 and an altar in the city of thy habitation,
 a copy of the holy tent which thou didst prepare from the
  beginning.
9 With thee is wisdom, who knows thy works
 and was present when thou didst make the world,
 and who understands what is pleasing in thy sight.
 and what is right according to thy commandments.
10 Send her forth from the holy heavens,
 and from the throne of thy glory send her,
 that she may be with me and toil,
 and that I may learn what is pleasing to thee.
11 For she knows and understands all things,
 and she will guide me wisely in my actions
 and guard me with her glory.
12 Then my works will be acceptable,
 and I shall judge thy people justly,
 and shall be worthy of the throne of my father.
13 For what man can learn the counsel of God?
 Or who can discern what the Lord wills?
14 For the reasoning of mortals is worthless,
 and our designs are likely to fail,
15 for a perishable body weighs down the soul,
 and this earthly tent burdens the thoughtful mind.

16 We can hardly guess at what is on earth,
  and what is at hand we find with labour;
  but who has traced out what is in the heavens?

17 Who has learned thy counsel, unless thou hast given wisdom
  and sent thy holy Spirit from on high?

18 And thus the paths of those on earth were set right,
  and men were taught what pleases thee,
  and were saved by wisdom."

VII

CHRISTIANITY

Matthew

Mark

Luke

John

Letter to the Ephesians

Christianity began as a small sect of Jews in Jerusalem, who claimed to be disciples of Jesus of Nazareth, a Jew who had been crucified under the Roman governor, Pontius Pilate and who, his disciples said, had appeared to them after his death. It was from this humble beginning that the Christian religion emerged. The earliest records of it are contained in the letters of Paul of Tarsus, a convert to the faith, who wrote in the early fifties, twenty years after the event. The first gospels or records of the life of Jesus were written in the second half of the first century, but they clearly depended on an oral tradition which had been preserved in the different Christian churches. In studying these records we must remember that they were written in Greek and translated from the original Aramaic, a Semitic dialect which Jesus and his disciples spoke. We have to allow also for the editing of the various stories and collections of teaching which had come down through the different churches. From Mark the first ten chapters have been taken which give the basic pattern of the life of Jesus as it came to be accepted in the synoptic tradition, and from Luke where he takes over from Mark and gives his own version of the teaching of Jesus, especially as seen in the great parables like the Good Samaritan and the Prodigal Son (Luke 10–21). To this Matthew and Luke added the infancy stories together with the appearances after the resurrection and the records of the teaching of Jesus, which had come down to them. We have given the Sermon on the Mount from Matthew and the parables and discourses from Luke which illustrate one aspect of the universal wisdom. John's gospel comes later at the end of the first century and opens up another world. It is generally believed to have been written in Ephesus in what is now Turkey, which was a centre of gnostic spirituality and it is here that the gospel story was brought into contact with the wider tradition of universal wisdom.

The Fourth Gospel, as we shall call it, as its author, the 'beloved disciple' is unknown, speaks of Jesus as the *Logos*, the Word or Wisdom of God, and this gives the key to the whole gospel. It is a record of the life and teaching of Jesus seen in the light of the Universal Wisdom, in which every event in the life of Jesus is given a symbolic meaning. Symbolism is the language of the universal wisdom. It sees the whole universe as a symbol of God, a sign by which the divine Wisdom makes itself known. In Jesus of Nazareth the gospel sees the supreme symbol of God, the sign by which the divine wisdom makes itself known and becomes present to humanity in its fullness. It reveals that the divine wisdom, or the ultimate truth, is known not only by words written in a book or by philosophy enshrined in doctrine but in the "flesh", that is, in the actual, concrete conditions of human existence. Jesus was crucified "under Pontius Pilate" at a particular time and place and in a particular historic situation. On the other hand, the Fourth Gospel reveals above all the intimate relation between Jesus and God. The earliest tradition does not speak of Jesus as God: that was a later theological development. The original revelation was that Jesus was a "man approved by God" (Acts 2: 22), whom God "anointed" with the Holy Spirit and with power (Acts 10: 38). Jesus himself in the Fourth Gospel constantly speaks of himself in relation to God and refers everything he says and does to its source in the "Father". This is the particular Christian revelation, not that Jesus was God, as Rama and Krishna can be said to be God, but that he stood in a unique relation to God as Son to the Father.

It is significant that Muhammad in the Quran insisted that God had no son. This would have undermined the solitary isolation of the monotheistic God in whom he believed. By calling himself Son, Jesus recognized relationship in God, in the ultimate Truth and Reality. God in this understanding is not a solitary Monad. The Godhead, the divine being itself, is constituted by relationship. But this means not only that Jesus is the son of God but that all humanity in Jesus is brought into this relationship with God. Creation itself, according to Thomas Aquinas, is a relation to God. It has no existence in itself but exists only in relation to God. In Jesus the whole creation and the whole of humanity are brought into this living relationship which Jesus shares with the Father. We are made "partakers of the divine nature" (Peter, Ch. 2). It is this that Semitic monotheism refuses to recognize, but the whole tradition of the Universal Wisdom recognizes this intimate relation between God and humanity, between God and creation. The world is not divided, there is no separation between God and the world. Relationship is not identity. Jesus is not identical with the Father. He is not the Father, and yet he is one with the Father. This is not monism or dualism but "non-dualism" (*advaita*) which is a transcendent relationship which cannot properly be expressed in human terms.

If Jesus is one with the Father, with God, in this unique relationship, so also are all those who respond to this call. The Word which "became flesh" in Jesus "enlightens everyone who comes into the world" (John 1:9). This Word is the Light, the Truth, the Word of Guru Nanak, the Name which is above every name, the Guru within to whom every external guru bears witness. When Jesus departed from his disciples he sent the Holy Spirit to be with them forever (John 16:7). The Holy Spirit is the indwelling presence of God, the source of all wisdom, truth and goodness. Above all it is the Love which created and sustains the world, which is grace and compassion, mercy and forgiveness. In the Trinity, God is revealed not as a person standing over against the world, but as the Communion of Love which embraces all humanity and all creation and is the Wisdom which orders the universe, for Wisdom is Knowledge by love.

THE GOSPEL ACCORDING
TO MATTHEW

CHAPTERS 3–7 v. 29

MATTHEW

This translation is taken from
the Revised Standard Version of the Bible

CHAPTER THREE

1 In those days came John the Baptist, preaching in the wilderness of
Judea,

2 "Repent, for the kingdom of heaven is at hand."

3 For this is he who was spoken of by the prophet Isaiah when he
said,
"The voice of one crying in the wilderness:
Prepare the way of the Lord,
make his paths straight."

4 Now John wore a garment of camel's hair, and a leather girdle
around his waist; and his food was locusts and wild honey.

5 Then went out to him Jerusalem and all Judea and all the region
about the Jordan,

6 and they were baptized by him in the river Jordan, confessing their
sins.

7 But when he saw many of the Pharisees and Sadducees coming for
baptism, he said to them, "You brood of vipers! Who warned
you to flee from the wrath to come?

8 Bear fruit that befits repentance,

9 and do not presume to say to yourselves, 'We have Abraham as our
father'; for I tell you, God is able from these stones to raise up
children to Abraham.

10 Even now the axe is laid to the root of the trees; every tree therefore
that does not bear good fruit is cut down and thrown into the
fire.

11 "I baptize you with water for repentance, but he who is coming after
me is mightier than I, whose sandals I am not worthy to carry; he
will baptize you with the Holy Spirit and with fire.

12 His winnowing fork is in his hand, and he will clear his threshing
floor and gather his wheat into the granary, but the chaff he will
burn with unquenchable fire."

13 Then Jesus came from Galilee to the Jordan to John, to be baptized
by him.

14 John would have prevented him, saying, "I need to be baptized by
you, and do you come to me?"

15 But Jesus answered him, "Let it be so now; for thus it is fitting for us to fulfil all righteousness." Then he consented.

16 And when Jesus was baptized, he went up immediately from the water, and behold, the heavens were opened and he saw the Spirit of God descending like a dove, and alighting on him;

17 and lo, a voice from heaven, saying, "This is my beloved Son, with whom I am well pleased."

CHAPTER FOUR

1 Then Jesus was led up by the Spirit into the wilderness to be tempted by the devil.

2 And he fasted forty days and forty nights, and afterward he was hungry.

3 And the tempter came and said to him, "If you are the Son of God, command these stones to become loaves of bread."

4 But he answered, "It is written,
  'Man shall not live by bread alone,
  but by every word that proceeds from the mouth of God.'"

5 Then the devil took him to the holy city, and set him on the pinnacle of the temple,

6 and said to him, "If you are the Son of God, throw yourself down; for it is written,
  'He will give his angels charge of you,' and 'On their hands they will bear you up,
  lest you strike your foot against a stone.'"

7 Jesus said to him, "Again it is written,
  'You shall not tempt the Lord your God.'"

8 Again, the devil took him to a very high mountain, and showed him all the kingdoms of the world and the glory of them;

9 and he said to him, "All these I will give you, if you will fall down and worship me."

10 Then Jesus said to him, "Begone, Satan! for it is written,
  'You shall worship the Lord your God
  and him only shall you serve.'"

11 Then the devil left him, and behold,
  angels came and ministered to him.

12 Now when he heard that John had been arrested, he withdrew into Galilee;

13 and leaving Nazareth he went and dwelt in Caper'na-um by the sea, in the territory of Zeb'ulun and Naph'tali,

14 that what was spoken by the prophet Isaiah might be fulfilled;

15 "The land of Zeb'ulun and the land of Naph'tali,
  toward the sea, across the Jordan,
  Galilee of the Gentiles—
16 the people who sat in darkness
  have seen a great light,
  and for those who sat in the region and shadow of death
  light has dawned."
17 From that time Jesus began to preach, saying, "Repent, for the
  kingdom of heaven is at hand."
18 As he walked by the Sea of Galilee, he saw two brothers, Simon
  who is called Peter and Andrew his brother, casting a net into
  the sea; for they were fishermen.
19 And he said to them, "Follow me, and I will make you fishers of
  men."
20 Immediately they left their nets and followed him.
21 And going on from there he saw two other brothers, James the son
  of Zeb'edee and John his brother, in the boat with Zeb'edee
  their father, mending their nets, and he called them.
22 Immediately they left the boat and their father, and followed him.

23 And he went about all Galilee, teaching in their synagogues and
  preaching the gospel of the kingdom and healing every disease and
  every infirmity among the people.
24 So his fame spread throughout all Syria, and they brought him all
  the sick, those afflicted with various diseases and pains, demoniacs,
  epileptics, and paralytics, and he healed them.
25 And great crowds followed him from Galilee and the Decap'olis
  and Jerusalem and Judea and from beyond the Jordan.

CHAPTER FIVE

1 Seeing the crowds, he went up the mountain, and when he sat down
  his disciples came to him.
2 And he opened his mouth and taught them, saying:
3 "Blessed are the poor in spirit, for theirs is the kingdom of heaven.
4 "Blessed are those who mourn, for they shall be comforted.
5 "Blessed are the meek, for they shall inherit the earth.
6 "Blessed are those who hunger and thirst for righteousness, for they
  shall be satisfied.
7 "Blessed are the merciful, for they shall obtain mercy.
8 "Blessed are the pure in heart, for they shall see God.
9 "Blessed are the peacemakers, for they shall be called sons of God.

10 "Blessed are those who are persecuted for righteousness' sake, for theirs is the kingdom of heaven.

11 "Blessed are you when men revile you and persecute you and utter all kinds of evil against you falsely on my account.

12 Rejoice and be glad, for your reward is great in heaven, for so men persecuted the prophets who were before you.

13 "You are the salt of the earth; but if salt has lost its taste, how shall its saltness be restored? It is no longer good for anything except to be thrown out and trodden under foot by men.

14 "You are the light of the world. A city set on a hill cannot be hid.

15 Nor do men light a lamp and put it under a bushel, but on a stand, and it gives light to all in the house.

16 Let your light so shine before men, that they may see your good works and give glory to your Father who is in heaven.

17 "Think not that I have come to abolish the law and the prophets; I have come not to abolish them but to fulfil them.

18 For truly, I say to you, till heaven and earth pass away, not an iota, not a dot, will pass from the law until all is accomplished.

19 Whoever then relaxes one of the least of these commandments and teaches men so, shall be called least in the kingdom of heaven; but he who does them and teaches them shall be called great in the kingdom of heaven.

20 For I tell you, unless your righteousness exceeds that of the scribes and Pharisees, you will never enter the kingdom of heaven.

21 "You have heard that it was said to the men of old, 'You shall not kill; and whoever kills shall be liable to judgement.'

22 But I say to you that every one who is angry with his brother shall be liable to judgement; whoever insults his brother shall be liable to the council, and whoever says, 'You fool!' shall be liable to the hell of fire.

23 So if you are offering your gift at the altar, and there remember that your brother has something against you,

24 leave your gift there before the altar and go; first be reconciled to your brother, and then come and offer your gift.

25 Make friends quickly with your accuser, while you are going with him to court, lest your accuser hand you over to the judge, and the judge to the guard, and you be put in prison;

26 truly, I say to you, you will never get out till you have paid the last penny.

27 "You have heard that it was said, 'You shall not commit adultery.'

28 But I say to you that every one who looks at a woman lustfully has already committed adultery with her in his heart.

29 If your right eye causes you to sin, pluck it out and throw it away;

it is better that you lose one of your members than that your
whole body be thrown into hell.

30 And if your right hand and causes you to sin, cut it off and throw
it away; it is better that you lose one of your members than that
your whole body go into hell.

31 "It was also said, 'Whoever divorces his wife, let him give her a
certificate of divorce.'

32 But I say to you that every one who divorces his wife, except on the
ground of unchastity, makes her an adulteress; and whoever
marries a divorced woman commits adultery.

33 "Again you have heard that it was said to the men of old, 'You shall
not swear falsely, but shall perform to the Lord what you have
sworn.'

34 But I say to you, Do not swear at all, either by heaven, for it is the
throne of God,

35 or by the earth, for it is his footstool, or by Jerusalem, for it is the
city of the great King.

36 And do not swear by your head, for you cannot make one hair white
or black.

37 Let what you say be simply 'Yes' or 'No'; anything more than this
comes from evil.

38 "You have heard that it was said, 'An eye for an eye and a tooth
for a tooth.'

39 But I say to you, Do not resist one who is evil. But if any one strikes
you on the right cheek, turn to him the other also;

40 and if any one would sue you and take your coat, let him have your
cloak as well;

41 and if any one forces you to go one mile, go with him two miles.

42 Give to him who begs from you, and do not refuse him who would
borrow from you.

43 "You have heard that it was said, 'You shall love your neighbour
and hate your enemy.'

44 But I say to you, Love your enemies and pray for those who
persecute you,

45 so that you may be sons of your Father who is in heaven; for he
makes his sun rise on the evil and on the good, and sends rain on
the just and on the unjust.

46 For if you love those who love you, what reward have you? Do not
even the tax collectors do the same?

47 And if you salute only your brethren, what more are you doing than
others? Do not even the Gentiles do the same?

48 You, therefore, must be perfect, as your heavenly Father is perfect.

CHAPTER SIX

1 "Beware of practising your piety before men in order to be seen by them; for then you will have no reward from your Father who is in heaven.

2 "Thus, when you give alms, sound no trumpet before you, as the hypocrites do in the synagogues and in the streets, that they may be praised by men. Truly, I say to you, they have received their reward.

3 But when you give alms, do not let your left hand know what your right hand is doing,

4 so that your alms may be in secret; and your Father who sees in secret will reward you.

5 "And when you pray, you must not be like the hypocrites; for they love to stand and pray in the synagogues and at the street corners, that they may be seen by men. Truly, I say to you, they have received their reward.

6 But when you pray, go into your room and shut the door and pray to your Father who is in secret; and your Father who sees in secret will reward you.

7 "And in praying do not heap up empty phrases as the Gentiles do; for they think that they will be heard for their many words.

8 Do not be like them, for your Father knows what you need before you ask him.

9 Pray then like this:
Our Father who art in heaven,
Hallowed be thy name.

10 Thy kingdom come,
Thy will be done,
On earth as it is in heaven.

11 Give us this day our daily bread;

12 And forgive us our debts,
As we also have forgiven our debtors;

13 And lead us not into temptation,
But deliver us from evil.

14 For if you forgive men their trespasses, your heavenly Father also will forgive you;

15 but if you do not forgive men their trespasses, neither will your Father forgive your trespasses.

16 "And when you fast, do not look dismal, like the hypocrites, for they disfigure their faces that their fasting may be seen by men. Truly, I say to you, they have received their reward.

17 But when you fast, anoint your head and wash your face,

18 that your fasting may not be seen by men but by your Father who is in secret; and your Father who sees in secret will reward you.

19 "Do not lay up for yourselves treasures on earth, where moth and rust consume and where thieves break in and steal,

20 but lay up for yourselves treasure in heaven, where neither moth nor rust consumes and where thieves do not break in and steal.

21 For where your treasure is, there will your heart be also.

22 "The eye is the lamp of the body. So, if your eye is sound, your whole body will be full of light;

23 but if your eye is not sound, your whole body will be full of darkness. If then the light in you is darkness, how great is the darkness!

24 "No one can serve two masters; for either he will hate the one and love the other, or he will be devoted to the one and despise the other. You cannot serve God and mammon.

25 "Therefore I tell you, do not be anxious about your life, what you shall eat or what you shall drink, nor about your body, what you shall put on. Is not life more than food, and the body more than clothing?

26 Look at the birds of the air: they neither sow nor reap nor gather into barns, and yet your heavenly Father feeds them. Are you not of more value than they?

27 And which of you by being anxious can add one cubit to his span of life?

28 And why are you anxious about clothing? Consider the lilies of the field, how they grow; they neither toil nor spin;

29 yet I tell you, even Solomon in all his glory was not arrayed like one of these.

30 But if God so clothes the grass of the field, which today is alive and tomorrow is thrown into the oven, will he not much more clothe you, O men of little faith?

31 Therefore do not be anxious, saying, 'What shall we eat?' or 'What shall we drink?' or 'What shall we wear?'

32 For the Gentiles seek all these things; and your heavenly Father knows that you need them all.

33 But seek first his kingdom and his righteousness, and all these things shall be yours as well.

34 "Therefore do not be anxious about tomorrow, for tomorrow will be anxious for itself. Let the day's own trouble be sufficient for the day.

CHAPTER SEVEN

1 "Judge not, that you be not judged.

2 For with the judgement you pronounce you will be judged, and the measure you give will be the measure you get.

3 Why do you see the speck that is in your brother's eye, but do not notice the log that is in your own eye?

4 Or how can you say to your brother, 'Let me take the speck out of your eye,' when there is the log in your own eye?

5 You hypocrite, first take the log out of your own eye, and then you will see clearly to take the speck out of your brother's eye.

6 "Do not give dogs what is holy; and do not throw your pearls before swine, lest they trample them under foot and turn to attack you.

7 "Ask, and it will be given you; seek, and you will find; knock, and it will be opened to you.

8 For every one who asks receives, and he who seeks finds, and to him who knocks it will be opened.

9 Or what man of you, if his son asks him for bread, will give him a stone?

10 Or if he asks for a fish, will give him a serpent?

11 If you then, who are evil, know how to give good gifts to your children, how much more will your Father who is in heaven give good things to those who ask him!

12 So whatever you wish that men would do to you, do so to them; for this is the law and the prophets.

13 "Enter by the narrow gate; for the gate is wide and the way is easy, that leads to destruction, and those who enter by it are many.

14 For the gate is narrow and the way is hard, that leads to life, and those who find it are few.

15 "Beware of false prophets, who come to you in sheep's clothing but inwardly are ravenous wolves.

16 You will know them by their fruits. Are grapes gathered from thorns, or figs from thistles?

17 So, every sound tree bears good fruit, but the bad tree bears evil fruit.

18 A sound tree cannot bear evil fruit, nor can a bad tree bear good fruit.

19 Every tree that does not bear good fruit is cut down and thrown into the fire.

20 Thus you will know them by their fruits.

21 "Not every one who says to me, 'Lord, Lord,' shall enter the

kingdom of heaven, but he who does the will of my Father who is in heaven.

22 On that day many will say to me, 'Lord, Lord, did we not prophesy in your name, and cast out demons in your name, and do many mighty works in your name?'

23 And then will I declare to them, 'I never knew you; depart from me, you evildoers.'

24 "Every one then who hears these words of mine and does them will be like a wise man who built his house upon the rock;

25 and the rain fell, and the floods came, and the winds blew and beat upon that house, but it did not fall, because it had been founded on the rock.

26 And every one who hears these words of mine and does not do them will be like a foolish man who built his house upon the sand;

27 and the rain fell, and the floods came, and the winds blew and beat against that house, and it fell; and great was the fall of it."

28 And when Jesus finished these sayings, the crowds were astonished at his teaching,

29 for he taught them as one who had authority, and not as their scribes.

THE GOSPEL ACCORDING TO MARK

CHAPTERS 1–10

MARK

*This translation is taken from
the Revised Standard Version of the Bible*

CHAPTER ONE

1 The beginning of the gospel of Jesus Christ, the Son of God.

2 As it is written in Isaiah the prophet,
> "Behold, I send my messenger before thy face,
> who shall prepare thy way;

3 the voice of one crying in the wilderness:
> Prepare the way of the Lord,
> make his paths straight—"

4 John the baptizer appeared in the wilderness, preaching a baptism of repentance for the forgiveness of sins.

5 And there went out to him all the country of Judea, and all the people of Jerusalem; and they were baptized by him in the river Jordan, confessing their sins.

6 Now John was clothed with camel's hair, and had a leather girdle around his waist, and ate locusts and wild honey.

7 And he preached, saying, "After me comes he who is mightier than I, the thong of whose sandals I am not worthy to stoop down and untie.

8 I have baptized you with water; but he will baptize you with the Holy Spirit."

9 In those days Jesus came from Nazareth of Galilee and was baptized by John in the Jordan.

10 And when he came up out of the water, immediately he saw the heavens opened and the Spirit descending upon him like a dove;

11 and a voice came from heaven, "Thou art my beloved Son; with thee I am well pleased."

12 The Spirit immediately drove him out into the wilderness.

13 And he was in the wilderness forty days, tempted by Satan; and he was with the wild beasts; and the angels ministered to him.

14 Now after John was arrested, Jesus came into Galilee, preaching the gospel of God,

15 and saying, "The time is fulfilled, and the Kingdom of God is at hand; repent, and believe in the gospel."

the brother of Simon casting a net in the sea; for they were
fishermen.

17 And Jesus said to them, "Follow me and I will make you become
fishers of men."

18 And immediately they left their nets and followed him.

19 And going on a little farther, he saw James the son of Zeb'edee and
John his brother, who were in their boat mending the nets.

20 And immediately he called them; and they left their father Zeb'edee
in the boat with the hired servants, and followed him.

21 And they went into Caper'na-um; and immediately on the sabbath
he entered the synagogue and taught.

22 And they were astonished at his teaching, for he taught
them as one who had authority, and not as the
scribes.

23 And immediately there was in their synagogue a man with an unclean
spirit;

24 and he cried out, "What have you to do with us, Jesus of Nazareth?
Have you come to destroy us? I know who you are, the Holy One
of God."

25 But Jesus rebuked him, saying, "Be silent, and come out of him!"

26 And the unclean spirit, convulsing him and crying with a loud voice,
came out of him.

27 And they were all amazed, so that they questioned among
themselves, saying, "What is this? A new teaching! With authority
he commands even the unclean spirits, and they obey him."

28 And at once his fame spread everywhere throughout all the
surrounding region of Galilee.

29 And immediatey he left the synagogue, and entered the house of
Simon and Andrew, with James and John.

30 Now Simon's mother-in-law lay sick with a fever, and immediately
they told him of her.

31 And he came and took he by the hand and lifted her up, and the
fever left her; and she served them.

32 That evening, at sundown, they brought to him all who were sick
or possessed with demons.

33 And the whole city was gathered together about the
door.

34 And he healed many who were sick with various diseases, and cast
out many demons; and he would not permit the demons to
speak, because they knew him.

35 And in the morning, a great while before day, he rose and went out
to a lonely place, and there he prayed.

36 And Simon and those who were with him pursued him,

37 and they found him and said to him, "Every one is searching for you."

38 And he said to them, "Let us go on to the next towns, that I may preach there also; for that is why I came out."

39 And he went throughout all Galilee, preaching in their synagogues and casting out demons.

40 And a leper came to him beseeching him, and kneeling said to him, "If you will, you can make me clean."

41 Moved with pity, he stretched out his hand and touched him, and said to him, "I will; be clean."

42 And immediately the leprosy left him, and he was made clean.

43 And he sternly charged him, and sent him away at once,

44 and said to him, "See that you say nothing to any one; but go, show yourself to the priest, and offer for your cleansing what Moses commanded, for a proof to the people."

45 But he went out and began to talk freely about it, and to spread the news, so that Jesus could no longer openly enter a town, but was out in the country; and people came to him from every quarter.

CHAPTER TWO

1 And when he returned to Caper′na-um after some days, it was reported that he was at home.

2 And many were gathered together, so that there was no longer room for them, not even about the door; and he was preaching the word to them.

3 And they came, bringing to him a paralytic carried by four men.

4 And when they could not get near him because of the crowd, they removed the roof above him; and when they had made an opening, they let down the pallet on which the paralytic lay.

5 And when Jesus saw their faith, he said to the paralytic, "My son, your sins are forgiven."

6 Now some of the scribes were sitting there, questioning in their hearts,

7 "Why does this man speak thus? It is blasphemy! Who can forgive sins but God alone?"

8 And immediately Jesus, perceiving in his spirit that they thus questioned within themselves, said to them, "Why do you question thus in your hearts?

9 Which is easier, to say to the paralytic, "Your sins are forgiven," or to say, "Rise, take up your pallet and walk"?

10 But that you may know that the Son of man has authority on earth to forgive sins" – he said to the paralytic –

11 "I say to you, rise, take up your pallet and go home."

12 And he rose, and immediately took up the pallet and went out before them all; so that they were all amazed and glorified God, saying, "We never saw anything like this!"

13 He went out again beside the sea; and all the crowd gathered about him, and he taught them.

14 And as he passed on, he saw Levi the son of Alphaeus sitting at the tax office, and he said to him, "Follow me." And he rose and followed him.

15 And as he sat at table in his houses, many tax collectors and sinners were sitting with Jesus and his disciples; for there were many who followed him.

16 And the scribes of the Pharisees, when they saw that he was eating with sinners and tax collectors, said to his disciples, "Why does he eat with tax collectors and sinners?"

17 And when Jesus heard it, he said to them, "Those who are well have no need of a physicians, but those who are sick; I came not to call the righteous, but sinners."

18 Now John's disciples and the Pharisees were fasting; and people came and said to him, "Why do John's disciples and the disciples of the Pharisees fast, but your disciples do not fast?"

19 And Jesus said to them, "Can the wedding guests fast while the bridegroom is with them? As long as they have the bridegroom with them, they cannot fast.

20 The days will come, when the bridegroom is taken away from them, and then they will fast in that day.

21 No one sews a piece of unshrunk cloth on an old garment; if he does, the patch tears away from it, the new from the old, and a worse tear is made.

22 And no one puts new wine into old wineskins; if he does, the wine will burst the skins, and the wine is lost, and so are the skins; but new wine is for fresh skins."

23 One sabbath he was going through the grainfields; and as they made their way his disciples began to pluck heads of grain.

24 And the Pharisees said to him, "Look, why are they doing what is not lawful on the sabbath?"

25 And he said to them, "Have you never read what David did, when he was in need and was hungry, he and those who were with him:

26 how he entered the house of God, when Abi'atha was high priest, and ate the bread of the Presence, which it is not lawful for any

but the priests to eat, and also gave it to those who were with him?"

27 And he said to them, "The sabbath was made for man, not man for the sabbath;

28 so the Son of man is lord even of the sabbath."

CHAPTER THREE

1 Again he entered the synagogue, and a man was there who had a withered hand.

2 And they watched him, to see whether he would heal him on the sabbath, so that they might accuse him.

3 And he said to the man who had the withered hand, "Come here."

4 And he said to them, "Is it lawful on the sabbath to do good or to do harm, to save life or to kill?" But they were silent.

5 And he looked around at them with anger, grieved at their hardness of heart, and said to the man, "Stretch out your hand." He stretched it out, and his hand was restored.

6 The Pharisees went out, and immediately held counsel with the Hero'di-ans against him, how to destroy him.

7 Jesus withdrew with his disciples to the sea, and a great multitude from Galilee followed; also from Judea

8 and Jerusalem and Idume'a and from beyond the Jordan and from about Tyre and Sidon a great multitude, hearing all that he did, came to him.

9 And he told his disciples to have a boat ready for him because of the crowd, lest they should crush him;

10 for he had healed many, so that all who had diseases pressed upon him to touch him.

11 And whenever the unclean spirits beheld him, they fell down before him and cried out, "You are the Son of God."

12 And he strictly ordered them not to make him known.

13 And he went up on the mountain, and called to him those whom he desired; and they came to him.

14 And he appointed twelve, to be with him, and to be sent out to preach

15 and have authority to cast out demons:

16 Simon whom he surnamed Peter;

17 James the son of Zeb'edee and John the brother of James, whom he surnamed Boaner'ges, that is, sons of thunder;

18 Andrew, and Philip, and Bartholomew, and Matthew, and Thomas, and James the son of Alphaeus, and Thaddaeus, and Simon the Cananaean,

19 and Judas Iscariot, who betrayed him.

Then he went home;

20 and the crowd came together again, so that they could not even eat.

21 And when his family heard it, they went out to seize him, for people were saying, "He is beside himself."

22 And the scribes who came down from Jerusalem said, "He is possessed by Be-el'zebul, and by the prince of demons he casts out the demons."

23 And he called them to him, and said to them in parables, "How can Satan cast out Satan?

24 If a kingdom is divided against itself, that kingdom cannot stand.

25 And if a house is divided against itself, that house will not be able to stand.

26 And if Satan has risen up against himself and is divided, he cannot stand, but is coming to an end.

27 But no one can enter a strong man's house and plunder his goods, unless he first binds the strong man; then indeed he may plunder his house.

28 "Truly, I say to you, all sins will be forgiven the sons of men, and whatever blasphemies they utter;

29 but whoever blasphemes against the Holy Spirit never has forgiveness, but is guilty of an eternal sin" –

30 for they had said, "He has an unclean spirit."

31 And his mother and his brothers came; and standing outside they sent to him and called him.

32 And a crowd was sitting about him; and they said to him, "Your mother and your brothers are outside, asking for you."

33 And he replied, "Who are my mother and my brothers?"

34 And looking around on those who sat about him, he said, "Here are my mother and my brothers!

35 Whoever does the will of God is my brother and sister, and mother."

CHAPTER FOUR

1 Again he began to teach beside the sea. And a very large crowd gathered about him, so that he got into a boat and sat in it on the sea; and the whole crowd was beside the sea on the land.

2 And he taught them many things in parables, and in his teaching he said to them:

3 "Listen! A sower went out to sow.

4 And as he sowed, some seed fell along the path, and the birds came and devoured it.

5 Other seed fell on rocky ground, where it had not much soil, and immediately it sprang up, since it had no depth of soil;

6 and when the sun rose it was scorched, and since it had no root it withered away.

7 Other seed fell among thorns and the thorns grew up and choked it, and it yielded no grain.

8 And other seeds fell into good soil and brought forth grain, growing up and increasing and yielding thirtyfold and sixtyfold and a hundredfold."

9 And he said, "He who has ears to hear, let him hear."

10 And when he was alone, those who were about him with the twelve asked him concerning the parables.

11 And he said to them, "To you has been given the secret of the kingdom of God, but for those outside everything is in parables;

12 so that they may indeed see but not perceive, and may indeed hear but not understand; lest they should turn again, and be forgiven."

13 And he said to them, "Do you not understand this parable? How then will you understand all the parables?

14 The sower sows the word.

15 And these are the ones along the path, where the word is sown; when they hear, Satan immediately comes and takes away the word which is sown in them.

16 And these in like manner are the ones sown upon rocky ground, who, when they hear the word, immediately receive it with joy;

17 and they have no root in themselves, but endure for a while; then, when tribulation or persecution arises on account of the word, immediately they fall away.

18 And others are the ones sown among thorns; they are those who hear the word,

19 but the cares of the world, and the delight in riches, and the desire for other things, enter in and choke the word, and it proves unfruitful.

20 But those that were sown upon the good soil are the ones who hear the word and accept it and bear fruit, thirtyfold and sixtyfold and a hundredfold."

21 And he said to them, "Is a lamp brought in to be put under a bushel, or under a bed, and not on a stand?

22 For there is nothing hid, except to be made manifest; nor is anything secret, except to come to light.

23 If any man has ears to hear, let him hear."

24 And he said to them, "Take heed what you hear; the measure you give will be the measure you get, and still more will be given you.

25 For to him who has will more be given; and from him who has not, even what he has will be taken away."

26 And he said, "The kingdom of God is as if a man should scatter seed upon the ground,

27 and should sleep and rise night and day, and the seed should sprout and grow, he knows not how.

28 The earth produces of itself, first the blade, then the ear, then the full grain in the ear.

29 But when the grain is ripe, at once he puts in the sickle, because the harvest has come."

30 And he said, "With what can we compare the kingdom of God, or what parable shall we use for it?

31 It is like a grain of mustard seed, which, when sown upon the ground, is the smallest of all the seeds on earth;

32 yet when it is sown it grows up and becomes the greatest of all shrubs, and puts forth large branches, so that the birds of the air can make nests in its shade."

33 With many such parables he spoke the word to them, as they were able to hear it;

34 he did not speak to them without a parable, but privately to his own disciples he explained everything.

35 On that day, when evening had come, he said to them, "Let us go across to the other side."

36 And leaving the crowd, they took him with them in the boat, just as he was. And other boats were with him.

37 And a great storm of wind arose, and the waves beat into the boat, so that the boat was already filling.

38 But he was in the stern, asleep on the cushion; and they woke him and said to him, "Teacher, do you not care if we perish?"

39 And he awoke and rebuked the wind, and said to the sea, "Peace! Be still!" And the wind ceased, and there was a great calm.

40 He said to them, "Why are you afraid? Have you no faith?"

41 And they were filled with awe, and said to one another, "Who then is this, that even wind and sea obey him?"

CHAPTER FIVE

1 They came to the other side of the sea, to the country of the Gerasenes.

2 And when he had come out of the boat, there met him out of the tombs a man with an unclean spirit,

3 who lived among the tombs; and no one could bind him any more, even with a chain;

4 for he had often been bound with fetters and chains, but the chains he wrenched apart, and the fetters he broke in pieces; and no one had the strength to subdue him.

5 Night and day among the tombs and on the mountains he was always crying out, and bruising himself with stones.

6 And when he saw Jesus from afar, he ran and worshipped him;

7 and crying out with a loud voice, he said, "What have you to do with me, Jesus, Son of the Most High God? I adjure you by God, do not torment me."

8 For he had said to him, "Come out of the man, you unclean spirit!"

9 And Jesus asked him, "What is your name?" He replied, "My name is Legion; for we are many."

10 And he begged him eagerly not to send them out of the country.

11 Now a great herd of swine was feeding there on the hillside;

12 and they begged him, "Send us to the swine, let us enter them."

13 So he gave them leave. And the unclean spirits came out, and entered the swine; and the herd, numbering about two thousand, rushed down the steep bank into the sea, and were drowned in the sea.

14 The herdsmen fled, and told it in the city and in the country. And people came to see what it was that had happened.

15 And they came to Jesus, and saw the demoniac sitting there, clothed and in his right mind, the man who had had the legion; and they were afraid.

16 And those who had seen it told what had happened to the demoniac and to the swine.

17 And they began to beg Jesus to depart from their neighbourhood.

18 And as he was getting into the boat, the man who had been possessed with demons begged him that he might be with him.

19 But he refused, and said to him, "Go home to your friends, and tell them how much the Lord has done for you, and how he has had mercy on you."

20 And he went away and began to proclaim in the Decap'olis how much Jesus had done for him; and all men marvelled.

21 And when Jesus had crossed again in the boat to the other side, a great crowd gathered about him; and he was beside the sea.

22 Then came one of the rulers of the synagogue, Ja'irus by name; and seeing him, he fell at his feet,

23 and besought him, saying, "My little daughter is at the point of death. Come and lay your hands on her, so that she may be made well, and live."

24 And he went with him.

And a great crowd followed him and thronged about him.

25 And there was a woman who had had a flow of blood for twelve
   years,

26 and who had suffered much under many physicians, and had spent
   all that she had, and was no better but rather grew worse.

27 She had heard the reports about Jesus, and came up behind him in
   the crowd and touched his garment.

28 For she said, "If I touch even his garments, I shall be made well."

29 And immediately the haemorrhage ceased; and she felt in her body
   that she was healed of her disease.

30 And Jesus, perceiving in himself that power had gone forth from
   him, immediately turned about in the crowd, and said, "Who
   touched my garments?"

31 And his disciples said to him, "You see the crowd pressing around
   you, and yet you say, 'Who touched me?'"

32 And he looked around to see who had done it.

33 But the woman, knowing what had been done to her, came in fear
   and trembling and fell down before him, and told him the whole
   truth.

34 And he said to her, "Daughter, your faith has made you well; go in
   peace, and be healed of your disease."

35 While he was still speaking, there came from the ruler's house some
   who said, "Your daughter is dead. Why trouble the Teacher any
   further?"

36 But ignoring what they said, Jesus said to the ruler of the synagogue,
   "Do not fear, only believe."

37 And he allowed no one to follow him except Peter and James and
   John the brother of James.

38 When they came to the house of the ruler of the synagogue, he saw
   a tumult, and people weeping and wailing loudly.

39 And when he had entered, he said to them, "Why do you make a
   tumult and weep? The child is not dead but sleeping."

40 And they laughed at him. But he put them all outside, and took the
   child's father and mother and those who were with him, and
   went in where the child was.

41 Taking her by the hand he said to her, "*Tal' itha cu' mi*"; which
   means, "Little girl, I say to you, arise."

42 And immediately the girl got up and walked (she was twelve years
   of age), and they were immediately overcome with amazement.

43 And he strictly charged them that no one should know this, and
   told them to give her something to eat.

CHAPTER SIX

1 He went away from there and came to his own country; and his disciples followed him.

2 And on the sabbath he began to teach in the synagogue; and many who heard him were astonished, saying, "Where did this man get all this? What is the wisdom given to him? What mighty works are wrought by his hands!

3 Is not this the carpenter, the son of Mary and brother of James and Joses and Judas and Simon, and are not his sisters here with us?" And they took offence at him.

4 And Jesus said to them, "A prophet is not without honour, except in his own country, and among his own kin, and in his own house."

5 And he could do no mighty work there, except that he laid his hands upon a few sick people and healed them.

6 And he marvelled because of their unbelief.
And he went about among the villages teaching.

7 And he called to him the twelve, and began to send them out two by two, and gave them authority over the unclean spirits.

8 He charged them to take nothing for their journey except a staff; no bread, no bag, no money in their belts;

9 but to wear sandals and not put on two tunics.

10 And he said to them, "Where you enter a house, stay there until you leave the place.

11 And if any place will not receive you and they refuse to hear you, when you leave, shake off the dust that is on your feet for a testimony against them."

12 So they went out and preached that men should repent.

13 And they cast out many demons, and anointed with oil many that were sick and healed them.

14 King Herod heard of it; for Jesus' name had become known. Some said, "John the baptizer has been raised from the dead; that is why these powers are at work in him."

15 But others said, "It is Eli'jah." And others said, "It is a prophet, like one of the prophets of old."

16 But when Herod heard of it he said, "John, whom I beheaded, has been raised."

17 For Herod had sent and seized John, and bound him in prison for the sake of Hero'di-as, his brother Philip's wife; because he had married her.

18 For John said to Herod, "It is not lawful for you to have your brother's wife."

19 And Hero'di-as had a grudge against him, and wanted to kill him.
But she could not,

20 for Herod feared John, knowing that he was a righteous and holy
man, and kept him safe. When he heard him, he was much
perplexed; and yet he heard him gladly.

21 But an opportunity came when Herod on his birthday gave a banquet
for his courtiers and officers and the leading men of Galilee.

22 For when Hero'di-as' daughter came in and danced, she pleased
Herod and his guests; and the king said to the girl, "Ask me
for whatever you wish, and I will grant it."

23 And he vowed to her, "Whatever you ask me, I will give you, even
half of my kingdom."

24 And she went out, and said to her mother, "What shall I ask?" And
she said, "The head of John the baptizer."

25 And she came in immediately with haste to the king, and asked,
saying, "I want you to give me at once the head of John the
Baptist on a platter."

26 And the king was exceedingly sorry; but because of his oaths and
his guests he did not want to break his word to her.

27 And immediately the king sent a soldier of the guard and gave orders
to bring his head. He went and beheaded him in the prison,

28 and brought his head on a platter, and gave it to the girl; and the
girl gave it to her mother.

29 When his disciples heard of it, they came and took his body, and
laid it in a tomb.

30 The apostles returned to Jesus, and told him all that they had done
and taught.

31 And he said to them, "Come away by yourselves to a lonely place,
and rest a while." For many were coming and going, and they had
no leisure even to eat.

32 And they went away in the boat to a lonely place by themselves.

33 Now many saw them going, and knew them, and they ran there on
foot from all the towns, and got there ahead of them.

34 As he went ashore he saw a great throng, and he had compassion
on them, because they were like sheep without a shepherd; and
he began to teach them many things.

35 And when it grew late, his disciples came to him and said, "This is
a lonely place, and the hour is now late;

36 send them away, to go into the country and villages round about
and buy themselves something to eat."

37 But he answered them, "You give them something to eat." And
they said to him, "Shall we go and buy two hundred denarii worth
of bread, and give it to them to eat?"

38 And he said to them, "How many loaves have you? Go and see." And when they had found out, they said, "Five, and two fish."

39 Then he commanded them all to sit down by companies upon the green grass.

40 So they sat down in groups, by hundreds and by fifties.

41 And taking the five loaves and the two fish he looked up to heaven, and blessed, and broke the loaves, and gave them to the disciples to set before the people; and he divided the two fish among them all.

42 And they all ate and were satisfied.

43 And they took up twelve baskets full of broken pieces and of the fish.

44 And those who ate the loaves were five thousand men.

45 Immediately he made his disciples get into the boat and go before him to the other side, to Beth-sa'ida, while he dismissed the crowd.

46 And after he had taken leave of them, he went up on the mountain to pray.

47 And when evening came, the boat was out on the sea, and he was alone on the land.

48 And he saw that they were making headway painfully, for the wind was against them. And about the fourth watch of the night he came to them, walking on the sea. He meant to pass by them,

49 but when they saw him walking on the sea they thought it was a ghost, and cried out;

50 for they all saw him, and were terrified. But immediately he spoke to them and said, "Take heart, it is I; have no fear."

51 And he got into the boat with them and the wind ceased. And they were utterly astounded,

52 for they did not understand about the loaves, but their hearts were hardened.

53 And when they had crossed over, they came to land at Gennes'aret, and moored to the shore.

54 And when they got out of the boat, immediately the people recognised him,

55 and ran about the whole neighbourhood and began to bring sick people on their pallets to any place where they heard he was.

56 And wherever he came, in villages, cities, or country, they laid the sick in the market places, and besought him that they might touch even the fringe of his garment; and as many as touched it were made well.

CHAPTER SEVEN

1 Now when the Pharisees gathered together to him, with some of
  the scribes, who had come from Jerusalem,
2 they saw that some of his disciples ate with hands defiled, that is,
  unwashed.
3 (For the Pharisees, and all the Jews, do not eat unless they wash
  their hands, observing the tradition of the elders;
4 and when they come from the market place, they do not eat unless
  they purify themselves; and there are many other traditions
  which they observe, the washing of cups and pots and vessels of
  bronze.)
5 And the Pharisees and the scribes asked him, "Why do your disciples
  not live according to the tradition of the elders, but eat with
  hands defiled?"
6 And he said to them, "Well did Isaiah prophesy of you hypocrites,
  as it is written,
  'This people honours me with their lips,
  but their heart is far from me;
7 in vain do they worship me,
  teaching as doctrines the precepts of men.'
8 You leave the commandment of God, and hold fast the tradition of
  men."
9 And he said to them, "You have a fine way of rejecting
  the commandment of God, in order to keep your tradition!
10 For Moses said, 'Honour your father and your mother'; and, 'He
  who speaks evil of father or mother, let him surely die';
11 but you say, 'If a man tells his father or his mother, What you would
  have gained from me is Corban' (that is, given to God) –
12 then you no longer permit him to do anything for his father or
  mother,
13 thus making void the word of God through your tradition which you
  hand on. And many such things you do."
14 And he called the people to him again, and said to them, "Hear
  me, all of you, and understand:
15 there is nothing outside a man which by going into him can defile
  him; but the things which come out of a man are what defile him."
17 And when he had entered the house, and left the people, his
  disciples asked him about the parable.
18 And he said to them, "Then are you also without understanding?
  Do you not see that whatever goes into a man from outside cannot
  defile him,

19 since it enters, not his heart but his stomach, and so passes on?"
(Thus he declared all foods clean.)

20 And he said, "What comes out of a man is what defiles a man.

21 For from within, out of the heart of man, come evil thoughts,
fornication, theft, murder, adultery,

22 coveting, wickedness, deceit, licentiousness, envy, slander, pride,
foolishness.

23 All these evil things come from within, and they defile a man."

24 And from there he arose and went away to the region of Tyre and
Sidon. And he entered a house, and would not have any one know
it; yet he could not be hid.

25 But immediately a woman, whose little daughter was possessed by
an unclean spirit, heard of him, and came and fell down at his
feet.

26 Now the woman was a Greek, a Syrophoeni'cian by birth. And she
begged him to cast the demon out of her daughter.

27 And he said to her, "Let the children first be fed, for it is not right
to take the children's bread and throw it to the dogs."

28 But she answered him, "Yes, Lord; yet even the dogs under the
table eat the children's crumbs."

29 And he said to her, "For this saying you may go your way; the
demon has left your daughter."

30 And she went home, and found the child lying in bed, and the
demon gone.

31 Then he returned from the region of Tyre, and went through Sidon
to the Sea of Galilee, through the region of the Decap'olis.

32 And they brought to him a man who was deaf and had an
impediment in his speech; and they besought him to lay his hand
upon him.

33 And taking him aside from the multitude privately, he put his fingers
into his ears, and he spat and touched his tongue;

34 and looking up to heaven, he sighed, and said to him, "Eph'phatha,"
that is, "Be opened."

35 And his ears were opened, his tongue was released, and he spoke
plainly.

36 And he charged them to tell no one; but the more he charged them,
the more zealously they proclaimed it.

37 And they were astonished beyond measure, saying, "He has done
all things well; he even makes the deaf hear and the dumb
speak."

CHAPTER EIGHT

1 In those days, when again a great crowd had gathered, and they had nothing to eat, he called his disciples to him, and said to them,

2 "I have compassion on the crowd, because they have been with me now three days, and have nothing to eat;

3 and if I send them away hungry to their homes, they will faint on the way; and some of them have come a long way."

4 And his disciples answered him, "How can one feed these men with bread here in the desert?"

5 And he asked them, "How many loaves have you?" They said, "Seven."

6 And he commanded the crowd to sit down on the ground; and he took the seven loaves, and having given thanks he broke them and gave them to his disciples to set before the people; and they set them before the crowd.

7 And they had a few small fish; and having blessed them, he commanded that these also should be set before them.

8 And they ate, and were satisfied; and they took up the broken pieces left over, seven baskets full.

9 And there were about four thousand people.

10 And he sent them away; and immediately he got into the boat with his disciples, and went to the district of Dalmanu'tha.

11 The Pharisees came and began to argue with him, seeking from him a sign from heaven, to test him.

12 And he sighed deeply in his spirit, and said, "Why does this generation seek a sign? Truly, I say to you, no sign shall be given to this generation."

13 And he left them, and getting into the boat again he departed to the other side.

14 Now they had forgotten to bring bread; and they had only one loaf with them in the boat.

15 And he cautioned them, saying, "Take heed, beware of the leaven of the Pharisees and the leaven of Herod."

16 And they discussed it with one another, saying, "We have no bread."

17 And being aware of it, Jesus said to them, "Why do you discuss the fact that you have no bread? Do you not yet perceive or understand? Are your hearts hardened?

18 Having eyes do you not see, and having ears do you not hear? And do you not remember?

19 When I broke the five loaves for the five thousand, how many baskets

full of broken pieces did you take up?" They said to him, "Twelve."

20 "And the seven for the four thousand, how many baskets full of broken pieces did you take up?" And they said to him, "Seven."

21 And he said to them, "Do you not yet understand?"

22 And they came to Beth-sa'-ida. And some people brought to him a blind man, and begged him to touch him.

23 And he took the blind man by the hand, and led him out of the village; and when he had spit on his eyes and laid his hands upon him, he asked him, "Do you see anything?"

24 And he looked up and said, "I see men; but they look like trees, walking."

25 Then again he laid his hands upon his eyes; and he looked intently and was restored, and saw everything clearly.

26 And he sent him away to his home, saying, "Do not even enter the village."

27 And Jesus went on with his disciples, to the villages of Caesare'a Philippi; and on the way he asked his disciples, "Who do men say that I am?"

28 And they told him, "John the Baptist; and others say, Eli'jah; and others one of the prophets."

29 And he asked them, "But who do you say that I am?" Peter answered him, "You are the Christ."

30 And he charged them to tell no one about him.

31 And he began to teach them that the Son of man must suffer many things, and be rejected by the elders and the chief priests and the scribes, and be killed, and after three days rise again.

32 And he said this plainly. And Peter took him, and began to rebuke him.

33 But turning and seeing his disciples, he rebuked Peter, and said, "Get behind me, Satan! For you are not on the side of God, but of men."

34 And he called to him the multitude with his disciples, and said to them, "If any man would come after me, let him deny himself and take up his cross and follow me.

35 For whoever would save his life will lose it; and whoever loses his life for my sake and the gospel's will save it.

36 For what does it profit a man, to gain the whole world and forfeit his life?

37 For what can a man give in return for his life?

38 For whoever is ashamed of me and of my words in this adulterous and sinful generation, of him will the Son of man also be ashame, when he comes in the glory of his Father with the holy angels."

CHAPTER NINE

1 And he said to them, "Truly, I say to you, there are some standing here who will not taste death before they see that the kingdom of God has come with power."

2 And after six days Jesus took with him Peter and James and John, and led them up a high mountain apart by themselves; and he was transfigured before them,

3 and his garments became glistening, intensely white, as no fuller on earth could bleach them.

4 And there appeared to them Eli'jah with Moses; and they were talking to Jesus.

5 And Peter said to Jesus, "Master, it is well that we are here; let us make three booths, one for you and one for Moses and one for Eli'jah."

6 For he did not know what to say, for they were exceedingly afraid.

7 And a cloud overshadowed them, and a voice came out of the cloud, "This is my beloved Son; listen to him."

8 And suddenly looking around they no longer saw any one with them but Jesus only.

9 And as they were coming down the mountain, he charged them to tell no one what they had seen, until the Son of man should have risen from the dead.

10 So they kept the matter to themselves, questioning what the rising from the dead meant.

11 And they asked him, "Why do the scribes say that first Eli'jah must come?"

12 And he said to them, "Eli'jah does come first to restore all things; and how is it written of the Son of man, that he should suffer many things and be treated with contempt?

13 But I tell you that Eli'jah has come, and they did to him whatever they pleased, as it is written of him."

14 And when they came to the disciples, they saw a great crowd about them, and scribes arguing with them.

15 And immediately all the crowd, when they saw him, were greatly amazed, and ran up to him and greeted him.

16 And he asked them, "What are you discussing with them?"

17 And one of the crowd answered him, "Teacher, I brought my son to you, for he has a dumb spirit;

18 and wherever it seizes him, it dashes him down; and he foams and grinds his teeth and becomes rigid; and I asked your disciples to cast it out, and they were not able."

19 And he answered them, "O faithless generation, how long am I to be with you? How long am I to bear with you? Bring him to me."

20 And they brought the boy to him; and when the spirit saw him, immediately it convulsed the boy, and he fell on the ground and rolled about, foaming at the mouth.

21 And Jesus asked his father, "How long has he had this?" And he said, "From childhood.

22 And it has often cast him into the fire and into the water, to destroy him; but if you can do anything, have pity on us and help us."

23 And Jesus said to him, "If you can! All things are possible to him who believes."

24 Immediately the father of the child cried out and said, "I believe; help my unbelief!"

25 And when Jesus saw that a crowd came running together, he rebuked the unclean spirit, saying to it, "You dumb and deaf spirit, I command you, come out of him, and never enter him again."

26 And after crying out and convulsing him terribly, it came out, and the boy was like a corpse; so that most of them said, "He is dead."

27 But Jesus took him by the hand and lifted him up, and he arose.

28 And when he had entered the house, his disciples asked him privately, "Why could we not cast it out?"

29 And he said to them, "This kind cannot be driven out by anything but prayer."

30 They went on from there and passed through Galilee. And he would not have any one know it;

31 for he was teaching his disciples, saying to them, "The Son of man will be delivered into the hands of men, and they will kill him; and when he is killed, after three days he will rise."

32 But they did not understand the saying, and they were afraid to ask him.

33 And they came to Caper'na-um; and when he was in the house he asked them, "What were you discussing on the way?"

34 But they were silent; for on the way they had discussed with one another who was the greatest.

35 And he sat down and called the twelve; and he said to them, "If any one would be first, he must be last of all and servant of all."

36 And he took a child, and put him in the midst of them; and taking him in his arms, he said to them,

37 "Whoever receives one such child in my name receives me; and whoever receives me, receives not me but him who sent me."

38 John said to him, "Teacher, we saw a man casting out demons in your name, and we forbade him, because he was not following us."

39 But Jesus said, "Do not forbid him; for no one who does a mighty work in my name will be able soon after to speak evil of me.

40 For he that is not against us is for us.

41 For truly, I say to you, whoever gives you a cup of water to drink because you bear the name of Christ, will by no means lose his reward.

42 "Whoever causes one of these little ones who believe in me to sin, it would be better for him if a great millstone were hung round his neck and he were thrown into the sea.

43 And if your hand causes you to sin, cut it off; it is better for you to enter life maimed than with two hands to go to hell, to the unquenchable fire.

45 And if your foot causes you to sin, cut it off; it is better for you to enter life lame than with two feet to be thrown into hell.

47 And if your eye causes you to sin, pluck it out; it is better for you to enter the kingdom of God with one eye than with two eyes to be thrown into hell,

48 where their worm does not die, and the fire is not quenched.

49 For every one will be salted with fire.

50 Salt is good; but if the salt has lost its saltness, how will you season it? Have salt in yourselves, and be at peace with one another."

CHAPTER TEN

1 And he left there and went to the region of Judea and beyond the Jordan, and crowds gathered to him again; and again, as his custom was, he taught them.

2 And Pharisees came up and in order to test him asked, "Is it lawful for a man to divorce his wife?"

3 He answered them, "What did Moses command you?"

4 They said, "Moses allowed a man to write a certificate of divorce, and to put her away."

5 But Jesus said to them, "For your hardness of heart he wrote you this commandment.

6 But from the beginning of creation, 'God made them male and female.'

7 'For this reason a man shall leave his father and mother and be joined to his wife,

8 and the two shall become one flesh.' So they are no longer two but one flesh.

9 What therefore God has joined together, let not man put asunder."

10 And in the house the disciples asked him again about this matter.

11 And he said to them, "Whoever divorces his wife and marries another, commits adultery against her;

12 and if she divorces her husband and marries another, she commits adultery."

13 And they were bringing children to him, that he might touch them; and the disciples rebuked them.

14 But when Jesus saw it he was indignant, and said to them, "Let the children come to me, do not hinder them; for to such belongs the kingdom of God.

15 Truly, I say to you, whoever does not receive the kingdom of God like a child shall not enter it."

16 And he took them in his arms and blessed them, laying his hands upon them.

17 And as he was setting out on his journey, a man ran up and knelt before him, and asked him, "Good Teacher, what must I do to inherit eternal life?"

18 And Jesus said to him, "Why do you call me good? No one is good but God alone.

19 You know the commandments: 'Do not kill, Do not commit adultery, Do not steal, Do not bear false witness, Do not defraud, Honour your father and mother.'"

20 And he said to him, "Teacher, all these I have observed from my youth."

21 And Jesus looking upon him loved him, and said to him, "You lack one thing; go, sell what you have, and give to the poor, and you will have treasure in heaven; and come, follow me."

22 At that saying his countenance fell, and he went away sorrowful; for he had great possessions.

23 And Jesus looked around and said to his disciples, "How hard it will be for those who have riches to enter the kingdom of God!"

24 And the disciples were amazed at his words. But Jesus said to them again, "Children, how hard it is to enter the kingdom of God!

25 It is easier for a camel to go through the eye of a needle than for a rich man to enter the kingdom of God."

26 And they were exceedingly astonished, and said to him, "Then who can be saved?"

27 Jesus looked at them and said, "With men it is impossible, but not with God; for all things are possible with God."

28 Peter began to say to him, "Lo, we have left everything and followed you."

29 Jesus said, "Truly, I say to you, there is no one who has left house or brothers or sisters or mother or father or children or lands, for my sake and for the gospel,

30 who will not receive a hundredfold now in this time, houses and brothers and sisters and mothers and children and lands, with persecutions, and in the age to come eternal life.

31 But many that are first will be last, and the last first."

32 And they were on the road, going up to Jerusalem, and Jesus was walking ahead of them; and they were amazed, and those who followed were afraid. And taking the twelve again, he began to tell them what was to happen to him,

33 saying, "Behold, we are going up to Jerusalem; and the Son of man will be delivered to the chief priests and the scribes, and they will condemn him to death, and deliver him to the Gentiles;

34 and they will mock him, and spit upon him, and scourge him, and kill him; and after three days he will rise."

35 And James and John, the sons of Zeb'edee, came forward to him, and said to him, "Teacher, we want you to do for us whatever we ask of you."

36 And he said to them, "What do you want me to do for you?"

37 And they said to him, "Grant us to sit, one at your right hand and one at your left, in your glory."

38 But Jesus said to them, "You do not know what you are asking. Are you able to drink the cup that I drink, or to be baptized with the baptism with which I am baptized?"

39 And they said to him, "We are able." And Jesus said to them, "The cup that I drink you will drink; and with the baptism with which I am baptized, you will be baptized;

40 but to sit at my right hand or at my left is not mine to grant, but it is for those for whom it has been prepared."

41 And when the ten heard it, they began to be indignant at James and John.

42 And Jesus called them to him and said to them, "You know that those who are supposed to rule over the Gentiles lord it over them, and their great men exercise authority over them.

43 But it shall not be so among you; but whoever would be great among you must be your servant,

44 and whoever would be first among you must be slave of all.

45 For the Son of man also came not to be served but to serve, and to give his life as a ransom for many."

46 And they came to Jericho; and as he was leaving Jericho with his disciples and a great multitude, Bartimae'us, a blind beggar, the son of Timae'us, was sitting by the roadside.

47 And when he heard that it was Jesus of Nazareth, he began to cry out and say, "Jesus, Son of David, have mercy on me!"

48 And many rebuked him, telling him to be silent; but he cried out all the more, "Son of David, have mercy on me!"

49 And Jesus stopped and said, "Call him." And they called the blind man; saying to him, "Take heart; rise, he is calling you."

50 And throwing off his mantle he sprang up and came to Jesus.

51 And Jesus said to him, "What do you want me to do for you?" And the blind man said to him, "Master, let me receive my sight."

52 And Jesus said to him, "Go your way; your faith has made you well." And immediately he received his sight and followed him on the way.

THE GOSPEL ACCORDING
TO LUKE

CHAPTERS 10–22 v. 38

LUKE

*This translation is taken from
the Revised Standard Version of the Bible*

CHAPTER TEN

1 After this the Lord appointed seventy others, and sent them on ahead of him, two by two, into every town and place where he himself was about to come.

2 And he said to them, "The harvest is plentiful, but the labourers are few; pray therefore the Lord of the harvest to send out labourers into his harvest.

3 Go your way; behold, I send you out as lambs in the midst of wolves.

4 Carry no purse, no bag, no sandals; and salute no one on the road.

5 Whatever house you enter, first say, 'Peace be to this house!'

6 And if a son of peace is there, your peace shall rest upon him; but if not, it shall return to you.

7 And remain in the same house, eating and drinking what they provide, for the labourer deserves his wages; do not go from house to house.

8 Whenever you enter a town and they receive you, eat what is set before you;

9 heal the sick in it and say to them, 'The kingdom of God has come near to you.'

10 But whenever you enter a town and they do not receive you, go into its streets and say,

11 'Even the dust of your town that clings to our feet, we wipe off against you; nevertheless know this, that the kingdom of God has come near.'

12 I tell you, it shall be more tolerable on that day for Sodom than for that town.

13 "Woe to you, Chora'zin! woe to you, Beth-sa'ida! for if the mighty works done in you had been done in Tyre and Sidon, they would have repented long ago, sitting in sackcloth and ashes.

14 But it shall be more tolerable in the judgment for Tyre and Sidon than for you.

15 And you, Caper'na-um, will you be exalted to heaven? You shall be brought down to Hades.

16 "He who hears you hears me, and he who rejects you rejects me, and he who rejects me rejects him who sent me."

17 The seventy returned with joy, saying, "Lord, even the demons are subject to us in your name!"

18 And he said to them, "I saw Satan fall like lightning from heaven.

19 Behold, I have given you authority to tread upon serpents and scorpions, and over all the power of the enemy; and nothing shall hurt you.

20 Nevertheless do not rejoice in this, that the spirits are subject to you; but rejoice that your names are written in heaven."

21 In that same hour he rejoiced in the Holy Spirit and said, "I think thee, Father, Lord of heaven and earth, that thou hast hidden these things from the wise and understanding and revealed them to babes; yea, Father, for such was thy gracious will.

22 All things have been delivered to me by my Father; and no one knows who the Son is except the Father, or who the Father is except the Son and any one to whom the Son chooses to reveal him."

23 Then turning to the disciples he said privately, "Blessed are the eyes which see what you see!

24 For I tell you that many prophets and kings desired to see what you see, and did not see it, and to hear what you hear, and did not hear it."

25 And behold, a lawyer stood up to put him to the test, saying, "Teacher, what shall I do to inherit eternal life?"

26 He said to him, "What is written in the law? How do you read?"

27 And he answered, "You shall love the Lord your God with all your heart, and with all your soul, and with all your strength, and with all your mind; and your neighbour as yourself."

28 And he said to him, "You have answered right; do this, and you will live."

29 But he, desiring to justify himself, said to Jesus, "And who is my neighbour?"

30 Jesus replied, "A man was going down from Jerusalem to Jericho, and he fell among robbers, who stripped him and beat him, and departed, leaving him half dead.

31 Now by chance a priest was going down that road; and when he saw him he passed by on the other side.

32 So likewise a Levite, when he came to the place and saw him, passed by on the other side.

33 But a Samaritan, as he journeyed, came to where he was; and when he saw him, he had compassion,

34 and went to him and bound up his wounds, pouring on oil and wine; then he set him on his own beast and brought him to an inn, and took care of him.

35 And the next day he took out two denarii and gave them to the innkeeper, saying, 'Take care of him; and whatever more you spend, I will repay you when I come back.'

36 Which of these three, do you think, proved neighbour to the man who fell among the robbers?"

37 He said, "The one who showed mercy on him." And Jesus said to him, "Go and do likewise."

38 Now as they went on their way, he entered a village; and a woman named Martha received him into her house.

39 And she had a sister called Mary, who sat at the Lord's feet and listened to his teaching.

40 But Martha was distracted with much serving; and she went to him and said, "Lord, do you not care that my sister has left me to serve alone? Tell her then to help me."

41 But the Lord answered her, "Martha, Martha, you are anxious and troubled about many things;

42 one thing is needful. Mary has chosen the good portion, which shall not be taken away from her."

CHAPTER ELEVEN

1 He was praying in a certain place, and when he ceased, one of his disciples said to him, "Lord, teach us to pray, as John taught his disciples."

2 And he said to them, "When you pray, say:
  "Father, hallowed be thy name. Thy kingdom come.

3 Give us each day our daily bread;

4 and forgive us our sins, for we ourselves forgive every one who is indebted to us; and lead us not into temptation."

5 And he said to them, "Which of you who has a friend will go to him at midnight and say to him, 'Friend, lend me three loaves;

6 for a friend of mine has arrived on a journey, and I have nothing to set before him';

7 and he will answer from within, 'Do not bother me; the door is now shut, and my children are with me in bed; I cannot get up and give you anything'?

8 I tell you, though he will not get up and give him anything because he is his friend, yet because of his importunity he will rise and give him whatever he needs.

9 And I tell you, Ask, and it will be given you; seek, and you will find; knock, and it will be opened to you.

10 For every one who asks receives, and he who seeks finds, and to him who knocks it will be opened.

11 What father among you, if his son asks for a fish, will instead of a
   fish give him a serpent;

12 or if he asks for an egg, will give him a scorpion?

13 If you then, who are evil, know how to give good gifts to your
   children, how much more will the heavenly Father give the Holy
   Spirit to those who ask him!"

14 Now he was casting out a demon that was dumb; when the demon
   had gone out, the dumb man spoke, and the people marvelled.

15 But some of them said, "He casts out demons by Be-el'zebul, the
   prince of demons";

16 while others, to test him, sought from him a sign from heaven.

17 But he, knowing their thoughts, said to them, "Every kingdom
   divided against itself is laid waste, and a divided household falls.

18 And if Satan also is divided against himself, how will his kingdom
   stand? For you say that I cast out demons by Be-el'zebul.

19 And if I cast out demons by Be-el'zebul, by whom do your sons
   cast them out? Therefore they shall be your judges.

20 But if it is by the finger of God that I cast out demons, then the
   kingdom of God has come upon you.

21 When a strong man, fully armed, guards his own palace, his goods
   are in peace;

22 but when one stronger than he assails him and overcomes him, he
   takes away his armour in which he trusted, and divides his spoil.

23 He who is not with me is against me, and he who does not gather
   with me scatters.

24 "When the unclean spirit has gone out of a man, he passes through
   waterless places seeking rest; and finding none he says, 'I will
   return to my house from which I came.'

25 And when he comes he finds it swept and put in
   order.

26 Then he goes and brings seven other spirits more evil than himself,
   and they enter and dwell there; and the last state of that man
   becomes worse than the first."

27 As he said this, a woman in the crowd raised her voice and said to
   him, "Blessed is the womb that bore you, and the breasts that
   you sucked!"

28 But he said, "Blessed rather are those who hear the word of God
   and keep it!"

29 When the crowds were increasing, he began to say, "This generation
   is an evil generation; it seeks a sign, but no sign shall be given to
   it except the sign of Jonah.

30 For as Jonah became a sign to the men of Nin'eveh, so will the Son
   of man be to this generation.

31 The queen of the South will arise at the judgement with the men
of this generation and condemn them; for she came from the ends
of the earth to hear the wisdom of Solomon, and behold,
something greater than Solomon is here.

32 The men of Nin'eveh will arise at the judgement with this generation
and condemn it; for they repented at the preaching of Jonah, and
behold, something greater than Jonah is here

33 "No one after lighting a lamp puts it in a cellar or under a bushel,
but on a stand, that those who enter may see the light.

34 Your eye is the lamp of your body; when your eye is sound, your
whole body is full of light; but when it is not sound, your body is
full of darkness.

35 Therefore be careful lest the light in you be darkness.

36 If then your whole body is full of light, having no part dark, it will
be wholly bright, as when a lamp with its rays gives you light."

37 While he was speaking, a Pharisee asked him to dine with him; so
he went in and sat at table.

38 The Pharisee was astonished to see that he did not first wash before
dinner.

39 And the Lord said to him, "Now you Pharisees cleanse the outside
of the cup and of the dish, but inside you are full of extortion and
wickedness.

40 You fools! Did not he who made the outside make the inside also?

41 But give for alms those things which are within; and behold,
everything is clean for you.

42 "But woe to you Pharisees! for you tithe mint and rue and every
herb, and neglect justice and the love of God; these you ought
to have done, without neglecting the others.

43 Woe to you Pharisees! for you love the best seat in the synagogues
and salutations in the market places.

44 Woe to you! for you are like graves which are not seen, and men
walk over them without knowing it."

45 One of the lawyers answered him, "Teacher, in saying this you
reproach us also."

46 And he said, "Woe to you lawyers also! for you load men with
burdens hard to bear, and you yourselves do not touch the burdens
with one of your fingers.

47 Woe to you! for you build the tombs of the prophets whom your
fathers killed.

48 So you are witnesses and consent to the deeds of your fathers; for
they killed them, and you build their tombs.

49 Therefore also the Wisdom of God said, 'I will send them prophets
and apostles, some of whom they will kill and persecute,'

50 that the blood of all the prophets, shed from the foundation of the
world, may be required of this generation,

51 from the blood of Abel to the blood of Zechari′ah, who perished
between the altar and the sanctuary. Yes, I tell you, it shall be
required of this generation.

52 Woe to you lawyers! for you have taken away the key of knowledge;
you did not enter yourselves and you hindered those who were
entering.”

53 As he went away from there, the scribes and the Pharisees began
to press him hard, and to provoke him to speak of many things,

54 lying in wait for him, to catch at something he might say.

CHAPTER TWELVE

1 In the meantime, when so many thousands of the multitude had
gathered together that they trod upon one another, he began to
say to his disciples first, “Beware of the leaven of the Pharisees,
which is hypocrisy.

2 Nothing is covered up that will not be revealed, or hidden that will
not be known.

3 Therefore whatever you have said in the dark shall be heard in the
light, and what you have whispered in private rooms shall be
proclaimed upon the housetops.

4 “I tell you, my friends, do not fear those who kill the body, and
after that have no more that they can do.

5 But I will warn you whom to fear: fear him who, after he has killed,
has power to cast into hell; yes, I tell you, fear him!

6 Are not five sparrows sold for two pennies? And not one of them is
forgotten before God.

7 Why, even the hairs of your head are all numbered. Fear not; you
are of more value than many sparrows.

8 “And I tell you, every one who acknowledges me before men, the
Son of man also will acknowledge before the angels of God;

9 but he who denies me before men will be denied before the angels
of God.

10 And every one who speaks a word against the Son of man will be
forgiven; but he who blasphemes against the Holy Spirit will
not be forgiven.

11 And when they bring you before the synagogues and the rulers and
the authorities, do not be anxious how or what you are to answer
or what you are to say;

12 for the Holy Spirit will teach you in that very hour what you ought
to say.”

13 One of the multitude said to him, "Teacher, bid my brother divide the inheritance with me."

14 But he said to him, "Man, who made me a judge or divider over you?"

15 And he said to them, "Take heed, and beware of all covetousness; for a man's life does not consist in the abundance of his possessions."

16 And he told them a parable, saying, "The land of a rich man brought forth plentifully;

17 and he thought to himself, 'What shall I do, for I have nowhere to store my crops?'

18 And he said, 'I will do this: I will pull down my barns, and build larger ones; and there I will store all my grain and my goods.

19 And I will say to my soul, Soul, you have ample goods laid up for many years; take your ease, eat, drink, be merry.'

20 But God said to him, 'Fool! This night your soul is required of you; and the things you have prepared, whose will they be?'

21 So is he who lays up treasure for himself, and is not rich toward God."

22 And he said to his disciples, "Therefore I tell you, do not be anxious about your life, what you shall eat, nor about your body, what you shall put on.

23 For life is more than food, and the body more than clothing.

24 Consider the ravens: they neither sow nor reap, they have neither storehouse nor barn, and yet God feeds them. Of how much more value are you than the birds!

25 And which of you by being anxious can add a cubit to his span of life?

26 If then you are not able to do as small a thing as that, why are you anxious about the rest?

27 Consider the lilies, how they grow; they neither toil nor spin; yet I tell you, even Solomon in all his glory was not arrayed like one of these.

28 But if God so clothes the grass which is alive in the field today and tomorrow is thrown into the oven, how much more will he clothe you, O men of little faith!

29 And do not seek what you are to eat and what you are to drink, nor be of anxious mind.

30 For all the nations of the world seek these things; and your Father knows that you need them.

31 Instead, seek his kingdom, and these things shall be yours as well.

32 "Fear not, little flock, for it is your Father's good pleasure to give you the kingdom.

33 Sell your possessions, and give alms; provide yourselves with purses
   that do not grow old, with a treasure in the heavens that does
   not fail, where no thief approaches and no moth destroys.

34 For where your treasure is, there will your heart be also.

35 "Let your loins be girded and your lamps burning,

36 and be like men who are waiting for their master to come home
   from the marriage feast, so that they may open to him at once
   when he comes and knocks.

37 Blessed are those servants whom the master finds awake when he
   comes; truly, I say to you, he will gird himself and have them
   sit at table, and he will come and serve them.

38 If he comes in the second watch, or in the third, and finds them so,
   blessed are those servants!

39 But know this, that if the householder had known at what hour the
   thief was coming, he would not have left his house to be broken
   into.

40 You also must be ready; for the Son of man is coming at an
   unexpected hour."

41 Peter said, "Lord, are you telling this parable for us or for all?"

42 And the Lord said, "Who then is the faithful and wise steward,
   whom his master will set over his household, to give them their
   portion of food at the proper time?

43 Blessed is that servant whom his master when he comes will find
   so doing.

44 Truly, I say to you, he will set him over all his possessions.

45 But if that servant says to himself, 'My master is delayed in coming,'
   and begins to beat the menservants and the maidservants, and
   to eat and drink and get drunk,

46 the master of that servant will come on a day when he does not
   expect him and at an hour he does not know, and will punish
   him, and put him with the unfaithful.

47 And that servant who knew his master's will, but did not make ready
   or act according to his will, shall receive a severe beating.

48 But he who did not know, and did what deserved a beating, shall
   receive a light beating. Every one to whom much is given, of him
   will much be required; and of him to whom men commit much
   they will demand the more.

49 "I came to cast fire upon the earth; and would that it were already
   kindled!

50 I have a baptism to be baptized with; and how I am constrained
   until it is accomplished!

51 Do you think that I have come to give peace on earth? No, I tell
   you, but rather division;

52 for henceforth in one house there will be five divided, three against two and two against three;

53 they will be divided, father against son and son against father, mother against daughter and daughter against her mother, mother-in-law against her daughter-in-law and daughter-in-law against her mother-in-law."

54 He also said to the multitudes, "When you see a cloud rising in the west, you say at once, 'A shower is coming'; and so it happens.

55 And when you see the south wind blowing, you say, 'There will be scorching heat'; and it happens.

56 You hypocrites! You know how to interpret the appearance of earth and sky; but why do you not know how to interpret the present time?

57 "And why do you not judge for yourselves what is right?

58 As you go with your accuser before the magistrate, make an effort to settle with him on the way, less he drag you to the judge, and the judge hand you over to the officer, and the officer put you in prison.

59 I tell you, you will never get out till you have paid the very last copper."

CHAPTER THIRTEEN

1 There were some present at that very time who told him of the Galileans whose blood Pilate had mingled with their sacrifices.

2 And he answered them, "Do you think that these Galileans were worse sinners than all the other Galileans, because they suffered thus?

3 I tell you, No; but unless you repent you will all likewise perish.

4 Or those eighteen upon whom the tower in Silo'am fell and killed them, do you think that they were worse offenders than all the others who dwelt in Jerusalem?

5 I tell you, No; but unless you repent you will all likewise perish."

6 And he told this parable: "A man had a fig tree planted in his vineyard; and he came seeking fruit on it and found none.

7 And he said to the vinedresser, 'Lo, these three years I have come seeking fruit on this fig tree, and I find none. Cut it down; why should it use up the ground?'

8 And he answered him, 'Let it alone, sir, this year also, till I dig about it and put on manure.

9 And if it bears fruit next year, well and good; but if not, you can cut it down.' "

10 Now he was teaching in one of the synagogues on the sabbath.

11 And there was a woman who had had a spirit of infirmity for eighteen years; she was bent over and could not fully straighten herself.

12 And when Jesus saw her, he called her and said to her, "Woman, you are freed from your infirmity."

13 And he laid his hands upon her, and immediately she was made straight, and she praised God.

14 But the ruler of the synagogue, indignant because Jesus had healed on the sabbath, said to the people, "There are six days on which work ought to be done; come on those days and be healed, and not on the sabbath day."

15 Then the Lord answered him, "You hypocrites! Does not each of you on the sabbath untie his ox or his ass from the manger, and lead it away to water it?

16 And ought not this woman, a daughter of Abraham whom Satan bound for eighteen years, be loosed from this bond on the sabbath day?"

17 As he said this, all his adversaries were put to shame; and all the people rejoiced at all the glorious things that were done by him.

18 He said therefore, "What is the kingdom of God like? And to what shall I compare it?

19 It is like a grain of mustard seed which a man took and sowed in his garden; and it grew and became a tree, and the birds of the air made nests in its branches."

20 And again he said, "To what shall I compare the kingdom of God?

21 It is like leaven which a woman took and hid in three measures of flour, till it was all leavened."

22 He went on his way through towns and villages, teaching, and journeying toward Jerusalem.

23 And some one said to him, "Lord, will those who are saved be few?" And he said to them,

24 "Strive to enter by the narrow door; for many, I tell you, will seek to enter and will not be able.

25 When once the householder has risen up and shut the door, you will begin to stand outside and to knock at the door, saying, 'Lord, open to us.' He will answer you, 'I do not know where you come from.'

26 Then you will begin to say, 'We ate and drank in your presence, and you taught in our streets.'

27 But he will say, 'I tell you, I do not know where you come from; depart from me, all you workers of iniquity!'

28 There you will weep and gnash your teeth, when you see Abraham and Isaac and Jacob and all the prophets in the kingdom of God and you yourselves thrust out.

29 And men will come from east and west, and from north and south,
and sit at table in the kingdom of God.

30 And behold, some are last who will be first, and some are first who
will be last.'

31 At that very hour some Pharisees came, and said to him, "Get away
from here, for Herod wants to kill you."

32 And he said to them, "Go and tell that fox, 'Behold, I cast out
demons and perform cures today and tomorrow, and the third
day I finish my course.

33 Nevertheless I must go on my way today and tomorrow and the day
following; for it cannot be that a prophet should perish away from
Jerusalem.'

34 O Jerusalem, Jerusalem, killing the prophets and stoning those who
are sent to you! How often would I have gathered your children
together as a hen gathers her brood under her wings, and you
would not!

35 Behold, your house is forsaken. And I tell you, you will not see me
until you say, 'Blessed is he who comes in the name of the
Lord!' "

CHAPTER FOURTEEN

1 One sabbath when he went to dine at the house of a ruler who
belonged to the Pharisees, they were watching him.

2 And behold, there was a man before him who had dropsy.

3 And Jesus spoke to the lawyers and Pharisees, saying, "Is it lawful
to heal on the sabbath, or not?"

4 But they were silent. Then he took him and healed him, and let
him go.

5 And he said to them, "Which of you, having a son or an ox that has
fallen into a well, will not immediately pull him out on a sabbath
day?"

6 And they could not reply to this.

7 Now he told a parable to those who were invited, when he marked
how they chose the places of honour, saying to them,

8 "When you are invited by any one to a marriage feast, do not sit
down in a place of honour, lest a more eminent man than you be
invited by him;

9 and he who invited you both will come and say to you, 'Give place
to this man,' and then you will begin with shame to take the lowest
place.

10 But when you are invited, go and sit in the lowest place, so that

when your host comes he may say to you, 'Friend, go up higher'; then you will be honoured in the presence of all who sit at table with you.

11 For every one who exalts himself will be humbled, and he who humbles himself will be exalted."

12 He said also to the man who had invited him, "When you give a dinner or a banquet, do not invite your friends or your brothers or your kinsmen or rich neighbours, lest they also invite you in return, and you be repaid.

13 But when you give a feast, invite the poor, the maimed, the lame, the blind,

14 and you will be blessed, because they cannot repay you. You will be repaid at the resurrection of the just."

15 When one of those who sat at table with him heard this, he said to him, "Blessed is he who shall eat bread in the kingdom of God!"

16 But he said to him, "A man once gave a great banquet, and invited many;

17 and at the time for the banquet he sent his servant to say to those who had been invited, 'Come; for all is now ready.'

18 But they all alike began to make excuses. The first said to him, 'I have bought a field, and I must go out and see it; I pray you, have me excused.'

19 And another said, 'I have bought five yoke of oxen, and I go to examine them; I pray you, have me excused.'

20 And another said, 'I have married a wife, and therefore I cannot come.'

21 So the servant came and reported this to his master. Then the householder in anger said to his servant, 'Go out quickly to the streets and lanes of the city, and bring in the poor and maimed and blind and lame.'

22 And the servant said, 'Sir, what you commanded has been done, and still there is room.'

23 And the master said to the servant, 'Go out to the highways and hedges, and compel people to come in, that my house may be filled.

24 For I tell you, none of those men who were invited shall taste my banquet.'"

25 Now great multitudes accompanied him; and he turned and said to them,

26 "If any one comes to me and does not hate his own father and mother and wife and children and brothers and sisters, yes, and even his own life, he cannot be my disciple.

27 Whoever does not bear his own cross and come after me, cannot be my disciple.

28 For which of you, desiring to build a tower, does not first sit down and count the cost, whether he has enough to complete it?

29 Otherwise, when he has laid a foundation, and is not able to finish, all who see it begin to mock him,

30 saying, 'This man began to build, and was not able to finish.'

31 Or what king, going to encounter another king in war, will not sit down first and take counsel whether he is able with ten thousand to meet him who comes against him with twenty thousand?

32 And if not, while the other is yet a great way off, he sends an embassy and asks terms of peace.

33 So therefore, whoever of you does not renounce all that he has cannot be my disciple.

34 "Salt is good; but if salt has lost its taste, how shall its saltness be restored?

35 It is fit neither for the land nor for the dunghill; men throw it away. He who has ears to hear, let him hear."

CHAPTER FIFTEEN

1 Now the tax collectors and sinners were all drawing near to hear him.

2 And the Pharisees and the scribes murmured, saying, "This man receives sinners and eats with them."

3 So he told them this parable:

4 "What man of you, having a hundred sheep, if he has lost one of them, does not leave the ninety-nine in the wilderness, and go after the one which is lost, until he finds it?

5 And when he has found it, he lays it on his shoulders, rejoicing.

6 And when he comes home, he calls together his friends and his neighbours, saying to them, 'Rejoice with me, for I have found my sheep which was lost.'

7 Just so, I tell you, there will be more joy in heaven over one sinner who repents than over ninety-nine righteous persons who need no repentance.

8 "Or what woman, having ten silver coins, if she loses one coin, does not light a lamp and sweep the house and seek diligently until she finds it?

9 And when she has found it, she calls together her friends and neighbours, saying, 'Rejoice with me, for I have found the coin which I had lost.'

10 Just so, I tell you, there is joy before the angels of God over one
sinner who repents.''

11 And he said, ''There was a man who had two sons;

12 and the younger of them said to his father, 'Father, give me the
share of property that falls to me.' And he divided his living
between them.

13 Not many days later, the younger son gathered all he had and took
his journey into a far country, and there he squandered his property
in loose living.

14 And when he had spent everything, a great famine arose in that
country, and he began to be in want.

15 So he went and joined himself to one of the citizens of
that country, who sent him into his fields to feed
swine.

16 And he would gladly have fed on the pods that the swine ate; and
no one gave him anything.

17 But when he came to himself he said, 'How many of my father's
hired servants have bread enough and to spare, but I perish here
with hunger!

18 I will arise and go to my father, and I will say to him, "Father, I
have sinned against heaven and before you;

19 I am no longer worthy to be called your son; treat me as one of your
hired servants.'' '

20 And he arose and came to his father. But while he was yet at a
distance, his father saw him and had compassion, and ran and
embraced him and kissed him.

21 And the son said to him, 'Father, I have sinned against heaven and
before you; I am no longer worthy to be called your son.'

22 But the father said to his servants, 'Bring quickly the best robe, and
put it on him; and put a ring on his hand, and shoes on his
feet;

23 and bring the fatted calf and kill it, and let us eat and make merry;

24 for this my son was dead, and is alive again; he was lost, and is
found.' And they began to make merry.

25 ''Now his elder son was in the field; and as he came and drew near
to the house, he heard music and dancing.

26 And he called one of the servants and asked what this meant.

27 And he said to him, 'Your brother has come, and your father has
killed the fatted calf, because he has received him safe and
sound.'

28 But he was angry and refused to go in. His father came out and
entreated him,

29 but he answered his father, 'Lo, these many years I have served

you, and I never disobeyed your command; yet you never gave me a kid, that I might make merry with my friends.

30 But when this son of yours came, who has devoured your living with harlots, you killed for him the fatted calf!'

31 And he said to him, 'Son, you are always with me, and all that is mine is yours.

32 It was fitting to make merry and be glad, for this your brother was dead, and is alive; he was lost, and is found.'"

CHAPTER SIXTEEN

1 He also said to the disciples, "There was a rich man who had a steward, and charges were brought to him that this man was wasting his goods.

2 And he called him and said to him, 'What is this that I hear about you? Turn in the account of your stewardship, for you can no longer be steward.'

3 And the steward said to himself, 'What shall I do, since my master is taking the stewardship away from me? I am not strong enough to dig, and I am ashamed to beg.

4 I have decided what to do, so that people may receive me into their houses when I am put out of the stewardship.'

5 So, summoning his master's debtors one by one, he said to the first, 'How much do you owe my master?'

6 He said, 'A hundred measures of oil.' And he said to him, 'Take your bill, and sit down quickly and write fifty.'

7 Then he said to another, 'And how much do you owe?' He said, 'A hundred measures of wheat.' He said to him, 'Take your bill, and write eighty.'

8 The master commended the dishonest steward for his shrewdness; for the sons of this world are more shrewd in dealing with their own generation than the sons of light.

9 And I tell you, make friends for yourselves by means of unrighteous mammon, so that when it fails they may receive you into the eternal habitations.

10 "He who is faithful in a very little is faithful also in much; and he who is dishonest in a very little is dishonest also in much.

11 If then you have not been faithful in the unrighteous mammon, who will entrust to you the true riches?

12 And if you have not been faithful in that which is another's, who will give you that which is your own?

13 No servant can serve two masters; for either he will hate the one

and love the other, or he will be devoted to the one and despise the other. You cannot serve God and mammon."

14 The Pharisees, who were lovers of money, heard all this, and they scoffed at him.

15 But he said to them, "You are those who justify yourselves before men, but God knows your hearts; for what is exalted among men is an abomination in the sight of God.

16 "The law and the prophets were until John; since then the good news of the kingdom of God is preached, and every one enters it violently.

17 But it is easier for heaven and earth to pass away, than for one dot of the law to become void.

18 "Every one who divorces his wife and marries another commits adultery, and he who marries a woman divorced from her husband commits adultery.

19 "There was a rich man, who was clothed in purple and fine linen and who feasted sumptuously every day.

20 And at his gate lay a poor man named Laz'arus, full of sores,

21 who desired to be fed with what fell from the rich man's table; moreover the dogs came and licked his sores.

22 The poor man died and was carried by the angels to Abraham's bosom. The rich man also died and was buried;

23 and in Hades, being in torment, he lifted up his eyes, and saw Abraham far off and Laz'arus in his bosom.

24 And he called out, 'Father Abraham, have mercy upon me, and send Laz'arus to dip the end of his finger in water and cool my tongue; for I am in anguish in this flame.'

25 But Abraham said, 'Son, remember that you in your lifetime received your good things, and Laz'arus in like manner evil things; but now he is comforted here, and you are in anguish.

26 And besides all this, between us and you a great chasm has been fixed, in order that those who would pass from here to you may not be able, and none may cross from there to us.'

27 And he said, 'Then I beg you, father, to send him to my father's house,

28 for I have five brothers, so that he may warn them, lest they also come into this place of torment.'

29 But Abraham said, 'They have Moses and the prophets; let them hear them.'

30 And he said, 'No, father Abraham; but if some one goes to them from the dead, they will repent.'

31 He said to him, 'If they do not hear Moses and the prophets, neither will they be convinced if some one should rise from the dead.'"

CHAPTER SEVENTEEN

1 And he said to his disciples, "Temptations to sin are sure to come; but woe to him by whom they come!

2 It would be better for him if a millstone were hung round his neck and he were cast into the sea, than that he should cause one of these little ones to sin.

3 Take heed to yourselves; if your brother sins, rebuke him, and if he repents, forgive him;

4 and if he sins against you seven times in the day, and turns to you seven times, and says, 'I repent,' you must forgive him."

5 The apostles said to the Lord, "Increase our faith!"

6 And the Lord said, "If you had faith as a grain of mustard seed, you could say to this sycamine tree, 'Be rooted up, and be planted in the sea,' and it would obey you.

7 "Will any one of you, who has a servant ploughing or keeping sheep, say to him when he has come in from the field, 'Come at once and sit down at table'?

8 Will he not rather say to him, 'Prepare supper for me, and gird yourself and serve me, till I eat and drink; and afterward you shall eat and drink'?

9 Does he thank the servant because he did what was commanded?

10 So you also, when you have done all that is commanded you, say, 'We are unworthy servants; we have only done what was our duty.'"

11 On the way to Jerusalem he was passing along between Samar'ia and Galilee.

12 And as he entered a village, he was met by ten lepers, who stood at a distance

13 and lifted up their voices and said, "Jesus, Master, have mercy on us."

14 When he saw them he said to them, "Go and show yourselves to the priests." And as they went they were cleansed.

15 Then one of them, when he saw that he was healed, turned back, praising God with a loud voice;

16 and he fell on his face at Jesus' feet, giving him thanks. Now he was a Samaritan.

17 Then said Jesus, "Were not ten cleansed? Where are the nine?

18 Was no one found to return and give praise to God except this foreigner?"

19 And he said to him, "Rise and go your way; your faith has made you well."

20 Being asked by the Pharisees when the kingdom of God was coming,

he answered them, "The kingdom of God is not coming with signs to be observed;

21 nor will they say, 'Lo, here it is!' or 'There!' for behold, the kingdom of God is in the midst of you."

22 And he said to the disciples, "The days are coming when you will desire to see one of the days of the Son of man, and you will not see it.

23 And they will say to you, 'Lo, there!' or 'Lo, here!' Do not go, do not follow them.

24 For as the lightning flashes and lights up the sky from one side to the other, so will the Son of man be in his day.

25 But first he must suffer many things and be rejected by this generation.

26 As it was in the days of Noah, so will it be in the days of the Son of man.

27 They ate, they drank, they married, they were given in marriage, until the day when Noah entered the ark, and the flood came and destroyed them all.

28 Likewise as it was in the days of Lot – they ate, they drank, they bought, they sold, they planted, they built,

29 but on the day when Lot went out from Sodom fire and sulphur rained from heaven and destroyed them all –

30 so will it be on the day when the Son of man is revealed.

31 On that day, let him who is on the housetop, with his goods in the house, not come down to take them away; and likewise let him who is in the field not turn back.

32 Remember Lot's wife.

33 Whoever seeks to gain his life will lose it, but whoever loses his life will preserve it.

34 I tell you, in that night there will be two in one bed; one will be taken and the other left.

35 There will be two women grinding together; one will be taken and the other left."

37 And they said to him, "Where, Lord?" He said to them, "Where the body is, there the eagles will be gathered together."

CHAPTER EIGHTEEN

1 And he told them a parable, to the effect that they ought always to pray and not lose heart.

2 He said, "In a certain city there was a judge who neither feared God nor regarded man;

3 and there was a widow in that city who kept coming to him and saying, 'Vindicate me against my adversary.'

4 For a while he refused; but afterward he said to himself, 'Though I neither fear God nor regard man,

5 yet because this widow bothers me, I will vindicate her, or she will wear me out by her continual coming.'"

6 And the Lord said, "Hear what the unrighteous judge says.

7 And will not God vindicate his elect, who cry to him day and night? Will he delay long over them?

8 I tell you, he will vindicate them speedily. Nevertheless, when the Son of man comes, will he find faith on earth?"

9 He also told this parable to some who trusted in themselves that they were righteous and despised others:

10 "Two men went up into the temple to pray, one a Pharisee and the other a tax collector.

11 The Pharisee stood and prayed thus with himself, 'God, I thank thee that I am not like other men, extortioners, unjust, adulterers, or even like this tax collector.

12 I fast twice a week, I give tithes of all that I get.'

13 But the tax collector, standing far off, would not even lift-up his eyes to heaven, but beat his breast, saying, 'God, be merciful to me a sinner!'

14 I tell you, this man went down to his house justified rather than the other; for every one who exalts himself will be humbled, but he who humbles himself will be exalted."

15 Now they were bringing even infants to him that he might touch them; and when the disciples saw it, they rebuked them.

16 But Jesus called them to him, saying, "Let the children come to me, and do not hinder them; for to such belongs the kingdom of God.

17 Truly, I say to you, whoever does not receive the kingdom of God like a child shall not enter it."

18 And a ruler asked him, "Good Teacher, what shall I do to inherit eternal life?"

19 And Jesus said to him, "Why do you call me good? No one is good but God alone.

20 You know the commandments: 'Do not commit adultery, Do not kill, Do not steal, Do not bear false witness, Honour your father and mother.'"

21 And he said, "All these I have observed from my youth."

22 And when Jesus heard it, he said to him, "One thing you still lack. Sell all that you have and distribute to the poor, and you will have treasure in heaven; and come, follow me."

23 But when he heard this he became sad, for he was very rich.

24 Jesus looking at him said, "How hard it is for those who have riches to enter the kingdom of God!

25 For it is easier for a camel to go through the eye of a needle than for a rich man to enter the kingdom of God."

26 Those who heard it said, "Then who can be saved?"

27 But he said, "What is impossible with men is possible with God."

28 And Peter said, "Lo, we have left our homes and followed you."

29 And he said to them, "Truly, I say to you, there is no man who has left house or wife or brothers or parents or children, for the sake of the kingdom of God,

30 who will not receive manifold more in this time, and in the age to come eternal life."

31 And taking the twelve, he said to them, "Behold, we are going up to Jerusalem, and everything that is written of the Son of man by the prophets will be accomplished.

32 For he will be delivered to the Gentiles, and will be mocked and shamefully treated and spit upon;

33 they will scourge him and kill him, and on the third day he will rise."

34 But they understood none of these things; this saying was hid from them, and they did not grasp what was said.

35 As he drew near to Jericho, a blind man was sitting by the roadside begging;

36 and hearing a multitude going by, he inquired what this meant.

37 They told him, "Jesus of Nazareth is passing by."

38 And he cried, "Jesus, Son of David, have mercy on me!"

39 And those who were in front rebuked him, telling him to be silent; but he cried out all the more, "Son of David, have mercy on me!"

40 And Jesus stopped, and commanded him to be brought to him; and when he came near, he asked him,

41 "What do you want me to do for you?" He said, "Lord, let me receive my sight."

42 And Jesus said to him, "Receive your sight; your faith has made you well."

43 And immediately he received his sight and followed him, glorifying God; and all the people, when they saw it, gave praise to God.

CHAPTER NINETEEN

1 He entered Jericho and was passing through.

2 And there was a man named Zacchae′us; he was a chief tax collector,
and   rich.

3 And he sought to see who Jesus was, but could not, on account of
the crowd, because he was small of stature.

4 So he ran on ahead and climbed up into a sycamore tree to see him,
for he was to pass that way.

5 And when Jesus came to the place, he looked up and said to him,
"Zacchae′us, make haste and come down; for I must stay at your
house   today."

6 So he made haste and came down, and received him joyfully.

7 And when they saw it they all murmured, "He has gone in to be
the guest of a man who is a sinner."

8 And Zacchae′us stood and said to the Lord, "Behold, Lord, the
half of my goods I give to the poor; and if I have defrauded any
one of anything, I restore it fourfold."

9 And Jesus said to him, 'Today salvation has come to this house,
since he also is a son of Abraham.

10 For the Son of man came to seek and to save the lost."

11 As they heard these things, he proceeded to tell a parable, because
he was near to Jerusalem, and because they supposed that the
kingdom of God was to appear immediately.

12 He said therefore, "A nobleman went into a far country to receive
a kingdom and then return.

13 Calling ten of his servants, he gave them ten pounds, and said to
them, 'Trade with these till I come.'

14 But his citizens hated him and sent an embassy after him, saying,
'We do not want this man to reign over us.'

15 When he returned, having received the kingdom, he commanded
these servants, to whom he had given the money, to be called to
him, that he might know what they had gained by trading.

16 The first came before him, saying, 'Lord, your pound has made ten
pounds   more.'

17 And he said to him, 'Well done, good servant! Because you have
been faithful in a very little, you shall have authority over ten
cities.'

18 And the second came, saying, 'Lord, your pound has made five
pounds.'

19 And he said to him, 'And you are to be over five cities.'

20 Then another came, saying, 'Lord, here is your pound, which I kept
laid away in a napkin;

21 for I was afraid of you, because you are a severe man; you take up what you did not lay down, and reap what you did not sow.'

22 He said to him, "I will condemn you out of your own mouth, you wicked servant! You knew that I was a severe man, taking up what I did not lay down and reaping what I did not sow?

23 Why then did you not put my money into the bank, and at my coming I should have collected it with interest?

24 And he said to those who stood by, 'Take the pound from him, and give it to him who has the ten pounds.'

25 (And they said to him, 'Lord, he has ten pounds!')

26 I tell you, that to every one who has will more be given; but from him who has not, even what he has will be taken away.

27 But as for these enemies of mine, who did not want me to reign over them, bring them here and slay them before me.'"

28 And when he had said this, he went on ahead, going up to Jerusalem.

29 When he drew near to Beth'phage and Bethany, at the mount that is called Olivet, he sent two of the disciples,

30 saying, "Go into the village opposite, where on entering you will find a colt tied, on which no one has ever yet sat; untie it and bring it here.

31 If any one asks you, 'Why are you untying it?' you shall say this, 'The Lord has need of it.'"

32 So those who were sent went away and found it as he had told them.

33 And as they were untying the colt, its owners said to them, "Why are you untying the colt?"

34 And they said, "The Lord has need of it."

35 And they brought it to Jesus, and throwing their garments on the colt they set Jesus upon it.

36 And as he rode along, they spread their garments on the road.

37 As he was now drawing near, at the descent of the Mount of Olives, the whole multitude of the disciples began to rejoice and praise God with a loud voice for all the mighty works that they had seen,

38 saying, "Blessed is the King who comes in the name of the Lord! Peace in heaven and glory in the highest!"

39 And some of the Pharisees in the multitude said to him, "Teacher, rebuke your disciples."

40 He answered, "I tell you, if these were silent, the very stones would cry out."

41 And when he drew near and saw the city he wept over it,

42 saying, "Would that even today you knew the things that make for peace! But now they are did from your eyes.

43 For the days shall come upon you, when your enemies will cast up a bank about you and surround you, and hem you in on every side,

44 and dash you to the ground, you and your children within you, and they will not leave one stone upon another in you; because you did not know the time of your visitation."

45 And he entered the temple and began to drive out those who sold,

46 saying to them, "It is written, 'My house shall be a house of prayer'; but you have made it a den of robbers."

47 And he was teaching daily in the temple. The chief priests and the scribes and the principal men of the people sought to destroy him;

48 but they did not find anything they could do, for all the people hung upon his words.

CHAPTER TWENTY

1 One day, as he was teaching the people in the temple and preaching the gospel, the chief priests and the scribes with the elders came up

2 and said to him, "Tell us by what authority you do these things, or who it is that gave you this authority."

3 He answered them, "I also will ask you a question; now tell me,

4 Was the baptism of John from heaven or from men?"

5 And they discussed it with one another, saying, "If we say, 'From heaven,' he will say, 'Why did you not believe him?'

6 But if we say, 'From men,' all the people will stone us; for they are convinced that John was a prophet."

7 So they answered that they did not know whence it was.

8 And Jesus said to them, "Neither will I tell you by what authority I do these things."

9 And he began to tell the people this parable: "A man planted a vineyard, and let it out to tenants, and went into another country for a long while.

10 When the time came, he sent a servant to the tenants, that they should give him some of the fruit of the vineyard; but the tenants beat him, and sent him away empty-handed.

11 And he sent another servant; him also they beat and treated shamefully, and sent him away empty-handed.

12 And he sent yet a third; this one they wounded and cast out.

13 Then the owner of the vineyard said, 'What shall I do? I will send my beloved son; it may be they will respect him.'

14 But when the tenants saw him, they said to themselves, 'This is the heir; let us kill him, that the inheritance may be ours.'

15 And they cast him out of the vineyard and killed him. What then will the owner of the vineyard do to them?

16 He will come and destroy those tenants, and give the vineyard to others." When they heard this, they said, "God forbid!"

17 But he looked at them and said, "What then is this that is written: 'The very stone which the builders rejected has become the head of the corner'?

18 Every one who falls on that stone will be broken to pieces; but when it falls on any one it will crush him."

19 The scribes and the chief priests tried to lay hands on him at that very hour, but they feared the people; for they perceived that he had told this parable against them.

20 So they watched him, and sent spies, who pretended to be sincere, that they might take hold of what he said, so as to deliver him up to the authority and jurisdiction of the governor.

21 They asked him, "Teacher, we know that you speak and teach rightly, and show no partiality, but truly teach the way of God.

22 Is it lawful for us to give tribute to Caesar, or not?"

23 But he perceived their craftiness, and said to them,

24 "Show me a coin. Whose likeness and inscription has it?" They said, "Caesar's."

25 He said to them, "Then render to Caesar the things that are Caesar's, and to God the things that are God's."

26 And they were not able in the presence of the people to catch him by what he said; but marvelling at his answer they were silent.

27 There came to him some Sad'ducees, those who say that there is no resurrection,

28 and they asked him a question, saying, "Teacher, Moses wrote for us that if a man's brother dies, having a wife but no children, the man must take the wife and raise up children for his brother.

29 Now there were seven brothers; the first took a wife, and died without children;

30 and the second

31 and the third took her, and likewise all seven left no children and died.

32 Afterward the woman also died.

33 In the resurrection, therefore, whose wife will the woman be? For the seven had her as wife."

34 And Jesus said to them, "The sons of this age marry and are given in marriage;

35 but those who are accounted worthy to attain to that age and to the resurrection from the dead neither marry nor are given ill marriage,

36 for they cannot die any more, because they are equal to angels and are sons of God, being sons of the resurrection.

37 But that the dead are raised, even Moses showed, in the passage about the bush, where he calls the Lord the God of Abraham and the God of Isaac and the God of Jacob.

38 Now he is not God of the dead, but of the living; for all live to him."

39 And some of the scribes answered, "Teacher, you have spoken well."

40 For they no longer dared to ask him any question.

41 But he said to them, "How can they say that the Christ is David's son?

42 For David himself says in the Book of Psalms,
'The Lord said to my Lord,
Sit at my right hand,

43 till I make thy enemies a stool for thy feet.'

44 David thus calls him Lord; so how is he his son?"

45 And in the hearing of all the people he said to his disciples,

46 "Beware of the scribes, who like to go about in long robes, and love salutations in the market places and the best seats in the synagogues and the places of honour at feasts,

47 who devour widows' houses and for a pretence make long prayers. They will receive the greater condemnation."

CHAPTER TWENTY-ONE

1 He looked up and saw the rich putting their gifts into the treasury;

2 and he saw a poor widow put in two copper coins.

3 And he said, "Truly I tell you, this poor widow has put in more than all of them;

4 for they all contributed out of their abundance, but she out of her poverty put in all the living that she had."

5 And as some spoke of the temple, how it was adorned with noble stones and offerings, he said,

6 "As for these things which you see, the days will come when there shall not be left here one stone upon another that will not be thrown down."

7 And they asked him, "Teacher, when will this be, and what will be the sign when this is about to take place?"

8 And he said, "Take heed that you are not led astray; for many will come in my name, saying, 'I am he!' and, 'The time is at hand!' Do not go after them.

9 And when you hear of wars and tumults, do not be terrified; for this must first take place, but the end will not be at once."

10 Then he said to them, "Nation will rise against nation, and kingdom against kingdom;

11 there will be great earthquakes, and in various places famines and pestilences; and there will be terrors and great signs from heaven.

12 But before all this they will lay their hands on you and persecute you, delivering you up to the synagogues and prisons, and you will be brought before kings and governors for my name's sake.

13 This will be a time for you to bear testimony.

14 Settle it therefore in your minds, not to meditate beforehand how to answer;

15 for I will give you a mouth and wisdom, which none of your adversaries will be able to withstand or contradict.

16 You will be delivered up even by parents and brothers and kinsmen and friends, and some of you they will put to death;

17 you will be hated by all for my name's sake.

18 But not a hair of your head will perish.

19 By your endurance you will gain your lives.

20 "But when you see Jerusalem surrounded by armies, then know that its desolation has come near.

21 Then let those who are in Judea flee to the mountains, and let those who are inside the city depart, and let not those who are out in the country enter it;

22 for these are days of vengeance, to fulfil all that is written.

23 Alas for those who are with child and for those who give suck in those days! For great distress shall be upon the earth and wrath upon this people;

24 they will fall by the edge of the sword, and be led captive among all nations; and Jerusalem will be trodden down by the Gentiles, until the times of the Gentiles are fulfilled.

25 "And there will be signs in sun and moon and stars, and upon the earth distress of nations in perplexity at the roaring of the sea and the waves,

26 men fainting with fear and with foreboding of what is coming on the world; for the powers of the heavens will be shaken.

27 And then they will see the Son of man coming in a cloud with power and great glory.

28 Now when these things begin to take place, look up and raise your heads, because your redemption is drawing near."

29 And he told them a parable: "Look at the fig tree, and all the trees;

30 as soon as they come out in leaf, you see for yourselves and know that the summer is already near.

31 So also, when you see these things taking place, you know that the kingdom of God is near.

32 Truly, I say to you, this generation will not pass away till all has taken place.

33 Heaven and earth will pass away, but my words will not pass away.

34 "But take heed to yourselves lest your hearts be weighed down with dissipation and drunkenness and cares of this life, and that day come upon you suddenly like a snare;

35 for it will come upon all who dwell upon the face of the whole earth.

36 But watch at all times, praying that you may have strength to escape all these things that will take place, and to stand before the Son of man."

37 And every day he was teaching in the temple, but at night he went out and lodged on the mount called Olivet.

38 And early in the morning all the people came to him in the temple to hear him.

THE GOSPEL ACCORDING TO JOHN

JOHN

This translation is taken from
the Revised Standard Version of the Bible

CHAPTER ONE

1 In the beginning was the Word, and the Word was with God, and the Word was God.

2 He was in the beginning with God;

3 all things were made through him, and without him was not anything made that was made.

4 In him was life, and the life was the light of men.

5 The light shines in the darkness, and the darkness has not overcome it.

6 There was a man sent from God, whose name was John.

7 He came for testimony, to bear witness to the light, that all might believe through him.

8 He was not the light, but came to bear witness to the light.

9 The true light that enlightens every man was coming into the world.

10 He was in the world, and the world was made through him, yet the world knew him not.

11 He came to his own home, and his own people received him not.

12 But to all who received him, who believed in his name, he gave power to become children of God;

13 who were born, not of blood nor of the will of the flesh nor of the will of man, but of God.

14 And the Word became flesh and dwelt among us, full of grace and truth; we have beheld his glory, glory as of the only Son from the Father.

15 (John bore witness to him, and cried, "This was he of whom I said, 'He who comes after me ranks before me, for he was before me.'")

16 And from his fullness have we all received, grace upon grace.

17 For the law was given through Moses; grace and truth came through Jesus Christ.

18 No one has ever seen God; the only Son, who is in the bosom of the Father, he has made him known.

19 And this is the testimony of John, when the Jews sent priests and Levites from Jerusalem to ask him, "Who are you?"

20 He confessed, he did not deny, but confessed, "I am not the Christ."

21 And they asked him, "What then? Are you Eli'jah?" He said, "I am not." "Are you the prophet?" And he answered, "No."

22 They said to him then, "Who are you? Let us have an answer for those who sent us. What do you say about yourself?"

23 He said, "I am the voice of one crying in the wilderness, 'Make straight the way of the Lord,' as the prophet Isaiah said."

24 Now they had been sent from the Pharisees.

25 They asked him, "Then why are you baptizing, if you are neither the Christ, nor Eli'jah, nor the prophet?"

26 John answered them, "I baptize with water; but among you stands one whom you do not know,

27 even he who comes after me, the thong of whose sandal I am not worthy to untie."

28 This took place in Bethany beyond the Jordan, where John was baptizing.

29 The next day he saw Jesus coming toward him, and said, "Behold, the Lamb of God, who takes away the sin of the world!

30 This is he of whom I said, 'After me comes a man who ranks before me, for he was before me.'

31 I myself did not know him; but for this I came baptizing with water, that he might be revealed to Israel."

32 And John bore witness, "I saw the Spirit descend as a dove from heaven, and it remained on him.

33 I myself did not know him; but he who sent me to baptize with water said to me, 'He on whom you see the Spirit descend and remain, this is he who baptizes with the Holy Spirit.'

34 And I have seen and have borne witness that this is the Son of God."

35 The next day again John was standing with two of his disciples;

36 and he looked at Jesus as he walked, and said, "Behold, the Lamb of God!"

37 The two disciples heard him say this, and they followed Jesus.

38 Jesus turned, and saw them following, and said to them, "What do you seek?" And they said to him, "Rabbi" (which means Teacher), "where are you staying?"

39 He said to them, "Come and see." They came and saw where he was staying; and they stayed with him that day, for it was about the tenth hour.

40 One of the two who heard John speak, and followed him, was
Andrew, Simon Peter's brother.

41 He first found his brother Simon, and said to him, "We have found
the Messiah" (which means Christ).

42 He brought him to Jesus. Jesus looked at him, and said, "So you
are Simon the son of John? You shall be called Cephas" (which
means Peter).

43 The next day Jesus decided to go to Galilee. And he found Philip
and said to him, "Follow me."

44 Now Philip was from Beth-sa'ida, the city of Andrew and Peter.

45 Philip found Nathan'a-el, and said to him, "We have found him of
whom Moses in the law and also the prophets wrote, Jesus of
Nazareth, the son of Joseph."

46 Nathan'a-el said to him, "Can anything good come out of
Nazareth?" Philip said to him, "Come and see."

47 Jesus saw Nathan'a-el coming to him, and said of him, "Behold,
an Israelite indeed, in whom is no guile!"

48 Nathan'a-el said to him, "How do you know me?" Jesus answered
him, "Before Philip called you, when you were under the fig
tree, I saw you."

49 Nathan'a-el answered him, "Rabbi, you are the Son of God! You
are the King of Israel!"

50 Jesus answered him, "Because I said to you, I saw you under the
fig tree, do you believe? You shall see greater things than these."

51 And he said to him, "Truly, truly, I say to you, you will see heaven
opened, and the angels of God ascending and descending upon
the Son of man."

CHAPTER TWO

1 On the third day there was a marriage at Cana in Galilee, and the
mother of Jesus was there;

2 Jesus also was invited to the marriage, with his disciples.

3 When the wine gave out, the mother of Jesus said to him, "They
have no wine."

4 And Jesus said to her, "O woman, what have you to do with me?
My hour has not yet come."

5 His mother said to the servants, "Do whatever he tells you."

6 Now six stone jars were standing there, for the Jewish rites of
purification, each holding twenty or thirty gallons.

7 Jesus said to them, "Fill the jars with water." And they filled them
up to the brim.

8 He said to them, "Now draw some out, and take it to the steward of the feast." So they took it.

9 When the steward of the feast tasted the water now become wine, and did not know where it came from (though the servants who had drawn the water knew), the steward of the feast called the bridegroom

10 and said to him, "Every man serves the good wine first; and when men have drunk freely, then the poor wine; but you have kept the good wine until now."

11 This, the first of his signs, Jesus did at Cana in Galilee, and manifested his glory; and his disciples believed in him.

12 After this he went down to Caper′na-um, with his mother and his brothers and his disciples; and there they stayed for a few days.

13 The Passover of the Jews was at hand, and Jesus went up to Jerusalem.

14 In the temple he found those who were selling oxen and sheep and pigeons, and the money-changers at their business.

15 And making a whip of cords, he drove them all, with the sheep and oxen, out of the temple; and he poured out the coins of the money-changers and overturned their tables.

16 And he told those who sold the pigeons, "Take these things away; you shall not make my Father's house a house of trade."

17 His disciples remembered that it was written, "Zeal for thy house will consume me."

18 The Jews then said to him, "What sign have you to show us for doing this?"

19 Jesus answered them, "Destroy this temple, and in three days I will raise it up."

20 The Jews then said, "It has taken forty-six years to build this temple, and will you raise it up in three days?"

21 But he spoke of the temple of his body.

22 When therefore he was raised from the dead, his disciples remembered that he had said this; and they believed the scripture and the word which Jesus had spoken.

23 Now when he was in Jerusalem at the Passover feast, many believed in his name when they saw the signs which he did;

24 but Jesus did not trust himself to them,

25 because he knew all men and needed no one to bear witness of man; for he himself knew what was in man.

CHAPTER THREE

1 Now there was a man of the Pharisees, named Nicode'mus, a ruler of the Jews.

2 This man came to Jesus by night and said to him, "Rabbi, we know that you are a teacher come from God; for no one can do these signs that you do, unless God is with him."

3 Jesus answered him, "Truly, truly, I say to you, unless one is born anew, he cannot see the kingdom of God."

4 Nicode'mus said to him, "How can a man be born when he is old? Can he enter a second time into his mother's womb and be born?"

5 Jesus answered, "Truly, truly, I say to you, unless one is born of water and the Spirit, he cannot enter the kingdom of God.

6 That which is born of the flesh is flesh, and that which is born of the Spirit is spirit.

7 Do not marvel that I said to you, 'You must be born anew.'

8 The wind blows where it wills, and you hear the sound of it, but you do not know whence it comes or whither it goes; so it is with every one who is born of the Spirit."

9 Nicode'mus said to him, "How can this be?"

10 Jesus answered him, "Are you a teacher of Israel, and yet you do not understand this?

11 Truly, truly, I say to you, we speak of what we know, and bear witness to what we have seen; you do not receive our testimony.

12 If I have told you earthly things and you do not believe, how can you believe if I tell you heavenly things?

13 No one has ascended into heaven but he who descended from heaven, the Son of man.

14 And as Moses lifted up the serpent in the wilderness, so must the Son of man be lifted up,

15 that whoever believes in him may have eternal life."

16 For God so loved the world that he gave his only Son, that whoever believes in him should not perish but have eternal life.

17 For God sent the Son into the world, not to condemn the world, but that the world might be saved through him.

18 He who believes in him is not condemned; he who does not believe is condemned already, because he has not believed in the name of the only Son of God.

19 And this is the judgement, that the light has come into the world, and men loved darkness rather than light, because their deeds were evil.

20 For every one who does evil hates the light, and does not come to the light, lest his deeds should be exposed.

21 But he who does what is true comes to the light, that it may be clearly seen that his deeds have been wrought in God.

22 After this Jesus and his disciples went into the land of Judea; there he remained with them and baptized.

23 John also was baptizing at Ae'non near Salim, because there was much water there; and people came and were baptized.

24 For John had not yet been put in prison.

25 Now a discussion arose between John's disciples and a Jew over purifying.

26 And they came to John, and said to him, "Rabbi, he who was with you beyond the Jordan, to whom you bore witness, here he is, baptizing, and all are going to him."

27 John answered, "No one can receive anything except what is given him from heaven.

28 You yourselves bear me witness, that I said, I am not the Christ, but I have been sent before him.

29 He who has the bride is the bridegroom; the friend of the bridegroom, who stands and hears him, rejoices greatly at the bridegroom's voice; therefore this joy of mine is now full.

30 He must increase, but I must decrease."

31 He who comes from above is above all; he who is of the earth belongs to the earth, and of the earth he speaks; he who comes from heaven is above all.

32 He bears witness to what he has seen and heard, yet no one receives his testimony;

33 he who receives his testimony sets his seal to this, that God is true.

34 For he whom God has sent utters the words of God, for it is not by measure that he gives the Spirit;

35 the Father loves the Son, and has given all things into his hand.

36 He who believes in the Son has eternal life; he who does not obey the Son shall not see life, but the wrath of God rests upon him.

CHAPTER FOUR

1 Now when the Lord knew that the Pharisees had heard that Jesus was making and baptizing more disciples than John

2 (although Jesus himself did not baptize, but only his disciples),

3 he left Judea and departed again to Galilee.

4 He had to pass through Samar'ia.

5　So he came to a city of Samar′ia, called Sy′char, near the field that Jacob gave to his son Joseph.

6　Jacob's well was there, and so Jesus, wearied as he was with his journey, sat down beside the well. It was about the sixth hour.

7　There came a woman of Samar′ia to draw water. Jesus said to her, "Give me a drink."

8　For his disciples had gone away into the city to buy food.

9　The Samaritan woman said to him, "How is it that you, a Jew, ask a drink of me, a woman of Samar′ia?" For Jews have no dealings with Samaritans.

10　Jesus answered her, "If you knew the gift of God, and who it is that is saying to you, 'Give me a drink,' you would have asked him, and he would have given you living water."

11　The woman said to him, "Sir, you have nothing to draw with, and the well is deep; where do you get that living water?

12　Are you greater than our father Jacob who gave us the well, and drank from it himself, and his sons, and his cattle?"

13　Jesus said to her, "Every one who drinks of this water will thirst again,

14　but whoever drinks of the water that I shall give him will never thirst; the water that I shall give him will become in him a spring of water welling up to eternal life."

15　The woman said to him, "Sir, give me this water, that I may not thirst, nor come here to draw."

16　Jesus said to her, "Go, call your husband, and come here."

17　The woman answered him, "I have no husband." Jesus said to her, "You are right in saying, 'I have no husband';

18　for you have had five husbands, and he whom you now have is not your husband; this you said truly."

19　The woman said to him, "Sir, I perceive that you are a prophet.

20　Our fathers worshipped on this mountain; and you say that in Jerusalem is the place where men ought to worship."

21　Jesus said to her, "Woman, believe me, the hour is coming when neither on this mountain nor in Jerusalem will you worship the Father.

22　You worship what you do not know; we worship what we know, for salvation is from the Jews.

23　But the hour is coming, and now is, when the true worshippers will worship the Father in spirit and truth, for such the Father seeks to worship him.

24　God is spirit, and those who worship him must worship in spirit and truth."

25 The woman said to him, "I know that Messiah is coming (he who is called Christ); when he comes, he will show us all things."

26 Jesus said to her, "I who speak to you am he."

27 Just then his disciples came. They marvelled that he was talking with a woman, but none said, "What do you wish?" or, "Why are you talking with her?"

28 So the woman left her water jar, and went away into the city, and said to the people,

29 "Come, see a man who told me all that I ever did. Can this be the Christ?"

30 They went out of the city and were coming to him.

31 Meanwhile the disciples besought him, saying, "Rabbi, eat."

32 But he said to them, "I have food to eat of which you do not know."

33 So the disciples said to one another, "Has any one brought him food?"

34 Jesus said to them, "My food is to do the will of him who sent me, and to accomplish his work.

35 Do you not say, "There are yet four months, then comes the harvest"? I tell you, lift up your eyes, and see how the fields are already white for harvest.

36 He who reaps receives wages, and gathers fruit for eternal life, so that sower and reaper may rejoice together.

37 For here the saying holds true, "One sows and another reaps."

38 I sent you to reap that for which you did not labour; others have laboured, and you have entered into their labour."

39 Many Samaritans from that city believed in him because of the woman's testimony, "He told me all that I ever did."

40 So when the Samaritans came to him, they asked him to stay with them; and he stayed there two days.

41 And many more believed because of his word.

42 They said to the woman, "It is no longer because of your words that we believe, for we have heard for ourselves, and we know that this is indeed the Saviour of the world."

43 After the two days he departed to Galilee.

44 For Jesus himself testified that a prophet has no honour in his own country.

45 So when he came to Galilee, the Galileans welcomed him, having seen all that he had done in Jerusalem at the feast, for they too had gone to the feast.

46 So he came again to Cana in Galilee, where he had made the water wine. And at Caper′na-um there was an official whose son was ill.

47 When he heard that Jesus had come from Judea to Galilee, he went

and begged him to come down and heal his son, for he was at the point of death.

48 Jesus therefore said to him, "Unless you see signs and wonders you will not believe."

49 The official said to him, "Sir, come down before my child dies."

50 Jesus said to him, "Go; your son will live." The man believed the word that Jesus spoke to him and went his way.

51 As he was going down, his servants met him and told him that his son was living.

52 So he asked them the hour when he began to mend, and they said to him, "Yesterday at the seventh hour the fever left him."

53 The father knew that was the hour when Jesus had said to him, "Your son will live"; and he himself believed, and all his household.

54 This was now the second sign that Jesus did when he had come from Judea to Galilee.

CHAPTER FIVE

1 After this there was a feast of the Jews, and Jesus went up to Jerusalem.

2 Now there is in Jerusalem by the Sheep Gate a pool, in Hebrew called Beth-za'tha, which has five porticoes.

3 In these lay a multitude of invalids, blind, lame, paralysed.

5 One man was there, who had been ill for thirty-eight years.

6 When Jesus saw him and knew that he had been lying there a long time, he said to him, "Do you want to be healed?"

7 The sick man answered him, "Sir, I have no man to put me into the pool when the water is troubled, and while I am going another steps down before me."

8 Jesus said to him, "Rise, take up your pallet, and walk."

9 And at once the man was healed, and he took up his pallet and walked.

Now that day was the sabbath,

10 So the Jews said to the man who was cured, "It is the sabbath, it is not lawful for you to carry your pallet."

11 But he answered them, "The man who healed me said to me, "Take up your pallet, and walk.'"

12 They asked him, "Who is the man who said to you, 'Take up your pallet, and walk'?"

13 Now the man who had been healed did not know who it was, for Jesus had withdrawn, as there was a crowd in the place.

14 Afterward, Jesus found him in the temple, and said to him, "See,

you are well! Sin no more, that nothing worse befall you."

15 The man went away and told the Jews that it was Jesus who had healed him.

16 And this was why the Jews persecuted Jesus, because he did this on the sabbath.

17 But Jesus answered them, "My Father is working still, and I am working."

18 This was why the Jews sought all the more to kill him, because he not only broke the sabbath but also called God his own Father, making himself equal with God.

19 Jesus said to them, "Truly, truly, I say to you, the Son can do nothing of his own accord, but only what he sees the Father doing; for whatever he does, that the Son does likewise.

20 For the Father loves the Son, and shows him all that he himself is doing; and greater works than these will he show him, that you may marvel.

21 For as the Father raises the dead and gives them life, so also the Son gives life to whom he will.

22 The Father judges no one, but has given all judgement to the Son,

23 that all may honour the Son, even as they honour the Father. He who does not honour the Son does not honour the Father who sent him.

24 Truly, truly, I say to you, he who hears my word and believes him who sent me, has eternal life; he does not come into judgement, but has passed from death to life.

25 "Truly, truly, I say to you, the hour is coming, and now is, when the dead will hear the voice of the Son of God, and those who hear will live.

26 For as the Father has life in himself, so he has granted the Son also to have life in himself,

27 and has given him authority to execute judgement, because he is the Son of man.

28 Do not marvel at this; for the hour is coming when all who are in the tombs will hear his voice

29 and come forth, those who have done good, to the resurrection of life, and those who have done evil, to the resurrection of judgement.

30 "I can do nothing on my own authority; as I hear, I judge; and my judgement is just, because I seek not my own will but the will of him who sent me.

31 If I bear witness to myself, my testimony is not true;

32 there is another who bears witness to me, and I know that the testimony which he bears to me is true.

33 You sent to John, and he has borne witness to the
truth.

34 Not that the testimony which I receive is from man; but I say this
that you may be saved.

35 He was a burning and shining lamp, and you were willing to rejoice
for a while in his light.

36 But the testimony which I have is greater than that of John; for the
works which the Father has granted me to accomplish, these
very works which I am doing, bear me witness that the Father
has sent me.

37 And the Father who sent me has himself borne witness to me. His
voice you have never heard, his form you have never seen;

38 and you do not have his word abiding in you, for you do not believe
him whom he has sent.

39 You search the scriptures, because you think that in them you have
eternal life; and it is they that bear witness to me;

40 yet you refuse to come to me that you may have life.

41 I do not receive glory from men.

42 But I know that you have not the love of God within you.

43 I have come in my Father's name, and you do not receive me; if
another comes in his own name, him you will receive.

44 How can you believe, who receive glory from one another and do
not seek the glory that comes from the only God?

45 Do not think that I shall accuses you to the Father; it is Moses who
accuses you, on whom you set your hope.

46 If you believed Moses, you would believe me, for he wrote of me.

47 But if you do not believe his writings, how will you believe my
words?"

CHAPTER SIX

1 After this Jesus went to the other side of the Sea of Galilee, which
is the Sea of Tibe'ri-as.

2 And a multitude followed him, because they saw the signs which he
did on those who were diseased.

3 Jesus went up on the mountain, and there sat down with his
disciples.

4 Now the Passover, the feast of the Jews, was at hand.

5 Lifting up his eyes, then, and seeing that a multitude was coming
to him, Jesus said to Philip, "How are we to buy bread, so that
these people may eat?"

6 This he said to test him, for he himself knew what he would do.

7 Philip answered him, "Two hundred denarii would not buy enough
   bread for each of them to get a little."

8 One of his disciples, Andrew, Simon Peter's brother, said to him,

9 "There is a lad here who has five barley loaves and two fish; but
   what are they among so many?"

10 Jesus said, "Make the people sit down." Now there was much grass
   in the place; so the men sat down, in number about five
   thousand.

11 Jesus then took the loaves, and when he had given thanks, he
   distributed them to those who were seated; so also the fish, as
   much as they wanted.

12 And when they had eaten their fill, he told his disciples, "Gather
   up the fragments left over, that nothing may be lost."

13 So they gathered them up and filled twelve baskets with fragments
   from the five barley loaves, left by those who had eaten.

14 When the people saw the sign which he had done, they said, "This
   is indeed the prophet who is to come into the world!"

15 Perceiving then that they were about to come and take him by force
   to make him king, Jesus withdrew again to the mountain by
   himself.

16 When evening came, his disciples went down to the sea,

17 got into a boat, and started across the sea to Caper'naum. It was
   now dark, and Jesus had not yet come to them.

18 The sea rose because a strong wind was blowing.

19 When they had rowed about three or four miles, they saw Jesus
   walking on the sea and drawing near to the boat. They were
   frightened,

20 but he said to them, "It is I; do not be afraid."

21 Then they were glad to take him into the boat, and immediately the
   boat was at the land to which they were going.

22 On the next day the people who remained on the other side of the
   sea saw that there had been only one boat there, and that Jesus
   had not entered the boat with his disciples, but that his disciples
   had gone away
   alone.

23 However, boats from Tibe'ri-as came near the place where they ate
   the bread after the Lord had given thanks.

24 So when the people saw that Jesus was not there, nor his disciples,
   they themselves got into the boats and went to Caper'naum,
   seeking Jesus.

25 When they found him on the other side of the sea, they said to him
   "Rabbi, when did you come here?

26 Jesus answered them, "Truly, truly, I say to you, you seek me, not

because you saw signs, but because you ate your fill of the loaves.

27 Do not labour for the food which perishes, but for the food which endures to eternal life, which the Son of man will give to you; for on him has God the Father set his seal.

28 Then they said to him, "What must we do, to be doing the works of God?

29 Jesus answered them, "This is the work of God, that you believe in him whom he has sent."

30 So they said to him, "Then what sign do you do, that we may see, and believe you? What work do you perform?

31 Our fathers ate the manna in the wilderness; as it is written, 'He gave them bread from heaven to eat.'"

32 Jesus then said to them, "Truly, truly, I say to you, it was not Moses who gave you the bread from heaven; my Father gives you the true bread from heaven.

33 For the bread of God is that which comes down from heaven, and gives life to the world."

34 They said to him, "Lord, give us this bread always."

35 Jesus said to them, "I am the bread of life; he who comes to me shall not hunger, and he who believes in me shall never thirst.

36 But I said to you that you have seen me and yet do not believe.

37 All that the Father gives me will come to me; and him who comes to me I will not cast out.

38 For I have come down from heaven, not to do my own will, but the will of him who sent me;

39 and this is the will of him who sent me, that I should lose nothing of all that he has given me, but raise it up at the last day.

40 For this is the will of my Father, that every one who sees the Son and believes in him should have eternal life; and I will raise him up at the last day."

41 The Jews then murmured at him because he said, "I am the bread which came down from heaven."

42 They said, "Is not this Jesus, the son of Joseph, whose father and mother we know? How does he now say, 'I have come down from heaven'?"

43 Jesus answered them, "Do not murmur among yourselves.

44 No one can come to me unless the Father who sent me draws him; and I will raise him up at the last day.

45 It is written in the prophets, 'And they shall all be taught by God.' Every one who has heard and learned from the Father comes to me.

46 Not that any one has seen the Father except him who is from God; he has seen the Father.

47 Truly, truly, I say to you, he who believes has eternal life.

48 I am the bread of life.

49 Your fathers ate the manna in the wilderness, and they died.

50 This is the bread which comes down from heaven, that a man may eat of it and not die.

51 I am the living bread which came down from heaven; if any one eats of this bread, he will live for ever; and the bread which I shall give for the life of the world is my flesh."

52 The Jews then disputed among themselves, saying, "How can this man give us his flesh to eat?"

53 So Jesus said to them, "Truly, truly, I say to you, unless you eat the flesh of the Son of man and drink his blood, you have no life in you;

54 he who eats my flesh and drinks my blood has eternal life, and I will raise him up at the last day.

55 For my flesh is food indeed, and my blood is drink indeed.

56 He who eats my flesh and drinks my blood abides in me, and I in him.

57 As the living Father sent me, and I live because of the Father, so he who eats me will live because of me.

58 This is the bread which came down from heaven, not such as the fathers ate and died; he who eats this bread will live for ever."

59 This he said in the synagogue, as he taught at Caper'na-um.

60 Many of his disciples, when they heard it, said, "This is a hard saying; who can listen to it?"

61 But Jesus, knowing in himself that his disciples murmured at it, said to them, "Do you take offence at this?

62 Then what if you were to see the Son of man ascending where he was before?

63 It is the spirit that gives life, the flesh is of no avail; the words that I have spoken to you are spirit and life.

64 But there are some of you that do not believe." For Jesus knew from the first who those were that did not believe, and who it was that would betray him.

65 And he said, "This is why I told you that no one can come to me unless it is granted him by the Father."

66 After this many of his disciples drew back and no longer went about with him.

67 Jesus said to the twelve, "Do you also wish to go away?"

68 Simon Peter answered him, "Lord, to whom shall we go? You have the words of eternal life;

69 and we have believed, and have come to know, that you are the Holy One of God."

70 Jesus answered them, "Did I not choose you, the twelve, and one of you is a devil?"

71 He spoke of Judas the son of Simon Iscariot, for he, one of the twelve, was to betray him.

CHAPTER SEVEN

1 After this Jesus went about in Galilee; he would not go about in Judea, because the Jews sought to kill him.

2 Now the Jews' feast of Tabernacles was at hand.

3 So his brothers said to him, "Leave here and go to Judea, that your disciples may see the works you are doing.

4 For no man works in secret if he seeks to be known openly. If you do these things, show yourself to the world."

5 For even his brothers did not believe in him.

6 Jesus said to them, "My time has not yet come, but your time is always here.

7 The world cannot hate you, but it hates me because I testify of it that its works are evil.

8 Go to the feast yourselves; I am not going up to this feast, for my time has not yet fully come."

9 So saying, he remained in Galilee.

10 But after his brothers had gone up to the feast, then he also went up, not publicly but in private.

11 The Jews were looking for him at the feast, and saying, "Where is he?"

12 And there was much muttering about him among the people. While some said, "He is a good man," others said, "No, he is leading the people astray."

13 Yet for fear of the Jews no one spoke openly of him.

14 About the middle of the feast Jesus went up into the temple and taught.

15 The Jews marvelled at it, saying, "How is it that this man has learning, when he has never studied?"

16 So Jesus answered them, "My teaching is not mine, but his who sent me;

17 if any man's will is to do his will, he shall know whether the teaching is from God or whether I am speaking on my own authority.

18 He who speaks on his own authority seeks his own glory; but he who seeks the glory of him who sent him is true, and in him there is no falsehood.

19 Did not Moses give you the law? Yet none of you keeps the law. Why do you seek to kill me?"

20 The people answered, "You have a demon! Who is seeking to kill you?"

21 Jesus answered them, "I did one deed, and you all marvel at it.

22 Moses gave you circumcision (not that it is from Moses, but from the fathers), and you circumcise a man upon the sabbath.

23 If on the sabbath a man receives circumcision, so that the law of Moses may not be broken, are you angry with me because on the sabbath I made a man's whole body well?

24 Do not judge by appearances, but judge with right judgement."

25 Some of the people of Jerusalem therefore said, "Is not this the man whom they seek to kill?

26 And here he is, speaking openly, and they say nothing to him! Can it be that the authorities really know that this is the Christ?

27 Yet we know where this man comes from; and when the Christ appears, no one will know where he comes from."

28 So Jesus proclaimed, as he taught in the temple, "You know me, and you know where I come from? But I have not come of my own accord; he who sent me is true, and him you do not know.

29 I know him, for I come from him, and he sent me."

30 So they sought to arrest him; but no one laid hands on him, because his hour had not yet come.

31 Yet many of the people believed in him; they said, "When the Christ appears, will he do more signs than this man has done?"

32 The Pharisees heard the crowd thus muttering about him, and the chief priests and Pharisees sent officers to arrest him.

33 Jesus then said, "I shall be with you a little longer, and then I go to him who sent me;

34 you will seek me and you will not find me; where I am you cannot come."

35 The Jews said to one another, "Where does this man intend to go that we shall not find him? Does he intend to go to the Dispersion among the Greeks and teach the Greeks?

36 What does he mean by saying, 'You will seek me and you will not find me,' and, 'Where I am you cannot come'?"

37 On the last day of the feast, the great day, Jesus stood up and proclaimed, "If any one thirst, let him come to me and drink.

38 He who believes in me, as the scripture has said, 'Out of his heart shall flow rivers of living water.'"

39 Now this he said about the Spirit, which those who believed in him were to receive; for as yet the Spirit had not been given, because Jesus was not yet glorified.

40 When they heard these words, some of the people said, "This is really the prophet."

41 Others said, "This is the Christ." But some said, "Is the Christ to come from Galilee?

42 Has not the scripture said that the Christ is descended from David, and comes from Bethlehem, the village where David was?"

43 So there was a division among the people over him.

44 Some of them wanted to arrest him, but no one laid hands on him.

45 The officers then went back to the chief priests and Pharisees, who said to them, "Why did you not bring him?"

46 The officers answered, "No man ever spoke like this man!"

47 The Pharisees answered them, "Are you led astray, you also?

48 Have any of the authorities or of the Pharisees believed in him?

49 But this crowd, who do not know the law, are accursed."

50 Nicode'mus, who had gone to him before, and who was one of them, said to them,

51 "Does our law judge a man without first giving him a hearing and learning what he does?"

52 They replied, "Are you from Galilee too? Search and you will see that no prophet is to rise from Galilee."

CHAPTER EIGHT

1 They went each to his own house,
but Jesus went to the Mount of Olives.

2 Early in the morning he came again to the temple; all the people came to him, and he sat down and taught them.

3 The scribes and the Pharisees brought a woman who had been caught in adultery, and placing her in the midst

4 they said to him, "Teacher, this woman has been caught in the act of adultery.

5 Now in the law Moses commanded us to stone such. What do you say about her?"

6 This they said to test him, that they might have some charge to bring against him. Jesus bent down and wrote with his finger on the ground.

7 And as they continued to ask him, he stood up and said to them, "Let him who is without sin among you be the first to throw a stone at her."

8 And once more he bent down and wrote with his finger on the ground.

9 But when they heard it, they went away, one by one, beginning with the eldest, and Jesus was left alone with the woman standing before him.

10 Jesus looked up and said to her, "Woman, where are they? Has no one condemned you?"

11 She said, "No one, Lord." And Jesus said, "Neither do I condemn you; go, and do not sin again."

12 Again Jesus spoke to them, saying, "I am the light of the world; he who follows me will not walk in darkness, but will have the light of life."

13 The Pharisees then said to him, "You are bearing witness to yourself; your testimony is not true."

14 Jesus answered, "Even if I do bear witness to myself, my testimony is true, for I know whence I have come and whither I am going, but you do not know whence I come or whither I am going.

15 You judge according to the flesh, I judge no one.

16 Yet even if I do judge, my judgement is true, for it is not I alone that judge, but I and he who sent me.

17 In your law it is written that the testimony of two men is true;

18 I bear witness to myself, and the Father who sent me bears witness to me."

19 They said to him therefore, "Where is your Father?" Jesus answered, "You know neither me nor my Father; if you knew me, you would know my Father also."

20 These words he spoke in the treasury, as he taught in the temple; but no one arrested him, because his hour had not yet come.

21 Again he said to them, "I go away, and you will seek me and die in your sin; where I am going, you cannot come."

22 Then said the Jews, "Will he kill himself, since he says, 'Where I am going, you cannot come'?"

23 He said to them, "You are from below, I am from above; you are of this world, I am not of this world.

24 I told you that you would die in your sins, for you will die in your sins unless you believe that I am he."

25 They said to him, "Who are you?" Jesus said to them, "Even what I have told you from the beginning.

26 I have much to say about you and much to judge; but he who sent me is true, and I declare to the world what I have heard from him."

27 They did not understand that he spoke to them of the Father.

28 So Jesus said, "When you have lifted up the Son of man, then you will know that I am he, and that I do nothing on my own authority but speak thus as the Father taught me.

29 And he who sent me is with me; he has not left me alone, for I
always do what is pleasing to him."

30 As he spoke thus, many believed in him.

31 Jesus then said to the Jews who had believed in him,
"If you continue in my word, you are truly my
disciples,

32 and you will know the truth, and the truth will make you free."

33 They answered him, "We are descendants of Abraham, and have
never been in bondage to any one. How is it that you say, 'You
will be made free'?"

34 Jesus answered them, "Truly, truly, I say to you, every one who
commits sin is a slave to sin.

35 The slave does not continue in the house for ever; the son continues
for ever.

36 So if the Son makes you free, you will be free indeed.

37 I know that you are descendants of Abraham; yet you seek to kill
me, because my word finds no place in you.

38 I speak of what I have seen with my Father, and you do what you
have heard from your father."

39 They answered him, "Abraham is our father." Jesus said to them,
"If you were Abraham's children, you would do what Abraham
did,

40 but now you seek to kill me, a man who has told you the truth which
I heard from God; this is not what Abraham did.

41 You do what your father did." They said to him, "We were not
born of fornication; we have one Father, even God."

42 Jesus said to them, "If God were your Father, you would love me,
for I proceeded and came forth from God; I came not of my own
accord, but he sent me.

43 Why do you not understand what I say? It is because you cannot
bear to hear my word.

44 You are of your father the devil, and your will is to do
your father's desires. He was a murderer from the beginning,
and has nothing to do with the truth, because there is no truth in
him. When he lies, he speaks according to his own nature, for
he is a liar and the father of lies.

45 But, because I tell the truth, you do not believe me.

46 Which of you convicts me of sin? If I tell the truth, why do you not
believe me?

47 He who is of God hears the words of God; the reason why you do
not hear them is that you are not of God."

48 The Jews answered him, "Are we not right in saying that you are a
Samaritan and have a demon?"

49 Jesus answered, "I have not a demon; but I honour my Father, and you dishonour me.

50 Yet I do not seek my own glory; there is One who seeks it and he will be the judge.

51 Truly, truly, I say to you, if any one keeps my word, he will never see death."

52 The Jews said to him, "Now we know that you have a demon. Abraham died, as did the prophets; and you say, 'If any one keeps my word, he will never taste death.'

53 Are you greater than our father Abraham, who died? And the prophets died! Who do you claim to be?"

54 Jesus answered, "If I glorify myself, my glory is nothing; it is my Father who glorifies me, of whom you say that he is your God.

55 But you have not known him; I know him. If I said, I do not know him, I should be a liar like you; but I do know him and I keep his word.

56 Your father Abraham rejoiced that he was to see my day; he saw it and was glad."

57 The Jews then said to him, "You are not yet fifty years old, and have you seen Abraham?"

58 Jesus said to them, "Truly, truly, I say to you, before Abraham was, I am."

59 So they took up stones to throw at him; but Jesus hid himself and went out of the temple.

CHAPTER NINE

1 As he passed by, he saw a man blind from his birth.

2 And his disciples asked him, "Rabbi, who sinned, this man or his parents, that he was born blind?"

3 Jesus answered, "It was not that this man sinned, or his parents, but that the works of God might be made manifest in him.

4 We must work the works of him who sent me, while it is day; night comes, when no one can work.

5 As long as I am in the world, I am the light of the world."

6 As he said this, he spat on the ground and made clay of the spittle and anointed the man's eyes with the clay,

7 saying to him, "Go, wash in the pool of Silo'am" (which means Sent). So he went and washed and came back seeing.

8 The neighbours and those who had seen him before as a beggar, said, "Is not this the man who used to sit and beg?"

9 Some said, "It is he"; others said, "No, but he is like him." He said, "I am the man."

10 They said to him, "Then how were your eyes opened?"

11 He answered, "The man called Jesus made clay and anointed my
    eyes and said to me, 'Go to Silo'am and wash'; so went and washed
    and received my sight."

12 They said to him, "Where is he?" He said, "I do not know."

13 They brought to the Pharisees the man who had formerly been
    blind.

14 Now it was a sabbath day when Jesus made the clay and opened his
    eyes.

15 The Pharisees again asked him how he had received his sight. And
    he said to them, "He put clay on my eyes, and I washed, and I
    see."

16 Some of the Pharisees said, "This man is not from God, for he
    does not keep the sabbath." But others said, "How can a man
    who is a sinner do such signs?" There was a division among
    them.

17 So they again said to the blind man, "What do you say about him,
    since he has opened your eyes?" He said, "He is a prophet."

18 The Jews did not believe that he had been blind and had received
    his sight, until they called the parents of the man who had
    received his sight,

19 and asked them, "Is this your son, who you say was born blind?
    How then does he now see?"

20 His parents answered, "We know that this is our son, and that he
    was born blind;

21 but how he now sees we do not know, nor do we know who opened
    his eyes. Ask him; he is of age, he will speak for himself."

22 His parents said this because they feared the Jews, for the Jews had
    already agreed that if any one should confess him to be Christ,
    he was to be put out of the synagogue.

23 Therefore his parents said, "He is of age, ask him."

24 So for the second time they called the man who had been blind,
    and said to him, "Give God the praise; we know that this man
    is a sinner."

25 He answered, "Whether he is a sinner, I do not know; one thing I
    know, that though I was blind, now I see."

26 They said to him, "What did he do to you? How did he open your
    eyes?"

27 He answered them, "I have told you already, and you would not
    listen. Why do you want to hear it again? Do you too want to
    become his disciples?."

28 And they reviled him, saying, "You are his disciple, but we are
    disciples of Moses.

29 We know that God has spoken to Moses, but as for this man, we do not know where he comes from."

30 The man answered, "Why, this is a marvel! You do not know where he comes from, and yet he opened my eyes.

31 We know that God does not listen to sinners, but if any one is a worshipper of God and does his will, God listens to him.

32 Never since the world began has it been heard that any one opened the eyes of a man born blind.

33 If this man were born from God, he could do nothing."

34 They answered him, "You were born in utter sin, and would you teach us?" And they cast him out.

35 Jesus heard that they had cast him out, and having found him he said, "Do you believe in the Son of man?"

36 He answered, "And who is he, sir, that I may believe in him?"

37 Jesus said to him, "You have seen him, and it is he who speaks to you."

38 He said, "Lord, I believe"; and he worshipped him.

39 Jesus said; "For judgement I came into this world, that those who do not see may see, and that those who see may become blind."

40 Some of the Pharisees near him heard this, and they said to him, "Are we also blind?"

41 Jesus said to them, "If you were blind, you would have no guilt; but now that you say, "We see," your guilt remains.

CHAPTER TEN

1 "Truly, truly, I say to you, he who does not enter the sheepfold by the door but climbs in by another way, that man is a thief and a robber;

2 but he who enters by the door is the shepherd of the sheep.

3 To him the gatekeeper opens; the sheep hear his voice, and he calls his own sheep by name and leads them out.

4 When he has brought out all his own, he goes before them, and the sheep follow him, for they know his voice.

5 A stranger they will not follow, but they will flee from him, for they do not know the voice of strangers."

6 This figure Jesus used with them, but they did not understand what he was saying to them.

7 So Jesus again said to them, "Truly, truly, I say to you, I am the door of the sheep.

8 All who came before me are thieves and robbers; but the sheep did not heed them.

9 I am the door; if any one enters by me, he will be saved, and will go in and out and find pasture.

10 The thief comes only to steal and kill and destroy; I came that they may have life, and have it abundantly.

11 I am the good shepherd. The good shepherd lays down his life for the sheep.

12 He who is a hireling and not a shepherd, whose own the sheep are not, sees the wolf coming and leaves the sheep and flees; and the wolf snatches them and scatters them.

13 He flees because he is a hireling and cares nothing for the sheep.

14 I am the good shepherd; I know my own and my own know me,

15 as the Father knows me and I know the Father; and I lay down my life for the sheep.

16 And I have other sheep, that are not of this fold; I must bring them also, and they will heed my voice. So there shall be one flock, one shepherd.

17 For this reason the Father loves me, because I lay down my life, that I may take it again.

18 No one takes it from me, but I lay it down of my own accord. I have power to lay it down, and I have power to take it again; this charge I have received from my Father."

19 There was again a division among the Jews because of these words.

20 Many of them said, "He has a demon, and he is mad; why listen to him?"

21 Others said, "These are not the sayings of one who has a demon. Can a demon open the eyes of the blind?"

22 It was the feast of the Dedication at Jerusalem;

23 it was winter, and Jesus was walking in the temple, in the portico of Solomon.

24 So the Jews gathered round him and said to him, "How long will you keep us in suspense? If you are the Christ, tell us plainly."

25 Jesus answered them, "I told you, and you do not believe. The works that I do in my Father's name, they bear witness to me;

26 but you do not believe, because you do not belong to my sheep.

27 My sheep hear my voice, and I know them, and they follow me;

28 and I give them eternal life, and they shall never perish, and no one shall snatch them out of my hand.

29 My Father, who has given them to me, is greater than all, and no one is able to snatch them out of the Father's hand.

30 and the Father are one."

31 The Jews took up stones again to stone him.

32 Jesus answered them, "I have shown you many good works from the Father; for which of these do you stone me?"

33 The Jews answered him, "It is not for a good work that we stone you but for blasphemy; because you being a man, make yourself God."

34 Jesus answered them, "Is it not written in your law, 'I said, you are gods'?

35 If he called them gods to whom the word of God came (and scripture cannot be broken),

36 do you say of him whom the Father consecrated and sent into the world, 'You are blaspheming,' because I said, 'I am the Son of God'?

37 If I am not doing the works of my Father, then do not believe me;

38 but if I do them, even though you do not believe me, believe the works, that you may know and understand that the Father is in me and I am in the Father."

39 Again they tried to arrest him, but he escaped from their hands.

40 He went away again across the Jordan to the place where John at first baptized, and there he remained.

41 And many came to him; and they said, "John did no sign, but everything that John said about this man was true."

42 And many believed in him there.

CHAPTER ELEVEN

1 Now a certain man was ill, Laz'arus of Bethany, the village of Mary and her sister Martha.

2 It was Mary who anointed the Lord with ointment and wiped his feet with her hair, whose brother Laz'arus was ill.

3 So the sisters sent to him, saying, "Lord, he whom you love is ill."

4 But when Jesus heard it he said, "This illness is not unto death; it is for the glory of God, so that the Son of God may be glorified by means of it."

5 Now Jesus loved Martha and her sister and Laz'arus.

6 So when he heard that he was ill, he stayed two days longer in the place where he was.

7 Then after this he said to the disciples, "Let us go into Judea again."

8 The disciples said to him, "Rabbi, the Jews were but now seeking to stone you, and are you going there again?"

9 Jesus answered, "Are there not twelve hours in the day? If any one walks in the day, he does not stumble, because he sees the light of this world.

10 But if any one walks in the night, he stumbles, because the light is not in him."

11 Thus he spoke, and then he said to them, "Our friend Laz'arus has fallen asleep, but I go to awake him out of sleep."

12 The disciples said to him, "Lord, if he has fallen asleep, he will recover."

13 Now Jesus had spoken of his death, but they thought that he meant taking rest in sleep.

14 Then Jesus told them plainly, "Laz'arus is dead;

15 and for your sake I am glad that I was not there, so that you may believe. But let us also go to him."

16 Thomas, called the Twin, said to his fellow disciples, "Let us also go, that we may die with him."

17 Now when Jesus came, he found that Laz'arus had already been in the tomb four days.

18 Bethany was near Jerusalem, about two miles off,

19 and many of the Jews had come to Martha and Mary to console them concerning their brother.

20 When Martha heard that Jesus was coming, she went and met him, while Mary sat in the house.

21 Martha said to Jesus, "Lord, if you had been here, my brother would not have died.

22 And even now I know that whatever you ask from God, God will give you."

23 Jesus said to her, "Your brother will rise again."

24 Martha said to him, "I know that he will rise again in the resurrection at the last day."

25 Jesus said to her, "I am the resurrection and the life; he who believes in me, though he die, yet shall he live,

26 and whoever lives and believes in me shall never die. Do you believe this?"

27 She said to him, "Yes, Lord; I believe that you are the Christ, the Son of God, he who is coming into the world."

28 When she had said this, she went and called her sister Mary, saying quietly, "The Teacher is here and is calling for you."

29 And when she heard it, she rose quickly and went to him.

30 Now Jesus had not yet come to the village, but was still in the place where Martha had met him.

31 When the Jews who were with her in the house, consoling her, saw Mary rise quickly and go out, they followed her, supposing that she was going to the tomb to weep there.

32 Then Mary, when she came where Jesus was and saw him, fell at his feet, saying to him, "Lord, if you had been here, my brother would not have died."

33 When Jesus saw her weeping, and the Jews who came with her also weeping, he was deeply moved in spirit and troubled;

34 and he said, "Where have you laid him?" They said to him, "Lord, come and see."

35 Jesus wept.

36 So the Jews said, "See how he loved him!"

37 But some of them said, "Could not he who opened the eyes of the blind man have kept this man from dying?"

38 Then Jesus, deeply moved again, came to the tomb; it was a cave, and a stone lay upon it.

39 Jesus said, "Take away the stone." Martha, the sister of the dead man, said to him, "Lord, by this time there will be an odor, for he has been dead four days."

40 Jesus said to her, "Did I not tell you that if you would believe you would see the glory of God?"

41 So they took away the stone. And Jesus lifted up his eyes and said, "Father, I thank thee that thou hast heard me.

42 I knew that thou hearest me always, but I have said this on account of the people standing by, that they may believe that thou didst send me."

43 When he had said this, he cried with a loud voice, "Laz'arus, come out."

44 The dead man came out, his hands and feet bound with bandages, and his face wrapped with a cloth. Jesus said to them, "Unbind him, and let him go."

45 Many of the Jews therefore, who had come with Mary and had seen what he did, believed in him;

46 but some of them went to the Pharisees and told them what Jesus had done.

47 So the chief priests and the Pharisees gathered the council, and said, "What are we to do? For this man performs many signs.

48 If we let him go on thus, every one will believe in him, and the Romans will come and destroy both our holy place and our nation."

49 But one of them, Ca'iaphas, who was high priest that year, said to them, "You know nothing at all;

50 you do not understand that it is expedient for you that one man should die for the people, and that the whole nation should not perish."

51 He did not say this of his own accord, but being high priest that year he prophesied that Jesus should die for the nation,

52 and not for the nation only, but to gather into one the children of
   God who are scattered abroad.
53 So from that day on they took counsel how to put him to death.
54 Jesus therefore no longer went about openly among the Jews, but
   went from there to the country near the wilderness, to a town
   called E'phraim; and there he stayed with the disciples.
55 Now the Passover of the Jews was at hand, and many went up from
   the country to Jerusalem before the Passover, to purify themselves.
56 They were looking for Jesus and saying to one another as they stood
   in the temple, "What do you think? That he will not come to the
   feast?"
57 Now the chief priests and the Pharisees had given orders that if any
   one knew where he was, he should let them know, so that they
   might arrest him.

CHAPTER TWELVE

1 Six days before the Passover, Jesus came to Bethany, where Laz'arus
   was, whom Jesus had raised from the dead.
2 There they made him a supper; Martha served, and Laz'arus was
   one of those at table with him.
3 Mary took a pound of costly ointment of pure nard and anointed
   the feet of Jesus and wiped his feet with her hair; and the house
   was filled with the fragrance of the ointment.
4 But Judas Iscariot, one of his disciples (he who was to betray him),
   said,
5 "Why was this ointment not sold for three hundred denarii and
   given to the poor?"
6 This he said, not that he cared for the poor but because he was a
   thief, and as he had the money box he used to take what was put
   into it.
7 Jesus said, "Let her alone, let her keep it for the day of my burial.
8 The poor you always have with you, but you do not always have
   me."
9 When the great crowd of the Jews learned that he was there, they
   came, not only on account of Jesus but also to see Laz'arus,
   whom he had raised from the dead.
10 So the chief priests planned to put Laz'arus also to death,
11 because on account of him many of the Jews were going away and
   believing in Jesus.
12 The next day a great crowd who had come to the feast heard that
   Jesus was coming to Jerusalem.
13 So they took branches of palm trees and went out to meet him,

crying, "Hosanna Blessed is he who comes in the name of the Lord, even the King of Israel!'

14 And Jesus found a young ass and sat upon it; as it is written,

15 "Fear not, daughter of Zion;
   behold, your king is coming,
   sitting on an ass's colt!"

16 His disciples did not understand this at first; but when Jesus was glorified, then they remembered that this had been written of him and had been done to him.

17 The crowd that had been with him when he called Laz'arus out of the tomb and raised him from the dead bore witness.

18 The reason why the crowd went to meet him was that they heard he had done this sign.

19 The Pharisees then said to one another, "You see that you can do nothing; look, the world has gone after him."

20 Now among those who went up to worship at the feast were some Greeks.

21 So these came to Philip, who was from Beth-sai'ida in Galilee, and said to him, "Sir, we wish to see Jesus.'

22 Philip went and told Andrew; Andrew went with Philip and they told Jesus.

23 And Jesus answered them "The hour has come for the Son of man to be glorified.

24 Truly, truly, I say to you, unless a grain of wheat falls into the earth and dies, it remains alone; but if it dies, it bears much fruit.

25 He who loves his life loses it, and he who hates his life in this world will keep it for eternal life.

26 If any one serves me, he must follow me; and where I am, there shall my servant be also; if any one serves me, the Father will honour him.

27 "Now is my soul troubled. And what shall I say? 'Father, save me from this hour'? No, for this purpose I have come to this hour.

28 Father, glorify thy name." Then a voice came from heaven, "I have glorified it, and I will glorify it again."

29 The crowd standing by heard it and said that it had thundered. Others said, "An angel has spoken to him."

30 Jesus answered, "This voice has come for your sake, not for mine.

31 Now is the judgement of this world, now shall the ruler of this world be cast out;

32 and I, when I am lifted up from the earth, will draw all men to myself."

33 He said this to show by what death he was to die.

34 The crowd answered him, "We have heard from the law that the

Christ remains for ever. How can you say that the Son of man must be lifted up? Who is this Son of man?"

35 Jesus said to them, "The light is with you for a little longer. Walk while you have the light, lest the darkness overtake you; he who walks in the darkness does not know where he goes.

36 While you have the light, believe in the light, that you may become son of the light."
When Jesus had said this, he departed and hid himself from them.

37 Though he had done so many signs before them, yet they did not believe in him;

38 it was that the word spoken by the prophet Isaiah might be fulfilled:
"Lord, who has believed our report,
and to whom has the arm of the Lord been revealed?"

39 Therefore they could not believe. For Isaiah again said,

40 "He has blinded their eyes and hardened their heart,
lest they should see with their eyes and perceive with their heart,
and turn for me to heal them."

41 Isaiah said this because he saw his glory and spoke of him.

42 Nevertheless many even of the authorities believed in him, but for fear of the Pharisees they did not confess it, lest they should be put out of the synagogue:

43 for they loved the praise of men more then the praise of God.

44 And Jesus cried out and said, "He who believes in me, believes not in me but in him who sent me.

45 And he who sees me sees him who sent me.

46 I have come as light into the world, that whoever believes in me may not remain in darkness.

47 If any one hears my sayings and does not keep them, I do not judge him; for I did not come to judge the world but to save the world.

48 He who rejects me and does not receive my sayings has a judge; the word that I have spoken will be his judge on the last day.

49 For I have not spoken on my own authority; the Father who sent me has himself given me commandment what to say and what to speak.

50 And I know that his commandment is eternal life. What I say, therefore, I say as the Father has bidden me."

CHAPTER THIRTEEN

1 Now before the feast of the Passover, when Jesus knew that his hour had come to depart out of this world to the Father, having loved his own who were in the world, he loved them to the end.

2 And during supper, when the devil had already put it into the heart of Judas Iscariot, Simon's son, to betray him,

3 Jesus, knowing that the Father had given all things into his hand, and that he had come from God and was going to God,

4 rose from supper, laid aside his garments, and girded himself with a towel.

5 Then he poured water into a basin, and began to wash the disciples' feet, and to wipe them with the towel with which he was girded.

6 He came to Simon Peter; and Peter said to him, "Lord, do you wash my feet?"

7 Jesus answered him, "What I am doing you do not know now, but afterward you will understand."

8 Peter said to him, "You shall never wash my feet." Jesus answered him, "If I do not wash you, you have no part in me."

9 Simon Peter said to him, "Lord, not my feet only but also my hands and my head!"

10 Jesus said to him, "He who has bathed does not need to wash, except for his feet, but he is clean all over; and you are clean, but not every one of you."

11 For he knew who was to betray him; that was why he said, "You are not all clean."

12 When he had washed their feet, and taken his garments, and resumed his place, he said to them, "Do you know what I have done to you?

13 You call me Teacher and Lord; and you are right, for so I am.

14 If I then, your Lord and Teacher, have washed your feet, you also ought to wash one another's feet.

15 For I have given you an example, that you also should do as I have done to you.

16 Truly, truly, I say to you, a servant is not greater than his master; nor is he who is sent greater than he who sent him.

17 If you know these things, blessed are you if you do them.

18 I am not speaking of you all; I know whom I have chosen; it is that the scripture may be fulfilled, 'He who ate my bread has lifted his heel against me.'

19 I tell you this now, before it takes place, that when it does take place you may believe that I am he.

20 Truly, truly, I say to you, he who receives any one whom I send receives me; and he who receives me receives him who sent me."

21 When Jesus had thus spoken, he was troubled in spirit, and testified, "Truly, truly, I say to you, one of you will betray me."

22 The disciples looked at one another, uncertain of whom he spoke.

23 One of his disciples, whom Jesus loved, was lying close to the breast of Jesus;

24 so Simon Peter beckoned to him and said, "Tell us who it is of whom he speaks."

25 So lying thus, close to the breast of Jesus, he said to him, "Lord, who is it?"

26 Jesus answered, "It is he to whom I shall give this morsel when I have dipped it." So when he had dipped the morsel, he gave it to Judas, the son of Simon
Iscariot.

27 Then after the morsel, Satan entered into him. Jesus said to him, "What you are going to do, do quickly."

28 Now no one at the table knew why he said this to him.

29 Some thought that, because Judas had the money box, Jesus was telling him, "Buy what we need for the feast"; or, that he should give something to the poor.

30 So, after receiving the morsel, he immediately went out; and it was night.

31 When he had gone out, Jesus said, "Now is the Son of man glorified, and in him God is glorified;

32 if God is glorified in him, God will also glorify him in himself, and glorify him at once.

33 Little children, yet a little while I am with you. You will seek me; and as I said to the Jews so now I say to you, 'Where I am going you cannot come.'

34 A new commandment I give to you, that you love one another; even as I have loved you, that you also love one another.

35 By this all men will know that you are my disciples, if you have love for one another."

36 Simon Peter said to him, "Lord, where are you going?" Jesus answered, "Where I am going you cannot follow me now; but you shall follow afterward."

37 Peter said to him, "Lord, why cannot I follow you now? I will lay down my life for you."

38 Jesus answered, "Will you lay down your life for me? Truly, truly, I say to you, the cock will not crow, till you have denied me three times.

CHAPTER FOURTEEN

1 "Let not your hearts be troubled; believe in God, believe also in me.

2 In my Father's house are many rooms; if it were not so, would I have told you that I go to prepare a place for you?

3 And when I go and prepare a place for you, I will come again and will take you to myself, that where I am you may be also.

4 And you know the way where I am going."

5 Thomas said to him, "Lord, we do not know where you are going; how can we know the way?"

6 Jesus said to him, "I am the way, and the truth, and the life; no one comes to the Father, but by me.

7 If you had known me, you would have known my Father also; henceforth you know him and have seen him."

8 Philip said to him, "Lord, show us the Father, and we shall be satisfied."

9 Jesus said to him, "Have I been with you so long, and yet you do not know me, Philip? He who has seen me has seen the Father; how can you say 'Show us the Father'?

10 Do you not believe that I am in the Father and the Father in me? The words that I say to you I do not speak on my own authority; but the Father who dwells in me does his works.

11 Believe me that I am in the Father and the Father in me; else believe me for the sake of the work themselves.

12 "Truly, truly, I say to you, he who believes in me will also do the works that I do; and greater works than these will he do, because I go to the Father.

13 Whatever you ask in my name, I will do it, that the Father may be glorified in the Son;

14 if you ask anything in my name, I will do it.

15 "If you love me, you will keep my commandments.

16 And I will pray the Father, and he will give you another Counsellor, to be with you for ever,

17 even the Spirit of truth, whom the world cannot receive, because it neither sees him nor knows him; you know him, for he dwells with you, and will be in you.

18 "I will not leave you desolate; I will come to you.

19 Yet a little while, and the world will see me no more, but you will see me; because I live, you will live also.

20 In that day you will know that I am in my Father, and you in me, and I in you.

21 He who has my commandments and keeps them, he it is who loves me; and he who loves me will be loved by my Father, and I will love him and manifest myself to him."

22 Judas (not Iscariot) said to him, "Lord, how is it that you will manifest yourself to us, and not to the world?"

23 Jesus answered him, "If a man loves me, he will keep my word, and my Father will love him, and we will come to him and make our home with him.

24 He who does not love me does not keep my words; and the word which you hear is not mine but the Father's who sent me.

25 "These things I have spoken to you, while I am still with you.

26 But the Counsellor, the Holy Spirit, whom the Father will send in my name, he will teach you all things, and bring to your remembrance all that I have said to you.

27 Peace I leave with you; my peace I give to you; not as the world gives do I give to you. Let not your hearts be troubled, neither let them be afraid.

28 You heard me say to you, 'I go away, and I will come to you.' If you loved me, you would have rejoiced, because I go to the Father; for the Father is greater than I.

29 And now I have told you before it takes place, so that when it does take place, you may believe.

30 I will no longer talk much with you, for the ruler of this world is coming. He has no power over me;

31 but I do as the Father has commanded me, so that the world may know that I love the Father. Rise, let us go hence.

CHAPTER FIFTEEN

1 "I am the true vine, and my Father is the vinedresser.

2 Every branch of mine that bears no fruit, he takes away, and every branch that does bear fruit he prunes, that it may bear more fruit.

3 You are already made clean by the word which I have spoken to you.

4 Abide in me, and I in you. As the branch cannot bear fruit by itself, unless it abides in the vine, neither can you, unless you abide in me.

5 I am the vine, you are the branches. He who abides in me, and I in him, he it is that bears much fruit, for apart from me you can do nothing.

6 If a man does not abide in me, he is cast forth as a branch and

withers; and the branches are gathered, thrown into the fire and burned.

7 If you abide in me, and my words abide in you, ask whatever you will, and it shall be done for you.

8 By this my Father is glorified, that you bear much fruit, and so prove to be my disciples.

9 As the Father has loved me, so have I loved you; abide in my love.

10 If you keep my commandments, you will abide in my love, just as I have kept my Father's commandments and abide in his love.

11 These things I have spoken to you, that my joy may be in you, and that your joy may be full.

12 "This is my commandment, that you love one another as I have loved you.

13 Greater love has no man than this, that a man lay down his life for his friends.

14 You are my friends if you do what I command you.

15 No longer do I call you servants, for the servant does not know what his master is doing; but I have called you friends, for all that I have heard from my Father I have made known to you.

16 You did not choose me, but I chose you and appointed you that you should go and bear fruit and that your fruit should abide; so that whatever you ask the Father in my name, he may give it to you.

17 This I command you, to love one another.

18 "If the world hates you, know that it has hated me before it hated you.

19 If you were of the world, the world would love its own; but because you are not of the world, but I chose you out of the world, therefore the world hates you.

20 Remember the word that I said to you, "A servant is not greater than his master." If they persecuted me, they will persecute you; if they kept my word, they will keep yours also.

21 But all this they will do to you on my account, because they do not know him who sent me.

22 If I had not come and spoken to them, they would not have sin; but now they have no excuse for their sin.

23 He who hates me hates my Father also.

24 If I had not done among them the works which no one else did, they would not have sin; but now they have seen and hated both me and my Father.

25 It is to fulfil the word that is written in their law, "They hated me without a cause."

26 But when the Counsellor comes, whom I shall send to you from the

Father, even the Spirit of truth, who proceeds from the Father, he will bear witness to me;

27 and you also are witnesses, because you have been with me from the beginning.

CHAPTER SIXTEEN

1 "I have said all this to you to keep you from falling away.

2 They will put you out of the synagogues; indeed, the hour is coming when whoever kills you will think he is offering service to God.

3 And they will do this because they have not known the Father, nor me.

4 But I have said these things to you, that when their hour comes you may remember that I told you of them.

"I did not say these things to you from the beginning, because I was with you.

5 But now I am going to him who sent me; yet none of you asks me, 'Where are you going?'

6 But because I have said these things to you, sorrow has filled your hearts.

7 Nevertheless I tell you the truth: it is to your advantage that I go away, for if I do not go away, the Counsellor will not come to you; but if I go, I will send him to you.

8 And when he comes, he will convince the world concerning sin and righteousness and judgement:

9 concerning sin, because they do not believe in me;

10 concerning righteousness, because I go to the Father, and you will see me no more;

11 concerning judgement, because the ruler of this world is judged.

12 "I have yet many things to say to you, but you cannot bear them now

13 When the Spirit of truth comes, he will guide you into all the truth; for he will not speak on his own authority, but whatever he hears he will speak, and he will declare to you the things that are to come.

14 He will glorify me, for he will take what is mine and declare it to you.

15 All that the Father has is mine, therefore I said that he will take what is mine and declare it to you.

16 "A little while, and you will see me no more; again a little while, and you will see me."

17 Some of his disciples said to one another, "What is this that he says to us, 'A little while and you will not see me, and again a little

while, and you will see me'; and 'because I go to the Father'?"

18 They said, "What does he mean by 'a little while'? We do not know what he means."

19 Jesus knew that they wanted to ask him; so he said to them, "Is this what you are asking yourselves, what I meant by saying, 'A little while, and you will not see me, and again a little while, and you will see me'?

20 Truly, truly, I say to you, you will weep and lament, but the world will rejoice; you will be sorrowful, but your sorrow will turn into joy.

21 When a woman is in travail she has sorrow, because her hour has come; but when she is delivered of the child, she no longer remembers the anguish, for joy that a child is born into the world.

22 So you have sorrow now, but I will see you again and your hearts will rejoice, and no one will take your joy from you.

23 In that day you will ask nothing of me. Truly, truly, I say to you, if you ask anything of the Father, he will give it to you in my name.

24 Hitherto you have asked nothing in my name; ask, and you will receive, that your joy may be full.

25 "I have said this to you in figures; the hour is coming when I shall no longer speak to you in figures but tell you plainly of the Father.

26 In that day you will ask in my name; and I do not say to you that I shall pray the Father for you;

27 for the Father himself loves you, because you have loved me and have believed that I came from the Father.

28 I came from the Father and have come into the world; again, I am leaving the world and going to the Father."

29 His disciples said, "Ah, now you are speaking plainly, not in any figure!

30 Now we know that you know all things, and need none to question you; by this we believe that you came from God."

31 Jesus answered them, "Do you now believe?

32 The hour is coming, indeed it has come, when you will be scattered, every man to his home, and will leave me alone; yet I am not alone, for the Father is with me.

33 I have said this to you, that in me you may have peace. In the world you have tribulation; but be of good cheer, I have overcome the world."

CHAPTER SEVENTEEN

1 When Jesus had spoken these words, he lifted up his eyes to heaven and said, "Father, the hour has come; glorify thy Son that the Son may glorify thee,

2 since thou hast given him power over all flesh, to give eternal life to all whom thou hast given him.

3 And this is eternal life, that they know thee the only true God, and Jesus Christ whom thou hast sent.

4 I glorified thee on earth, having accomplished the work which thou gavest me to do;

5 and now, Father, glorify thou me in thy own presence with the glory which I had with thee before the world was made.

6 "I have manifested thy name to the men whom thou gavest me out of the world; thine they were, and thou gavest them to me, and they have kept thy word.

7 Now they know that everything that thou hast given me is from thee;

8 for I have given them the words which thou gavest me, and they have received them and know in truth that I came from thee; and they have believed that thou didst send me.

9 I am praying for them; I am not praying for the world but for those whom thou hast given me, for they are thine;

10 all mine are thine, and thine are mine, and I am glorified in them.

11 And now I am no more in the world, but they are in the world, and I am coming to thee. Holy Father, keep them in thy name, which thou hast given me, that they may be one, even as we are one.

12 While I was with them, I kept them in thy name, which thou hast given me; I have guarded them, and none of them is lost but the son of perdition, that the scripture might be fulfilled.

13 But now I am coming to thee; and these things I speak in the world, that they may have my joy fulfilled in themselves.

14 I have given them thy word; and the world has hated them because they are not of the world, even as I am not of the world.

15 I do not pray that thou shouldst take them out of the world, but that thou shouldst keep them from the evil one.

16 They are not of the world, even as I am not of the world.

17 Sanctify them in the truth; thy word is truth.

18 As thou didst send me into the world, so I have sent them into the world.

19 And for their sake I consecrate myself, that they also may consecrated in truth.

20 "I do not pray for these only, but also for those who believe in me through their word,

21 that they may all be one; even as thou, Father, art in me, and I in thee, that they also may be in us, so that the world may believe that thou hast sent me.

22 The glory which thou hast given me I have given to them, that they may be one even as we are one,

23 I in them and thou in me, that they may become perfectly one, so that the world may know that thou hast sent me and hast loved them even as thou hast loved me.

24 Father, I desire that they also, whom thou hast given me, may be with me where I am, to behold my glory which thou hast given me in thy love for me before the foundation of the world.

25 O righteous Father, the world has not known thee, but I have known thee, and these know that thou hast sent me.

26 I made known to them thy name, and I will make it known, that the love with which thou hast loved me may be in them, and I in them."

CHAPTER EIGHTEEN

1 When Jesus had spoken these words, he went forth with his disciples across the Kidron valley, where there was a garden, which he and his disciples entered.

2 Now Judas, who betrayed him, also knew the place; for Jesus often met there with his disciples.

3 So Judas, procuring a band of soldiers and some officers from the chief priests and the Pharisees, went there with lanterns and torches and weapons.

4 Then Jesus, knowing all that was to befall him, came forward and said to them, "Whom do you seek?"

5 They answered him, "Jesus of Nazareth." Jesus said to them, "I am he." Judas, who betrayed him, was standing with them.

6 When he said to them, "I am he," they drew back and fell to the ground.

7 Again he asked them, "Whom do you seek?" And they said, "Jesus of Nazareth."

8 Jesus answered, "I told you that I am he; so, if you seek me, let these men go."

9 This was to fulfil the word which he had spoken, "Of those whom thou gavest me I lost not one."

10 Then Simon Peter, having a sword, drew it and struck the high

priest's slave and cut off his right ear. The slave's name was Malchus.

11 Jesus said to Peter, "Put your sword into its sheath; shall I not drink the cup which the Father has given me?"

12 So the band of soldiers and their captain and the officers of the Jews seized Jesus and bound him.

13 First they led him to Annas; for he was the father-in-law of Ca'iaphas, who was high priest that year.

14 It was Ca'iaphas who had given counsel to the Jews that it was expedient that one man should die for the people.

15 Simon Peter followed Jesus, and so did another disciple. As this disciple was known to the high priest, he entered the court of the high priest along with Jesus,

16 while Peter stood outside at the door. So the other disciple, who was known to the high priest, went out and spoke to the maid who kept the door, and brought Peter in.

17 The maid who kept the door said to Peter, "Are not you also one of this man's disciples?" He said, "I am not."

18 Now the servants and officers had made a charcoal fire, because it was cold, and they were standing and warming themselves; Peter also was with them, standing and warming himself.

19 The high priest then questioned Jesus about his disciples and his teaching.

20 Jesus answered him, "I have spoken openly to the world; I have always taught in synagogues and in the temple, where all Jews come together; I have said nothing secretly.

21 Why do you ask me? Ask those who have heard me, what I said to them; they know what I said."

22 When he had said this, one of the officers standing by struck Jesus with his hand, saying, "Is that how you answer the high priest?"

23 Jesus answered him, "If I have spoken wrongly, bear witness to the wrong; but if I have spoken rightly, why do you strike me?"

24 Annas then sent him bound to Ca'iaphas the high priest.

25 Now Simon Peter was standing and warming himself. They said to him, "Are not you also one of his disciples?" He denied it and said, "I am not."

26 One of the servants of the high priest, a kinsman of the man whose ear Peter had cut off, asked, "Did I not see you in the garden with him?"

27 Peter again denied it; and at once the cock crowed.

28 Then they led Jesus from the house of Ca'iaphas to the praetorium. It was early. They themselves did not enter the praetorium, so that they might not be defiled, but might eat the passover.

29 So Pilate went out to them and said, "What accusation do you bring against this man?"

30 They answered him, "If this man were not an evildoer, we would not have handed him over."

31 Pilate said to them, "Take him yourselves and judge him by your own law." The Jews said to him, "It is not lawful for us to put any man to death."

32 This was to fulfil the word which Jesus had spoken to show by what death he was to die.

33 Pilate entered the praetorium again and called Jesus, and said to him, "Are you the King of the Jews?"

34 Jesus answered, "Do you say this of your own accord, or did others say it to you about me?"

35 Pilate answered, "Am I a Jew? Your own nation and the chief priests have handed you over to me; what have you done?"

36 Jesus answered, "My kingship is not of this world; if my kingship were of this world, my servants would fight, that I might not be handed over to the Jews; but my kingship is not from the world."

37 Pilate said to him, "So you are a king?" Jesus answered, "You say that I am a king. For this I was born, and for this I have come into the world, to bear witness to the truth. Every one who is of the truth hears my voice."

38 Pilate said to him, "What is the truth?"
After he had said this, he went out to the Jews again, and told them, "I find no crime in him.

39 But you have a custom that I should release one man for you at the Passover; will you have me release for you the King of the Jews?"

40 They cried out again, "Not this man, but Barab'bas!" Now Barab'bas was a robber.

CHAPTER NINETEEN

1 Then Pilate took Jesus and scourged him.

2 And the soldiers plaited a crown of thorns, and put it on his head, and arrayed him in a purple robe;

3 they came up to him, saying, "Hail, King of the Jews!" and struck him with their hands.

4 Pilate went out again, and said to them, "See, I am bringing him out to you, that you may know that I find no crime in him."

5 So Jesus came out, wearing the crown of thorns and the purple robe. Pilate said to them, "Behold the man!"

6 When the chief priests and the officers saw him, they cried out, "Crucify him, crucify him!" Pilate said to them, "Take him yourselves and crucify him, for I find no crime in him."

7 The Jews answered him, "We have a law, and by that law he ought to die, because he has made himself the Son of God."

8 When Pilate heard these words, he was the more afraid;

9 he entered the praetorium again and said to Jesus, "Where are you from?" But Jesus gave no answer.

10 Pilate therefore said to him, "You will not speak to me? Do you not know that I have power to release you, and power to crucify you?"

11 Jesus answered him, "You would have no power over me unless it had been given you from above; therefore he who delivered me to you has the greater sin."

12 Upon this Pilate sought to release him, but the Jews cried out, "If you release this man, you are not Caesar's friend; everyone who makes himself a king sets himself against Caesar."

13 When Pilate heard these words, he brought Jesus out and sat down on the judgment seat at a place called The Pavement, and in Hebrew, Gab'batha.

14 Now it was the day of Preparation of the Passover; it was about the sixth hour. He said to the Jews, "Behold your King!"

15 They cried out, "Away with him, away with him, crucify him!" Pilate said to them, "Shall I crucify your King?" The chief priests answered, "We have no king but Caesar."

16 Then he handed him over to them to be crucified.

17 So they took Jesus, and he went out, bearing his own cross, to the place called the place of a skull, which is called in Hebrew Gol'gotha.

18 There they crucified him, and with him two others, one on either side, and Jesus between them.

19 Pilate also wrote a title and put it on the cross; it read, "Jesus of Nazareth, the King of the Jews."

20 Many of the Jews read this title, for the place where Jesus was crucified was near the city; and it was written in Hebrew, in Latin, and in Greek.

21 The chief priests of the Jews then said to Pilate, "Do not write, 'The King of the Jews,' but, 'This man said, I am King of the Jews.'"

22 Pilate answered, "What I have written I have written."

23 When the soldiers had crucified Jesus they took his garments and made four parts, one for each soldier; also his tunic. But the tunic was without seam, woven from top to bottom;

24 so they said to one another, "Let us not tear it, but cast lots for it to see whose it shall be." This was to fulfil the scripture,
   "They parted my garments among them,
   and for my clothing they cast lots."

25 So the soldiers did this. But standing by the cross of Jesus were his mother, and his mother's sister, Mary the wife of Clopas, and Mary Mag'dalene.

26 When Jesus saw his mother, and the disciple whom he loved standing near, he said to his mother, "Woman, behold, your son!"

27 Then he said to the disciple, "Behold, your mother!" And from that hour the disciple took her to his own home.

28 After this Jesus, knowing that all was now finished, said (to fulfil the scripture), "I thirst."

29 A bowl full of vinegar stood there; so they put a sponge full of the vinegar on hyssop and held it to his mouth.

30 When Jesus had received the vinegar, he said, "It is finished"; and he bowed his head and gave up his spirit.

31 Since it was the day of Preparation, in order to prevent the bodies from remaining on the cross on the sabbath (for that sabbath was a high day), the Jews asked Pilate that their legs might be broken, and that they might be taken way.

32 So the soldiers came and broke the legs of the first, and of the other who had been crucified with him;

33 but when they came to Jesus and saw that he was already dead, they did not break his legs.

34 But one of the soldiers pierced his side with a spear, and at once there came out blood and water.

35 He who saw it has borne witness – his testimony is true, and he knows that he tells the truth – that you also may believe.

36 For these things took place that the scripture might be fulfilled, "Not a bone of him shall be broken."

37 And again another scripture says, "They shall look on him whom they have pierced."

38 After this Joseph of Arimathe'a, who was a disciple of Jesus, but secretly, for fear of the Jews, asked Pilate that he might take away the body of Jesus, and Pilate gave him leave. So he came and took away his body.

39 Nicode'mus also, who had at first come to him by night, came bringing a mixture of myrrh and aloes about a hundred pounds' weight.

40 They took the body of Jesus, and bound it in linen cloths with the spices, as is the burial custom of the Jews.

41 Now in the place where he was crucified there was a garden, and

in the garden a new tomb where no one had ever been laid.

42 So because of the Jewish day of Preparation, as the tomb was close at hand, they laid Jesus there.

CHAPTER TWENTY

1 Now on the first day of the week Mary Mag'dalene came to the tomb early, while it was still dark, and saw that the stone had been taken away from the tomb.

2 So she ran, and went to Simon Peter and the other disciple, the one whom Jesus loved, and said to them, "They have taken the Lord out of the tomb, and we do not know where they have laid him."

3 Peter then came out with the other disciple, and they went toward the tomb.

4 They both ran, but the other disciple outran Peter and reached the tomb first;

5 and stooping to look in, he saw the linen cloths lying there, but he did not go in.

6 Then Simon Peter came, following him, and went into the tomb; he saw the linen cloths lying,

7 and the napkin, which had been on his head, not lying with the linen cloths but rolled up in a place by itself.

8 Then the other disciple, who reached the tomb first also went in, and he saw and believed

9 for as yet they did not know the scripture, that he must rise from the dead

10 Then the disciples went back to their homes.

11 But Mary stood weeping outside the tomb, and as she wept she stooped to look into the tomb;

12 and she saw two angels in white, sitting where the body of Jesus had lain, one at the head and one at the feet.

13 They said to her "Woman, why are you weeping?" She said to them, "Because they have taken away my Lord, and I do not know where they have laid him."

14 Saying this, she turned round and saw Jesus standing, but she did not know that was Jesus.

15 Jesus said to her, "Woman, why are you weeping? Whom do you seek?" Supposing him to be the gardener,
she said to him, "Sir, if you have carried him away,
tell me where you have laid him, and I will take him away."

16 Jesus said to her, "Mary." She turned and said to him in Hebrew, "Rab-bo'ni!" (which means Teacher).

17 Jesus said to her, "Do not hold me, for I have not yet ascended to the Father; but go to my brethren and say to them, I am ascending to my Father and your Father, to my God and your God."

18 Mary Mag'dalene went and said to the disciples, "I have seen the Lord"; and she told them that he had said these things to her.

19 On the evening of that day, the first day of the week, the doors being shut where the disciples were, for fear of the Jews, Jesus came and stood among them and said to them, "Peace be with you."

20 When he had said this, he showed them his hands and his side. Then the disciples were glad when they saw the Lord.

21 Jesus said to them again, "Peace be with you. As the Father has sent me, even so I send you."

22 And when he had said this, he breathed on them, and said to them, "Receive the Holy Spirit.

23 If you forgive the sins of any, they are forgiven; if you retain the sins of any, they are retained."

24 Now Thomas, one of the twelve, called the Twin, was not with them when Jesus came.

25 So the other disciples told him, "We have seen the Lord." But he said to them, "Unless I see in his hands the print of the nails, and place my finger in the mark of the nails, and place my hand in his side, I will not believe."

26 Eight days later, his disciples were again in the house, and Thomas was with them. The doors were shut, but Jesus came and stood among them, and said, "Peace be with you."

27 Then he said to Thomas, "Put your finger here, and see my hands; and put out your hand, and place it in my side; do not be faithless, but believing."

28 Thomas answered him, "My Lord and my God!"

29 Jesus said to him, "Have you believed because you have seen me? Blessed are those who have not seen and yet believe."

30 Now Jesus did many other signs in the presence of the disciples, which are not written in this book;

31 but these are written that you may believe that Jesus is the Christ, the Son of God, and that believing you may have life in his name.

CHAPTER TWENTY-ONE

1 After this Jesus revealed himself again to the disciples by the Sea of Tibe'ri-as; and he revealed himself in this way.

2 Simon Peter, Thomas called the Twin, Nathan'a-el of Cana in Galilee, the sons of Zeb'edee, and two others of his disciples were together.

3 Simon Peter said to them, "I am going fishing." They said to him, "We will go with you." They went out and got into the boat; but that night they caught nothing.

4 Just as day was breaking, Jesus stood on the beach; yet the disciples did not know that it was Jesus.

5 Jesus said to them, "Children, have you any fish?" They answered him, "No."

6 He said to them, "Cast the net on the right side of the boat, and you will find some." So they cast it, and now they were not able to haul it in, for the quantity of fish.

7 That disciple whom Jesus loved said to Peter, "It is the Lord!" When Simon Peter heard that it was the Lord, he put on his clothes, for he was stripped for work, and sprang into the sea.

8 But the other disciples came in the boat, dragging the net full of fish, for they were not far from the land, but about a hundred yards off.

9 When they got out on land, they saw a charcoal fire there, with fish lying on it, and bread.

10 Jesus said to them, "Bring some of the fish that you have just caught."

11 So Simon Peter went aboard and hauled the net ashore, full of large fish, a hundred and fifty-three of them; and although there were so many, the net was not torn:

12 Jesus said to them, "Come and have breakfast." Now none of the disciples dared ask him, "Who are you?" They knew it was the Lord.

13 Jesus came and took the bread and gave it to them, and so with the fish.

14 This was now the third time that Jesus was revealed to the disciples after he was raised from the dead.

15 When they had finished breakfast, Jesus said to Simon Peter, "Simon, son of John, do you love me more than these?" He said to him, "Yes, Lord; you know that I love you." He said to him, "Feed my lambs."

16 A second time he said to him, "Simon, son of John, do

you love me?" He said to him, "Yes, Lord; you
know that I love you." He said to him, "Tend my
sheep."

17 He said to him the third time, "Simon, son of John, do you love
me?" Peter was grieved because he said to him the third time,
"Do you love me?" And he said to him, "Lord, you know
everything; you know that I love you." Jesus said to him, "Feed
my sheep.

18 Truly, truly, I say to you, when you were young, you
girded yourself and walked where you would; but when you are
old, you will stretch out your hands, and another will gird you and
carry you where you do not wish to go."

19 (This he said to show by what death he was to glorify God.) And
after this he said to him, "Follow me."

20 Peter turned and saw following them the disciple whom Jesus loved,
who had lain close to his breast at the supper and had said,
"Lord, who is it that is going to betray you?"

21 When Peter saw him, he said to Jesus, "Lord, what about this man?"

22 Jesus said to him, "If it is my will that he remain until I come, what
is that to you? Follow me!"

23 The saying spread abroad among the brethren that this disciple was
not to die; yet Jesus did not say to him that he was not to die,
but, "If it is my will that he remain until I come, what is that to
you?"

24 This is the disciple who is bearing witness to these things, and who
has written these things; and we know that his testimony is true.

25 But there are also many other things which Jesus did; were every
one of them to be written, I suppose that the world itself could
not contain the books that would be written.

THE LETTER OF PAUL
TO THE EPHESIANS

EPHESIANS

*This translation is taken from
the Revised Standard Version of the Bible*

CHAPTER ONE

1 Paul, an apostle of Christ Jesus by the will of God,
　　To the saints who are also faithful in Christ Jesus:
2 Grace to you and peace from God our Father and the Lord Jesus
　　Christ.

3 Blessed be the God and Father of our Lord Jesus Christ, who has
　　blessed us in Christ with every spiritual blessing in the heavenly
　　places,
4 even as he chose us in him before the foundation of the world, that
　　we should be holy and blameless before him.
5 He destined us in love to be his sons through Jesus Christ, according
　　to the purpose of his will,
6 to the praise of his glorious grace which he freely bestowed on us
　　in the Beloved.
7 In him we have redemption through his blood, the forgiveness of
　　our trespasses, according to the riches of his grace
8 which he lavished upon us.
9 For he has made known to us in all wisdom and insight the mystery
　　of his will, according to his purpose which he set forth in Christ
10 as a plan for the fullness of time, to unite all things in him, things
　　in heaven and things on earth.
11 In him, according to the purpose of him who accomplishes all things
　　according to the counsel of his will,
12 we who first hoped in Christ have been destined and appointed to
　　live for the praise of his glory.
13 In him you also, who have heard the word of truth, the gospel of
　　your salvation, and have believed in him, were sealed with the
　　promised Holy Spirit,
14 which is the guarantee of our inheritance until we acquire possession
　　of it, to the praise of his glory.
15 For this reason, because I have heard of your faith in the Lord Jesus
　　and your love toward all the saints,
16 I do not cease to give thanks for you, remembering you in my
　　prayers,

17 that the God of our Lord Jesus Christ, the Father of glory, may
give you a spirit of wisdom and of revelation in the knowledge of
him,

18 having the eyes of your hearts enlightened, that you may know what
is the hope to which he has called you, what are the riches of
his glorious inheritance in the saints,

19 and what is the immeasurable greatness of his power in us who
believe, according to the working of his great might

20 which he accomplished in Christ when he raised him from the dead
and made him sit at his right hand in the heavenly places,

21 far above all rule and authority and power and dominion, and above
every name that is named, not only in this age but also in that
which is to come;

22 and he has put all things under his feet and has made him the head
over all things for the church,

23 which is his body, the fullness of him who fills all in all.

CHAPTER TWO

1 And you he made alive, when you were dead through the trespasses
and sin

2 in which you once walked, following the course of this world,
following the prince of the power of the air, the spirit that is now
at work in the sons of disobedience.

3 Among these we all once lived in the passions of our flesh, following
the desires of body and mind, and so we were by nature children
of wrath, like the rest of mankind.

4 But God, who is rich in mercy, out of the great love with which he
loved us,

5 even when we were dead through our trespasses, made us alive
together with Christ (by grace you have been saved),

6 and raised us up with him and made us sit with him in the heavenly
places in Christ Jesus,

7 that in the coming ages he might show the immeasurable riches of
his grace in kindness toward us in Christ Jesus.

8 For by grace you have been saved through faith; and this is not your
own doing, it is the gift of God –

9 not because of works, lest any man should boast.

10 For we are his workmanship, created in Christ Jesus for good works,
which God prepared beforehand, that we should walk in them.

11 Therefore remember that at one time you Gentiles in the flesh,
called the uncircumcision by what is called the circumcision,
which is made in the flesh by hands –

12 remember that you were at that time separated from Christ,
alienated from the commonwealth of Israel, and strangers to the
covenants of promise, having no hope and without God in the
world.

13 But now in Christ Jesus you who once were far off have been brought
near in the blood of Christ.

14 For he is our peace, who has made us both one, and has broken
down the dividing wall of hostility,

15 by abolishing in his flesh the law of commandments and ordinances,
that he might create in himself one new man in place of the
two, so making peace,

16 and might reconcile us both to God in one body through the cross,
thereby bringing the hostility to an end.

17 And he came and preached peace to you who were far off and peace
to those who were near;

18 for through him we both have access in one Spirit to the Father.

19 So then you are no longer strangers and sojourners, but you are
fellow citizens with the saints and members of the household of
God,

20 built upon the foundation of the apostles and prophets, Christ Jesus
himself being the cornerstone,

21 in whom the whole structure is joined together and grows into a
holy temple in the Lord;

22 in whom you also are built into it for a dwelling place of God in
the Spirit.

CHAPTER THREE

1 For this reason I, Paul, a prisoner for Christ Jesus on behalf of you
Gentiles –

2 assuming that you have heard of the stewardship of God's grace
that was given to me for you,

3 how the mystery was made known to me by revelation, as I have
written briefly.

4 When you read this you can perceive my insight into the mystery of
Christ,

5 which was not made known to the sons of men in other generations
as it has now been revealed to his holy apostles and prophets
by the Spirit;

6 that is, how the Gentiles are fellow heirs, members of the same
body, and partakers of the promise in Christ Jesus through the
gospel.

7 Of this gospel I was made a minister according to the gift of God's grace which was given me by the working of his power.

8 To me, though I am the very least of all the saints, this grace was given, to preach to the Gentiles the unsearchable riches of Christ,

9 and to make all men see what is the plan of the mystery hidden for ages in God who created all things;

10 that through the church the manifold wisdom of God might now be made known to the principalities and powers in the heavenly places.

11 This was according to the eternal purpose which he has realised in Christ Jesus our Lord,

12 in whom we have boldness and confidence of access through our faith in him.

13 So I ask you not to lose heart over what I am suffering for you, which is your glory.

14 For this reason I bow my knees before the Father,

15 from whom every family in heaven and on earth is named,

16 that according to the riches of his glory he may grant you to be strengthened with might through his Spirit in the inner man,

17 and that Christ may dwell in your hearts through faith; that you, being rooted and grounded in love,

18 may have power to comprehend with all the saints what is the breadth and length and height and depth,

19 and to know the love of Christ which surpasses knowledge, that you may be filled with all the fullness of God.

20 Now to him who by the power at work within us is able to do far more abundantly than all that we ask or think,

21 to him be glory in the church and in Christ Jesus to all generations, for ever and ever. Amen.

CHAPTER FOUR

1 I therefore, a prisoner for the Lord, beg you to lead a life worthy of the calling to which you have been called,

2 with all lowliness and meekness, with patience, forbearing one another in love,

3 eager to maintain the unity of the Spirit in the bond of peace.

4 There is one body and one Spirit, just as you were called to the one hope that belongs to your call,

5 one Lord, one faith, one baptism,

6 one God and Father of us all, who is above all and through all and in all.

7 But grace was given to each of us according to the measure of
Christ's gift.

8 Therefore it is said,
"When he ascended on high he led a host of captives,
and he gave gifts to men."

9 (In saying, "He ascended," what does it mean but that he had also
descended into the lower parts of the earth?

10 He who descended is he who also ascended far above all the heavens,
that he might fill all things.)

11 And his gifts were that some should be apostles, some prophets,
some evangelists, some pastors and teachers,

12 to equip the saints for the work of ministry, for building up the body
of Christ,

13 until we all attain to the unity of the faith and of the knowledge of
the Son of God, to mature manhood, to the measure of the stature
of the fullness of Christ;

14 so that we may no longer be children, tossed to and fro and carried
about with every wind of doctrine, by the cunning of men, by their
craftiness in deceitful wiles.

15 Rather, speaking the truth in love, we are to grow up in every way
into him who is the head, into Christ,

16 from the whole body, joined and knit together by every joint with
which it is supplied, when each part is working properly, makes
bodily growth and upbuilds itself in love.

17 Now this I affirm and testify in the Lord, that you must no longer
live as the Gentiles do, in the futility of their minds;

18 they are darkened in their understanding, alienated from the life of
God because of the ignorance that is in them, due to their
hardness of heart;

19 they have become callous and have given themselves up to
licentiousness, greedy to practise every kind of uncleanless.

20 You did not so learn Christ! –

21 assuming that you have heard about him and were taught in him,
as the truth is in Jesus.

22 Put off your old nature which belongs to your former manner of
life and is corrupt through deceitful lusts,

23 and be renewed in the spirit of your minds,

24 and put on the new nature, created after the likeness of God in true
righteousness and holiness.

25 Therefore, putting away falsehood, let every one speak the truth
with his neighbour, for we are members one of another.

26 Be angry but do not sin; do not let the sun go down on your anger,

27 and give no opportunity to the devil.

28 Let the thief no longer steal, but rather let him labour, doing honest work with his hands, so that he may be able to give to those in need.

29 Let no evil talk come out of your mouths, but only such as is good for edifying, as fits the occasion, that it may impart grace to those who hear.

30 And do not grieve the Holy Spirit of God, in whom you were sealed for the day of redemption.

31 Let all bitterness and wrath and anger and clamour and slander be put away from you, with all malice,

32 and be kind to one another, tenderhearted, forgiving one another, as God in Christ forgave you.

CHAPTER FIVE

1 Therefore be imitators of God, as beloved children.

2 And walk in love, as Christ loved us and gave himself up for us, a fragrant offering and sacrifice to God.

3 But fornication and all impurity or covetousness must not even be named among you, as is fitting among saints.

4 Let there be no filthiness, nor silly talk, nor levity, which are not fitting; but instead let there be thanksgiving.

5 Be sure of this, that no fornicator or impure man, or one who is covetous (that is, an idolater), has any inheritance in the kingdom of Christ and of God.

6 Let no one deceive you with empty words, for it is because of these things that the wrath of God comes upon the sons of disobedience.

7 Therefore do not associate with them,

8 for once you were darkness, but now you are light in the Lord; walk as children of light

9 (for the fruit of light is found in all that is good and right and true),

10 and try to learn what is pleasing to the Lord.

11 Take no part in the unfruitful works of darkness, but instead expose them.

12 For it is a shame even to speak of the things that they do in secret;

13 but when anything is exposed by the light it becomes visible, for anything that becomes visible is light.

14 Therefore it is said,
"Awake, O sleeper, and arise from the dead,
and Christ shall give you light."

15 Look carefully then how you walk not as unwise men but as wise,

16 making the most of the time, because the days are evil.

17 Therefore do not be foolish, but understand what the will of the Lord is.

18 And do not get drunk with wine, for that is debauchery; but be filled with the Spirit,

19 addressing one another in psalms and hymns and spiritual songs, singing and making melody to the Lord with all your heart,

20 always and for everything giving thanks in the name of our Lord Jesus Christ to God the Father.

21 Be subject to one another out of reverence for Christ.

22 Wives, be subject to your husbands, as to the Lord.

23 For the husband is the head of the wife as Christ is the head of the church, his body, and is himself its Saviour.

24 As the church is subject to Christ, so let wives also be subject in everything to their husbands.

25 Husbands, love your wives, as Christ loved the church and gave himself up for her,

26 that he might sanctify her, having cleansed her by the washing of water with the word,

27 that he might present the church to himself in splendour, without spot or wrinkle or any such thing, that she might be holy and without blemish.

28 Even so husbands should love their wives as their own bodies. He who loves his wife loves himself.

29 For no man ever hates his own flesh, but nourishes and cherishes it, as Christ does the church,

30 because we are members of his body.

31 "For this reason a man shall leave his father and mother and be joined to his wife, and the two shall become one flesh."

32 This mystery is a profound one, and I am saying that it refers to Christ and the church;

33 however, let each one of you love his wife as himself, and let the wife see that she respects her husband.

CHAPTER SIX

1 Children, obey your parents in the Lord, for this is right.

2 "Honour your father and mother" (this is the first commandment with a promise),

3 "that it may be well with you and that you may live long on the earth."

4 Fathers, do not provoke your children to anger, but bring them up in the discipline and instruction of the Lord.

5 Slaves, be obedient to those who are your earthly masters, with fear and trembling, in singleness of heart, as to Christ;

6 not in the way of eyeservice, as men-pleasers, but as servants of Christ, doing the will of God from the heart,

7 rendering service with a good will as to the Lord and not to men,

8 knowing that whatever good any one does, he will receive the same again from the Lord, whether he is a slave or free.

9 Masters, do the same to them, and forbear threatening, knowing that he who is both their Master and yours is in heaven, and that there is no partiality with him.

10 Finally, be strong in the Lord and in the strength of his might.

11 Put on the whole armour of God, that you may be able to stand against the wiles of the devil.

12 For we are not contending against flesh and blood, but against the principalities, against the powers, against the world rulers of this present darkness, against the spiritual hosts of wickedness in the heavenly places.

13 Therefore take the whole armour of God, that you may be able to withstand in the evil day, and having done all, to stand.

14 Stand therefore, having girded your loins with truth, and having put on the breastplate of righteousness,

15 and having shod your feet with the equipment of the gospel of peace;

16 besides all these, taking the shield of faith, with which you can quench all the flaming darts of the evil one.

17 And take the helmet of salvation, and the sword of the Spirit, which is the word of God.

18 Pray at all times in the Spirit, with all prayer and supplication. To that end keep alert with all perseverance, making supplication for all the saints,

19 and also for me, that utterance may be given me in opening my mouth boldly to proclaim the mystery of the gospel,

20 for which I am an ambassador in chains; that I may declare it boldly, as I ought to speak.

21 Now that you also may know how I am and what I am doing, Tych'icus the beloved brother and faithful minister in the Lord will tell you everything.

22 I have sent him to you for this very purpose, that you may know how we are, and that he may encourage your hearts.

23 Peace be to the brethren, and love with faith, from God the Father
    and the Lord Jesus Christ.

24 Grace be with all who love our Lord Jesus Christ with love undying.

NOTES

1 Mircea Eliade: *Patterns in Comparative Religion* (Sheed and Ward 1958)

2 Rudolf Otto: *The Idea of the Holy* (Oxford University Press 1923)

3 Mircea Eliade: *Patterns in Comparative Religion* (Sheed and Ward 1958)

4 Jacques Maritain: *Sign and Symbol* (Sheed and Ward)

5 cf The Saying of Goethe: "A man born and bred in the so-called exact sciences, on the height of his analytical reason, will not easily comprehend that there is something like an exact concrete imagination." Quoted by Erich Heiler in *The Disinherited Mind*

6 Rupert Sheldrake: *A New Science of Life* (Blond and Briggs 1981)

7 Christopher Dawson: *Progress and Religion* (Greenwood Press, London 1983)

8 Jeanine Miller: *The Vedas* (Rider and Company, London 1974)

9 Karl Popper and John Eccles: *The Self and its Brain* (Routledge, London 1990)

10 David Bohm: *Wholeness and the Implicate Order* (Routledge and Kegan Paul 1980)

Nevertheless I tell you the truth: it is your advantage
that I go away, for if I do not go away, the Advocate will
not come to you, but if I go, I will send him to you.

St John 16:7

That they may all be one.   St John 17:21

THE RENEWAL OF
CONTEMPLATIVE LIFE

The spiritual legacy of Dom Bede Griffiths

Bede Griffiths, English Benedictine monk and one of the outstanding
spiritual leaders, sages and mystics of the twentieth century, passed over
into the eternity of God (Sanskrit: *maha samadhi*) on 13 May 1993 at
4.30 pm. He was 86 years of age. In the presence of his most devoted
and closest disciple Camaldolese Father Christudas (= *Servant of Christ*),
who had followed him for almost 30 years in unconditional devotion and
love. Dom Bede died in the anticipation of the Holy Spirit two weeks
before the feast of the Ascension of Christ in his hut in Saccidananda
Ashram, not far from the town of Tiruchirapalli in Tamil Nadu, South
India. On the occasion of his last birthday on 17 December 1992, Bede
Griffiths, *Swami Dayananda* (Sanskrit: *Bliss of Compassion*) had announced
in the presence of 2000 visitors that his early life would not last for much
longer. Two serious strokes on 20 December 1992 and 24 January 1993
marked the beginning of the final and decisive phase of a transformation
process, which appeared to those in the vicinity of the master as agonized
suffering, but which for the man involved represented a journey into the
innermost and eternal essence of his original being. Referring to the
suffering of the famous Indian sage Ramana Maharshi (1879–1950), who
lived and taught only 200 km north of Shantivanam in a cave of the holy
Mount Arunachala, Dom Bede said of himself, when I saw him for the
last time on the morning of New Year's Eve 1992, "*My body and my soul*

may suffer, but not my spirit, which will continue to live after my death. I am experiencing total oneness and a permanent stream of everlasting love."

On the occasion of a ceremony in honour of Bede Griffiths on 14 January 1993 in London, the English cardinal and Benedictine monk Basil Hume made the following moving statement: "*Dom Bede is a source of inspiration and encouragement for many all over the world. He is a mystic in touch with absolute love and beauty. Dom Bede thinks and writes as a disciple of Christ.*" An unusual testimony to a Catholic monk during his own lifetime!

Alan Richard Griffiths was born on 17 December 1906 in Walton-on-Thames, near London. He was the fourth child of a middle-class Anglican family. Even as a boy he underwent a central experience of oneness during an exploration of the countryside. Towards the end of his schooldays at Christ's Hospital, he had another profound experience which he was later to describe as one of the most important in his life. He was walking alone at sunset when his senses were suddenly heightened. He heard the birds singing as never before; a hawthorn bush, the setting sun, the song of a lark as it fluttered in the sky, and the evening mist descending across the scene, overwhelmed him with an "awe-inspiring" feeling of God's presence. On this evening, his consciousness became aware for the first time of another dimension of existence. Even at this stage in his life he understood that the force which Hinduism describes as the manifestation of God was responsible for his becoming aware of the divine reality behind the material forms of creation. He had penetrated the secret of the cosmos.

Alan Richard Griffiths's scholarship and thirst for knowledge were remarkable. In Oxford he studied literature and philosophy and met C. S. Lewis, the famous writer and eminent university professor, who was later to become a long-standing friend. C. S. Lewis said of his friend Alan: "He was one of the most brilliant dialecticians I have ever met".

Throughout his life, Alan Richard Griffiths was fascinated by the English poet, painter and mystic visionary William Blake (1757–1827), who provided him with the inspiration for the title of his beautiful autobiography, *The Golden String*.

> *I give you the end of a golden string;*
> *Only wind it into a ball,*
> *it will lead you in at Heaven's gate,*
> *Built in Jerusalem's wall.*

William Blake

On 20 December 1932, sixty years to the day before he suffered his serious stroke, Alan Richard Griffiths entered the novitiate in the Benedictine monastery of Prinknash Abbey. He assumed the name of

Bede, the great English holy man whose life had deeply impressed him. Four years later he took his final vows and was ordained priest on 9 March 1940. In 1955, after a promising period as a Benedictine monk in England, during the last years of which he served as Prior at Farnborough Abbey, Bede Griffiths embarked, at the age of almost 50, on his journey to India in search of the other side of his soul. "*I had begun to realize*", said Father Bede, "*that there was something missing in the Western church; we only live out half of our soul; the conscious rational side. We still have to discover the other half, the unconscious, intuitive dimension. I wanted to experience during my own lifetime the marriage of these two dimensions of human existence, the rational and the intuitive, the masculine and the feminine.*"

After his arrival in India, Father Bede lived at first in a Western-oriented Benedictine monastery near Bangalore (South India), but soon felt that Gregorian chants, the familiar monk's habits and the entire Western lifestyle bore no relationship to the life of the village inhabitants. The next station on his journey was the Kurisumala Ashram in the mountains of Kerala, where together with Francis Mahieu, a Belgian Trappist monk (now known as Francis Acharya) and a small group of Indian monks, he attempted a *rapprochement* between Indian and Western Christian spirituality.

At the end of 1968 Bede Griffiths and two Indian fellow-monks moved to the plains of Tamil Nadu to take over the Saccidananda Ashram on the River Cauvery, the holy river of South India. The founder of Shantivanam, the French monk Jules Monchanin, had died of cancer in his native country. The joint founder of the ashram, the French Benedictine monk Henri Le Saux, well known under his Indian name Swami Abhishiktananda, had withdrawn during the summer of 1968 to his hermitage in Uttarkarshi in North India; he died in December 1973 in Indore.

Since its foundation in 1950, the Saccidananda Ashram Shantivanam had remained virtually unchanged. The arrival of Bede Griffiths marked the beginning of a fundamental transformation. Since 1969, Shantivanam has become an important centre for dialogue and contemplation. The ashram has acquired an international reputation for being open to all those who come; and they do come from all corners of the world. Dom Bede became a true guru, the main attraction for all those who made the journey to Shantivanam. His person made the ashram world famous. People came from all over the world to be inspired by his wisdom and touched by his example, his love, his presence, by his incorporation of the quality known in India as *darshan*.

"*All religious teachings are a symbolic expression of a truth which cannot adequately be expressed*", Dom Bede so often said, continuing, "*Each religion, be it Christian, Hindu, Buddhist, Muslim or whatever, is limited by time, space and circumstances. All forms of organization, priesthood, ritual and doctrine belong to the world of signs, which will pass away. But in all these superficial forms of religion, an eternal truth manifests itself. Idolatry consists of remaining in the realm of these signs; true religion goes beyond the sign to reality."*

And so the Saccidananda Ashram became a true meeting place for the religions of the world. A course in meditation led by a Zen Buddhist master is as much a part of its life as a lecture by a Christian theologian, together with yoga lessons given by one of the monks and an encounter with a Hindu *swami* (teacher). Bede Griffiths has played an important role in the reconciliation of the religions of the world. In his epoch-making work *Universal Wisdom*, the sage and prophet of Shantivanam has compiled a sort of Holy Scripture for men throughout the world who are searching for God's presence and oneness.

One of Bede Griffiths's prime concerns was the renewal of contemplative life. For this reason, together with close friends, he had initiated a movement in California in September 1992 (*The Society for the Renewal of Contemplative Life*), which aims to link together a worldwide network of individuals searching for God without the legal forms and organized structures of Roman canon law. In this context, Dom Bede summarized in memorable form the meaning of the word "contemplation":

"Contemplation is the awakening to the presence of God in the human heart and in the universe which is around us. Contemplation is knowledge by love."

May 1993. For the past two weeks, Bede Griffiths had been suffering from a feverish pneumonia, exacerbated by the oppressive tropical heat (43°C) and the extremely high humidity. During the previous years, Dom Bede had spent these weeks in the more temperate Indian highlands or travelling in Europe, America and Australia. He was attended night and day by Father Christudas, Sister Marie-Louise and Sister Valsa as well as the other brethren of the community. In spite of being racked by fever with a temperature of over 40°C for several weeks, Bede Griffiths had moments of extreme lucidity. He uttered no complaint about his suffering, but called continually for the presence of his closest friends.

Christudas, who had observed every breath of his master for decades, felt that death was not far away and said: "*My beloved* guruji, *the hour is come when only God can help.*" Together they sang Dom Bede's favourite hymns in Sanskrit, repeating the Lord's Prayer three times. Dom Bede gazed one last time at his devoted disciple Christudas and died peacefully on Thursday, 13 May 1993 in his hut in the paradisal enclave of

Shantivanam, where for 25 years he had lovingly welcomed and taught visitors from all over the world.

On 14 May, Bishop Gabriel of Tiruchirapalli presided over a memorial service and said in his moving address: *"Dom Bede Griffiths is a great gift to the Indian Church. He is a saint."*

The official requiem and burial were planned for 15 May. Bede Griffiths lay in state before the altar in the chapel where for so long he had celebrated the Eucharist every day in the presence of so many people from all over the world. In his hands he held a chalice as a sign of his priesthood, together with a Benedictine cross and a rosary. The face of the saintly man glowed peacefully in the blazing tropical sunlight. A local priest celebrated with Father Christudas the ceremonial Mass for the Dead. The Ashram community and countless friends from the surrounding villages (Christians, Hindus, Muslims etc.) took their leave of the Benedictine monk and Sannyasin Bede Griffiths, who had made Shantivanam into a place of reconicliation for the religions of the world.

Before the coffin was closed, Bede Griffiths's closest friends washed their master's feet for the last time, kissing his forehead and feet and taking leave of him in gratitude and love. Christudas, his faithful companion, placed his shawl in the coffin of his guru.

In a great procession of lights and a sea of flowers, the funeral procession moved towards the burial place near the chapel. Suddenly the heavens darkened for a few moments and a violent storm roared across the ashram. Nature bowed in obeisance before Dom Bede. Leaves and flowers were blown into the grave and covered the coffin of the mystic and saint of Shantivanam. Many saw in this portent a sign and recalled the Gospel according to St John, Chapter 3, Verse 8: *"The wind blows where it chooses, and you hear the sound of it, but you do not know where it comes from or where it goes. So it is with everyone who is born of the Spirit.*

Two years previously, when Bede Griffiths celebrated the festival of Pentecost with friends in a mountain village in Upper Bavaria, he proclaimed: *"It was a great joy to celebrate Pentecost here and to see it as the culmination of the Christian year. The moment when all the mysteries of Christ, birth, epiphany, death and resurrection are all realized in the depth of the spirit within. It is the moment of self-realization, when all that has been experienced externally is gathered into the centre and is realized as the way of inner transformation, by which we pass continually from death to life and prepare for the final transformation, when the whole creation will be taken up into the fullness of Christ, and God will be all in all."*

Roland Romuald Ropers Obl OSB
Saccidananda Ashram
15–17 May 1993

ACKNOWLEDGEMENTS

The publishers gratefully acknowledge permission to the following, for use of their copyright texts:

A. P. Watt on behalf of Benares University for the translations of the Isha, Kena, Katha, Mundaka and Mandukya Upanishads by W. B. Yeats and Shree Purohit Swami. Penguin Books Ltd for the translation of the Svetasvatara Upanishad by Juan Mascaro. The Regents of the University of California for the translation of the Bhagavadgita by Kees W. Bolle, © 1979. Dutton, an imprint of New American Library, a division of Penguin Books USA Inc, for the translation of Awakening of Faith by Dwight Goddard from *A Buddhist Bible*, © 1938, renewed © 1966. Gower Publishing Co Ltd and Alfred A. Knopf, Inc for the translation of the Tao Te Ching by Gia-Fu Feng and Jane English, © 1972. George Allen & Unwin, an imprint of HarperCollins Publishers, for the translation of Sikh Morning, Evening and Bedtime Prayer, from *Sacred Writings of the Sikhs*. Allen & Unwin, an imprint of HarperCollins Publishers, for the translation of Al Ghazali's Deliverance from Error by W. Montgomery Watt, and for the translation of the Poems of Rumi by Reynold A. Nicholson. HarperColling Publishers and the Department of Education, The National Council of Churches of Christ in the USA for extracts from the Revised Standard Version of the Bible.